Mwynhewch stori Powell Bach

Enjoy the story of Powell Bach

Denley Owen

Signed photograph of W. R. H. Powell, from *Baily's Monthly Magazine of Sports and Pastimes,* No. 282, Vol. XLI, August 1883.

Powell Maesgwynne

Philanthropist, Sporting Great and Radical Hero

An account of the life and times of
W. R. H. POWELL, MP,
Llanboidy, Carmarthenshire
(1819-1889)

Denley Owen

Published by
Cymdeithas Hynafiaethau Sir Gaerfyrddin/Carmarthenshire Antiquarian Society
with support from Llanboidy Community Council

Carmarthenshire Antiquarian Society Monograph Series Volume 9

Copyright © 2012 William Denley Owen/Carmarthenshire Antiquarian Society

Published in 2012 by
Cymdeithas Hynafiaethau Sir Gaerfyrddin/Carmarthenshire Antiquarian Society
with support from Llanboidy Community Council

ISBN 978-0-906972-08-3

Cover photograph
courtesy Mrs Mary Taylor

Printed and bound in Wales by
Dinefwr Press Ltd
Rawlings Road, Llandybie, Carmarthenshire, SA18 3YD

I

Owain, Steffan, Cai, Llyr, Iestyn a Beca Hedd

CONTENTS

FOREWORD

MY GREAT uncle Herbert Vaughan was the author of *The South Wales Squires*, first published in 1926, and a man alleged to be too dangerous to ask to tea for fear of how he might report his visit.

In his book he referred to my great-great-grandfather W. R. H. Powell in a chapter headed 'Oddities and Quiddities' in not very flattering terms. Guests at W. R. H. Powell's home at Maesgwynne were described as being mostly of the horsey-foxy-doggy type and there were then dubious remarks questioning his ethics both on the racecourse and politically. His brother had by then married W. R. H. Powell's granddaughter and was living happily at Maesgwynne with his young family perhaps in greater comfort than my Uncle Herbert.

Coming down within my family, Uncle Herbert aside, there is still a wealth of admiration and affection for the manner in which W. R. H. Powell lived his life and for his achievements. Detail has, however, become rather blurred with the passing of each generation and I greatly welcome Denley Owen's well researched book which fills in the detail of a remarkable life, lived to the full.

DAVID VAUGHAN

(Courtesy Lon Owen).

PREFACE

SIX GENERATIONS have passed since Powell Bach 'ruled' in Carmarthenshire from his strong-hold of Maesgwynne, Llanboidy. An unassuming man, he never sought praise or fame for himself but rather he dedicated his life to the task of improving the lives of others, especially of the working classes and the poor. His progressive influence was felt in social, economic, sporting and political fields but, today, his considerable achievements are unknown to most.

Dr Denley Owen, born and bred in Llanboidy Parish, has performed a marvellous job in researching the life and times of W. R. H. Powell and has produced a book which will provide the reader with a feast of information about the supreme Squire of Maesgwynne. You can read about his passion for hunting and horse racing; his ways of improving farming methods and his campaign for butter factories; his insistence on education being free of religious dogma; his provision of cottages, sickness benefit and old age pension for labourers; his emergence as a radical politician calling for disestablishment of the Church, rights for tenants, democratic control of local taxation and spending, and Home Rule . . . and much more. Powell's progressive politics upset the Conservative press but on a personal level he had no enemies; he was admired and loved by everyone who had the privilege of meeting him.

We are greatly indebted to Denley because he has fulfilled a need, long overdue, in producing an account of the life and times of W. R. H. Powell and, in so doing, he has paid homage to one who contributed so much to the community as well as to the radical liberal movement in nineteenth century Carmarthenshire.

EDDIE EVANS
Llanboidy

'. . . may Powell Maesgwynne be our hero this time again.'

(Carmarthenshire Nonconformists during the
1885 General Election)

INTRODUCTION

I<small>T WAS</small> in the 1940s that I first heard of Powell Bach Maesgwynne. My grandmother's farm, Canerw, bordered onto Maesgwynne land and I remember going on walks along an old and fast disappearing track past the ruin of Lleine and on to Llyn Maesgwynne. Wild ducks would suddenly and noisily flee their sanctuary among the sedges leaving a lake almost completely overgrown and a sorry reminder of the times when it was, or so I was told, a haven for water fowl, domestic and wild. My father would comment to the effect that things had been allowed to run down (*pethe wedi'u gadel i fynd*). Clearly 'things' were in better shape twenty years earlier, when he was a child at Canerw. But even then, Walter Rice Howell Powell, sometime Squire of Maesgwynne, had been dead for forty years or so, and my father's knowledge was based on word of mouth.

But the Maesgwynne Arms Hotel, the Market Hall, the village school and the houses of Piccadilly Square were solid enough evidence to support the hearsay that much of Llanboidy village owed its existence to the Squire of Maesgwynne.

Somehow it was no surprise to hear that he was a good man (*wedd e'n ddyn da*) who had done his utmost to improve the lot of everyone in the community. And a grateful people showed their appreciation in the usual endearing Welsh way: they called him Powell Bach or *Y Dyn Bach.* Just the sort to become a Member of Parliament. And Powell had indeed won Carmarthenshire for the Liberals although, presumably, as a squire he should have been a Tory. But with his belief in education for all, disestablishment of the Church and security for tenants, Powell was 'manna from heaven' to the radical Liberal Nonconformists whose army of canvassing preachers saw him home and dry.

It was not 'all work' for Powell because my father reckoned he had built a racecourse near Cefnbrafle Hamlet where his steeplechasers and hunters took on all-comers and usually beat them to the post. And in the first half of the 1860s his annual week-long festival of racing and hunting at Llanboidy attracted the best steeplechasers from Wales, Ireland and England as well as reporters from London's top sporting journals, *The Field* and *Bell's Life in London and Sporting Chronicle.* The races were run under 'The Grand National Steeple Chase Rules' and, clearly, they predated the point-to-point era and Llanboidy's inheritor is present-day Ffos Las.

When the troubled Carmarthenshire Races called for his help, Powell's remarkable organising ability transformed them into what was claimed to be the 'top steeplechase meeting in Wales', whose 'Open' winner gained automatic entry for the Grand National at Aintree.

But Powell's staple diet of sport had been fox hunting for which purpose he kept a pack of hounds at his own expense for fifty years.

The information about this extraordinary character that I was fed as a child gave me much food for thought and over the years I occasionally entertained the idea of finding out more about the life and times of Powell Bach. But my periodic whims of admiration for the Squire were always tempered by my mother's childhood experience of squires when living on the Dolwilym estate of the Protheroes, a few miles away near Llanglydwen. She and her brother had been severely reprimanded by their parents after the squire's sister, Miss Protheroe, complained of their failure to salute her when their paths crossed on the track from Glyntaf to Dolwilym. Thereafter, whenever 'Miss' came into sight my mother saluted and muttered repeatedly 'Good morning Miss' until the woman passed by and was out of sight. Curiously, my mother was not bothered by the incident but rather, or so it seemed to me, she was somewhat proud of having attracted the attention of the upper class. I should add that the Protheroes were well thought of by their tenants.

For myself, my mother's tale induced a prejudice against squires which, for years, put me off following up my interest in the Squire of Maesgwynne and his involvement with the local and wider community in the nineteenth century. I should not have been so hesitant; Walter Rice Howell Powell was no ordinary squire; he was, indeed, a man apart!

DENLEY OWEN

ACKNOWLEDGEMENTS

COLLECTING information for writing this book meant visiting places such as the National Library of Wales in Aberystwyth, the British Library in London, the magnificent new Central Library in Cardiff, the Regional Library in Llanelli, the County Library in Haverfordwest, the Record Offices in Bristol and in Haverfordwest, the Carmarthenshire Archive Service in Carmarthen and the Carmarthenshire County Museum in Abergwili. I am grateful to the staff at all those institutions for their ready assistance. Most of my research time over the past three years was spent reading nineteenth-century copies of the *Carmarthen Journal* and of *The Welshman* in the reference department of the Regional Library in Carmarthen and the fact that the staff there were invariably courteous and helpful was a great bonus. It is a pleasure to thank them all. *Diolch yn fawr iawn.*

One person who epitomised the commitment of Carmarthen's librarians to help amateur searchers like myself was the late Rhun Jones. It was a pleasure for Rhun to assist and he always produced something positive to follow up . . . he will be sorely missed. *Diolch o galon, Rhun.*

Llanboidy's own local historian, Eddie Evans, author of *Llanboidy: Hanes Plwyf, Pentref a Chapel*, was a mine of information and he made available to me his collection of documents relevant to Maesgwynne. With assistance from his wife Merle they provided most of the photographs for this book. It is a pleasure to thank them for their interest and their encouragement. I am especially grateful to Eddie for the Preface.

It is a pleasure to thank Thomas Lloyd, OBE, FSA, Wales Herald Extraordinary and Vice-President of Carmarthenshire Antiquarian Society, for his readiness to lend photographs and for his invaluable advice and encouragement during the final stages of preparing the book.

I gratefully acknowledge the assistance received from Powell descendants, Mrs Mary Taylor and David and Michael Vaughan, and I am particularly thankful to David for the Foreword.

My search for photographs benefited from the generosity of the following to whom I offer my sincere thanks: Robert King, Harry Lloyd, Parchedig Beti-Wyn, Mrs Nansi Evans and Mrs Pat Phillips.

I am grateful to the National Library of Wales for permission to reproduce the photographs so noted.

My thanks to Brian Lee of Cardiff, chronicler of point-to-point horse racing and a regular contributor to the *Western Mail*, for an informative discussion on matters of steeplechasers and steeplechasing.

Journalist Handel Jones was kind enough to look over the 'proofs' and I am hugely thankful for his helpful suggestions and corrections.

I thank my wife Lon for her ever-ready help, advice and infinite patience and for being a completely reliable chauffeuse and for photographing silverware, the Powell 'coat of arms' banner and the beautiful paintings of hounds, horses and men, all of which appear in colour in the book.

Guidance on publishing from Phil Alder, Carmarthenshire County Council's Arts Development Officer, helped turn a wish into reality and I am especially grateful for his advice.

Carmarthenshire Antiquarian Society's support made it possible to publish the book and I am particularly indebted to the Society's Miss Muriel Bowen Evans, MA, for her constructive comments.

It is a pleasure to thank Llanboidy Community Council for its generous financial award to the Carmarthenshire Antiquarian Society to help meet the costs of publication.

Staff at Gwasg Dinefwr, and in particular Mr Eddie John, could not have been more helpful during the process of producing the book for which I am especially grateful.

Finally, I should point out that the inaccuracies that remain are all my own.

DENLEY OWEN

Part I

MAINLY FAMILY MATTERS

Walter Rice Howell Powell was born in Foley House, in the parish of St Thomas', Haverfordwest, on 4 April 1819. On the following day he was baptised at home which suggests that he was a weakling and not expected to survive. But survive he did. And by the middle of the nineteenth century Walter Rice Howell Powell, Squire of Maesgwynne, was an adored community leader in Carmarthenshire and a well-known and highly respected racehorse owner on courses in Wales, England and Ireland. He ended his days as a radical Member of Parliament admired for his devotion to duty at Westminster and for his reforming zeal in his constituency. Ironically, because of his small physical stature, he was commonly referred to by a Welsh term of endearment, *Y Dyn Bach*.

He was the third generation of his family to inherit Maesgwynne in the parish of Llanboidy. It was W. R. H. Powell's grandfather, Walter Powell, a dry-salter at Bristol, who acquired the estate in 1789 when he was left it in the will of his unmarried godfather, Walter Rice Howell, the last of the Howell line dating back to the early seventeenth century to have occupied Maesgwynne. Walter Powell was the son of John Powell, collector of customs at Bristol. A family tree chart[1] obtained from a Powell descendent shows that John was a first cousin to Walter Rice Howell of Maesgwynne, confirming the family relationship stated in one source.[2] At the same time it disproves the claim in another source[3] that no evidence exists to show any kinship with the Howell family of Maesgwynne.

After the death of Walter Rice Howell on 20 December 1789, his lucky godson and cousin-once-removed, Walter Powell, moved from Bristol and settled at Maesgwynne. His inheritance included the mansion of Maesgwynne and an estate of nearly 3,500 acres comprising 22 farms in the locality of Llanboidy together with about 10 houses in the village. An indication of where Maesgwynne fitted into the estates-league in west Wales may be obtained from figures given in *The Return of the Owners of Land* of 1874.[4] The main landowner in Carmarthenshire at that time was Earl Cawdor of Stackpole Court in Pembrokeshire who owned 33,782 acres in the county. Other major landowners were J. H. Williams Drummond of Edwinsford near Llansawel (9,281), Earl Ashburnham of Sussex who owned about 5,865 around Pembrey, Lord Dynevor of Newton House, Llandeilo (7,208), J. Gwynne-Hughes of Tregib, Llandeilo (6,797), Alfred Jones of Pantglas, Llanfynydd (7,909) and Mansel Lewis of Stradey Castle, Llanelli (3,139). Clearly his inheritance did not place him in the top league of landowners but once he was settled in Maesgwynne, Walter Powell hitched himself to the clergy and to the minor and major gentry in west Wales. In 1794 he married a local lady, Elizabeth, the elder daughter of the Reverend John Lewis Philipps, MA, of Llwyncrwn, Llangynin, who was the vicar of St Clears. Her grandfather was John Adams Esq. of Whitland. Her sister Charlotte married, in

Foley House, Haverfordwest, birthplace of Powell Bach.
(*Gathering the Jewels*, Web site. Item GTJ 75421, as at 21/11/11).

1800, Sir John Owen Bart. Lord Lt. and MP for Pembrokeshire and Governor of Milford Haven.[5]

Walter and Elizabeth had three children. The first, a boy, was born on 26 February 1795 at Maesgwynne. He was named after the godfather who had secured the future of the Powells, namely Walter Rice Howell. The second, a girl born in 1797 at Maesgwynne, was called Elizabeth Jane Oliver Hungerford Powell. For a girl to be loaded with those names, was an indication of how important it was for the parents to claim kinship with them. In fact, she was made to carry her mother's maiden surname, Oliver, together with the surname of her great-great-grandfather, Sir John Hungerford of Hungerford. The third child, a girl born at Maesgwynne in 1799, was named Margaret Maria Georgiana Powell.

In June 1799 Walter almost killed himself by drinking posset with added ginger. The ginger had been accidentally contaminated with arsenic used to kill rats. After three days of suffering Walter and one of his guests, a Mr Davies, recovered but his other guest, a Mr Sanxay late of the Pembrokeshire yeomanry cavalry, lingered for eight days and then died. 'From the moment he (Mr Sanxay) discovered the cause of his indisposition he felt aware of the impossibility of recovery and exhibited a picture of resignation and real fortitude. The Coroner's Inquest was *Accidental Death.*'[6] Accident it may have been but, surely, an avoidable one. The tragic result of someone's irresponsibility would have weighed heavily on Walter's conscience and this together with possible after-effects of his arsenic-spiked drink might well have contributed to his premature death a year later at only 41-years-of-age.

Walter Powell, died at Maesgwynne and was buried at St Clears. His son and heir was only five years of age and for the next twenty years, it appears from available records[7] that the Powells spent much of their time at Haverfordwest rather than at Maesgwynne. In fact, W. R. H. Powell (senior) rented Foley House in Goat Street, Haverfordwest, a Georgian town house where Lord Nelson received the freedom of the town in 1802.[8] Designed for solicitor Richard

2

Foley by John Nash in *c*.1795, it was 'one of the best houses in town . . . and the rent would presumably have been high. So Powell (senior) was obviously not poor.'[9] The reason for living part of the time in Haverfordwest is unclear. It is possible that the mansion at Maesgwynne was rebuilt or refurbished at that time and that the family moved out to facilitate the programme of works. Francis Jones wrote[3] that the 'mansion is said to have been built in the 1790s but appears to be somewhat later in date and was added to and altered during the nineteenth century.' Thomas Lloyd et al[10] stated that Maesgwynne 'was a five-bay hipped house with verandas each side of an enclosed hipped porch, built *c*.1830 for W. R. H. Powell [senior].' On the other hand it may be that the Powells used Foley House as their 'town house' in Haverfordwest to where they removed for the 'season' as well as on other occasions. According to David Howell,[11] Haverfordwest in winter was a great attraction for the squires, and to avoid the discomfort of travelling great distances many families maintained winter houses in the town. 'Balls, dinners, card-parties and plays were organised for their amusement. During Assize week, balls were given by the sheriff, the county representative and the foreman of the jury. The ladies arrived at these balls in sedan chairs and the dancing continued into the early hours of the morning.' It should also be remembered that in those days Haverfordwest was one of the few places in west Wales where schools, including a grammar school, had been established. In his will, dated 1799, Walter Powell charged his brother Thomas Hungerford Powell, together with an Attorney at Law, Thomas Lewis of Llandeilo, with 'tuition, Guardianship and education of all my children until they shall respectively attain the age of twenty-one years or my daughters shall be married with such consent aforesaid.' Therefore, it may well be that the opportunity to have their children educated locally was the main reason for the Powells living for much of the time between 1800 and 1820 in Haverfordwest.

During that period, the heir to the estate, Walter Rice Howell Powell (senior) made good educational progress and on 28 January 1813, at 17 years of age, he entered Christ Church, Oxford. He was still at Oxford in 1816.[12] In the same year his mother, who had remarried to a certain John Marten, died at Haverfordwest. Walter Rice Howell Powell (senior) made more progress on 8 May 1817 when he married a girl with the same surname as himself and who, like his father, came from Bristol. His bride, Mary Powell, had been born in the parish of Brislington, Somerset (now part of Bristol) and the marriage took place in the parish church of Brislington.[7,13] The couple continued the Powell practice of living some of the time at Haverfordwest. They were at Maesgwynne on 26 August 1818 when Dr Evan Protheroe of Dolwilym Mansion, Llanglydwen and his daughter Emma rode the four miles or so 'to call upon Mr and Mrs Powell'. The following day the Protheroe coach collected W.R.H. and his wife as well as his sisters, Elizabeth Jane Oliver Hungerford and Margaret Maria Georgiana and conveyed them to Dolwilym for dinner. Mr Griffiths of Glandŵr (the minister of the Independent Chapel) was there as well and stayed the night. A week later, W. R. H. Powell (senior) sent three braces of partridges to Mrs Protheroe.[14] He must have enjoyed the dinner!

Evan Protheroe, like W. R. H. Powell's father Walter, had not inherited his estate through being the next of kin. He was in fact plain Dr Evan Jones, MD, when he was left the Dolwilym Estate by his brother-in-law, Evan Protheroe, who had changed his will to the benefit of Evan Jones in a fit of indignation on hearing of his next of kin's premature preparations to celebrate his 'death'. To inherit the estate Evan Jones had to satisfy two conditions: change his surname to Protheroe and live in Dolwilym Mansion. He duly agreed to both and became a squire. A hundred-and-twenty-two years later Dr Evan Protheroe's great-great-grandson John (Jack) Protheroe Beynon married W. R. H. Powell's (senior) great-great-granddaughter (Wilma 'Bobs' Vaughan) thus bringing together the two major land-owning families within Llanboidy Parish.

In 1818 'W. R. H. Powell of Maesgwynne' was recorded as one of a hundred-and-ten annual subscribers to the recently formed Cambrian Society established 'for the preservation of the remains of ancient British Literature and for the encouragement of the National Musik [sic]'. The first-ever gorsedd ceremony, organised by Iolo Morganwg, took place at an eisteddfod organised by the Cambrian Society at the Ivy Bush, Carmarthen, in 1819.[15,16]

On 18 May 1819, a month after the birth of Powell Bach, the Powells were celebrating again. At the parish church of St Thomas', Haverfordwest, 22-year-old Elizabeth Jane Oliver Hungerford Powell of the parish of St. Mary's, Haverfordwest (aunt of the month-old baby), was married to her 26-year-old cousin Timothy Powell, Esquire of the parish of St Thomas', Haverfordwest.[17] Timothy Powell had been born in the parish of Brislington, Somerset, the son of one Jonathan Powell. It may have been that Timothy Powell's parents had also moved from Brislington to Haverfordwest. If so, their presence would have been another reason why the Powells of Maesgwynne spent a lot of time there during the first two decades of the nineteenth century.

Timothy and Elizabeth Jane Oliver Hungerford Powell settled in the area and their first child was born in 1820 in Trewern, a mansion near Whitland but over the border in Pembrokeshire. By the mid-1820s they were settled at Penycoed, St Clears, where they spent the rest of their lives. They had three children. Hungerford's unmarried sister, Margaret Maria Georgiana Powell, spent much of her time at Penycoed up to the death of Hungerford in 1854. Timothy was a magistrate and pretty right wing in his views which, as we shall see later, was in stark contrast to the progressive left wing views of his cousin W. R. H. Powell. Timothy Powell re-married in 1856 to Margaret Williams of Llanfihangel Parish, Carmarthenshire, who was 45-years his junior. After the death of Timothy in 1889 Margaret got friendly, or friendlier, with her footman Thomas Nicholas whom she promoted to butler by 1891 and married in 1897. The butler did rather well out of the union because in the 1901 census 62-year-old Thomas was recorded as 'Head' of the household, living on own means and employing a cook and three maids. But he died a year later. The twice-widowed Margaret lived for another 23 years, reaching the age of 88 years.

After the excitement of 1819 W. R. H. Powell (senior) and his wife Mary and son continued to live at Haverfordwest and only occasionally at Maesgwynne. However it was as 'W. R. H. Powell of Maesgwynne' that his name appeared in *The Times* of 6 February 1821 which reported his appointment as High Sheriff of Carmarthenshire for that year. Their second child, a daughter named Maria Jane, was born at Haverfordwest on 12 April 1821. She was followed by another daughter, Georgiana Mary, born on 12 November 1822. Around that time the family seems to have settled at Maesgwynne where their last two children were born; Edward Henry on 26 September 1825 and Thomas Rees Oliver on 19 February 1832.

Like his father before him, W. R. H. Powell (senior) died when his children were still growing up. In June 1834 at the age of 39 years he passed away at Maesgwynne and was buried in the church graveyard at Llanboidy. In his will he nominated 'Timothy Samson Powell of

Henbury, Gloucestershire and Thomas Rees Thomas of Laugharne but now of Carmarthen as Trustees and in the event of my wife Mary re-marrying – to be Guardians of my children.' His eldest son W. R. H. Powell inherited his estate 'except as hereinafter is charged and more particularly detailed.' His 'beloved wife' Mary was given 'the whole of my household furniture, Plate, China, Books, Carvings and Household stuff to her use as long as she continues my widow together with the Mansion of Maesgwynne, Gardens and Plantation in Ring Fence around the house, Rent Free together with the lawn below the sunk fence subject to her paying my said son W. R. H. Powell for the said lawn the sum of £20 as Rent annually so long as she may choose to hold the same.' At that time the son and heir, 15-year-old W. R. H. Powell, was being educated by a private tutor. Previously he had been a boarder at a school in Swansea. But he was a sleep walker, which practice caused an accident in 1833 when Powell fell from 'the highest window in Swansea' and broke his nose and suffered injury which caused his schooling to be suspended for three years. But a private tutor was engaged to help and the tutor kept a pack of harriers so the young W. R. H. Powell had early experience of the mysteries of the noble science.[18]

On 19 October 1837, W. R. H. Powell followed in the tracks of his late father and entered Christ Church, Oxford.[12] His main interest there was sport, and hunting in particular. But his studies were interrupted and may well have been abandoned as a result of trouble at home in the form of the Rebecca uprising which initially concentrated on demolishing toll gates. The first gate to be destroyed was at Efailwen about six miles from Maesgwynne but the gate was renewed and was again destroyed on two occasions before the authorities gave up replacing it. The second impediment that received Rebecca's attention was the gate near Maesgwynne, Llanboidy, which was destroyed on the night of 15 June 1839. The 20-year-old W. R. H. Powell broke with convention and met with the local people to hear their grievances. He took steps to prevent erection and re-erection of toll gates in the Llanboidy area which ensured that no further trouble was experienced. W. R. H. Powell's success in dealing with the toll gates campaign and his understanding of the underlying causes of the unrest in the countryside were the earliest indications of his emergence as a community leader in west Carmarthenshire who was truly prepared to stand up for a better deal for the ordinary people.

On 5 May 1840 the Squire of Maesgwynne found time to marry Emily Anne Skrine daughter of landed proprietor, Henry Skrine Esq. and his wife Caroline Anne from Stubbings House, Bisham, Berkshire and of Warleigh Manor, Bath, Somerset. The marriage took place in St Marylebone Parish, London, Middlesex and it was the same parish that was entered as their place of residence at the time of their marriage. It may well be that the Skrine family had a third house in St Marylebone because it was in that parish that W.R.H. and Emily Anne Powell's daughter Caroline Mary was baptised on 20 May 1841. She had been born in Stubbings House on 23 February 1841. The 1841 census data was recorded on 7 June and by that time W. R. H. Powell, described as 'Gent', his wife and daughter were living at Maesgwynne Mansion, Llanboidy, Carmarthenshire. Living with them in the Mansion were four female servants. They had a gardener living in the round house of Maesgwynne Lodge. And it is more than likely the blacksmith, John Phillips at Panteg near Cefnypant found employment attending to the Squire's horses. Shoemakers Benjamin Lewis and son George at nearby Lleine may also have found work coming their way from Maesgwynne Mansion. Maesgwynne Farm was occupied by

Josiah John and his wife and two young children, and three female servants. A few of the many agricultural labourers living nearby in places such as Blaencwmfallen, Cefnbrafle and Llanboidy Village were also, no doubt, employed as required. In the same 1841 census the Squire's widowed mother, Mary, and his unmarried sisters, Maria Jane and Georgiana Mary, were recorded as living at 29 Green Park, Walcot Parish, Bath, Somerset. Mary was of 'independent means' and she employed two female servants and one male. It is possible that the social unrest in west Wales, manifested by the Rebecca uprising, influenced Mary and her daughters to leave Maesgwynne. On the other hand she may have disliked the idea of having to pay rent to her son for the use of the lawn at the Mansion as instructed in her late husband's will. Or she may have decided that the girls were more likely to meet suitable partners in Bath rather than in Llanboidy. It seems that Mary lived most of the rest of her life with her daughter Maria Jane in the west of England although it was at Maesgwynne with her son and his family that she passed away in 1868.

In 1843 W. R. H. Powell's sister Maria Jane married solicitor Edward Randolph in St Thomas' district, Devon and they went to live in Lympston, Devon. By 1861 Maria Jane and family lived in Bella Vista, Walcot, Bath and that is where she ended her days in 1885. She and her husband had four boys and three girls.

A son was born to the Squire and his wife at Maesgwynne in 1844 and he was named, inevitably, Walter Rice Howell Powell. In the same year W. R. H. Powell's brother Edward Henry, who in the 1841 census was listed as a 15-year-old pupil and boarder at King Edward VI Grammar School at Bromsgrove, Worcestershire, went up to St John's College, Oxford, with the intention of entering the Church. W. R. H. Powell's sister Georgiana Mary got married in 1845 to an army officer, John Weech Randolph, in St Thomas' district, Devon. So the two sisters, again, had the same surname. But Georgiana enjoyed only one year of marriage before dying in 1846 at 24 years of age on the birth of her child in Canterbury, Kent.

Another tragedy occurred at Maesgwynne in 1846 with the death of W. R. H. Powell's wife Emily Anne at 29 years of age. She left two young children, five-year-old Caroline Mary and two-year-old Walter Rice Howell. It is possible that the Squire's mother, Mary, returned to Maesgwynne from her daughter's home in Bath to help look after the children at that difficult time. But she was back in Bath by 30 March 1851 when census data was recorded.

There was good news from Oxford in 1848 when the Squire's brother Edward Henry Powell gained a BA degree. The following year Edward Henry got married to Ellen Daniel and in 1851 after gaining an MA degree at Christ Church, Oxford he was appointed curate at Lynton, Devon. Three years later Edward Henry was appointed curate at Ludchurch, Pembrokeshire, where he remained until the late 1850s before moving back to the west of England to become curate of Lockley, Somerset. In the late 1860s he became vicar of St Anne's, Congresbury, Axbridge, Somerset, where he remained until his death in 1892. Edward Henry Powell and his wife Ellen had eight children; four of each sex.

In 1849 W. R. H. Powell, at the age of 30, was appointed High Sheriff of Carmarthenshire. And two years later, on 14 March 1851, five years after the death of his first wife, W. R. H. Powell got married for the second time. His bride was from a well-known Carmarthenshire family, the Philipps of Cwmgwili near Abergwili, Carmarthen. Catherine Anne Prudence Philipps was 11 years younger than her husband. Her father, Grismond Philipps had passed away in the previous year and had been succeeded at Cwmgwili by his son, Capt. Grismond Philipps, RWF, JP. The marriage at Abergwili Church was performed by the Lord Bishop of St David's assisted by the Reverend Enoch Pugh, vicar.

The Maesgwynne Mansion household in 1851, as recorded in the census, consisted of 31-year-old W. R. H. Powell who was a J.P. for Carmarthenshire and a Deputy Lieutenant, his 20-year-old wife Catherine, his 10-year-old daughter Caroline Mary and his 7-year-old son Walter Rice Howell, both by his late first wife. Serving them were a cook, a house-maid and a kitchen-maid together with a nurse. Surprisingly, no governess was listed. Also listed as living in the Mansion were two grooms, 31-year-old John Rees and 21-year-old Levi Harries; horse-men clearly received pride of place in the Squire's priorities. We shall hear much more about John (Jack) Rees later. Bearing in mind the Squire's passion for hunters and racehorses it is surprising that he managed his stable with only two grooms, although it may well be that labourers such as those living nearby at Blaencwmfallen were hired to help out the grooms. John Morris the blacksmith at the Blacksmiths' Shop, listed in the 1851 census next to Blaen-cwmfallen, was able to offer a service closer to the stables than that provided at Panteg near Cefnypant by John Phillips. From the information in the 1851 census, seven persons, of whom six were living-in, can be identified as being employees of the Squire. The cottages of Plasybwci, near Blaencwmfallen, were not listed in the 1851 census which may mean that they had not been built at that time. Later they would house families earning their keep as employees of the Squire. At the round house of Maesgwynne Lodge there lived a gardener and his wife and their daughter, who was a dress-maker. W. R. H. Powell's younger brother Thomas Rees Oliver Powell was a law student in 1851, lodging at 52 Bernard Street, St George's, Bloomsbury, Middlesex.

The first half of 1855 brought with it a dreadful low to the lives of the Powell family with the death at Maesgwynne of the son and heir, Walter Rice Howell Powell, at the age of eleven years. He was buried at Llanboidy Church graveyard. During the second half of 1855 a daughter was born to the Squire and his second wife Catherine and she was named Emily Catherine.

By 1861, in addition to the Squire and his wife and two daughters, two of his relatives were also at Maesgwynne. One was his 29-year-old brother Thomas Rees Oliver Powell who was by then a practising barrister-at-law. Oliver got married in 1866 in London to Kate Pearls Lindsey and they went to live at Waungron Mansion, Lampeter Velfrey. The other relative was Powell Bach's un-married aunt, 60-year-old Georgiana Powell who had probably moved to Maes-gwynne from Penycoed, St Clears where she had been living with her sister Elizabeth Jane Oliver Hungerford Powell and her family. Elizabeth had died in 1854 and her widower, Timothy Powell, had taken a second wife in 1856 when he married his servant, Margaret Williams. In addition to a nurse, cook and two maids, the Powells of Maesgwynne now employed a footman. Also living in the Mansion was a stud-groom, 22-year-old John Wheal born in Lancaster and two stable-lads one of whom, 18-year-old John Pope, born in Tenby, was to become Powell Bach's leading jockey. A gamekeeper occupied Maesgwynne Lodge and a gardener was living at Maesgwynne Farm, whose wife was listed as the manager of the dairy farm. The identifiable staff attending to the Squire's stable of horses had increased substantially by 1861. In addition to the extra stable-lad living in the Mansion, two stable-men and their families lived at numbers 2 and 4 Blaencwmfallen. The forge near Blaencwmfallen was then called Plasmorgan Forge (it was later called California) where John Morris still plied his trade. Another blacksmith, 29-year-old Josiah Phillips, had set up in business at Hafod Hill in Llanboidy lower village.

Nos. 3 and 4 Plasybwci, semi-detached two-room workers' cottages.
(Eddie Evans collection).

Nos. 5 and 6 Plasybwci, semi-detached four-room workers' cottages, rebuilt by Powell *c*.1869.
In doorway: Phebe Jenkins (1865-1956) (author's great-grandmother) and son Emlyn (1904-1967).
(Eddie Evans collection).

Griffith Jenkins (1865-1933)
(author's great-grandfather), labourer
and coachman for W. R. H. Powell
and his successors from *c*.1884.
(Eddie Evans collection).

A few miles away in Cwmfelin Boeth village there lived a 78-year-old horse jockey, Daniel Howells, but he was probably past his best by that time. In 1861 a total of 12 staff, with 7 living-in, can be identified as being employed by the Squire at Maesgwynne.

In the 1861 census, one dwelling in the hamlet of Blaencwmfallen, half a mile or so from Maesgwynne, was named Plasybwci. Since 1851 the hamlet had increased from four dwellings, all named Blaencwmfallen, to seven; the extra dwellings were called Blaencwmfallen, Old Kennel and Plasybwci. (The name Blaencwmfallen should, probably, read Blaencwmafallen indicating an area rich in apple trees. The form Blaencwm-pally on the Cassini Historical map 158 surveyed between 1818 and 1831 was, surely, a mistake. On the equivalent map surveyed between 1842 and 1893 the hamlet was named Plas-y-bica, a name which might be derived from the place having been the residence of a clergyman because *bicer* is an old Welsh name for vicar.) By 1871 the hamlet was made up of six dwellings, two named Blaencwmfallen, three Plasybwci and one Old Kennel. By 1881, four dwellings bore the name of Blaencwmfallen and one Plasybwci; Old Kennel had been dropped. But the place known in 1871 as Old Kennel may well have been called Blaencwmfallen in 1881 since it was Thomas Davies and family that occupied both places. His job-title had changed from stable-man to groom but it is quite possible that his job specification remained the same. In 1891 and also in 1901 all six dwellings were labelled No. 1–6 Plasybwci but by 1911, Blaencwmfallen had made a come-back as the name of one of the dwellings in the hamlet, the other five claiming to be Plasybwci. The dwellings named Plasybwci in 1911 were likely to have been two blocks of semi-detached cottages. One block of two cottages had probably been rebuilt by W. R. H. Powell as part of his programme of improvement to workers' dwellings. Their construction in grey stone, is similar in appearance to that of the Market Hall and Piccadilly Square in Llanboidy Village known to have been put up in the early 1880s at the instructions of the Squire.

W. R. H. Powell's involvement in training and racing horses reached a peak in the 1860s when he established himself as one of, if not the, leading owner and trainer of racehorses in Wales. But in 1868 he suddenly 'retired from the turf' and sold many, if not most, of his steeplechasers, thereby reducing his stable of horses by about 40% to around 40, mainly hunters. Powell continued to run his hunters in the numerous hunt race meetings got up in those days in places such as Aberystwyth, Haverfordwest and Carmarthen, and his pack of hounds maintained its dominant position in the sport of fox-hunting in west Wales. The 1871 census entries show that a stable staff of stud-groom (John Pope), three grooms and a helper lived at the Mansion and a further two grooms and a stableman lived at nearby Blaencwmfallen and Plasybwci. The hounds were looked after by a kennel-man, 33-year-old Thomas John, born in St Nicholas, Pembrokeshire, who lived at Blaencwmfallen. The Hunt's whipper-in, 20-year-old Carmarthen-born Richard Griffiths, lived at the Mansion. The huntsman, John (Jack) Rees, was the landlord of the Lamb Inn, Llanboidy. In all, in 1871, 19 people can be identified as being full-time employees of the Squire of Maesgwynne. Thirteen of them lived in the Mansion. The number of employees remained the same for the following twenty years.

Successive squires took pride in developing lawns, gardens and woodland around the Mansion and the attractive environs were described by the Reverend John Jones, sometime curate at Morriston, but then signing himself as 'Joannes Towy' of Llanboidy, in a poem published in 1886:

Maesgwynne lies hid among the wood
In this secluded neighbourhood;
Environed with delightful trees,
Where birds chant forth their melodies.
Here gay plantations, green and fair,
Display their verdure everywhere.
Fair trees from many a foreign land
Adorn these walks on every hand;
The blushing rhododendron here
And modest copper-beech appear.
Laurels, laburnums, here abound
Through all the ornamental ground;
And graceful *arbor vitae* green
Adds beauty to the sylvan scene.

Embellished are these grounds again
With plots botanical, that thrives amain,
In native and exotic flowers,
The growth of sunshine and soft showers.
Gay flowers of exquisite fair dyes,
Bright as the wings of butterflies;
Blue, rose, vermilion, purple hues,
Adorn these children of the dews,
Whose colour, fragrance, bloom, and grace
Crown and imparadise the place;
The grateful perfumes they exhale
With balmy odours scent the gale.
And oh! The enchantment of sweet flowers
Reminds me of 'Arcadian Bowers'.

In such a flowering Paradise
The unobtrusive mansion lies;
Happy the man who dwells therein,
The famed Esquire of Maesgwynne;
Happy the view Llanboidy rise
A pleasing shade before his eyes;
Happy to see his tenants strive,
And happier still to see them thrive.
He loves to see the sons of toil
Progressing on the well-ploughed soil.
Long may he live; and may he still
Possess the same determined will
To carry out with vigorous hands
Enlarged improvements on his lands.[19]

The 1870s brought a mixture of ups and downs to the personal lives of the Powells. The second daughter, 19-year-old Emily Catherine, was married in 1874 to William Francis Roch of Butter Hill, St Ishmael's, Pembrokeshire, who was 10 years her senior. They had four children. It was, also, in 1874 that Powell Bach's head groom and number one jockey, Johnny Pope, married Margaret Jones. Two years later Margaret Pope died giving birth to a son, John Henry Pope. In the 1881 census, five-year-old John Henry Pope was recorded as 'Boarder' with 'Huntsman' Thomas Davies and his wife Esther and their four children at Plasybwci. Thirty-eight-year-old Thomas Davies had succeeded Jack Rees as the man in charge of the Maesgwynne pack.

In the 1870s and 1880s W. R. H. Powell's political radicalism and his popularity with the expanded electorate had made him a natural parliamentary candidate for the newly constituted Liberal party. In 1880 he was elected Liberal Member of Parliament for Carmarthenshire after narrowly failing to win a seat in 1874. He was re-elected in 1885 for the new seat of West Carmarthenshire and he represented that constituency for the rest of his life.

Death was never far away in nineteenth-century society and the Powells of Maesgwynne suffered like everyone else. In 1877 W. R. H. Powell lost his brother, Oliver, a barrister living at Waungron House, Lampeter Velfrey, at the age of 45 years. His widow, Kate Pearls Powell moved to Pwllywhead, Whitland. She took an active role in Llangan church and continued to provide clothes and culm for the poor at Christmas time. In about 1880 she left the area for Folkestone, Kent and spent most of her life there. She passed away in St Pancras, London, in 1903. In 1878, W. R. H. Powell's unmarried aunt, Margaret Maria Georgiana Powell died at the age of 79 years at Maesgwynne. She had spent much of her life with her sister, Elizabeth Jane Oliver Hungerford Powell, at Penycoed, St Clears. When W. R. H. Powell's sister Maria Jane Randolph died in Bath in 1885, at the age of 63, only Powell Bach and his brother Edward Henry were left of the five children born to W. R. H. Powell (senior) and his wife Mary between 1819 and 1832.

Four years later in 1889, W. R. H. Powell died at the age of 70 at Maesgwynne. It was also the year of the death of his son-in-law, William Francis Roch, at the age of 45 years. Powell Bach was buried at St Brynach's Church, Llanboidy. His brother, Edward Henry Powell died in Axbridge District, Somerset, in 1892 at the age of 67 years. With the passing of Powell Bach, the Maesgwynne Estate passed to his elder daughter Caroline Mary Powell, as stated in his will and reported in newspapers. 'Probate of the will, dated February 5 1890, of the late Mr Walter Rice Howell Powell, of Maesgwynne, Carmarthen, JP and DL (High Sheriff 1849) who died on June 25 1889, aged 70 years, has been granted to the sole executrix his daughter Miss Caroline Mary Powell to whom he bequeathed all his real and personal property, his wife, Mrs Caroline Ann Powell, being already provided for. The gross value of the testator's personal estate is £6,343.4s.2d. and its net value £2,788.17s.10d.'[20] The will was witnessed by John Pope (groom) and William Stephens (butler). The passing of W. R. H. Powell brought to a shuddering halt the sporting activities based at Maesgwynne. Nothing would have illustrated the change more clearly than the selling of the famous pack of hounds. The pack was bought for £800 by the Master of the Penllergaer Hunt, Mr W. J. Buckley who retained them as the 'Carmarthenshire' but they were moved from Maesgwynne to be kennelled at Travellers' Rest near Carmarthen. Thomas Davies was retained as huntsman but he, also, moved from Plasybwci to live in Carmarthen. With no racehorses to look after, Johnny Pope retired at 46 years of age and he also moved to Carmarthen where he found lodgings with his friend Thomas Davies. Pope passed away in 1900 and was buried in Llanllwch churchyard.

On 30 March 1896, only seven years after the death of her father, Caroline Mary passed away at 55 years of age. She had contracted scarlet fever after comforting a child suffering from the disease. A tribute by the Reverend John Jones, 'Joannes Towy', published in the *Carmarthen Journal* crystallized in verse the qualities that made the community refer to Caroline as 'the little angel'. One of the verses was:

> A lady bred, a lady born was she,
> Full of good works and rare humanity,
> Where sickness and where poverty were found,
> There always did her charity abound.
> The poor, indeed, will miss a valued friend,
> Who do their humble wants would condescend;
> How did the hearts of invalids rejoice
> To hear the kindly accents of her voice –
> And, as she spoke in language mild and bland,
> To feel the pressure of her generous hand.

Powell Bach's other daughter, Emily Catherine and her husband William Francis Roch had four children. After the death of Caroline Mary, it was the eldest of the four children, George Powell Roch, who had, by the 1901 census, become the Squire at Maesgwynne. Ten years later, as recorded in the 1911 census, he was an absentee landlord living on his own means with his wife in London; Maesgwynne Mansion was in the care of staff. George Powell Roch, as well as his youngest brother, William Protheroe Roch, was killed in action in the First World War; 42-year-old George lost his life on 21 May 1918 in Flanders and 35-year-old William died on 11 March 1918 in the Jordan Valley. Maesgwynne then passed to the surviving brother, Walter Francis Roch, born in Maesgwynne in 1880 and educated at Harrow. He qualified as a solicitor and became a barrister in 1913. In 1908 he was elected Liberal MP for Pembrokeshire but his support of Asquith rather than Lloyd George put paid not only to the talk that he might be a future Prime Minister but to his political career. In 1911 he married the Hon. Fflorens Mary Ursula Herbert who was a great-grand-daughter of the Welsh patriot Lady Llanover and her husband Benjamin Hall after whom Big Ben was named. Walter spent the last twenty-five years of his life at Tŷ Nant, Llanarth, Raglan, Monmouthshire.

Walter Francis Roch, after inheriting the almost 3,000-acre Maesgwynne Estate, wasted no time before selling nearly 2,500 acres by public auction at Whitland on 20 September 1918. The mansion and the 250-acre farm of Maesgwynne were retained and Walter Francis Roch's sister Mary Catherine and her husband Julian Wilmot Morris Vaughan returned from farming in Australia to take over the mansion and farm. Wilmot Vaughan was born in Llangoedmor, Cardiganshire and was a younger brother of the author Herbert Millingchamp Vaughan. Mary Catherine Vaughan, granddaughter of W. R. H. Powell, was the last of the Powell line to live at Maesgwynne. The Maesgwynne Estate comprising nearly 500 acres was finally disposed of by Walter Francis Roch at a public auction in Whitland on 15 September 1944. Mary Catherine and Wilmot Vaughan spent the last years of their lives near Gillingham, Dorset, England, where they ended their days, Wilmot in 1956 and Mary Catherine in 1963. Both were buried at St Brynach's churchyard, Llanboidy.

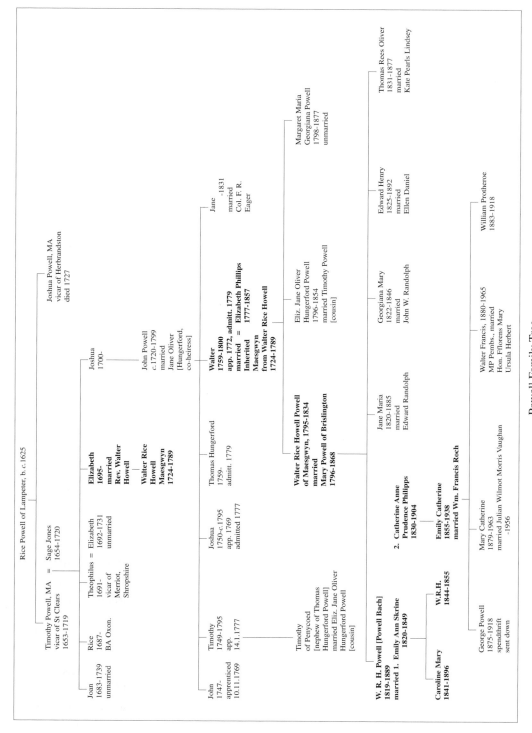

Powell Family Tree.
(Denley Owen collection).

Maesgwynne Mansion, *c.*1880.
(By permission of Llyfrgell Genedlaethol Cymru/The National Library of Wales).

Maesgwynne Mansion, *c.*1890. From right to left: Mrs Powell (1830-1904), Walter Francis Roch (1880-1965),
Emily Catherine Roch (née Powell) (1855-1938), Mary Catherine Roch (1879-1963), ?, William Protheroe Roch
(1883-1918), Caroline Mary Powell (1841-1896), George Powell Roch (1875-1918).
(Thomas Lloyd collection).

Identifiable employees at Maesgwynne from Census returns

	1841	1851	1861	1871	1882	1891
Nurse	0	1	1	0	0	0
Governess	0	0	0	0	0	1
Cook	0	1	1	1	0	1
Footman	0	0	1	0	0	1
Page	0	0	0	0	1	1
Butler	0	0	0	1	0	0
Servant	5	2	2	5	8	6
Gardener	1	1	1	1	2	3
Gamekeeper	0	0	1	1	0	0
Coachman	0	0	0	0	0	1
Groom	0	2	2	6	6	4
Stableman	0	0	3	2	2	0
Huntsman	0	0	0	1	0	0
Whipper-in	0	0	0	1	0	0
Kennelman	0	0	0	1	0	0
Total	**6**	**7**	**12**	**19**	**19**	**19**
County/country of origin	n/a	4C 3P	6C 5P	7C 10P	8C 8P	8C 8P 2E 1G

C = Carmarthenshire; P = Pembrokeshire; E = England; G = Germany.

Griffith Jenkins, Plasybwci, his son Jack (1896-1967), Maesgwynne Lodge, Glyn John, Maesgwynne Farm
Cottage, Ifan Lewis, Llwynteg, Llanboidy, at Maesgwynne in the 1920s.
(Denley Owen collection).

W. R. H. Powell (1819-1889).

(Thomas Lloyd collection).

Timothy Powell (1793-1889), Penycoed, St Clears.
Cousin-once-removed to Powell Bach.

(Thomas Lloyd collection).

Caroline Mary Powell (1841-1896), daughter
of Powell Bach from first marriage. She
inherited Maesgwynne on the death of her
father in 1889.

(Eddie Evans collection).

Emily Catherine Powell (1855-1938), daughter of
Powell Bach from second marriage. Her son
George Powell Roch (1875-1918) inherited
Maesgwynne in 1896.

(Eddie Evans collection).

Part II

WORKING FOR THE COMMUNITY: GLIMPSES OF THE SQUIRE'S INVOLVEMENT

2.1 Talking to Rebecca

EARLY IN 1839 trouble erupted in the borderlands of Carmarthenshire and Pembrokeshire which required the young Squire of Maesgwynne to return from Oxford to help deal with the crisis. In those days local governance was conducted by magistrates consisting of squires and clergy at meetings of petty sessions which in Llanboidy met at the Farmers' Arms. The sessions dealt with criminal cases and matters connected with the Poor Law, roads and the police. Many magistrates were absent from the locality. One of those was Lord Dynevor who lived at Barrington Park in the Cotswolds. Others were elderly and never attended the petty sessions. As a result, power and responsibility were in the hands of very few persons. In the St Clears area the dominant characters were Rice Pryce Beynon, Timothy Powell, John Waters and the Reverend John Evans of Nant-yr-eglwys, vicar of Llanboidy and rector of Llanglydwen. Married but without children; in addition to his clerical duties he ran the farm of Nant-yr-eglwys with the help of two house servants, three female and three male farm servants. Later he added the archdeaconry of Carmarthen to his portfolio.

Many of the magistrates were also members of the newer institutions of the turnpike trusts and of the Boards of Guardians which ran the workhouses.

It was a time of increasing cultural divide between the church-going English-speaking aristocracy and clergy on the one hand and the chapel-going Welsh-speaking common people and their ministers on the other. This caused increasing tension between the 'rulers' and the 'ruled'. *The Times* reporter, Thomas Campbell Foster, wrote that 'It cannot be denied that the people look upon the landlords and the gentry and magistrates as a class with hatred and suspicion . . . this arises solely from oppression and insulting, haughty, offensive demeanour.' A few landlords were vindictive towards tenants who offended them and there were several accusations that farmers had lost their holdings for voting independently on church rates and in parliamentary elections.[1] At a meeting of farmers in the Blue Bell Inn, Cynwyl Elfed, *The Times* correspondent was told that the county magistrates 'look upon the people as if they were beasts and not human beings and treat us with the greatest indignity.' Colonel Love, the military commander of the south Wales district, when asked to evaluate the responsibility of the leaders of society for the uprising that later broke out, replied that they had displayed a dangerous mix of insensitivity and inactivity. 'I grieve to say,' wrote Love's political superior, Sir James Graham, the Home Secretary, to his Prime Minister, 'that S. Wales bids fair to rival Ireland.

Poverty and the misconduct of landowners are at the root of crime and of discontent in both countries.'[2]

In addition the grim economic conditions made life a misery for the ordinary people in nineteenth-century Wales.[3] The fundamental reason for this economic misery was the rapid rise in population which occurred in the first decades of the nineteenth century and which in south-west Wales resulted in a chronic shortage of jobs. Deprivation was at its worst in the three counties of Carmarthenshire, Pembrokeshire and Cardiganshire where the conditions of the inhabitants was often compared to that of the Irish. *The Times* reporter, Thomas Campbell Foster, writing in 1843 described some of the homes he found in north Carmarthenshire: 'I entered several farm labourers' cottages by the roadside, out of curiosity to see the actual condition of the people, and found them mud hovels, the floors of mud and full of holes, without chairs or tables, generally half filled with peat packed up in every corner. Beds there were none; nothing but loose straw and filthy rags upon them. Peat-fires on the floors in a corner filling the cottages with smoke, and three or four children huddled around them. In the most miserable part (of the slums of London), in no part of England, did I ever witness such abject poverty.'[4]

The worst off were the farm labourers but it was the small farmers and tenants who felt most strongly the threat to their standard of living. It was they who paid the tolls to the turnpike companies when transporting their produce to market or when carting lime from the kilns; it was they who paid rent, rates and tithe. When extra rates were imposed on them to meet the costs of the new Narberth Workhouse, the building was set on fire on the evening of 16 January 1839. A reward of £300 for information included £50 from the Secretary of State, Lord John Russell, but it was never claimed.[5]

In the early 1830s, Squire W. R. H. Powell (senior) of Maesgwynne had been involved in some controversy about roads in Llanboidy Parish. He had obtained the support of the Parish to the tune of £1,500 to make a road from Llanboidy to St Clears.[6] In 1832 the road was inadvertently transferred to the control of the Whitland Trust which infuriated parishioners and the Trust's proposal to erect eight gates in the parish moved Squire Powell to declare 'No, never shall any gate be [erected] in my life.' Mr Powell died in June 1834.

The toll-gate erected by the Whitland Trust at Efailwen, Llandysilio Parish to 'catch' farmers carting lime from the Ludchurch kilns became the target for the uprising on 13 May 1839. The gate was destroyed and the tollhouse set on fire. But the gate was replaced and on 6 June a crowd of between 300 to 400 persons turned up at 10.30 p.m. some dressed in women's clothes with blackened faces. They chased the special constables guarding the gate into the surrounding countryside and used sledgehammers to destroy the gate and to dismantle the toll-house to within a yard of the ground. But the gate was again re-erected. It was destroyed for the third time on 17 July and it was on that occasion that the leader was addressed as 'Becca' and the name 'Rebecca Riots' came into use.

On the Saturday night of 15 June 1839 some two hundred disguised persons appeared at a gate near Maesgwynne, Llanboidy and destroyed it.[7] The 20-year-old Squire, W. R. H. Powell, intervened in a very positive manner, calling for and chairing a meeting of reconciliation with the farmers. Such meetings were anathema to most magistrates, including Powell's cousin-once-removed Timothy Powell of St Clears, whose insensitivity to the plight of the farmers and

A Rebecca attack and some of the causes of the uprising
as depicted in *Punch* in 1843.
(Wikipedia web site as at January 2012).

to the deprivation of the lower classes in general was a cause of the uprising. It became apparent that the immediate grievance felt by the farmers of Llanboidy was the decision by the Whitland Trust to order replacement gates for Efailwen and for Maesgwynne and new gates for other locations in the Llanboidy and St Clears area. Encouraged by the fact that the Trust had reached its decision by a majority of only two votes, W. R. H. Powell set about getting the Trust to revoke its order. Determined to introduce a more civilised way of dealing with the ordinary people and their grievances he made contact with some influential local leaders. He found an ally in John Jones of Ystrad, one of two Tory MPs for Carmarthenshire. Ystrad was a house near Carmarthen in what is now the village of Johnstown, named after the MP. John Jones' efforts to have the salt tax abolished earned him the nickname Jones yr Halen (Jones the Salt).

W. R. H. Powell also had support from the Pwlltrap Magistrate, Rice Pryce Beynon who was recorded in the 1851 census as being a 'landed proprietor' living in High Street, St Clears. According to D. J. V. Jones in *Rebecca's Children*, Beynon was 'notorious for [his] drunkeness, bad temper and moral lapses'. Evidence of his 'lapses' is found in his claim to six children although in successive censuses he was recorded as being a bachelor. By 1861 he was a Captain in the Royal Carmarthenshire Militia and lived in Pentowyn, Mydrim, a 300-acre farm which he was farming by 1871.

After much behind-the-scenes activity by W. R. H. Powell, Rice Pryce Beynon, John Jones MP together with the local Anglican clergymen, a packed public meeting of trustees, gentlemen and magistrates at the Blue Boar, St Clears, on 23 July 1839, chaired by the Reverend John Evans, Nant-yr-eglwys, advised the Whitland Trust to revoke the order for new gates. The notice to revoke, was signed by Trustees John Evans, R. P. Beynon and Nathaniel Rowland of Parciau, Henllan Amgoed.[8] Maesgwynne, Efailwen and Blue Boar Stables were to be free of tollgates and Tavernspite and Pantygroes near Cefnbrafle were saved from toll-bars.

Nathaniel Rowland was the grandson of the Methodist Revival leader, the Reverend Daniel Rowland of Llangeitho but Nathaniel's interests lay in earthly matters; he was a Captain in the Carmarthenshire Yeomanry, a magistrate, landowner and turnpike trust member. He died in 1849.

The decision to revoke was something of a triumph for the young Squire of Maesgwynne because those against were led by none other than Lord Dynevor, his son George Rice-Trevor MP and the influential local magistrate Timothy Powell of Penycoed, St Clears. Timothy Powell had warned that the concession being offered was bound to invite more trouble. But that claim proved unfounded. In fact, three years later, his claim was turned on its head when the erection of a new gate at St Clears by the Main Trust not only invited trouble but got it a-plenty! Between November 1842 and February 1843 twenty attacks were made on gates and toll-houses around St Clears. Magistrates Timothy Powell and Rice Pryce Beynon bore the brunt of the people's anger for these disturbances, but Timothy Powell alleged that the attackers were not from the St Clears area but from up-country, that is, Llanboidy!

Timothy Powell faced more trouble from ratepayers in 1843. It was alleged that the money from the county rate was being spent for the benefit of country gentlemen and their friends and magistrates including Timothy Powell were accused of dining on public money. The accusations were denied and corruption was never proved.

Things had been moving fast for the Squire of Maesgwynne. At the February 1842 meeting of the Carmarthenshire Quarter Sessions, chaired by John Jones MP, W. R. H. Powell together with his cousin-once-removed Timothy Powell of St Clears were admitted to serve as magistrates for the County of Carmarthenshire.[9] William Garrick Brydges Schaw Protheroe of Dolwilym, Llanglydwen, was already a magistrate. W. G. B. Schaw had transformed himself into a Protheroe by adding the surname when he married the heiress of Dolwilym, Emma Hart daughter of her mother of the same name and of Dr Evan Jones Protheroe who as mentioned previously was not a real Protheroe either.

The meeting of the quarter sessions considered the matter of the rate and, as reported in the *Carmarthen Journal*, 'a Rate of 1p in the £1 was ordered'. As a magistrate, W. R. H. Powell was by that time a member of the Whitland Trust with responsibility for toll-gates! In early February 1843 the *Carmarthen Journal* carried an advert signed by four trustees, W. R. H. Powell, Timothy Powell, R. P. Beynon and William Evans calling for a meeting of the Whitand Trust and the 17 February issue of the paper carried a report of the meeting held at the Blue Boar, St Clears. The meeting considered 'the best mode to restore peace to that district.' Among those present were W. R. H. Powell, R. P. Beynon, Nathaniel Rowland and Reverend John

Evans who chaired the meeting. It was reported that J. Lloyd Davies spoke powerfully in Welsh and 'we regret . . . our imperfect knowledge.' In other words the reporter could not understand a word of the 'powerful' speech. But he did understand that 50 farmers volunteered to be sworn in as special constables. However, the magistrates' forlorn hope of repelling the attacks by means of a few farmers, hastily sworn as special constables, stood no chance against hundreds of daughters of Rebecca but the Reverend John Evans' response was to condemn the cowardice of the poor farmers.

George Rice-Trevor MP was far more realistic in his assessment that most of the rural population was fully supportive of the Rebecca movement. But his answer that only a permanent police force could bring it to an end missed the fundamental point appreciated by W. R. H. Powell that the root causes of the discontent had to be addressed before Rebecca could be expected to disband her daughters.

During the disturbances, public meetings were called to discuss the grievances. Most of the gentry called on the government to ban such meetings, but W. R. H. Powell and a few others attended those held in their localities believing that such meetings helped defuse the situation. Where the gentry were absent, respectable farmers and Nonconformist ministers took the chair and by the end of the nineteenth century they had effectively displaced the gentry as community leaders. Thanks to W. R. H. Powell's foresight, the Llanboidy area enjoyed comparative peace during the troubles and his popularity was on the rise almost from the beginning of his inheriting the Maesgwynne estate. Moreover, he also understood that the riots were about more than toll-gates and appreciated the Home Secretary's assertion that at the root of the troubles were 'poverty and the misconduct of landowners.'

Powell's championing of 'reconciliation' between 'rulers' and 'ruled' during the riots was in stark contrast to the more usual practice of oppressing the ordinary people adopted by the magistrates and landowners of the time. And his cousin-once-removed, Timothy Powell of St Clears, was very much in the latter camp. W. R. H. Powell emerged as a leader that did not fit the picture of 'insensitivity and inactivity' painted by Colonel Love. Powell stood for fairness for the ordinary people and was prepared to take action to achieve it. He was, most certainly, a landowner apart.

2.2 Putting Llanboidy on the map

W. R. H. Powell's concern for the welfare of his fellow men and women was reflected in his support for Friendly Societies. According to their rules the main object of a Friendly Society was 'to raise from time to time, by subscription among the members thereof, or by voluntary contribution, or by donations, a stock or fund for the mutual relief and maintenance of such members, their wives or children, relations or nominees in sickness, infancy, advanced age or death'.[10] The 'True Ivorites Society' was an institution 'to encourage the Welsh language, to preserve its members as far as possible from want, and to unite every Welshman, as one man, to support each other.' Furthermore, 'that all books and accounts belonging to this society be kept in the Welsh Language, and the secretaries of every branch lodge are to deliver up the accounts of their respective lodges to the head lodge in Carmarthen.'

An Ivorite Lodge existed in Llanboidy in 1841 and in that year an Oddfellows Lodge named Goleu Cymru was established there as well, with its headquarters in the Farmers' Arms. It is likely that W. R. H. Powell was instrumental in establishing Goleu Cymru. Because of some disagreements the Ivorites in Carmarthen ended up with two lodges claiming seniority within the county. That may have been the reason for the Squire and others setting up the Oddfellows Lodge in Llanboidy. A report of a meeting on 14 September 1842 of Goleu Cymru at the Farmers' Arms stressed the cordial relations between the two lodges in Llanboidy. And the report contained a verse extolling the virtue of cooperation:[11]

Os Odydd ac Ifor
A fydd yn cyd-dynnu,
Paradwys y gelwir
Cymdogaeth Llanboidy.

The report also described a procession by members of Goleu Cymru to the home of W. R. H. Powell Esq. At Maesgwynne they were received in some style by Mr Powell after which they returned to their meeting room at the Farmers' Arms to partake of a sumptuous meal prepared by the landlady, Mrs Phillips. The popularity of the Friendly Societies waned in the second half of the nineteenth century especially in the rural areas. But W. R. H. Powell, ever alert to the needs of the rural population, formed a new society called 'The United Counties Friendly Society' or as it was popularly known, 'Clwb Powell Bach'. More of that later.

In 1849 W. R. H. Powell at the age of 30 was appointed High Sheriff of Carmarthenshire. Interestingly, he appointed his brother-in-law Edward Randolph, solicitor of Exeter as his Deputy and George Thomas jnr., solicitor of Carmarthen, as his Acting Deputy Sheriff.

W. R. H. Powell had a passion for horse racing and during 1851 he constructed his own racecourse, about one-and-a-half miles from Maesgwynne, on land half-a-mile west of the hamlet of Cefnbrafle or Cefnbriallu as it was labelled on the Ordnance Survey map of 1891. The site of the racecourse at Cefnbrafle must have been a hive of activity during 1851 as W. R. H. Powell organised his workforce consisting, probably, of local craftsmen and labourers to construct the courses. Some of the Squire's staff at Maesgwynne would have been involved in the preparation work on the course. For example, the two grooms, 31-year-old John Rees and 21-year-old Levi Harries would have been particularly interested because the new course would be the place where they would exercise and train the Maesgwynne horses. It must have been a marvellous sight to witness the horses being ridden over the Cefnbrafle ridge between their stables at Maesgwynne and the racecourse for their exercise and training. *Rhedegfa Cefnbrafle*, as the racecourse was identified on the Ordnance Survey map, was basically a 'banking' course over which horses had to jump or negotiate earth banks; a skill at which the Maesgwynne-trained horses became almost unbeatable. But races over a 'flying' course, a 'hurdles' course and on the flat could also be accommodated. The outer circuit was about one-and-a-half miles in length. A few years later in 1857 the course was improved and a grandstand was erected on the site; evidence of W. R. H. Powell's determination to make the course second to none in Wales and, as we shall see, Llanboidy Races became an unique annual event in the racing calendar.

Llanboidy's two parts: Pentre Ucha and Pentre Isha.
(Eddie Evans collection).

Cwmfelin Mynach.
(Eddie Evans collection).

In 1851 Llanboidy was blessed with a general medical practioner, Charles Lewis Crosswell who lived at Commercial House, a police officer, 35-year-old widower John Davies at Shop House and a schoolmaster, George Phillips, at East Gate, a house which belonged to the Maesgwynne Estate. George Phillips also acted as clerk to the Petty Sessions.

There was more good news for local craftsmen in 1856 when Powell decided to build a new hotel in Llanboidy to meet the needs of the hunting and racing fraternity. It was built on the site of the Farmers' Arms and was a major undertaking that would have provided employment for masons, carpenters and labourers. It has been suggested that Maesgwynne Arms might have been the work of local builder John Phillips. He may have been the John Phillips from Tavernspite who had been responsible for the ill thought-out assemblage of nearby Dolwilym Mansion between 1842 and 1845.[12] Either way, it is reasonable to assume that W. R. H. Powell would have taken advantage of the readily available local pool of craftsmen and labourers and likewise the local people would have been delighted at the amount of work coming their way as a result of the Squire's initiatives. The new hotel would have required extra staff to run it compared to the much smaller Farmers' Arms. According to the 1851 Census Benjamin Griffiths and his wife employed three maids and two labourers to run the Farmers' Arms and the 170-acre farm. By the time of the 1861 Census the Farmers' Arms had been converted into the Maesgwynne Arms and while they still employed two labourers their number of servants had increased to five and in addition their 18-year-old daughter and their 16 and 14-year-old sons were also on the staff of the new establishment.

With the coming of the railway to Carmarthen in 1852 and its extension to Haverfordwest by 1854, west Wales had never been so accessible or so easy to leave provided the fares were affordable. W. R. H. Powell appreciated that ease of accessibility to rail travel was vital to the development of settlements and that Llanboidy needed to be on the path of the proposed rail link between Whitland and Cardigan. He advocated a track that followed the River Gronw from Whitland to Llanboidy from where the track would need to cut its way to the valley of the Taf so as to access the Glogue Quarries, whose existence was the chief catalyst to developing the link. But the Taf Valley was the natural line of communication from the quarries at Pencelli, Penlan, Llanfyrnach and Glogue to Whitland and by 1868, John Owen, owner of the Glogue Quarry, was actively promoting the case for a Taf Valley railway from Whitland to Cardigan. The only company to be set up to develop a line from Whitland to Cardigan was one committed to the Taf Valley link but it experienced lengthy delays in acquiring the land as many landowners with no direct interest in the line held out for the maximum possible compensation. Work started on the Taf Valley line on 8 November 1870 and trains reached Llanglydwen on 4 January 1872. It may well be that Powell's efforts floundered on the intransigence of W. H. Yelverton, owner of Whitland Abbey, to allow Powell's proposed track to cross his land. Yelverton's opposition may have been political rather than financial because by that time, Powell had emerged as a Liberal radical in complete contrast to Yelverton's right-wing views.

As a magistrate, W. R. H. Powell attended the Carmarthenshire Quarter Sessions, the County ruling body which, in those days, dealt with most matters of local government including the 'care' of the mentally ill. For example, at the Easter 1856 quarter sessions at Carmarthen, one topic for discussion was a letter from the Secretary of State in London requiring the County to provide a 'Lunatic Asylum' for at least 110 'pauper lunatics'. Lord Cawdor, who seemed to act as a kind of leading spokesman at the meeting, expressed his opinion that the three counties of Carmarthen, Cardigan and Pembrokeshire should remain together on this matter and that the Secretary of State be informed that the United Counties Committee was already searching for a site. (The Secretary of State must have accepted the meeting's advice because one asylum for

Labour-intensive haymaking.
(Eddie Evans collection).

the three counties of west Wales was the eventual outcome.) Another item requiring decision was to appoint a member to serve on the County Roads Board to succeed the late Mr Neville. It was W. R. H. Powell who was duly appointed.

A matter of a rather delicate nature was the recommendation to the meeting that the Chaplain of Carmarthen Goal, Reverend Thomas Jones, be dismissed because he was no longer up to the job. After confirmation from the Clerk that the meeting had the power in law to dismiss him, the meeting agreed to Lord Cawdor's proposal that the Chaplain's employment be terminated on the grounds of 'age and infirmity in-order to soften the blow'. A major project under the jurisdiction of the magistrates was the repairs to Loughor Bridge. A report before the meeting indicated that the costs had escalated by 65%. The original estimate was for £315 but a further £200 was being requested! It was decided to seek further information.[13]

As would be expected, Powell was always ready to promote the interests of Llanboidy at the Quarter Session meetings. For example, at the October 1863 meeting, Powell proposed that a police house and cells be erected at Llanboidy. He expressed the view that Llanboidy 'was an outlet from Maenclochog and the upper part of Pembrokeshire and justified a police house and cells'.[14] He went on to claim that Llanboidy was 'infested with tramps and characters of the lowest sort'. The village was seven miles from the nearest railway station and a considerable distance from a lock-up or a station-house and when he had prisoners, the local police constable was obliged to keep them in his own house, a practice which was dangerous and improper. Powell's motion to the meeting requested a sum of £400 for a building with accommodation for two policemen or, £300 if they were restricted to one officer. He received support from other members of the committee including Sir James Drummond but Drummond pointed out that correct procedures needed to be followed. Since no notice of Powell's motion had been submitted at the previous Quarter Session, he should now withdraw his motion in favour of a notice that he wished the matter to be discussed at the next Quarter Session. Powell duly obliged.

Throughout his life, W. R. H. Powell spared no effort in attempting to improve the lot of his tenants by, for example, promoting better farming methods and trying to secure markets for their produce. In 1859 he founded the Llanboidy Agricultural Society which promoted the annual Llanboidy Agricultural Show which became one of the best known shows in the country. A feature of agricultural shows of the time was the dinner held after judging was complete. The practice at the dinners was the drinking of endless toasts to all and sundry in celebration of the occasion. Powell was against excessive drinking of alcohol and also considered the toasts to be an utter waste of time which should be better spent in discussing how the produce displayed in the show might be improved by better farming methods. To accommodate his wishes, Powell instigated the practice at Llanboidy Show of lumping together all those deemed worthy of a toast and celebrating their worthiness with a single drink! As a result, most of the time was given over to the judges to give reports of their findings and to make suggestions as to how products might be improved. The practice adopted at Llanboidy Show was followed to a greater or lesser degree at other shows in west Wales such as St Clears, Laugharne and Carmarthen.

Together with his brother, the lawyer T. R. Oliver Powell, he instigated the annual Llanboidy Ploughing Match, open to contestants from the parishes of the hundred of Derllys: Carmarthen Town and all parishes to the west in the county of Carmarthenshire. In February 1863 a 'Grand Ploughing Match at Llanboidy' was held on Bailymawr Farm where about 40 ploughmen took part in two competitions. The three judges were Evans of Castle Lloyd, Morse of Llandawke and John of Plas, Llanglydwen. In the first-class match, the winner was Isaac Davies, Goitre Uchaf, Llanwinio, followed by William Phillips, Castellmawr, Llanwinio; ploughman of David Evans, Cilgynydd, Llanboidy; Thomas Thomas, Cilgrymanfach, Llanwinio; David Lewis, Ffynonwen, Llanwinio and the ploughman of Mr Owen, Henllan, Henllan Amgoed. In the second-class match, the winner was James Phillips, Caerlleon, Llanwinio, followed by the ploughman of Castell Draenog, Llangan; William Thomas, Trehws, Llanwinio; David Lewis, Llechclawdd, Llanwinio; Isaac Davies, Cilgrymanfawr, Llanwinio and the ploughman of Cilhernin, Llanboidy. As pointed out in the *Journal* report, Llanwinio Parish got eight of the twelve places and 'at this rate they should dispel any fears of being displaced by steam.' Clearly, mechanisation was threatening jobs in the farming world. In the evening, 60 people including the competitors sat down to dinner at the Maesgwynne Arms Hotel.[15]

In 1868, T. R. O. Powell did away with the restriction that limited competitors to the hundred of Derllys and threw open the Llanboidy Ploughing Match to the whole of Great Britain. It was held on fields belonging to J. Morris of Wernberni and the stewards were J. Phillips, Castell Draenog; D. Picton, Cilanw; D. Thomas, Bailymawr and E. Jones, Ffynonfoida. The secretary was R. Howell, Gellidogyn.[16]

The high esteem in which W. R. H. Powell was held in the locality of Llanboidy and throughout the county of Carmarthenshire was acknowledged from time to time by public dinners held in his honour. For example, in October 1863, the Squire was described as 'a gentleman who for many years has been the foremost in promoting, by great personal patience and expense, the national sports of the county' and the intention to hold a dinner 'in recognition of the sports afforded by W. R. H. Powell but also of his cordial hospitality in connection with them' was announced. Also mentioned was the fact that a few years before, at another dinner in his honour, a splendid testimonial of plate had been presented to W. R. H. Powell by Lord Dynevor on behalf of the lovers of sport. *The Welshman*'s editorial reckoned that he provided sport in the county 'which are not surpassed in Wales'.[17] The speeches at the dinner made interesting reading. The occasion took place at the Boar's Head, Carmarthen, where Mrs Olive prepared the fare for about 50 gentlemen who sat down at 6 o'clock.[18] David Morris MP for Carmarthen Borough acted as chairman and praised W. R. H. Powell for sustaining and leading sport in the County. He said 'Everyone is welcomed at his "meets" . . . [and] . . . when his foxhounds are idle, he turns out a splendid pack of otter hounds which he takes all over the county. Intimately connected with those sports are the races . . . He has placed the Carmarthenshire Open higher than any other stakes in Wales.' He went on to claim that many advantages emanated from good sport. It was an inducement to gentlemen of fortune to live among them in the county and spend their money among their tenants and friends, instead of doing so in foreign lands.

Morris emphasised that W. R. H. Powell's contribution to society was not limited to sport; he worked hard for improving farming through the Llanboidy Agricultural Society and as a member and exhibitor of the Carmarthenshire Agricultural Society. He also promoted education and whatever was calculated to benefit Welshmen and Wales.

The County MP, David Pugh, of Manoravon, Llandeilo, said that they were honouring W. R. H. Powell not only as a sportsman but as a county gentleman, a good landlord, friend of the labourer and patron of education. 'What can be more calculated to unite all classes than sport of this kind?' he asked and went on: 'His virtues are those which are all the more able that they are not paraded before the eye of the public. He lives in the hearts of all classes of the people of this country. For proof look around.'

In his response, Powell said that it was 'some twenty-four years since I first kept hounds and have never regretted the efforts to provide good sport. My time and money have been well spent in that now we have a hunt and race meeting established in this county which at present is A1 in Wales. It now has the support of the Lord Lieutenant and of the County and Borough members . . . it will continue to prosper and improve.' He claimed that the Duke of Wellington kept a pack of hounds near his camp during the Peninsular War and during breaks in hostilities his officers went hunting and that avoided them falling into mischief and becoming indolent. 'Every county should possess a pack because it brings people together and creates social and happy intercourse.' He thanked the owners of covers and the farmers whose land the hunt crossed for their civility. And the fund to compensate farmers for any losses of animals to foxes breaking cover had 'already done good'.

A month earlier at the Llanboidy Agricultural Show Dinner his speech succinctly demonstrated his priorities.[19] The long list of flowery toasts to various members of the Royal Family, to the Armed Forces and to the Clergy usually proposed by the chairman on such occasions were trimmed to the bone by Powell so that the time could be spent far more profitably in discussions of farming matters. He lumped the Royal Family into a brief single toast and his toast to the Clergy specifically included 'and the Ministers of all other denominations' thus making plain his strongly held principle that all denominations were equal. The Reverend D. S.

Davies, minister of Ramoth Baptist Chapel, Cwmfelin Mynach, replied in Welsh . . . briefly no doubt! As an introduction to a general discussion on the quality of the exhibits Powell reminded the 60 or so diners that he had founded the Llanboidy Agricultural Society in order to get tenant farmers to unite with gentlemen of the district and to compete one with the other for the purpose of improving the stock. Improving stock was of paramount importance to Powell but farmers did not always respond to his urgings. For example, at the Carmarthenshire Agricultural Show Dinner in September 1863 the chairman, while complimenting Powell for his efforts to 'improve the quality and breed of horses in this county', was critical of the failure of farmers in general to follow his example. Powell replied: 'I am very fond of a good looking, well bred animal and I agree that farmers in this county do not pay sufficient attention to their horses. It will not pay them to breed horses as they do now; neither does it pay owners of good entire horses to send them into this country. Our farmers put their mares to horses who will serve them for 2 shillings or eighteen pence a mare (hear! hear! and laughter) . . . you must change your system or give up horse-breeding.'[20]

At the 1865 Llanboidy Agricultural Show Dinner, the brevity of the speeches by the two vicars present, one a humorous and droll address in Welsh, landed them in trouble for not including the absent Nonconformist ministers in their reply! Mr Williams of Penlan, Llangynin was called to reply on behalf of the dissenting ministers which he agreed to do but at the same time he could not understand why one of the vicars had not mentioned the dissenters in their replies; he could recall a Nonconformist minister doing so for absent vicars at past shows' dinners! That remark drew an apology from vicar D. R. Jenkins but he also took up a lot of time in explaining that he had nothing against the dissenters . . .

Mr Howell, Gellydogin, spoke in Welsh and praised the efforts of the Show's Hon. Sec., Oliver Powell 'the soul of the show' and of W. R. H. Powell in starting the Llanboidy Agricultural Society which had become 'a good school for farmers'. Howell considered that times were difficult and farmers had to improve their stock and economise on labour. Labour was the burning question of the times; it was scarce and wages high. Machinery offered one way around the problem. He warned that scarcity of labour was likely to increase as more and more labourers' children attended schools and benefited from the education they received. It made them long for 'other pursuits more congenial to their new tastes . . . They would become reporters to *The Welshman*.' He warned those present that by-and-by there would be a glut of reporters in the market and instead of 5 shillings a day they would have to put up with 18 pence a day. 'Such was the result of educating the children of labourers.'

James, Aberelwyn, Glandŵr reckoned that the stock on show that year was as good as any in Pembrokeshire. And there was little difference in standard between winners and losers. Their task was to ensure that the stock left at home was also improving in quality; that was the object of the Society.

Replying to a toast, W. R. H. Powell could not resist emphasising that he would not waste 'your time uselessly' in making a speech! W. R. H. Powell expressed his delight with the success of the Agricultural Society as demonstrated by the continually increased standard of exhibits at the show. He said that the success of the Llanboidy Show was the result of his brother Oliver's hard work as Hon. Sec. He then revealed his next project which was to establish at Llanboidy a Farmers Club 'for the discussion of agricultural subjects.' He had a young farmer in mind for the post of Hon. Sec. He would be happy to attend meetings himself 'as a learner and when he got older and tired of hunting he should probably settle down and turn farmer altogether.'

Oliver Powell in his few words said that as Hon. Sec. he could not please everyone. He referred to the previous year's show when it rained heavily all day and he was soaked to the skin. A bull and his owner turned up and were likewise soaked. He caught a cold and so did the bull . . . the owner blamed the Sec. and did not attend that year's show! J. H. Thomas proposed that the show should be open to all breeds of cattle and not be limited to Welsh Blacks. He thought that it was high time that Hereford and Shorthorn cattle were admitted.

In the 1867 show Oliver produced figures for the number of entries over the years: 1859-211, 1860-312, 1861-279, 1862-243, 1863-256, 1864-273, 1865-215, 1866-224 (Oliver Powell took a year off to get married), 1867-379. Naturally, the figures were well received.[21]

2.3 Friend of the poor: housing, education, hiring and health care

W. R. H. Powell was president of the day at the 1868 Llanboidy Show and at the dinner he took the opportunity to raise the matter of the unsatisfactory social conditions of the labouring population. The need to improve their dwellings and who was to effect the improvements had long exercised 'the brains of our public men'. Powell said that his wife and daughters were very anxious to see the gardens and cottages of the labourers improved. 'I assure you that no one takes a deeper interest in the conditions of the labouring classes than does my daughter (Caroline) . . . I promised to lay it before the committee.' He said that his wife and daughters would be happy to offer prizes to labourers for the best vegetables. 'Labourers make little or no use of their gardens.' He also thought that the dwellings of the labouring class required improvements urgently. 'You might say "why don't you do something about it then?"' He answered his own question 'Well, I have done a little and hope to do more. But I really think that the farmers should do something towards improving the dwellings of the labourers.' And then he injected a little humour, 'You are prospering in this locality and I hope to see you in scarlet coats next winter. The tenant farmers I assure you are flourishing in every respect. Look at the wives and daughters coming out in style compared with a few years ago (laughter).' He continued 'No doubt the landlords . . . and I for one . . . would be very happy to assist the tenants to improve the labourers dwellings . . . Those miserable huts that are in many places no better than Irish huts (hear, hear).' He also referred to another two matters. He wished that there was a little more morality amongst the servant boys and girls of the area (hear, hear). 'Sitting as I do at petty sessions, I have often noticed the want of shame or a want of delicacy of feeling on the part of country boys and girls. I think a good deal of blame is attached to the masters. They say they do not like to quarrel with the custom of the country, but you may depend upon it, the boys and girls would be a great deal better in all respects if they were taught to behave with decency and circumspection.'

His other concern was 'that disgraceful custom known as *caru yn y gwely* (hear, hear).' He claimed that he was often laughed at in England and was asked if that was the custom among the Welsh. 'I am obliged with shame to say that there is too much of it in this country.' He thought that the practice arose from the houses being too small, necessitating the crowding of

LLANBOIDY CHARACTERS

Top left:
Wil y Felin. William Griffiths (1812-*c.*1895) was a miller living at Felin Ganol, Llanboidy, with his wife Esther (1820-*c.*1895) and was assisted by his son John (b.1859).

Top right:
Harriet Phillips (1811-1896). She was married to castrator James Phillips (1810-1875) and in 1871 they lived in Swan Square, Pentre Ucha, Llanboidy, with two sons, both tailors. A widow by 1881, she then lived in No. 3 Piccadilly with her three sons, all tailors, a daughter who was a seamstress and two grand-daughters who were scholars at Ysgol Powell Bach. In 1891 she lived alone in Millbrook Cottage, Llanboidy.

Left:
John Davies. In 1891 tailor and widower John Davies (b.1812) lived at Penybont Fach next to Felin Ganol, Llanboidy, together with his daughter Amelia (b.1855) who was a baker.

(Photographs by permission of Llyfrgell Genedlaethol Cymru/ The National Library of Wales).

grown-up boys and girls in the same room. He thought that as landlords they ought to act to improve the dwellings on their property. 'I assure you that I have not come here to talk without the intention to act.' He announced that, as a start, he was subscribing a sovereign towards a prize for the best plan and estimate for cottages . . . double and single . . . 'to comprise, say, on the ground floor, what is called a living room, back kitchen, coal house, etc. and with three bedrooms up-stairs.' He had recently inspected Lord Penrhyn's model village and was 'much pleased with the exterior and interior of the cottages and the arrangements generally.' He added a suggestion that a few prizes be offered for the best-arranged gardens and cottages and for the best specimens of geraniums or window flowers. 'I think that window flowers in a cottage makes the place look neat and tidy – they certainly add to the appearance of the dwelling. In conclusion I may add that I shall be pleased at all times to do anything for you that lies in my power to do (cheers).'[22]

In 1866, a Lodge of the Manchester Order of Odd-Fellows number 5400 was established at the Salutation Inn, Whitland. It was named 'Howell the Good' Lodge and W. R. H. Powell was a leading member. On 1 June 1867, the Lodge members celebrated their first anniversary and hundreds came along to witness the proceedings. At 11.00 o'clock the brethren assembled at the Lodge room to put on their sashes and then walked in procession through the village of Whitland headed by the 21-strong Maesgwynne Brass Band which played 'several beautiful airs'. The procession marched to Trewern Mansion where Mr John Beynon supplied them with *cwrw da* after which they proceeded to Trevaughan and back to the Lodge room for a repast. John Beynon jnr. presided and his toast was responded to in Welsh by Mr Williams, Penlan, Llangynin who proposed a toast to the health of Mr W. R. H. Powell. In his reply, Mr Powell said that when he formed his brass band, some had said that it would be 'the means to lead members to inebriety but he contended otherwise . . . that it would have a different tendency and anyone who misconducted himself would be thrown out.' The health of the members of the Maesgwynne Band was then drunk.[23]

Everything was not always friendly with the Friendly Societies. For example, in March 1867, Josiah John of Esgairddeugoed, Cwmfelin Mynach, was up before the magistrates, Timothy Powell, John Beynon jnr. and W. R. H. Powell at Llanboidy Petty Session charged by the Trustees of the Goleu Cymru Lodge with misuse of Lodge monies. The matter was settled out of court, complainant paying costs.[24] At the same Petty Session, Police Constable John Jones No. 12 charged David Jacob of Middleway, Cyffig, with being drunk and riotous. He was fined five shillings plus costs in default of which he would be sent to the House of Correction for 14 days.

Powell was a believer in education for all children and to this end he had a school built in Llanboidy at his own expense which he opened on 5 October 1863. There had been a day school in Llanboidy since, at least, 1828. So why build another school? The answer probably lies in the fact that the existing school was a Church of England National School in which the teaching of the Church Catechism was being enforced. The vast majority of potential pupils in the Llanboidy area, as in the whole of Wales by that time, were from Nonconformist homes and would not attend a school where the Church of England catechism was mandatory. Since 1837, the Reverend John Evans had been vicar of Llanboidy and it is likely that he had insisted on the teaching of the Church Catechism being compulsory for all pupils at the National School. That

St Brynach's Church in Pentre Ucha.
(By permission of Llyfrgell Genedlaethol Cymru / The National Library of Wales).

Ysgol Powell Bach, built and managed by W. R. H. Powell. Opened in 1863 with 230 pupils.
(Eddie Evans collection).

would have effectively excluded children from Nonconformist homes from attending; something that W. R. H. Powell would have found abhorrent.

At least that interpretation of events is consistent with W. R. H. Powell's decision in 1863 to take sole control over the new school and to make the teaching of the Church Catechism non-compulsory. When the school was opened, the Reverend John Evans was excluded from having any say in the running of the school even though it was registered by Powell as a National Church School, subject to inspection by the National body. This was Powell's way of ensuring the highest standards at the school. Little wonder that the school was popularly known as Ysgol Powell Bach. Clearly, W. R. H. Powell was determined that his school should be open to every child in the catchment area. It is worth noting that during his time at Llanboidy the Reverend John Evans, in addition to his jobs as vicar of Llanboidy and rector of Llanglydwen, had also been appointed archdeacon of Carmarthen. So it was one of the most powerful churchmen in the County, and a magistrate as well, that the Squire of Maesgwynne had taken on in building a rival school! In response to his treatment, the Reverend John Evans kept open the old school, attached to the church building at Llanboidy, so that the village had two schools until 1865 when Evans' successor, the Reverend William Rees, closed the old school, happy in the knowledge that teaching of the Church Catechism was available in Mr Powell's school; but only for those who desired it. In 1866 the Reverend William Rees reported that the senior teacher at the School was paid between £80 and £90 and a second teacher was paid between £50 and £60 a year.[25]

For the re-opening of the school for the autumn term in 1866 the master Mr Edmund Barnes and 230 children displaying flags and banners gathered at 10.30 a.m. With a brass band at their head they marched to Maesgwynne where they were served with buns and milk. 'Rustic sports' followed supervised by the ladies while the committee and teachers sat down to lunch in the mansion. At 3.00 p.m. a return march was undertaken back to the school which had been decorated by the ladies of Maesgwynne. W. R. H. Powell addressed the gathered throng in the school yard and impressed on parents and scholars the necessity of regularity and punctuality to secure their improvement in education (loud cheers). That was followed by dancing until darkness when 'one of the most joyous holidays ever spent in Llanboidy' was brought to a close.[26]

W. R. H. Powell was fully supportive of Welsh cultural events. He was a vice-president of Cymdeithas yr Eisteddfod Genedlaethol,[27] the society founded in 1881 by educationalist Sir Hugh Owen, which initiated the current series of eisteddfodau cenedlaethol. Powell backed local eisteddfodau by his presence, often as president of the day and by his generous financial donations. For example, in May 1866 at Narberth Road (Clunderwen) Eisteddfod he performed the duties of president with style. He arrived with Mrs Powell, Miss Caroline Powell and a Miss Stallard and all were driven to the pavilion in their carriage accompanied by a brass band and a large concourse of persons. He was then installed in his presidential chair. A crowd variously estimated to have been between 2,000 and 4,000 attended and the organisers had allowed English to be used in some competitions and the occasion was described as 'The first of the now popular gatherings of bards and vocalists . . . held in Pembrokeshire for many ages, probably many centuries.' It was reckoned that the president's 'popularity over a wide district drew thither large numbers.' The one criticism was of the pavilion which 'took too much of the oblong character' with the result that those at either end 'could see nothing of what took place on the platform.' Gwilym Mai (Mr William Thomas, Carmarthen, who for a time worked as a compositor at the Tonn Press, Llandovery) led the eisteddfod and succeeded well 'under very trying circumstances.' Only one adjudicator was mentioned in *The Welshman*'s report and he was the famous journalist Llew Llwyfo (Lewis William Lewis) who succeeded in satisfying the majority 'for few were heard to grumble.'

In his opening speech, W. R. H. Powell assured the crowd that he was quite out of his element but could not refuse the earnest request of the committee. He went on to praise the holding of eisteddfodau 'for the purpose of endeavouring to revive the taste and genius for song and poetry which the ancient Bards, our forefathers, cultivated so keenly. . . . In the poems of Ossian [supposed author of a cycle of poems in Celtic mythology] we read of one prince having a hundred bards who played and sang in concert for his entertainment. These bards sang of the glorious deeds of their ancestors and before letters or writing were in use, they thus handed down the various achievements and records of families . . . during the reign of Edward the First the Bards became almost extinct, as described by the poet Gray,

> "Vocal no more, since Cambria's fatal day,
>   To high-born Hoel's harp, or soft Llewellyn's lay."'

He went on to say that since then 'many and great have been the changes. Trade and manufactures have occupied the leisure time our ancestors devoted to song and poetry. Many now leave these mountains to seek fortunes in distant parts, and though many return from amor patriae, or love of the old country, they have in general imbibed so much of foreign manners and customs as to despise all those of our ancestors. How fashions change! I see before me that the old Welsh hat and pais gwn bach or coat and jacket, are now nearly supplanted by the low-crowned hat and feathers and crinoline (much laughter). Let us hope that these eisteddfodau may be the means of cultivating more the natural good talents which the Welsh are admitted to have for music and be the means of establishing a good choir in every village and parish (loud cheers).' He then mentioned that the proceeds of the day would be given to 'one of our best and most charitable institutions, namely, the Carmarthenshire Infirmary.' He hoped that every competitor would be given a patient hearing and he advised the young men . . . 'do not sit too long with John Barleycorn to-day but remember the words of the old song,

> "Boys, do not get tipsy,
>   But be merry and wise."'

A party of four males then honoured the eisteddfod and the president in song to the tune of *Mae Robin yn Swil*:

> *O dyma Eisteddfod ryfeddaf y byd,*
>   *Y Cymry a'r Saeson yn casglu ynghyd*
> *I ganu am y gore mewn pabell o go'd*
>   *A drefnwyd i'r pwrpas gan wyr Narberth Road.*
>
>   *O dyma beth hardd, o dyma beth hardd*
>   *Mwy harddwych nas traethir gan awen un bardd.*

34

Y gŵr sy'n llywyddu yw Sgweiar Maesgwynne,
Mae'n Gymro o galon, ni fentrwn ddweud hyn,
A gwladgarwr pennaf a fagodd ein tir,
Fe gaiff fynd i'r Senedd dros Gymru cyn hir,
O bloeddied y wlad am i'r Cymro mâd
I fyned i eistedd i Senedd ein gwlad.

O dyma beth hardd . . . etc.

The references to Powell in the last verse are most revealing. Powell was described as the greatest of patriots raised in Wales. And the country was urged to 'call' him to 'represent Wales' in Parliament: this as early as 1866. Therefore, when he did become a parliamentary candidate in 1874, the *Carmarthen Journal*'s view that he was not a suitable person to be a Member of Parliament, was clearly at odds with the people's yearning for Powell to be their parliamentary representative as expressed eight years previously in the above verse.

The duet competition was won by brother and sister Edward and Elizabeth Thomas of Penclippin, Henllan Amgoed. The Penclippin family sometimes performed in concerts at the Llanboidy Market Hall.

The winning stanza in honour of the president was:

Gan gyfarch mae degau'n gofyn – pwy yw
Y Glyw sydd fel gloyn?
POWELL yw, ddaeth fel byw ddyn,
Gorrymus gawr o'r Maesgwyn.

I Narberth Road yn wir borth rheidiawl – daeth
Y doethwr gwladgarawl;
Ninau urddwn hwn drwy hawl
Yn dywysog dewisawl.

When Llew Llwyfo said that a stanza by John Davies, Plas, Llanglydwen, also deserved recognition, a Mr Ezra Roberts came up with another prize of 5 shillings 'and the two bards were invested amidst loud cheers'. John Davies' effort was:

Diareb yw'n Cadeirydd – am ei ddysg,
Am ei ddawn ysplenydd;
Ac a ei dda, yn ei ddydd,
I'w genedl ar fawr gynydd.

Er o achau gwir uchel – o'i fawr rin
Cyfrana i'r isel;
Un gar Gymru'n gu heb gel,
Dyna pwy ydyw'n POWELL.[28]

The Powell family's role in the local community was very much a hands-on involvement as, for example, was demonstrated by Mrs Powell and Miss Caroline Powell appearing as artists in a concert at the National School in April 1867. Their contribution was a pianoforte duet and a piano solo by Miss Powell. The Llanboidy choir took part as well as the Maesgwynne Brass Band under the direction of Mr Edmund Barnes who, in 1863, had been appointed headmaster at W. R. H. Powell's Llanboidy National School. Mr and Mrs Barnes sang a duet 'The Gipsy Countess' and gave a cornet and piano duet as an encore. The Thomas family of Penclippin near Henllan Amgoed were expected to sing the glee 'Yr Haf' but were unavoidably absent because of illness. Four Llanboidy schoolgirls sang 'Elfincall' and a certain Mr Gould, who happened to be present, was persuaded by Mr Powell to sing some comic songs! The Band played 'Garibaldi March' and the Glee Choir sang 'Sleep Gentle Lady' . . . both received much acclaim from those present among whom were, W. R. H. Powell and Mrs Powell, Miss Powell, Major and Mrs Philipps and Miss Philipps, Cwmgwili, Hon. W. Yelverton, Miss Yelverton, Reverend Roberts, W. O. Brigstocke, Gellidywyll, L. L. Price, Glangwili, W. H. Thomas, Swansea, George Thomas, Parke [sic] and party, W. E. B. Gwyn, Plas Cwrt Hyr, Reverend William Rees, vicar of Llanboidy and Mrs Rees.[29]

Clearly, the headmaster Edmund Barnes was very talented and must have made a big impression at the concert. But he was soon to be embroiled in a dispute about the language used in services at Llanboidy Parish Church.

The Welshman of 3 May 1867 published a letter of complaint about the practice of using both Welsh and English during a service. It was unsatisfactory for those who did not understand Welsh as they had to sit for an hour or so on hard uncomfortable seats while not understanding a word that was being said. The vicar had refused a request for services to be in one language and that the language used should alternate between Welsh and English. It was claimed that although the monoglot English in the parish were not numerically large, an extremely large majority of the parishioners could understand English. The letter was signed 'Members of the Established Church'.

During the following weeks numerous letters appeared in *The Welshman* attacking the idea of having English-only services which, it was felt, was sure to drive the overwhelmingly Welsh-speaking parishioners into swelling 'the already crowded Dissenting churches. The vicar wrote that Mr Barnes was the only person that had raised the matter with him. The practice at Llanboidy church was to have two sermons, one in Welsh and one in English, at every service which, as a consequence, lasted about two hours. There were two such services every Sunday. It was claimed that this arrangement was for the benefit of the few monoglot English listeners and one correspondent held the view that the vicar 'would be quite justified in banishing the English altogether instead of giving them a mixed service as he does now, doubtless at great personal inconvenience.' Even the few Welsh speakers who understood English preferred their sermon in Welsh. After the complainant admitted to having been in Llanboidy for 'only about eight months' (which ruled out the schoolmaster) another letter-writer claimed that 'sermons will not be changed to please one or two comparatively unknown persons who have been here for "only about eight months" and may well be gone before the wane of the next moon.' The vicar, the Reverend William Rees, in yet another letter gave a figure of 'more than 80' for the congregation and claimed that all preferred a Welsh service. The English communicants numbered only five and the previous vicar (Reverend John Evans) did not give an English service. He admitted that five or six had left the church but he claimed that they left the neighbourhood because he had closed the old school in favour of Mr Powell's school. The editor of *The Welshman* gave notice that correspondence on the matter of bilingual services in Llanboidy Church should cease.

Edmund Barnes did not stay long as headmaster of Llanboidy School and left in 1869. He was followed as headmaster by another Englishman, John Duckett, from Wells, Somerset.

In early 1867, residents in the Llanboidy area petitioned the Postmaster General to make Whitland the 'post town' rather than St Clears. The reply stated that the Postmaster General had granted a 'mounted post' from St Clears. Letters would then be delivered at 8.30 a.m. and the local office would close at 3 p.m. 'Indeed a boon to the village'.[30]

Back at Llanboidy, Powell found time to chair a meeting of the District Highway Board at Maesgwynne Arms attended by representatives of the parishes: W. J. Williams (Egremont), M. G. Davies (Llandysilio), O. James (Cilmaenllwyd), J. Davies (Llanglydwen), Thomas Jones (Castell Dwyran), George Thomas (Henllan) and J. John.[31] It seems to have been a trouble-free meeting with the District Surveyor giving a report for the previous quarter and his recommendations for the then current half year. All were accepted.

In the same month Powell was the only magistrate present at the Petty Session held in the Maesgwynne Arms. Before him were Thomas Rees, farm servant of Llanboidy Village, Robert Llewellyn, publican of Station House, Whitland and Evan Evans, railway policeman of Whitland. They were charged with stealing three sacks of potatoes from the platform of the railway station at Whitland, the property of Thomas Davies, merchant of Llanboidy who prosecuted his case. Powell's decision was to commit the prisoners for trial at the next quarter sessions to be held at Llandeilo Fawr. They were bailed for £50 each and one surety of £25.

The Llanboidy Agricultural Society, in addition to putting on an annual show, organised exhibitions of local produce. For example, on Friday, 11 September 1868, the society put on an exhibition of stock and in addition a competition was organised for Welsh cheese and butter.[32] In the 1868 General Election, David Pugh of Llandeilo, a retiring Conservative MP, was standing as an Independent in the two-seat Carmarthenshire constituency. He attended the Llanboidy Show where W. R. H. Powell took a full part in the proceedings, the previous year, ill-health limited his participation to one appearance on the field in his carriage. Pugh addressed electors outside the Maesgwynne Arms Hotel before attending a dinner inside, presided over by W. R. H. Powell with Pugh and Brigstocke as chief guests.

Pugh was unsuccessful in the election and the two seats were won by a Liberal, E. J. Sartoris and a Conservative, John Jones of Blaenos, Llandovery, who succeeded his brother, David Jones, Pantglas, Nantgaredig. They were the grandsons of David Jones, Blaenos, Llandovery, the famous drover and founder of the Black Ox Bank in 1799. (For an account of the Blaenos/Pantglas bankers, see *Carmarthenshire Historian*, 1975.)

In 1868 the Annual Llanboidy National School treat, given by the school's patron W. R. H. Powell, was held in October. More than 200 children paraded through the village before returning to the schoolroom which had been decorated by Mrs Powell and the ladies of Maesgwynne. The children and their mothers were entertained to a tea party but bad weather prevented the sports taking place. Farmers and traders accompanied by wives and children attended to hear an address by Powell in which he urged parents and children to accept the advantages offered to them. After alluding to the low state of morality in that part of the country and expressing a wish that the future be improved, Mr Powell suggested that every farm servant should receive a written character [reference] from his master or mistress and that printed forms should be circulated in all the county parishes. Several members of the school committee and other gentlemen addressed the audience in Welsh. The meeting was enlivened by the Juvenile Fife Band and by several part-songs and rounds which were sung by the school children in a highly creditable manner. The older children were able to read tonic sol-fa.

The matter of conduct and hiring of farm servants was further pursued by the Farm Servants Committee of the Carmarthenshire Agricultural Society at the Boar's Head, Carmarthen, at the special invitation of Sir James J. Hamilton Bart. of Plâs, Llansteffan. The meeting appointed W. R. H. Powell to the chair. Powell explained that labourers were now scarce and that they could demand good wages. But at hiring-fairs boys and girls were all mixed up and had no character reports to give prospective employers. Hirers should be able to ask servants for character references.

The view was expressed that it would be a good idea for farmers to shut up their houses at 11.00 p.m., and to allow young people certain nights in the week for meeting together instead of allowing them to be out all night and so be nearly worthless for work next morning. Sir James Hamilton agreed with W. R. H. Powell and he also drew the attention of landlords to the poor condition of the cottage accommodation they provided for their labourers. He also drew attention to the dreadfully demoralising system called 'bundling' (*caru yn y gwely*/ courting in bed) which produced its natural results in the unhappy cases frequently before magistrates.

The chairman in summing up said that labourers' cottages needed to be improved and he intended to begin building in the following spring. He contended that the cost per house would be in the region of £60 to £80. He further stated that a leaflet would be circulated to all of the leading farmers of the county: 'Respectful Friends: We ask you all to unite not to hire any candidate who cannot produce a bone-fida written character from the situation in which he or she last lived.' Powell then produced an example of the character reference form: 'John Davies has lived with me for the last 12 months. He has served me as an honest, faithful and industrious servant (female: she has been clean, honest, sober, industrious. (Hear! Hear!)).' A statement summarising the matters discussed finished with the sentence: 'We think it imperative to improve the moral and social conditions of those under your control' and was signed by Sir J. J. Hamilton and W. R. H. Powell Esq.[33]

In 1869 it was claimed that the Llanboidy Show had become, under the fostering care of W. R. H. Powell and his brother Oliver, the best and most important show for the exhibition of black cattle in the whole of Wales.[34] In 1869 Oliver Powell decided to retire from the post of Hon. Sec. of the Llanboidy Agricultural Society. He refused to change his mind despite the best efforts of his brother to persuade him to carry on. And thus it was that W. R. H. Powell, took on the duties of Hon. Sec. in addition to the Presidency of the Llanboidy Agricultural Society.[35]

The Welshman in September 1873 reported that the Agricultural Society was 'large and thriving' with W. R. H. Powell as its 'life and soul'. Its annual show was held in fields at the back of Maesgwynne Arms. In 1869, W. R. H. Powell had founded the Llanboidy Cottage Garden and Industrial Society and its annual show was held on the same day as the Agricultural Society's show. Mrs Powell was the Hon. Sec. and in 1873 the show of flowers, fruit and garden produce was held in a marquee where the crowd was entertained throughout the day by the Llanboidy Brass Band playing a choice selection under the leadership of Mr Davies.[36] Even in the matter of gardening the Maesgwynne family led by example and showed their produce in horticultural shows. For example, at the 1873 St Issell's Horticultural Show, the Maesgwynne entries were in the name of W. R. H. Powell and he gained the following success: 3rd prize for Cut Flowers-Asters; a special prize for Cockscombe; 2nd prize for a collection of potatoes; 2nd prize for collection of vegetables (not potatoes); 1st prize for best Coleus.[37]

In 1872 he instigated yet another show which became an annual event in the form of the Llanboidy Poultry and Green Crop Show.

As a Justice of the Peace, Powell served on the Llanboidy Petty Sessions and sometimes had to deal with unpleasant incidents. For example, in September 1873 the Reverend Evan Rowland, vicar of Llangynin, appeared before W. R. H. Powell, T. R. O. Powell, E. S. Protheroe and R. P. Beynon. He was charged with assaulting John Griffith Rees, clerk at Whitland Post Office, and of using language inciting a breach of the peace. He was bound over in the sum of £25 and one surety in the like sum to keep the peace for six months.[38]

During the 1874 General Election W. R. H. Powell, who at the last minute was persuaded to stand as one of the two Liberal candidates in the two-seat Carmarthenshire constituency, was accused of being 'against giving religious instruction in schools, and wished to let children grow up heathens.' Powell replied to the charges in a letter to *The Welshman* in which he explained that in 1863 he had established a National School at Llanboidy which he had maintained 'almost at (his) own expense.'

In 1870, Foster's Elementary Education Act made provision for local School Boards to be established, charged with providing non-denominational schools to educate children of 5 to 12 years of age (inclusive) and funded out of the local rates. Attendance fees were paid by parents. The 25th Clause in the Act allowed children of the poor to have their fees paid out of the rates and extended this provision to children attending denominational schools, overwhelmingly church schools, as well. Using public funds to pay church school fees aroused strong feelings against the 25th Clause in the Nonconformist communities because as W. R. H. Powell explained: 'School Boards . . . may spend ratepayers' money in supporting schools over which they have no control, and in which religious dogmas and rites, distasteful to perhaps a large number of the ratepayers are inculcated and practised. . . . Almost the only people who are anxious to retain the 25th Clause are those who wish to get their own denominational schools subsidised out of the rates. Holding, as I do, that it is not fair to tax one man to propagate the creed of another, I am opposed to the 25th Clause, but I do not wish to be judged by other than what I say and do. I am willing to appeal to what I have done for education in my own neighbourhood.'

As proof of the efficiency of his school at Llanboidy he referred to the reports of Her Majesty's Inspectors in 1869: 'The order in this school is excellent, the efficiency very superior. As regards management and instruction this is quite a model school.' In 1873 the HMI had reported: 'This school is in an excellent condition in regard to order, discipline and instruction.'

Powell went on: 'Many of the scholars in this school have passed some of the examinations of the Science and Art Department, and two pupil-teachers from it passed the examination for admission to training college last Christmas. 'Religious instruction has always been given in the school; but as a large proportion of the parents of the scholars are Dissenters, no catechism is taught. Now will any of my friends say that the children in my school get no religious education, or grow up like heathens? If they say "yes", I must say I differ from them, and add that if they had paid the same attention to education in their districts as I have in mine, and could show the same results as have been produced at Llanboidy, there would probably be fewer complaints of inefficient, half-empty schools, and fewer children would grow up like "heathens".'[39] That, surely, was proof enough that Powell's opposition to Clause 25 did not mean he was opposed to religious instruction in schools and to claim so was 'just as illogical as it would be to charge a man who wished to suppress habitual begging with wishing to starve the poor.'

He went on to outline his ideas of how religious instruction might be introduced in schools: 'I answer, let the clergy and ministers of all denominations undertake the religious education, a duty for which they ought to be the best fitted, and visit the schools at certain hours agreed upon, and also hold meetings in the churches and chapels, each teaching the children of his own flock. If this were done, the religious scruples of all would be respected, and I have no doubt the cause of religion would be benefited; whilst on the other hand the teachers of the day schools would be relieved of a part of their now onerous duties, and would be all the more able to discharge efficiently the duties which they are best fitted to perform. Another important advantage which would result from such a course is this; teachers would be selected according to their general qualifications and merits, and not according to the sect to which they might belong, or the particular shade of their views as Churchmen. While thus endeavouring to explain my views on points on which I feel persuaded, I have been misunderstood. I have no wish to enter into any newspaper controversy with any.'

W. R. H. Powell's enlightened proposal of equality of treatment for churchgoers and Non-conformists in matters of religion and education was yet another example of his progressive ideas from which the community benefited and it showed that he was way ahead of his time in this as he was on other issues that he involved himself with. He was labelled 'the hunting squire', but he was so much more.

The parishes of Llanboidy and Llangan formed the Llanboidy and Llangan United School Board. The Board's first meeting was at Powell's National School, Llanboidy on 18 March 1875. W. R. H. Powell of Maesgwynne was elected chairman, B. Griffiths jnr. of Maesgwynne Arms was appointed clerk at a salary of £10 per annum, and Mr Brewer of the London and Provincial Bank, Narberth, became treasurer. It was agreed that meetings of the Board would be held alternately at Whitland and Llanboidy. Before the meeting broke up, a few words were said about the transfer of the Llanboidy (National) and the Whitland (British) schools to the Board. Mr J. James proposed a vote of thanks to Mr Powell for the excellent way he had managed the Llanboidy school for many years (12 years). W. R. H. Powell, in his reply, said that it had given his family and himself great pleasure to look after their school though for some years he had been out of pocket with respect to its expenses. He complained bitterly of reports that had been circulating about him and the school. He denied in the most emphatic terms that he wished to make any lucrative transactions at the expense of the ratepayers. The claim that he wanted £1,800 for the school building was absurd. Powell continued by saying that it was up to the Board to acquire the school or not. He had use for the building if they decided to build a new school. He added that he was prepared to accept a rental, of an amount which the Board could decide upon for the three years of its existence. And to show how anxious he was to alleviate the burden which would of necessity fall upon the ratepayers, he would return the rent for that term of office to the rates. Great applause ensued!

The *Journal* went on to claim that many ratepayers felt that the building should be bought and made public property. And according to the reporter 'the Llanboidy school had been a bone of contention ever since it was built. Again and again has it divided the church people of Llanboidy into hostile parties. Had not Mr Powell had a proper coadjutor in the vicar of the parish, there would have been some excuse for the course he adopted. Everyone, however, who knows anything of the late Archdeacon Evans, know that a better parish priest could not have been found, nor one more earnest in the matter of education. Still, he was excluded from the management of the school; and, as a protest against its private character, he, up till his death, kept up the old school of the village. Then, at the appointment of the present vicar [William Rees], up crop the same questions again, causing the greatest unpleasantness, and the Squire of Llanboidy cannot congratulate himself on the manner in which, until recently, he has treated this gentleman.'[40]

The reporter, seemingly, could not stop digging for dirt to throw at Powell: 'Llanboidy schools were not erected at Mr Powell's expense. Every farmer in the neighbourhood lent his cart and horses and men to assist in the work; whilst relations of Mr Powell and others largely subscribed to the funds. These people feel it a great hardship that they should now have heavy rates levied upon them either to buy or rent these schools or to build new ones. Let the Board make a fair offer to Mr Powell, so as to decide the matter, and then, and not till then, will the public mind be at ease.'

How much basis was there to such criticism? The *Journal*'s attitude was undoubtedly clouded by its political stance. The *Carmarthen Journal* was a Tory newspaper and was therefore a strong supporter of the Church of England. Over the previous decade W. R. H. Powell's insistence on having a school in Llanboidy where the teaching was free of Church of England dogma and his declared support during the 1874 General Election for the disestablishment of the Church of England in Wales had marked him out as the leading Liberal *radical* in the County. He could therefore expect to be attacked on the flimsiest of evidence by a Tory newspaper.

The second meeting of the Llanboidy and Llangan United School Board on 5 April 1875 with W. R. H. Powell in the chair, took note of a letter from the Education Department which stated that a new school was needed at Whitland. The Board agreed to take over the management of the Whitland British School from 1 May. The Board further agreed to Mr Thomas of Forest's proposal that Powell's terms for transferring his Llanboidy National School to the Board's control be accepted. It also accepted the Reverend E. Rowland's proposal that the district be divided into four divisions: Llanboidy, Login, Henllan and Whitland for ascertaining the school accommodation required. The clerk was asked to take a census of children between 3 and 13 years. The matter of a site for the Whitland School was adjourned to a further meeting.[41]

At the end of May 1875 Llanboidy School was inspected by Mr E. H. Short, HMI, who found the School to be 'in excellent order and . . . exceedingly well instructed. The scholars passed a very good examination in the elementary subjects. The singing and sewing were exceedingly good and [did] the mistress much credit. The grant earned was £74/10/0 but £1/10/5 was deducted.' The headmaster at the time was Mr William Emsall.[42]

It was in 1874 that W. R. H. Powell founded a new Friendly Society in an attempt to fill the void left by the demise of the Ivorites and the Oddfellows in the rural areas. He called the new society The United Counties of Carmarthen, Pembroke and Cardigan Friendly Society although it was generally referred to as Clwb Powell Bach. Powell's purpose for the new society was to help the working class and he was praised for this in a letter in *The Welshman* of 3 April 1874: 'No one can but admire the philanthropic spirit of Mr Powell in undertaking to establish a friendly and prudential society for the labouring classes. Such a scheme demands the support of everyone who has the well being of the community at heart . . .'. It took some time for the society to establish itself and, once again, it seems as if politics had played its part with accusations flying around that Powell was setting up the society for political ends. In a meeting in Carmarthen in April 1875 the Reverend Latimer Maurice Jones, vicar of St Peter's Carmarthen, explained that the society was 'in working order' and said that workers should be encouraged to become members and to put aside some money for sickness and old age. He emphasised that Mr Powell had worked hard for two or three years to set up the society and that newspaper accounts of political bias were untrue. Although the president, W. R. H. Powell, was a Liberal he had not in any way attempted to raise his popularity through the society. 'And I say that as the greatest Tory in the world !' said the vicar.[41]

Powell's duty as a magistrate and chairman of Llanboidy Petty Sessions required him in September 1876 to consider a charge against Pheobe Evans of Lamb Inn, Blaenwaun of supplying beer at illegal hours to George Thomas and Benjamin Evans of Ffynnon Wen and John Rees of Dyffryn Broidin. They were each fined 6 shillings with 8 shillings costs.

In a speech at the Llanboidy Christmas Show Dinner attended by about 50 people in December 1876 W. R. H. Powell once again expressed his concern for some of the low standards of behaviour tolerated and indeed encouraged in the rural farming community. He reminded his audience that, come 1 January 1877 attendance at school was to be made compulsory and no farmer would be allowed to hire a boy under 12 years of age unless the boy could pass a certain standard of education. He referred to the 'nonsense talked about religious education in schools'. In his view teachers could not do much more than teach reading, writing and cipher.

He went on to trace the typical progress of children of working people. The children went nowhere except school. They had not been from home until they went into service. And then, the first place a boy was sent to was a hiring-fair which Powell equated to a 'mart'. In his view no greater place of iniquity existed in the country than the hiring-fairs of Narberth, St Clears, Llanboidy and other places where boys learnt to consume great quantities of spirits and tobacco. . . which he termed 'self imposed taxation'. The result was that pauperism in Wales was double that in England. He claimed that the liquor traffic in this country was enormous . . . £24 million spent annually on spirits, £25 million on beer and £7 million on tobacco. In other words people spent £56 million annually on things they could do without. He regretted seeing parents take their children to hiring-fairs and there holding them up to auction and selling them off to the highest bidder to be the slaves of somebody else for 12 months. The farmer then became responsible for the children. At the fairs children were introduced to drink and familiarisation began between boys and girls which eventually often led to court cases. Nothing good could be said about hiring-fairs and people needed to put their heads together to agree on an alternative system.

He was critical of the practice adopted by some farmers of snatching servants from other farmers by offering to increase their wages and encouraging them to return their 'earnest'. Sometimes this 'deal' would be perpetrated in the hay field during harvest time! He explained how he dealt with his own servants. He gave them a 12-month agreement with a provision for a months notice either way before the end of the period. If the servant gave a months notice he was then free to put his name down at the registration office for a fee of 2 or 3 pence and farmers would then be at liberty to hire those on the register. He also gave a written character reference to servants on leaving. He advocated giving higher wages to those servants with better references instead of paying the same to good and bad as was the practice at the time. He was very critical of farmers who offered a pint of beer to their carters for every load of lime delivered. Far better, said Powell, for farmers to encourage their servants to deliver more loads by paying contributions on their behalf to a Friendly Society.

He reported that the United Counties Friendly Society was making good progress with new branches opening. For example, at Maenclochog where Sir Owen Scourfield was the president; a meeting had been held at Eglwyswrw with Mr Colby in the chair and he had been asked to set up a branch at Letterston. He hoped that this would help reduce pauperism and he appealed to his audience to join with him in that task and thus 'improve the country.' They were, after all, improving their cattle, sheep and poultry . . . surely they should improve their men and women. He again expressed the hope that before the following year's fairs, a good plan could be devised for hiring servants without going to the fairs. There were loud cheers when he sat down. The chairman Mr Williams of Penlan, Llangynin, was fully in agreement with Powell and expressed his wish to see the speech published and circulated throughout the county.[43]

An announcement in *The Welshman* on 12 January 1877 declared that a public meeting was to be held in Llanboidy on 17 January to further discuss the hiring of servants. The meeting duly took place at the Maesgwynne Arms and was chaired by John Williams of Penlan, Llangynin, who was also the vice-chair of the Carmarthen Board of Guardians. Others present were W. R. H. Powell; Reverend D. Williams, Salem; James, Aberelwyn; W. Phillips; J. D. Morse, Llandawke; S. Owens, Hafod; J. Phillips, Caerlleon; C. Thomas, Castelldraenog; S. E. Richards, Llanboidy; James Evans, Danyrhendy; Davies, Ffynonfelyn; James, Pontygafel and farm servants Thomas Gibby and Amaziah Morris. James, Aberelwyn, proposed that 'a change be made in the mode of hiring servants and that register offices be established to take the place of the statute fairs.' He emphasised that it was not intended to try to 'lower wages' nor to form a union of masters. The scheme was to be 'entirely voluntary'. Thomas, Castelldraenog seconded and the motion was carried. It was further agreed that a meeting be held on 31 December at the Llanboidy School room to 'discuss the custom with the servants of the neighbourhood.' The outcome of that meeting seems to have been inconclusive because it does not appear that the new system of hiring farm servants, envisaged by W. R. H. Powell, ever came into fruition and the hiring-fairs remained as the basic mode of contact between masters and servants.

RULES AND TABLES

OF THE

UNITED COUNTIES OF CARMARTHEN, PEMBROKE, AND CARDIGAN

FRIENDLY SOCIETY.

FOUNDED A.D. 1874.

CARMARTHEN:
EVANS AND JONES "EXPRESS" AND "SEREN CYMRU" OFFICE.
1877.

THE UNITED COUNTIES FRIENDLY BENEFIT SOCIETY.

PATRONS:

The Right Rev. the LORD BISHOP OF ST. DAVID'S.
The Right Hon. LORD DYNEVOR.
The LORD KENSINGTON, M.P.
Col. PRYSE, Lord-Lieutenant of Cardiganshire.

PRESIDENT:

WALTER RICE HOWELL POWELL, Esq., Maesgwynne.

VICE-PRESIDENTS:

The CHAIRMEN and VICE-CHAIRMEN of the several Boards of Guardians in the Three Counties.

TRUSTEES:

Sir Thomas Davies Lloyd, Baronet, Bronwydd.
John Pugh Vaughan Pryse, Esq., Bwlchbychan.
James Buckley, Esq., Castle Gorfod.
H. C. Fryer, Esq., Lodge Park, Aberystwith.
Morgan Jones, Esq., Llanmiloe.
Herbert Evans, Esq., Highmead.
A. Thompson, Esq., Glyn Abbey.

ORGANISING COMMITTEE:

The Mayor of Carmarthen.
Rev. W. D. Phillips, Crunwear, Narberth.
E. B. Gwyn, Esq., Plas Cwrt Hir.
G. P. Brewer, Esq., London and Provincial Bank, Narberth.
William Rosser, Esq., Llanelly.
John Hughes, Esq., Surgeon, Carmarthen.
J. M. Davies, Esq., Froodvale.
R. Ward, Esq., Sodstone, Narberth.
Rev D. Williams, Penlan, Mydrim.
Everard W. Jones, Esq., Middleton, Narberth.
W. B. Roberts, Esq., Lovestone, Pembroke.
Baron F. de Rutzen, Slebech Hall, near Haverforwest.
George Thomas, Esq., Carmarthen.
Rev. W. Thomas, Parkglas, Carmarthen.
Henry Norton, Esq., Green Hill, Carmarthen.
Rev L. James, Carfan.

TREASURER:

G. P. Brewer, Esq., London and Provincial Bank, Narberth.

SECRETARY:

Mr. Thomas Thomas, No. 8, Quay-street, Carmarthen.

TABLE I.—SICK PAY UNTIL 65.

Shewing the Monthly Contributions, payable until 65 years of age, to provide the following allowances in sickness until that age.

Age at entry. Under	4s. a week.	6s. a week.	8s. a week.	10s. a week.
	s. d.	s. d.	s. d.	s. d.
15	0 5	0 7½	0 10	1 0
16	0 5	0 7½	0 10	1 0
17	0 5	0 7½	0 10	1 0
18	0 5	0 7½	0 10	1 0½
19	0 5	0 7½	0 10	1 0½
20	0 5	0 7½	0 10	1 0½
21	0 5	0 7½	0 10	1 0½
22	0 5½	0 8	0 10½	1 1
23	0 5½	0 8	0 10½	1 1
24	0 5½	0 8	0 10½	1 1
25	0 5½	0 8	0 10½	1 1½
26	0 5½	0 8	0 11	1 1½
27	0 5½	0 8½	0 11	1 1½
28	0 5½	0 8½	0 11	1 2
29	0 6	0 8½	0 11½	1 2
30	0 6	0 8½	0 11½	1 2½
31	0 6	0 9	0 11½	1 2½
32	0 6	0 9	1 0	1 2½
33	0 6½	0 9	1 0	1 3
34	0 6½	0 9½	1 0	1 3½
35	0 6½	0 9½	1 0½	1 3½
36	0 6½	0 9½	1 1	1 4
37	0 7	0 10	1 1	1 4½
38	0 7	0 10	1 1½	1 4½
39	0 7	0 10½	1 1½	1 5
40	0 7½	0 10½	1 2	1 5½
41	0 7½	0 11	1 2½	1 6
42	0 7½	0 11	1 2½	1 6
43	0 8	0 11½	1 3	1 6½
44	0 8	0 11½	1 3½	1 7
45	0 8	1 0	1 4	1 7½

ALEXANDER GLEN FINLAISON.

TABLE V.—PENSIONS AFTER 65.

Shewing the Monthly Contributions, payable until 65 years of age, to provide the following Pensions from that age until death.

Age at entry. Under	2s. a week.	3s. a week.	4s. a week.	5s. a week.
	s. d.	s. d.	s. d.	s. d.
15	0 4	0 6	0 8	0 10
16	0 4½	0 6½	0 8½	0 10½
17	0 4½	0 6½	0 9	0 11
18	0 5	0 7	0 9½	0 11½
19	0 5	0 7½	0 10	1 0
20	0 5½	0 8	0 10½	1 1
21	0 5½	0 8	0 11	1 1½
22	0 6	0 8½	0 11½	1 2
23	0 6	0 9	1 0	1 3
24	0 6½	0 9½	1 0½	1 3½
25	0 7	0 10	1 1	1 4½
26	0 7	0 10½	1 2	1 5½
27	0 7½	0 11	1 3	1 6½
28	0 8	0 11½	1 3½	1 7½
29	0 8½	1 0½	1 4½	1 8½
30	0 9	1 1	1 5½	1 9½
31	0 9½	1 2	1 6½	1 11
32	0 10	1 2½	1 7½	2 1
33	0 10½	1 3½	1 8½	2 2
34	0 11	1 4½	1 10	2 3½
35	1 0	1 5½	1 11½	2 5
36	1 0½	1 7	2 1	2 7
37	1 1½	1 8	2 2½	2 9
38	1 2½	1 9½	2 4½	2 11½
39	1 3½	1 11	2 6½	3 2
40	1 4½	2 0½	2 8½	3 4½
41	1 5½	2 2	2 11	3 8
42	1 7	2 4	3 1½	3 11
43	1 8½	2 6½	3 4½	4 2½
44	1 10	2 8½	3 7½	4 6½
45	1 11½	2 11½	3 11	4 11

ALEXANDER GLEN FINLAISON.

Cover, officers and sample pages of W. R. H. Powell's Friendly Society Handbook in 1877.
(Photocopies courtesy Carmarthenshire Archive Service).

The practice of *caru yn y gwely* (bundling) continued despite Powell's protestations to the masters for them to assume a degree of 'parental' responsibility in their dealings with their servants. Be that as it may, it remains a fact that Powell by his efforts to improve standards in the community and to effect an improvement in the living conditions of the people showed himself to be a social reformer who was prepared to use his resources to improve the people's lot in education, religious teaching, agriculture, housing, community facilities and social care.

In a letter published in *The Welshman* on 19 January 1877, Powell explained his reasoning in setting up the United Counties Friendly Society. He contended that the existing local clubs (branches of the Oddfellows and of the Ivorites Friendly Societies) were failing to meet their financial obligations to their members. Working men and agricultural labourers had invested their hard-earned savings in those societies in the hope that when the 'rainy day' came their promised benefits would be forthcoming. But he contended that 'hundreds were doomed to disappointment . . . the clubs to which they contributed nearly all their life-time had broken up through mismanagement or some other cause.' Contributions had been too small to secure the benefits promised and funds were paid out on a first-come-first-served basis; when the money ran out the club was 'broken up'.

The United Counties Club was based on sound financial principles and was now well established with 19 branches and invested capital of £604.10s.0d. Its Secretary was Mr Thomas Thomas, 9 Quay Street, Carmarthen. In May 1877, at a meeting of the Oddfellows Friendly Society at Maesgwynne Arms, Powell reminded those present that both the Oddfellows and his United Counties Society had the same aims. But he stressed that his society went a step further than the Oddfellows in that the benefit package offered included the provision of a 'pension in old age'. He pointed out that this provision did not come within the scope of the Oddfellows Society and he expressed the hope that the Oddfellows would join his Society inorder to obtain the benefit of an old age pension. He impressed on those present the need to 'inspire the working men and agricultural labourers in the three counties to invest their hard-earned savings' so that when the 'rainy day' came they would be able to enjoy the benefits.[44] It was to take three decades before David Lloyd George, Chancellor of the Exchequer in the Liberal government, introduced the Old Age Pension in 1908. Lloyd George's pension was paid for by new taxes on the wealthy, particularly landowners!

Powell's funding for his pension scheme was based on regular contributions from those joining the society. For example, figures published in the society's 'Rules and Tables' booklet for 1877 showed that those who joined the scheme before reaching 21 years of age and who paid a weekly contribution of 2½ % of their weekly wage would secure either a sickness benefit about equal to their weekly wage until they reached 65-years-of-age or a pension at 65 years of age equal to half their previous wage; a weekly contribution of 5% of their wage would secure both.[45] In addition to the basic funding through members' regular contributions Powell backed-up his scheme with funds raised from specially organised eisteddfodau. For example, with the help of a committee chaired by the Reverend David Saunders Davies, Cwmfelin Mynach, with Oliver Powell as Hon. Sec., he organised a Grand Eisteddfod at Whitland in June 1877. It was held in a marquee erected for the occasion and in those days attendance at eisteddfodau often numbered several thousands, with choirs attracting a following comparable to today's rugby teams. The chief choral competition was for a prize of £20 and the winning conductor was to receive 5 guineas donated by W. R. H. Powell. In addition to choral, brass band and poetry competitions there were two essay competitions on topics close to Powell's heart. One was entitled 'Priestcraft, War and Pauperism are incompatible with Christianity' for which a prize of 5 guineas was offered whereas the other: 'The best mode of cultivating root crops and sheep farming in the three counties' attracted a prize of £1.10s.0d. And there was a competition to compose a lecture on 'Advantage of the United Counties Friendly Society', the winner to receive £3.5s.0d. The winning lecture was to be not more than 20 minutes duration and was to be read at the eisteddfod.[46]

We get a glimpse of the Llanboidy Branch of the United Counties Friendly Society in action from a report of its 1878 annual meeting held at Llanboidy. It was chaired by Mr W. Bishop of Rosehill, Llanglydwen, who described the society as being 'excellent . . . [and] firmly established and gives such advantages to the working class, enabling them to provide when in good health against sickness, by paying a small monthly contribution to secure a sum of 10 shillings (50 pence) per week when disabled'. According to David Howell in his *Land and People in Nineteenth-Century Wales* the weekly wage for farm labourers in Carmarthenshire in 1870 ranged between 9s. and 11s.6d. Therefore, it is likely that the benefit of 10s per week was of the order of the average wage prevailing in 1878. Mr Bishop went on: 'I cannot see why every labourer should not join such a society.' He reported that the 'benefit membership' of the branch had increased over the year from 31 to 80 and the 'honorary membership' from 9 to 30. The income from the benefit membership for the year was £50, equivalent to an average payment from each member of 3d. (1.2p) per week. The honorary membership had contributed a total of £15 for the year which equated to an average payment by each member of 2.3p per week or 10s. (50p) for the year. The membership had enjoyed a year largely free of illness and the only charges incurred were a few pence for candles. The chairman expressed his hope that before long the society would be welcomed in every house in the three counties and that the working class would find it returning them a fair interest in the day of need. The chairman was re-elected for the ensuing year with Mr Tudor V. H. Thomas of Glyntaf as vice-chairman, Mr Davies as Agent and Surgeon Vaughan Bowen Jones as the Medical Officer. Eighteen benefit members joined at the end of the meeting.[47] At that time Vaughan Bowen Jones, born in Llanfallteg, was a 29-year-old bachelor at the beginning of his long service to the community of Llanboidy and district. He later lived at Glan-yr-afon, Llanboidy Lower Village with his wife Ann and son Douglas born in 1911. Dr Bowen Jones passed away in 1930.

In 1879 an Eisteddfod Gadeiriol, labelled the United Counties Eisteddfod, in aid of the United Counties Friendly Society was held at Crymych. As the instigator of the event, W. R. H. Powell had worked hard to sign up 34 patrons headed by W. P. Roch, the High Sheriff of Pembrokeshire, to support the event. It followed a similar eisteddfod held there in 1877. In 1879 the society had been in existence for five years; it had over 500 members in branches all over the three counties and had £2,000 invested funds. Between three and four thousand people attended the 1879 eisteddfod which was held in a pavilion erected near the railway station by Uriah Smart of Cardiff. The proceedings were conducted by the Reverend D. S. Davies of Cwmfelin Mynach. The adjudicators were Dr Joseph Parry of Aberystwyth (music) and the Reverend John Rhys Morgan D.D. (Lleurwg) of Zion Baptist Chapel, Llanelli (prose and poetry). Master Parry of Aberystwyth was the accompanist. A rendering by the band of the 37th Regiment from

Pentre Isha with Dr Bowen Jones in foreground.
(By permission of Llyfrgell Genedlaethol Cymru/The National Library of Wales).

Thatched cottage in Pentre Isha.
(By permission of Llyfrgell Genedlaethol Cymru/The National Library of Wales).

Pembroke Dock set things in motion at 12.00 noon. In the evening Joseph Parry's opera 'Blodwen' was performed by Fishguard Choral Union with guest soloists from the University College of Wales, Aberystwyth.[48] Eisteddfodau were great crowd-pullers in those days and at the end of June 1881 W. R. H. Powell MP was president at an eisteddfod at Pencader which 'attracted about 3,000 people.'

In 1882, according to an article in the *County Gentleman*, 'the United Counties Benefit Society [was] in a very flourishing condition.' In 1889, the St Clears Branch of the Friendly Society was quick to send a message of sympathy to Maesgwynne and 'to record its sense of great loss sustained . . . by the death of W. R. H. Powell MP, the founder and vice-president of the Society'. And again, a wreath at Powell's funeral with a card which read 'In memory of our beloved Founder' was from the Friendly Society. In fact the society (Clwb Powell Bach) continued to serve the community for another sixty years. In the final years of its existence the collector of contributions in the Llanboidy area was John (Jack) Jenkins, Greenhill, Llanboidy, formerly an employee of the Vaughans at Maesgwynne. In letters to the society's secretary, Mr Thomas of Carmarthen, dated 22 November 1951 and 11 February 1952, John Jenkins wrote that he had never recovered from the death of his wife [in 1948] and that he wished to give-up the job of collector for the society. His wish to be relieved of his duties was probably overtaken by events. By that time, government had set up the welfare state to provide ordinary people with sickness benefits and pensions which, thanks to the vision of Powell Bach, had been available in the three counties of west Wales for almost 80 years. At a special meeting held at St Peter's House, Carmarthen on Saturday, 4 July 1953, the United Counties of Carmarthen, Pembroke and Cardigan Friendly Society was wound-up.[45]

At the end of 1877 the *Carmarthen Journal* reported that the Llanboidy Farming Club was doing excellently and should continue to do so under its officers of Mr R. P. Beynon, Pentowyn, St Clears (President), Mr Owen Scourfield, Bart., Williamston (Vice-President) and W. R. H. Powell (Hon. Sec.). The Llanboidy Christmas Show had been 'highly successful' and at the afternoon dinner Mr Simon Davies, Nant-yr-eglwys Mill, had presented a paper on rearing and feeding poultry. He said that the country was importing 54 million eggs annually which was inexcusable as there was plenty of land on which to rear fowls so as to increase egg production. He claimed that 18 fowls eating 7 hundredweight of food yielded the same profit as one cow requiring 23 tons of fodder a year. Simon Davies advocated keeping 200 or 300 fowls which would pay the profit of 18 to 20 cows. He himself intended rearing 500 chickens that year feeding them on oatmeal and plenty of fresh water. However, the paper was criticised by several people who thought that the cost of feed would make it unprofitable to rear fowls on the scale advocated.[49]

In July 1878, Powell's efforts to get his tenants to improve their farming methods took a new turn when he treated them to an all-expenses-paid excursion to the Royal Agricultural Show in Bristol. The *Carmarthen Journal* in its 19 July issue reported that the 'tenants left Whitland Station together and seemed to form a very jolly company.' And in its report on the annual Llanboidy Agricultural Show the *Journal* was most generous in its praise of Powell's improving influence in the district: 'Though we have had occasion sometimes to differ widely with Mr Powell in certain matters, we cannot, in fairness, deny him praise for his merits as a landlord and his anxiety to benefit the agricultural community around him, and in no other way . . . has he done so much for the advantage of tenant farmers as in bringing Llanboidy Show to its present state of prosperity.'

More praise followed, 'The improvements . . . in the neighbourhood [are now] reflected in the village itself. Llanboidy is rapidly gaining the appearance of a neat country town. The church . . . has been put into excellent condition [it had been refurbished at Powell's expense in 1878] . . . On the other side of the street on the premises lately occupied by Mrs Richards, Messrs Ellis and Co. of Haverfordwest have opened a General Stores . . . where a great variety of goods . . . can be obtained as cheap as in Liverpool. . . . Llanboidy is looking up . . . largely owing to the successful management of the local agricultural society.'[50] (We shall come across the *Journal*'s wide differences with W. R. H. Powell in Part III.)

In December 1878, a weekly market was established at Llanboidy. 'About £400 worth of butter was sold last week as well as corn, fowls, ducks, geese, pigs, potatoes etc and there was a ready sale at fair prices. The market was a great boon to the district.'[47] Although not mentioned in the report, nevertheless, we can be sure that W. R. H. Powell had played his part in organising Llanboidy's weekly market. By that time Powell was a leading Liberal Radical. He had contested the Carmarthenshire constituency, unsuccessfully, in the 1874 General Election. Inevitably, his activities were then scrutinised by his Tory opponents in the hope of finding ammunition to attack him for political advantage. He was, for example, still being accused of setting up his Friendly Society for political reasons. To answer his critics, Powell pulled off a master-stroke at the 1877 Whitland Eisteddfod, by getting a leading Tory supporter, the Reverend Latimer Maurice Jones, vicar of St Peter's, Carmarthen, to lead the proceedings and to introduce the events. In the afternoon session, the Reverend Jones described the accusations against Powell as 'malicious libel'. Opponents had even spread rumours that the Whitland Eisteddfod was a Liberal eisteddfod . . . a Tory eisteddfod was to be somewhere else! Jones announced: 'I am a Tory but a supporter of Powell and his Friendly Society.' Although the vicar of Whitland, the Reverend E. Rowland, repeated the accusation in a letter to the *Western Mail*, he had reasons other than political for attacking Powell. Rowland's habit of physically assaulting his parishioners had landed him more than once in front of Powell's bench of magistrates.

Powell continued with his programme to improve living conditions of ordinary people by building the houses of Piccadilly Square in Llanboidy in 1880. His efforts to improve the lot of the community was supported by his wife who, every winter, gave away clothes to the poor. For example, in January 1880 Mrs Powell distributed clothes in the parishes of Llanboidy, Llangan, Henllan Amgoed and adjoining parishes.[51] And her sister-in-law Mrs Oliver Powell, widowed since 1877, and then living in Pwllywhead, Whitland, had 'had culm distributed to the aged poor and sick of Whitland and Llangan parishes.'

2.4 The butter campaign and Walter's last folly

In February 1880 a meeting was held at the Maesgwynne Arms which was described as being 'influential'. The meeting, presided over by Mr J. Bagnall Evans JP of Nant-yr-eglwys, agreed unanimously to the proposal 'that a railway be built from Llanboidy to Login and there to join the Whitland to Cardigan railway.' Nothing came of that proposal but a 'generous offer' made

Piccadilly Square workers' houses built by W. R. H. Powell in 1880.
(By permission of Llyfrgell Genedlaethol Cymru / The National Library of Wales).

in the same meeting by W. R. H. Powell soon came to fruition. Powell's offer was to build a 'market house, together with three houses attached to be used – one as a coffee tavern, one as a reading room and the other to keep the property belonging to the Llanboidy Agricultural Society.' It was further reported that plans for the building had been deposited. The only condition demanded by Mr Powell was that the material needed be hauled to the site by neighbouring farmers.[52]

When the horticultural produce at the September 1880 Llanboidy Show could hardly be fitted into the Board School, it was announced by one of the prime movers of the show, Mrs Powell, that next year's display would be in the new 'Market House'.[53] But when the Llanboidy Christmas Show was held on a very wet day towards the end of December 1880, the poultry was exhibited 'in the new Market Hall which is in the course of erection. The whole cost of the structure is borne by W. R. H. Powell MP.' The total cost of the Hall was about £1,500 and 'Mr Powell intends it for the use of the neighbourhood free of charge.'[54] The secretaryship of the Llanboidy Autumn and Christmas Shows had been taken on by Miss Caroline Powell after her father had been elected to parliament.

Establishing 'coffee taverns' had, for a few years, been a growing trend in large towns as a means of providing the public and particularly the working classes with places of refreshment and social recreation free of the temptation of alcoholic drinks served in the public houses. The model for the coffee taverns was the club set up in Pimlico, London by officers of the Household Brigade to 'elevate the common soldier.' The features of that club were the absence of intoxicating drinks, the provision of newspapers and magazines and the opportunity to play games such as backgammon, skittles and chess. There had been stirrings in Swansea where 'several influential gentlemen in Swansea have taken up the matter [of providing coffee taverns].'[55] Powell had enthused about public libraries in 1879 when as president of the evening at the first 'winter literary and musical entertainment' at the Town Hall, St Clears, he expressed his full support for establishing a reading room and library in the town.[56]

In Carmarthen a 'Coffee Tavern Club Room' had already been opened. The vicar of Carmarthen had been the driving force behind the project. But the vicar stressed that he intended the tavern to be 'as free from any sect or party as possible'. Undoubtedly the main intention in establishing the coffee taverns was to tackle the misuse of alcohol which was rampant in nineteenth-century society, particularly among the working class. Even the eminent brewer Allsop himself spoke against the abuses of drink. And although the Guinness family received praise for funding the restoration of St Patrick's Cathedral in Dublin, the sum involved, £200,000 – showing that 'Dublin stout must have been made in sufficient quantities to flood the Towy in order that church architecture might flourish' – was a sobering thought. The coffee taverns offered an alternative to the public houses for men to socialise after work.

Llanboidy Market Hall built by W. R. H. Powell in 1881.
(Eddie Evans collection).

The vicar of Carmarthen had enjoyed the support of 'such excellent men as Earl Cawdor, Lord Dynevor and Mr Powell of Maesgwynne which will . . . help bind all classes together in the county of Carmarthen which has long stood at the head of all the Welsh counties for the good feeling existing between the various classes of society.' None of the 'excellent men' were able to be present at the opening and they had sent their apologies with W. R. H. Powell, in his letter, stating: 'I sincerely hope the movement will tend to the comfort of the working men of Carmarthen. . . . I do not think that our artisans and labourers could anywhere find a better home and more employment than in this country, could we but do away with the places open "to provide the working man with his beer". Drink is a curse in this country – demoralising and impoverishing our people. The Carmarthen Coffee Tavern will, I hope, be imitated in our villages and fairs. Sincerely do I wish this undertaking every success and that the workmen of Carmarthen will value the boon.' Alderman W. de G. Warren pointed out that the coffee tavern could not be expected to bring about social reform at once. After all there were over 100 public houses in Carmarthen – one for every hundred inhabitants. But if so many pubs could be supported then the coffee tavern should be able to pay its way. At a fee of only 1s. (5p) per quarter, membership would have been within the reach of all bone-fide working men of 18 years of age and over. Honorary membership was available at a subscription of 10s.6d. (52.5p) per annum. The rules of the club stipulated that there was to be no drinking of intoxicating liquor, no quarrelling and no gambling.

In 1881, a few years after the opening of Carmarthen's coffee tavern, W. R. H. Powell had built and opened a coffee tavern and reading room as part of the Market Hall at Llanboidy. Powell referred to the new 'Market Hall' in his speech at the Llanboidy Agricultural Show Dinner in September 1881 as, possibly, 'Walter Powell's last folly'![57] But his comment was, no doubt, made as a light-hearted remark because his provisions in the village of Llanboidy . . . the Maesgwynne Arms Hotel, the school, the labourers houses of Piccadilly Square and the Market Hall with its adjoining coffee bar and library . . . were put in context by the Reverend John Wyndham Lewis, minister of Water Street Methodist Chapel, Carmarthen, who proclaimed that the 'model village' of Llanboidy was abundant proof that Powell was in touch with the people and that he understood and respected their aspirations. Powell went on to say that he did not for a moment expect the Hall to be filled with butter and poultry but that it would be turned to many a good account. He hoped that young farmers would form a library at the Hall or hold lectures there. And the working classes should not be forgotten; his wish for them was that the Hall would give them an evening's diversion and improve their minds. As long as he was their representative, nothing would be a trouble to him if he could possibly serve his country in any way.

Mrs and Miss Powell had spent much of the summer of 1881 organising and preparing a bazaar to be held on 20 September 1881 in the Market Hall for the purpose of raising money for the proposed library and for decorating the Hall. The Powells entertained lavishly at Maesgwynne in the afternoon and trade at the bazaar picked up when the throng arrived in the Hall. The refreshment stall was run by Miss Powell who offered tea at 6d. a head and tea and sandwiches for 1s.

We can only wonder as to how many workmen in the Llanboidy area changed their after-work habit of a pint at the Maesgwynne Arms or at the Lamb Inn to sip coffee and read newspapers in the coffee tavern and reading room attached to the Market Hall. Be that as it may, one of the wreaths at Powell's funeral in 1889 was from 'the members of the Reading room'.

Canerw, an early Nonconformist meeting place. Powell Bach recalled seeing hundreds gathered in the farmyard listening to eminent preachers in the 1820s.
(Eddie Evans collection).

In December 1879 the Bible Society held its AGM at Nazareth Baptist Chapel, Whitland. The society's chairman for the year was W. R. H. Powell and in his address he expressed his pleasure to be present and to aid in such a good cause. He expressed the view that in 'these times of national education there were few people who would not be able to read their Bibles.' It was reported that the Whitland Branch was in a good financial state and had been able to send £48 to the parent society during the year.[58]

As already mentioned, Powell insisted on equal treatment for all members of the community irrespective of religious beliefs. So it was no surprise that he responded positively in 1877 to a request from the minister of Glandŵr Independent Chapel, the Reverend O. R. Owen, for land to build a new chapel at Cefnypant. Powell released land opposite Llwynon Shop, half a mile or so nearer Llanglydwen than the old chapel or Ysgoldy Cefnypant which was demolished and

Cefnypant Independent Chapel
and memorial stone.
(Denley Owen collection).

its stones used for the new build. The building work started in April 1877 and on 1 May 1877 a 'memorial stone' was placed in the front wall and unveiled by Miss Caroline Mary Powell elder daughter of W. R. H. Powell. A large crowd attended the ceremony and the Reverend O. R. Owen presented Miss Powell with a silver trowel and hammer. W. R. H. Powell and others addressed the crowd and a collection brought in £108 towards the building costs.[59] W. R. H. Powell spoke about one of his earliest recollections of walking with his father on a Sunday afternoon across the fields to Canerw, a farmhouse and centre of worship for early Nonconformists. Powell was much struck with and never forgot 'the sight of some hundreds sitting on the courtyard walls, gates and hedges listening to an eminent Welsh preacher in the open air' and he felt 'great pleasure in now giving to that congregation a spot to build a place of worship . . . I trust that this building will tend to the honour of God and to man's salvation.'

Two years later a public lecture was held at Cefnypant on the subject *Bod yn Onest* (Being Truthful). The speaker's name was not printed on the ticket which cost 1 shilling with children under twelve being charged 6d. The proceeds went to the Chapel funds and no doubt a substantial sum was contributed by the chairman for the evening, W. R. H. Powell.

In December 1879, Powell and Mrs Powell were present at the first performance of the winter by the Carmarthen Dramatic Club at the Assembly Rooms.[60]

Powell's daughter Caroline followed in her father's footsteps in being dedicated to improving the well-being of the community. She acted as Hon. Sec. of the Llanboidy Agricultural Society, although as a woman she was not allowed to attend the annual dinner. She regularly gave assistance to the teachers at Llanboidy School and her commitment was reflected in the triennial elections to the Llanboidy and Llangan School Board in February 1881 when she topped the poll by a considerable margin. Elected were: Miss C. M. Powell (Church) 246, Mr J. Evans, Stationmaster (Independent) 229, Mr H. Phillips (I) 173, Reverend D. S. Davies (Baptist) 167, Mr D. Thomas (Unitarian) 163, Mr S. Owen (I) 132, Reverend W. Rees (C) 120. Five others were not elected. A month later Miss Powell was elected chairperson of the School Board despite her protests that she had never undertaken such a position previously and that they should choose someone better for the job. J. Evans was chosen as vice-chairman. The only other item on the meeting's agenda was to consider the plans for a third school for the Board to manage, namely a new school . . . Penygaer.[61] According to the report in the *Carmarthen Journal* of 18 March 1881, the Board questioned the need for another school and resolved that 'a memorial be sent to the Education Department to avoid Penygaer School; but should the reply be unfavourable the clerk be authorised to advertise for tenders and a special meeting be held.' The 'unfavourable' reply duly arrived and two years later Penygaer School was opened on 5 November 1883.

Powell was for ever urging the farming community to modernise their farming methods so as to improve their products and profitability. For example, at the 1882 St Clears Show Dinner, Powell spoke of the desirability of improving the cultivation of the soil. He claimed that 'in many cases productivity may be doubled. We want to see in this country more skilled labour expended upon and a greater amount of capital invested in the land. The question is, how is that to be done? How can we in England [*sic*] stimulate and encourage tenant farmers to lay out their skill as well as their capital?'[62] His use of 'England' is surprising bearing in mind his campaign for 'Welsh' butter and his championing of radical Liberal party policies such as the disestablishment of the Church of England in Wales. Powell supported Gladstone's policy of Home Rule for Ireland and would have been aware of the national awakening in Wales led at that time by Tom Ellis and Lloyd George. He may possibly have used 'England' when he meant Britain in the way that many people today use Britain when they really mean England.

It was very heartening for Powell to hear the judges at the Llanboidy Show Dinner in September 1882 praising the standard of entries and commenting on the improvement over the years. Sixty-one-year-old bachelor Tom Davies of Hayes Farm near Lamphey in Pembroke-shire, an expert horseman and former top-class jockey who had ridden many of Powell's star steeplechasers, was most eloquent in his praise of the high standard of the horses at that year's show. The cattle and sheep judge, Mr J. Lewis late of Grongar, said that a vast improvement had taken place in the [quality] of the cattle and sheep of the district during the years he had known the show (applause). Mr T. Evans, Treventy, reported on the prices of butter in London: Normandy, Brittany, Danish and superfine Irish were the best, sometime 14 shillings above Jersey in price. Welsh butter was put promiscuously with ordinary Irish as if there was no best or superfine Welsh. He reckoned that it was most unfair (applause).

In his speech, W. R. H. Powell referred to the Llanboidy Agricultural Show and its off-springs: the Christmas Show, root show, sheep dog trials and the flower show. He reminded his audience of the novel competition introduced the previous year in the flower show which gave a prize for taking honey from a bee-hive without killing the bees. The result was that eleven hives operated on the new principle in the village alone. Powell also referred to Llangeler Mountain and its cover of heather which he had witnessed in full-bloom when driving, recently, from Newcastle Emlyn Show. He felt sure that bee-keeping would prove most profitable in that area.

The Market Hall housed the flowers, fruit and vegetables of the cottagers and others at the 1882 Llanboidy Show and the 'spacious new market hall opposite the restored church [gave] visitors some idea of how things [were] progressing at Llanboidy.' The 'Cottagers' produce was out of all proportions better than a few years ago.' And 'One large apartment at the rear [was] fitted up as a reading room. Book cases were there and presently books too.' The popularity of the Powells meant that 'Volunteers assisting with the show at Llanboidy are far [more numerous] than elsewhere'.[63]

Three months later the Llanboidy Christmas Show (poultry) came off and in his speech at the inevitable dinner, Powell expressed his wish to see a 'branch of agricultural science introduced into our schools so that more interest be taken in the cultivation of soil.' He also explained that Mrs Powell was interested in bee-keeping and would give all information to neighbours and others. She was in the process of improving the breed by rearing Queen Bees.[64] The following year Mrs Powell was invited to join the committee of the Carmarthenshire Bee Keeping Association.

At the Carmarthenshire Agricultural Society annual Exhibition and Dinner in September 1882, Powell referred to criticism of his having brought up the matter of hiring servants at the previous year's show dinner. It was labelled 'politics'. But it was not so, claimed the MP, because the matter had been raised in Parliament with equal concern by members from both sides of the House. The show secretary, Mr David Prosser of Tygwyn Farm, Llangynwr, praised Powell but was sorry he followed Gladstone. Powell retorted that he and the electorate would have their chance at the next election to vote for him or not to.

Another glimpse of W. R. H. Powell's concern for the welfare of the farming community and of his vision can be seen in the practical measures he took to try to ensure that butter produced in the Llanboidy area was consistently of a high quality so as to increase both the demand for it and the price obtained for it. Throughout the 1880s his speeches at agricultural shows invariably referred to the problem of inconsistency in quality deterring consumers from buying Llanboidy butter. For example, at the September 1881 Llanboidy Agricultural Show Dinner, the Reverend Edward Hesketh Knowles, vicar of St Bees near Whitehaven in Cumberland, described how he had attended Llanboidy Show two years previously and had enjoyed their butter so much that when he returned to Cumberland he persuaded a man who had just opened a shop in Southport to source his butter from Llanboidy. 'Llanboidy Butter' had been transported by rail to Southport but unfortunately the variable quality of the butter had meant that it did not satisfy the customers. 'Llanboidy butter well made was first rate, but Llanboidy butter not well made was not first rate!' The Reverend Knowles expressed his disappointment at the failure of the enterprise because the shopkeeper in question could sell, at the very least, 1,000 lbs of butter a week. But he urged Llanboidy butter producers to profit from his remarks because the butter received in Southport from Westmoreland and Cumberland was far from pleasing the consumers because it was so hard that they could throw it against a wall without any damage to the butter! That comment drew a response from the Reverend D. S. Davies to the effect that although Llanboidy butter was improving he could recommend their [Llanboidy] cheeses as excellent wheels for wheelbarrows!

Powell described another example of the deficiency of Llanboidy butter involving himself and his family directly. They had been in London for five months (attending to his parliamentary work) and the butter that was served them at their guest house, they did not like. But when they enquired about its source they were told it was Llanboidy butter! So they changed to 'good Brittany butter', which sold at between 1s.6d. to 1s.8d. per pound. 'Normandy and Brittany butter held first place in London.' Powell reckoned that there was huge potential for Llanboidy butter if only they could improve the quality and consistency of their product.[65]

The culmination of his campaign was the exhibition by experts held at the Market Hall, Llanboidy, in October 1882. The Aylesbury Dairy Company had discovered the optimum conditions to be met at every stage of the butter-making process inorder to achieve the highest quality of product. The company had also discovered a process of preserving butter in which the salt content of the finished product was reduced from 5 or 6% to 1% which, in the company's view, would drive all salt butter out of the market. Bad news for the salty Llanboidy butter. The 'experts' brought to Llanboidy in 1882 by Powell were from the Aylesbury Company and he was quite sure that Wales could compete with other places if they devoted their attention a little to the improvement of the product. Powell introduced Mr Rickard, a skilled dairyman, who would churn butter and explain the whole process. The object was to show how such improvements might be brought about, and how they might prepare their butter in a marketable form so as to secure good prices. The cream to be used had been brought from neighbouring farms. There followed a detailed demonstration of the complete process of producing the finished product which, if followed every time, would produce butter of high quality and consistency matching that produced in Normandy and in Brittany which fetched 4d. per pound more than butter produced in Wales.[66] Powell's answer to the butter problem was to have butter-making factories which would make it far easier to produce butter of high and consistent quality. He campaigned ceaselessly for butter factories and took advantage of the area's agricultural show dinners to try to drum up support from reluctant farmers to change their ways. For example, at the 1886 St Clears Show he reported on his correspondence with a 'nobleman', Lord Vernon, who had established a butter factory and he had details of the venture which he hoped to make public at one of the coming meetings in Llanboidy, Laugharne or Carmarthen. He thought that Wales should be able to compete with the Dorset and Devonshire butter. He then described how he had taken a supply of butter with him to London and, on Saturdays when he had very little to do, had tried to get the Army and Navy stores to sell it for him. But they would have nothing to do with it; they objected to its colour and quality and did not want to get into bad odour with their customers by selling such butter. He did not mean that there was no good butter made in Wales but the general quality was not good enough. The trouble at that time was that Welsh butter did not have a good name in England. In another effort to get a sale for Welsh butter, he had got butter up from Wales for a messenger of the House of Commons who liked it very much. The messenger then got a pony and trap and, on days when he was not engaged in the House, the messenger went in search of customers. In fact he did get a lot of customers for Llanboidy butter but it only continued for a short time. The butter varied so much in quality that customers did not continue to take it.

Powell reminded the meeting of the Llanboidy man who secured an order for a thousand pounds of butter to be sent to Southport. But it was sent back for not being up to quality. There had been Llanboidy butter sent back from Cardiff and sold for 3d. per lb. Those were the things that damaged Welsh butter and they needed to be rectified. In Lord Vernon's factory the price they obtained in December was 1s.6d. per pound and in June it was 1s.4d. Butter was at a low price in Carmarthen at only about 10d. a pound. Powell wanted to see the situation rectified (hear! hear!). The butter should be of one colour, quality and style, like it used to be made by the late Mr Buckley of Castell Gorfod. He thought if they established butter factories in several places such as St Clears, Llanboidy, Whitland or Laugharne they would succeed in raising the quality. Lord Vernon had never had less than 1s.3d. per pound for his butter and he [W. R. H. Powell] had paid not less than 1s.6d. per pound when in London. There had to be something radically wrong with Welsh butter and he thought they might remedy it by establishing such factories (applause).[67]

A week later at the dinner held at the Maesgwynne Arms after the Llanboidy Show, Mr Treharne of Carmarthen, the judge of the butter competition, made the point that although the quality of the winning butter was excellent there were several lots of inferior butter shown. He said the entries reflected the complaints of butter dealers about the variable quality of Welsh butter which made it very difficult to sell it. Mr Treharne fully supported W. R. H. Powell's views as to the necessity for establishing butter factories or creameries which would give merchants more confidence in buying large quantities of Welsh butter. Butter factories would save a great deal of labour for the farmer, which must be a very heavy item [of expenditure] with wages being so high. Mr Williams of Penlan, Llangynin, referred to W. R. H. Powell's speech at St Clears on butter making. It was important to realise that the farmers as well as the landlords would benefit from having a butter factory. Powell said they should 'put their heads together and their shoulders to the wheel' to find a better way of making butter. He said a butter merchant had complained to him about the quality of Welsh butter and that he would not buy it if it were possible to get sufficient supply of Irish and Danish butter. Whatever they thought of the Irish, they certainly produced superior butter; they classified it and got the proper price for each kind. He had a hobby . . . the establishment of a butter factory . . . he would meet the farmers some evening in Llanboidy or elsewhere and discuss it with them. He was quite willing to put down £100 to start a factory and he had no doubt that Mr Pugh and other landlords would take shares but only if the farmers would join. They would have the factory in a convenient place so that farmers could bring in their milk every day. It would be made into butter all of one quality, and he had no doubt of its success. The mechanical operation of separating the cream from the milk was much better than the one they used; the cream was sweeter and the skim milk better than what they had; the labour was less and the farmer knew exactly how much he ought to have for his milk. They would save a lot of trouble and would have more time for other matters and looking after their dairy-maids. Lord Vernon's agent was willing to come down and show them how the factory was established and any of them who cared to go up and inspect the factory established by Lord Vernon for his tenants were welcome to do so.

Powell then went on to another matter, that of silage making and asked Mr John of Castell-garw to tell them about his silo. Mr John claimed he was a hill farmer and that, the previous year, instead of asking his landlord for a rent reduction he had asked for assistance to build a silo. He asked for £50, but Lord Kensington spent £150 and his agent and Mr John travelled to England to view some silos and get the best plan. He went on to describe how he had been filling his silo during the previous week. He allowed a certain amount of filling to heat up to 125 degrees and then put more on so that one filling pressed the other down. David Pugh, MP, had brought a sample of his silage for those present to examine although he stressed that it was an outside cut and was therefore inferior in quality to the mass of the rick. He spoke of the advantage of silage particularly in wet weather. If farmers could be made independent of the weather in respect of grass it would save a lot of time. And he said that ensilage would make as good butter as anything. There was an excellent book by the sub-editor of *The Field* on how to make silage. Both the vicar of Llanboidy and the Reverend D. S. Davies, minister of Ramoth Baptist Chapel, Cwmfelin Mynach, made short speeches in proposing toasts. D. S. Davies said he was glad to see better times for farmers; if farmers did not get on, he did not get on; if they flourished, so did he (laughter and applause).

But short speeches was the order of the evening and the chairman, Mr Gwynne-Hughes, told the gathering that he had been asked by the committee to curtail the formal toasts to allow more time for discussion on how farmers might improve their business. But it was not a question of 'all work and no play' because at intervals, Powell introduced singers to entertain the diners. Mr Stephens of Coedybrain sang 'Mind and put the brake on when you are going down the hill'. Later in the evening Mr Stephens entertained them with another song 'Kitty, with the buckles on her shoes'. During a third interval Mr Walter Evans of Lampeter sang a Welsh song. However, Powell admitted that he was behind the committee's 'few toasts and short speeches' instruction and he felt that the change had been a success (applause).[68]

Miss Caroline Powell, the Hon. Sec. of the show, was showered with praise for her organisation which had attracted a 'large and respectable gathering'. No ladies attended the dinner so that W. R. H. Powell replied on behalf of his daughter and thanked them for coming in such large numbers and mentioned the chairman Mr J. W. Gwynne-Hughes of Tregib, Llandeilo, the vice-chairman Mr Thomas of Caeglas, Llandeilo and Mr David Pugh, MP of Manoravon, Llandeilo, for travelling large distances to be present. Landowner David Pugh was a well known breeder of Shorthorn cattle and he also owned Garnant Colliery (Pwll Perkins mine).

On the same day as the Agricultural Show, the annual show of the Llanboidy Cottage Garden and Industrial Society was held at the Market Hall and 'was largely attended'. There were competitions for flowers, fruit and vegetables, for butter and classes for 'industrial and art'. There were two classes for the following fruit and vegetables: broad beans, French beans, Beans scarlet runners, beet, short carrots, red cabbage, eating cabbage, cauliflower, celery, leeks, lettuce, spring onions, potato onions, pickling onions, parsnips, rhubarb, shallots, double curled parsley, round potatoes, kidney potatoes, peas, pot herbs, turnips, backing apples, eating apples, plums, window plants 6 varieties, window plants 3 varieties, single plant. Extra prizes were given for: collection of vegetables (cottagers only), collection of potatoes, hank of onions, basket of mixed fruits, vegetable marrow, basket of fruit, nuts etc, bouquet of wild flowers, specimen of art, rabbit pie, cockle soup, salad, roll of oat cake, honey and comb in sections, extracted honey, sealed bar frames. Special prizes: collection of plants, 6lb. of fresh butter. All classes were reported to be well represented and the quality all-round was good.

On 26 April 1885 two men were killed in a railway accident at Llanglydwen, The dead men were train driver, Thomas Davies and stoker Thomas Phillips. In September, F. W. N. Bishop of nearby Rosehill called a meeting at the Bont Inn, Llanglydwen, to consider the circum-

The railway from Whitland reached Llanglydwen in January 1872.
(Eddie Evans collection).

stances of the widows and children. The meeting was chaired by W. R. H. Powell and those present were Mr James JP, Pontygafel, Glandŵr; Reverend S. Davies, Rector of Llanglydwen; Reverend D. Griffiths, vicar of Mynachlogddu; Reverend O. R. Owen, Glandŵr; Reverend D. S. Davies, Cwmfelinmynach; Reverend J. S. Lewis, Rector of Llanfyrnach; Reverend J. Stephens, Llwynyrhwrdd; Reverend D. Williams, Henllan Amgoed; Reverend Tegryn Phillips, Hebron; Mr Vaughan Bowen Jones, Surgeon, Llanboidy; J. Evans, Mines, Llanfyrnach; Henry John, Castellgarw; P. N. Owen, Whitland; S. Jones, Llwynyrhwrdd Farm; F. W. N. Bishop, Rosehill, Llanglydwen; J. Bishop, Gilfach Slate Quarries; W. Samuel, Boncath; J. Jones, Crymych; D. Davies, Llety; Morris, Llandre, Llanfyrnach. Frank Bishop had called the meeting and it was agreed to collect subscriptions over the area for which purpose books were distributed. It was decided to form a committee to organise matters. F. W. N. Bishop was elected chair and the Reverend S. Davies treasurer.[69]

The 1880s was a bad time for agriculture and one claim reckoned that a depression of 25% had occurred in the value of agricultural produce.[70] In 1886 a Tenant Farmers Association was formed at St Clears with the aims of petitioning landlords to grant a reduction of rent to assist tenants meet the depression. All members were required to pledge not to bid for another member's farm while that member was negotiating a rent re-adjustment with the landlord. At a meeting of the Association held at the Swan Hotel, St Clears, in early January 1886, chaired by John Williams, Penlan, Llangynin, D. Howell Thomas, Derllys, said that his landlord had promised to remit 20% of rent for that year. J. J. Jones, Castle Lloyd, Laugharne, said the Association was a partnership between tenant and landlord; the tenant put his money to work on the landlord's land and both should partake of profits and losses. Problems were mounting with no profits for the previous 18 months and farmers having to borrow money to pay rent. They also had to contend against foreign competition and the question of free trade should be considered. Imports of cattle should be prohibited. But at that point the chairman put a stop to any further talk about free trade as it was in his view a political problem![70]

On 6 January 1886 W. R. H. Powell MP gave a dinner at the Maesgwynne Arms, Llanboidy to between forty and fifty of his tenants. In his address, he mentioned the Tenants Rights Bill and expressed his willingness to support any bill that would assist the farmer. He referred to the depression in agriculture and intimated that he would respond to the crisis by reducing their half yearly rent by 15%. Not surprisingly, there was loud and prolonged cheering! Further, W. R. H. Powell's health was proposed by Mr S. Owen, Hafod, 'in a stirring Welsh speech'. The toast was drunk with musical honours and Powell thanked his tenants for their good feelings towards him and his family at all times. Addresses were also given by: Mr J. Owen, Llwynderw; Mr D. Picton, Cilanw; Mr Richards jnr., Ffoswine; Mr Morse jnr., Llandawke; Mr James, Blaencediw; Mr Evans, Velindre; Mr Jones, Fynnonfoida; Mr Griffiths, Ddôl; Mr Reynolds, Penllwyngwair; Mr Griffiths, Felin; Mr Levi Jones, Llanboidy and others. The company then went over to the Market Hall to join in the tea party given to children of Llanboidy Board School. Mrs and Miss Powell had erected a large Christmas tree with over 300 articles on it, which were raffled during the afternoon. Llanfyrnach Brass Band was in attendance. At 7.00 p.m. a concert was given by the Llanboidy and Cwmfelin glee parties with Mr T. Lewis, Cwmfelin, Miss Phillips, Sweet Briar, Miss Beti Rees, Llanboidy and others taking part.[71]

Later in the month *The Welshman* reported that two more landlords, Colonel Lewes of Llys-newydd and Mrs Brigstocke of Blaenpant, had allowed rent reductions of 10% and 15% respectively and at the beginning of February 1886, Mr J. Beynon, Trewern, gave his tenants a 20% reduction in rents although it was not made clear whether those figures were for six months or yearly rent. But in other parts of Wales, landlords were not so generous and tenants were forced to form organisations to put pressure for rent reductions. For example, the *Journal* reported in January that tenants of Lord Mostyn and of Lord Denbigh in north Wales were petitioning for a rent reduction.

In the Autumn of 1888, Powell was not enjoying the best of health and was only able to attend the shows at St Clears and Llanboidy. But at the shows he was as energetic as he could be in urging young men to join the agricultural societies that organised the events. He said that he had kept hounds at Maesgwynne for fifty years but he had always introduced young blood into the kennel. So it was with agricultural shows and other pursuits. And it was vital to keep improving farming activities to counter foreign competition. Powell described the change he had seen in London during the 1880s. For example, hotel staff had changed from English to French and German who were better educated and worked for lower wages. So they must learn their work or else others would take it from them. They must not let Normandy butter beat them. So far as his daughter was concerned he begged them to guide her in her work as Hon. Sec. of the Llanboidy Show. He felt quite useless [himself] (shouts of No! No! Not yet!). He felt like a broken-winded horse and would not advise anyone to work him now!

Powell's campaign for a butter factory and for improved farming methods received a boost when an editorial in *The Welshman* on 21 December 1888 highlighted progress in those matters taking place in north Wales. The counties of Caernarfon and Flint were about to see within their boundaries, dairy schools and butter factories. The progress followed from proposals made by a Professor Dobbie designed to improve farming operations and from the success of butter factories set up by farmers in Cheshire. The editorial claimed that progress of that kind was required in south Wales and posed the question 'what is being done here?'. In answering its own question the editorial praised W. R. H. Powell for his campaign to get agricultural science taught in schools and to set up a butter factory in the Llanboidy area and urged landlords to take the lead in setting up a factory on behalf of tenants. The editorial coincided with yet another speech by W. R. H. Powell calling for a butter factory to be established in Carmarthenshire. Powell was speaking at the 1888 Llanboidy Christmas Show and revealed that he had received a letter from a friend in America singing the praises of butter factories. He went on to challenge the farmers to come together for the purpose of establishing a butter factory; if they agreed he would put down £100, or more if required, to start the building work. He would also take £200 worth of shares. He was quite sure they would derive great advantage from having a factory; the quality of the butter would improve and the price would rise and they would be able to defy the competition from Normandy and every other country.

The farmers, eventually, did take up Powell's challenge and a butter factory was opened at St Clears on 11 June 1890 and a few years later another was opened at Llanboidy . . . too late for Powell Bach to see his dream fulfilled.[72]

W. R. H. Powell's last project for the people of Llanboidy was to design and plan a water supply for the 'model village'. He did not live to see the project delivered but his widow together

Llanboidy Butter Factory was housed in the single storey building at the side
and rear of the National Provincial Store.
(By permission of Llyfrgell Genedlaethol Cymru / The National Library of Wales).

with his daughter, Caroline Mary Powell, saw to that. The work cost about £500 to complete and included a drinking water fountain which served as a memorial to Powell. It was unveiled in 1890 by his granddaughter, 11-year-old Mary Catherine Roch.

A keen observer of the times, Tom Rees of Llansteffan, wrote that . . . 'when Maesgwynne was at its zenith, the village of Llanboidy was flourishing and prosperous . . .'[73] Few in the local community would have disagreed. Indeed, the villagers might well have thought that Rees had written the ideal epitaph to the remarkable Walter Rice Howell Powell . . . Powell Bach Maesgwynne.

Part III

CARMARTHENSHIRE'S FIRST RADICAL MP

3.1 'We have no voice'

AFTER he came of age in 1816 the elder W. R. H. Powell (1798-1834) played his part in political matters at local and at parliamentary level in Carmarthenshire. At that time 'gentlemen' living or owning property anywhere in the county qualified to stand for election to the town council of Carmarthen. W. R. H. Powell (senior) was elected a 'councilman' on 25 February 1825. He joined the likes of Sir George Griffies Williams of Llwynywermwd, near Llandovery, John Jones MP of Ystrad, near Carmarthen, Earl Cawdor of Stackpole Court and Lord Dynevor of Dynevor Castle on the twenty-member Carmarthen Town Council. Eleven of the members were non-residents of the town and this was a source of constant complaint by both the electors and the 'resident members'.

At parliamentary level, 1832 was the year of the Reform Act which granted seats in the House of Commons to large cities that had sprung up during the Industrial Revolution and took away seats from the 'rotten boroughs' – those with very small populations. The Act also increased the number of individuals entitled to vote to one out of six adult males in a population of some 14 million. The 1832 UK General Election, the first after the Reform Act, saw the Whigs win a large majority, with the Tories getting less than 30% of the vote. Earl Grey became Prime Minister of the first Parliament of Victoria's reign and the Duke of Wellington led the Tories. Carmarthenshire had been granted an extra seat and the Hon. George Rice-Trevor (Tory) of Dinefwr became the first member and Edward Hamlyn Adams (Whig) the second. During the election campaign W. R. H. Powell (the elder that is) served on Rice-Trevor's election committee. As a major landowner it was not surprising that the elder Powell supported the Tories. His son was to change all that – but not for a while!

Powell senior died in 1834 and in August 1837 his 18-year-old son attended a dinner at the de Rutzen Arms, Narberth, organised by the Friends of Conservatism. Baron de Rutzen, the Russian nobleman who had acquired the Slebech Park estate in Pembrokeshire from his Jamaican father-in-law, was chairman for the occasion and fifty people sat down to enjoy the food. At that time young Powell was about to emerge as one prepared to speak-up and take radical action to improve the lot of the common people and in attending the Tory 'do' he was probably simply doing what was expected of the son of his late father.

The Rebecca uprising soon added to Powell's awareness of the dire social conditions endured by ordinary people and his dealings at that time with farmers in the Llanboidy area showed he was fully in-tune with their demands (see Part II). At the same time south-west Wales' parliamentary representatives were pretty impotent. To their shame, during the Rebecca uprising,

Carmarthen County's John Jones and George Rice-Trevor (both Tories) and Carmarthen Boroughs' David Morris (Whig) were silent and so were their colleagues from Pembrokeshire and Cardiganshire. Their ineffectiveness was summed up by a farmer at a meeting near Cwm Ifor near Llangadog on 4 August 1843 which had been called for the purpose of forming a farmers' union: 'When we elect members of parliament they do just as they please. We have no voice.'[1] (Thirty-seven years were to elapse before the farmers, the labourers and the poor gained their voice through the election, in 1880, of W. R. H. Powell as Liberal MP for Carmarthenshire.)

Local newspaper editors did their best to raise the political temperature. One of the causes of rural discontent was the subject of an editorial in *The Welshman* on 18 November 1842. Headed 'To the Fifty Pound farmers of Carmarthenshire' it was a colourful attack on the Tories, claiming that the 'Tories have ruined us by supporting Sir Robert Peel in his Tariff and Corn Law sliding scale by which all our profits are reduced 40%. An opportunity has come by the death of Mr Jones [Yr Halen], one of our County members, when the damage caused by the Conservatives may be repaired. Your landlords will be shortly asking you to vote for some Conservative numbskull. Tell them boldly you cannot think of doing so unless they lower your rents at once 40% . . . and give you an undertaking in writing to make a still further reduction in the event of a still further injury to your interests. You need not be afraid of their blustering about turning you out as you can refer them for information as to the success of that scheme to Capt. Webley Parry of Noyadd near Newcastle Emlyn.' On the other hand, the Tories were backed by the *Carmarthen Journal* whose editor could not hide his loathing for the Whigs. He directed his venom against the Nonconformists, claiming that the preachers were 'not content with hurling political philippics and preaching political homilies from their pulpits and on the tented fields and the hedgerows' but that the 'political preachers and their no less political congregations held prayer meetings in different parts of the county to pray for the success of the radical candidate.' He went on to claim that: 'Much maudlin declamation has been directed against the coercion of Landlords. But what is that compared with the spiritual coercion exercised by the political preachers to induce tenants to "break through all restraints and vote against their Landlords".'[2]

But both Whig and Tory leadership in Carmarthenshire were largely unmoved by the vitriolic outpourings of the newspapers. Both camps were of the squirearchy and their rivalry was limited to competing for the prestige and authority within the county that came with being an MP. It was to take decades for the county's Whigs to join with Nonconformist radicals in a Liberal coalition ready to offer a real political challenge to the Tories.

Meanwhile, in November 1842 the Squire of Maesgwynne was present at a meeting in Carmarthen's Lion Royal Hotel to choose a successor to the recently deceased Tory MP John Jones, Ystrad. The meeting was chaired by Daniel Prytherch, magistrate, landed proprietor, father of thirteen and Carmarthen's mayor in 1824 and 1831. His great-grandfather was Rees Prytherch of Ystradwallter near Llandovery, Nonconformist leader in north Carmarthenshire and in the counties of Brecon and Radnor in the seventeenth century. It was he who led the area's persecuted dissenters during the reigns of Charles II and James II to worship in the relative safety of Craig-yr-Wyddon Cave near Pentre-tŷ-gwyn, Llandovery. But, clearly, his great-grandson had abandoned such 'wayward' activities for the 'safety' of the establishment. Prominent Carmarthenshire Tories such as the Reverend John Evans, Nant-yr-eglwys, Llanboidy, D. T. Bowen Davies, Maes-y-crigie, Pencader, Nathaniel Rowlands, Parciau, Henllan Amgoed, W. Evans of the *Carmarthen Journal*, Rice Pryce Beynon of St Clears and Timothy Powell were all 'noticed' at the meeting by the *Journal*'s reporter as was W. R. H. Powell. It was unanimously agreed to nominate one David Arthur Saunders Davies of Pentre, Manordeifi in north Pembrokeshire, a country gentleman, as the Tory candidate. *The Welshman*'s hoped-for-contest failed to materialise because the Whigs did not field a candidate and Saunders Davies duly joined another Tory, the Hon. George Rice-Trevor of Dinefwr, as MP for the two-seat Carmarthenshire constituency.

It was the age of rapid expansion of religious non-conformity in Wales and this went hand-in-hand with the growth of political radicalism. Between 1801 and 1851 a new chapel was opened every eight days on average! In the wider Llanboidy area, Henllan Amgoed Independent Chapel had been opened in 1697 and Rhydyceisied in 1701. And before the end of the eighteenth century Glandŵr Independent Chapel and Rhydyparc Unitarian Chapel were up and running. Trinity Independent Chapel was built in Llanboidy in 1800 and a split at Glandŵr resulted in the building of Hebron in 1805. Baptist chapels were built at Cwmfelin Mynach in 1823 and at Login in 1828 and Moriah Independent Chapel was opened in Blaenwaun in 1829. Soar Independent Chapel in Llanboidy Parish near Ietgoch, Whitland, was built in 1836. By 1851 there were a dozen chapels within a four mile radius of Llanboidy. Trinity was a branch of the Church at Henllan Amgoed which explains the absence of a minister resident in Llanboidy in 1851 because both chapels were served by the Reverend Joshua Lewis who lived in Henllan Amgoed Parish. In 1851 most (89%) of the population (4,383) of the six parishes of Llanboidy, Llanglydwen, Eglwysfair a Churrig, Llangan, Llanwinio and Llangynin, on average, attended a religious service on Sundays. And 75% (2,940) of the attendees went to the eleven Noncon-formist chapels within the six parishes.[3]

Powell's actions (see Part II) during the Rebecca uprising marked him out as a community leader with radical views prepared to stand up for the rights of the poor in sharp contrast to most of his fellow gentry. In the years following the troubles he gained experience of public service as a member of the magistracy. For example, in January 1850 he was one of forty members of the Bench of Magistrates of the Carmarthenshire Quarter Sessions that met at Llandeilo. The chair of the meeting was taken by David Pugh Esq. and among the Bench were the Earl Cawdor and his son John F. V. Campbell, Viscount Emlyn, MP for Pembrokeshire, Rice-Trevor MP for Carmarthenshire, Daniel Prytherch of Carmarthen, and three from St Clears, Rice Pryce Beynon, John Waters and Timothy Powell. One item on the agenda which amused, confused and raised the temperature of debate was the proposal to build a bridge at Llanfihangel-ar-Arth. According to the *Carmarthen Journal*, a sub-committee had met and its recommendation to the Quarter-Sessions was that 'a contract be entered into with Mr Garrett to erect a bridge on the terms which were stated in the *Journal* some weeks back.' One of the members remarked that the sub-committee 'had accepted the estimate without seeing the plan – a rather Irish mode of doing business.' But then he admitted that he was a member of the sub-committee that had acted in the mode that he was now criticising! The *Journal* reporter went on: 'A long con-versation, some of which was not of the most pleasant nature, then took place which was put an end to at the suggestion of Earl Cawdor.' It took several further meetings of the Quarter-Sessions before the bridge was given the go-ahead.

Another report considered at the January meeting recommended a reduction in the salaries of the paid officers of the county by 10%. Farming incomes had suffered a 10% drop which the magistrates now wished to pass on to their county employees. A proposal to consider individually each officer's salary was carried. It was also recommended that 'the Superintendent of Police perform the duties of Inspector of Weights and Measures and that police do the duty of Hall keepers.' Lord Cawdor added a proposal to sack the trumpeter who was in his opinion 'an official of no earthly use and when the office was abolished they [the members] might be safely left to blow their own trumpets!' All the recommendations together with Cawdor's proposal were agreed. A motion by J. H. Rees that the salary of the Chief Constable, Captain Scott, be reduced by 17% from £300 to £250, the minimum salary allowed by the Secretary of State, was put to the vote and was carried by 18 votes to 15. W. R. H. Powell voted for the motion.[4] The working-class was hit hard by the depression in agriculture and most of the numerous servants, male and female, at the 1850 hiring-fair at Haverfordwest were not hired.[5]

The 1859 UK General Election is considered to be the first to be contested by the Liberal Party – a name unofficially adopted to cover the alliance of Whigs, Peelites, Radicals and Irish Brigade who had previously voted against Lord Derby's administration in the House of Commons. It was also the last general election entered by the Chartists, before their organisation was dissolved. In 1859 Powell was still attending meetings of the Tory gentry and did in fact second the proposal that David Jones, Pantglas, Llanfynydd, be adopted as a Tory candidate for Carmarthenshire in that year's General Election. But it is worth noting that W. R. H. Powell in his speech emphasised the support given to local organisations by David Jones, as well as by the other Tory candidate David Pugh, as demonstrated by their 'liberal pecuniary assistance, which they were always ready to give and which I know is duly appreciated by a very large number of the constituency and will be remembered by them whenever the day arrives that a poll is demanded (Loud Cheers)'.[6] Again the two Tories, David Jones and David Pugh, who had succeeded Saunders Davies in 1857, were returned unopposed.

But party politics in Carmarthenshire was yet to emerge from domination by gentry families whose adoption of Tory or Whig labels was more a matter of habit or convenience rather than of policy differences and the two groups sought to find a consensus to avoid costly elections. The arrangement lasted from 1838 to 1867 and for almost thirty years there was no election and the two-seat county constituency was represented by a couple of Tories with Whig agreement. But Whig or Tory MPs drawn from the Anglican gentry did not reflect the outlook of their mainly Nonconformist constituents. For example, only two of Wales' thirty-two MPs voted for the Disestablishment of the Church in Ireland in 1856. And only twelve voted against church rates in 1861; the abolition of which was high on their constituents' agenda. The Corn Laws introduced in 1815 were another example where the ordinary people's interest was directly opposed to that of their landed representatives. The Laws introduced import tariffs designed to support domestic British corn prices against competition from less expensive foreign imports. They also enhanced the profits and political power associated with land ownership and the resulting high cost of food led to calls for their repeal. During 1844, the agitation subsided as there were fruitful harvests. However, the situation changed in late 1845 with poor harvests and the potato blight in Ireland; Britain faced scarcity and Ireland starvation. The repeal of the corn laws in 1846 and the end of the Rebecca uprising led to a period of relative prosperity in the countryside but the problems of land exhaustion and of land shortage remained and farming-life continued to be precarious.

3.2 A natural radical but a reluctant candidate

In the 1850s and the 1860s the displacement of the gentry as community leaders by Noncon-formist ministers accelerated as the preachers increasingly dominated the pulpit and the press. In the General Election of 1865 Wales, for the first time, returned a majority of Whigs to Westminster. But the Nonconformist leaders were not satisfied and in 1866 the Reverend Henry Richard called for an end to the over-lordship of the gentry. '*Trech gwlad nag arglwydd*' (a land is mightier than its lord) was his rallying cry which stirred fundamental passions in Wales. In 1867 Disraeli's Reform Act made a vital difference in urban areas where, for example, in Merthyr Tydfil the electorate increased from 1,387 to 14,577! The Liberal candidate in Merthyr in the 1868 General Election, Henry Richard, was openly challenging of the claims to authority of English-speaking landed gentry who had dominated the social and political life of Wales for over three centuries: 'The people who speak this language (Welsh), who read this literature, who own this history, who inherit these traditions, who venerate these names, who created and sustain these marvellous religious organisations, the people forming three-fourths of the people of Wales – have they not a right to say to this small propertied class . . . We are the Welsh people and not you? This country is ours and not yours, and therefore we claim to have our principles and sentiments and feelings represented in the Commons' House of Parliament.'[7] Liberal Henry Richard topped the poll in Merthyr, and elsewhere in Wales the Liberals generally saw off their Tory opponents in a remarkable upheaval in representation.

W. R. H. Powell's radicalism was established from the beginning of his time as Squire of Maesgwynne by his wide-ranging actions, from the late 1830s onwards, to improve community life. As the Liberal Party adopted more radical policies the old two-party system prevailing in west Wales became outdated. In Carmarthenshire, for example, the Tory/Whig consensus came to an end in a shambolic way at the general election of 1868. The Tories were hopelessly disorganised and three of them stood in the two-seat constituency. The county's Liberals were uncertain what to do and eventually settled on a candidate completely unknown to the area. E. J. Sartoris was a former unsuccessful Tory candidate from Hampshire and his links with Carmarthenshire were limited to the land he owned in the south-east of the county and to his friendship with Cowell-Stepney, a Whig, who in 1868 stood as a Liberal in Carmarthen Boroughs. But Sartoris, helped by the general swing to the Liberals and profiting from the three-way split in the Tory vote, topped the poll with the Tory John Jones (Blaenos) taking the other seat. Cowell-Stepney gained the Boroughs' seat for the Liberals. Some of the Tory gentry, whose parliamentary careers had been brought to an end or whose prospective careers had been throttled at birth, reacted most unwisely by evicting some of their tenants who had deserted them at the polls. In Carmarthenshire a total of 26 cases of eviction were proved. Tories countered with charges against the Liberal-supporting Nonconformist ministers whose effect they termed the 'chapel screw'. But it was Whig conservatism rather than Liberal radicalism that counted with the Carmarthenshire electorate at that time. When Sartoris had the opportunity in

1869 to vote for disestablishment of the Church of England in Wales, he was warned not to vote for the measure, so as not to risk jeopardising his chances of re-election! The days of Powell and the preachers were some way off.

In the early 1870s the Liberal Party's radical programme sorted out the sheep from the goats in Carmarthenshire and electors wishing to vote against the landlord class received a boost in 1872 with the introduction of the secret ballot. The Tories, unable to contemplate a deal with the Liberals, put up two candidates for the 1874 General Election. *The Welshman* commented on the Liberal Party's position in its issue of 30 January 1874 and considering it was supposed to be a Liberal-supporting newspaper it included some surprising comments on the Liberal programme. It reckoned that W. R. H. Powell would be the new Liberal candidate and that his running mate would be the independent-minded David Pugh provided he was prepared to adopt the Liberal programme including disestablishment of the Church and 'some other *destructive doctrines* [emphasis added]. Whether this was too much for him we shall see.' The 'Liberal programme' referred to was presumably a programme being advocated by Welsh Liberals under Nonconformist influence because disestablishment, for example, did not become party policy until 1887.

It appeared that the retiring Liberal member, E. J. Sartoris, was, at that stage, not being considered because according to *The Welshman* he 'does not seem to care about making friends in the county.' On the other hand W. R. H. Powell was 'perhaps the most popular man in the county.' However, it would appear that *The Welshman* was unaware of behind the scenes developments in the Liberal camp because Pugh had already turned down the Liberal ticket and E. J. Sartoris had agreed to take his place provided he had Powell as a running mate. Powell having failed to persuade his friend Pugh to stand, reluctantly agreed to be the second Liberal candidate. In his election address, printed in the same issue of *The Welshman*, he acknowledged the prosperity enjoyed by the country under the previous (Liberal) government and wrote that he would give it (if returned) his independent support. If that was intended to imply that his support of his own party's government would be in some way conditional, then he may have been trying to attract support from conservative minded electors. His beliefs, which were set out in the same paper, clearly defined Powell as a Liberal fully in tune with his party's radical programme and for the first time Carmarthenshire electors had a very clear choice in political terms. Powell's manifesto read: 'I am an advocate for the repeal of the Income Tax (originally imposed as a War Tax) and will support any measure tending to lessen the burden of local taxation. I think that the Farmers who contribute to the County Stock should have some voice and control over the expenditure through Representative Boards. I am in favour of the disestablishment of the Church as I believe it would tend to promote its real interests and check the acrimonious spirit prevailing. With respect to the Elementary Education Act, I trust to see it modified, particularly as regards the 25th Clause [which allowed children from poor homes attending church schools to have their fees paid from the rates], so as to put an end to the unseemly conflicts now so continually arising.' 'The Liberals can ask no more' was *The Welshman*'s verdict.

Inevitably Powell had to defend his support, in 1859, for the Tory David Jones and he did that at a meeting in Carmarthen by claiming that 'if my old friend [David Jones] were alive today he would tell you that my views were then as they are now (cheers).' In the same meeting he reminded the audience that in the 1868 general election he had proposed the Independent, David Pugh, who had approved of Powell's views then, and was now giving him his support. *The Welshman* was full of praise for Powell and claimed that he was 'perhaps the most popular man in the County . . . No one dares utter an evil word against him. In his own vicinity he is literally beloved and consulted by all classes. He has converted the Llanboidy district into one of the most improving parts of the County. He supports education, he endeavours to raise the peasant by creating within him a spirit of independence and self-respect, he encourages the farmer to adopt improved means of cultivating the land, he promotes the moral and religious condition of the people around. It was impossible for the Liberals to find personally a more desirable or a more popular candidate.' And then the reporter added: 'But no one was prepared for the opinions he now avows.'[8]

It is difficult to understand the reporter's statement. After-all, W. R. H. Powell's 'opinions' simply reflected his actions, over the previous 30 years, designed to improve the lot of the Welsh Nonconformist community of which he, although a churchman, was so much a part. However the reporter's opinion was undoubtedly influenced by the generally accepted values of the Victorian age in which 'Britishness' in the form of English institutions such as the monarchy and the Church of England stifled debate about the differing needs of the separate nations of Wales, Scotland and Ireland. Powell understood very well the unfairness felt by the Nonconformist majority at having to pay taxes and tithes to maintain churches which they never visited. He had come into direct conflict with the Church in the matter of schooling for the majority Nonconformist community of Llanboidy. No wonder Powell supported disestablishment of the Church of England in Wales. But it would appear that Powell's first-hand experience meant nothing to *The Welshman*'s reporter who probably could not endure the thought of disestablishment forcing him to think of Wales in a different way to England.

Powell did not succeed in gaining a seat in the 1874 General Election: 'The cry of disestablishment and secular education associated with the immense personal influence of Mr Powell has failed to captivate the county of Carmarthen. . . . The Conservatives were better canvassers.' Powell finished in third place behind the two Conservatives.[9] But he was not happy at the conduct of his opponents during the election. He claimed that the Tories had spread the belief that the ballot was not secret and had recorded the names of voters going to booths giving voters the impression that they would know how people had voted and that they would lose their employment if they failed to vote as instructed. Lord Emlyn was, apparently, very annoyed at Powell's charge but similar accusations were made by the town clerk of Haverfordwest.

3.3 Powell tops the poll in Carmarthenshire in the 1880 Election

Five years later another general election was looming. At a meeting of Liberals in October 1879 at the School Room of Water Street Methodist Chapel, Carmarthen the decision was taken to put up one candidate only to challenge the two Tories and W. R. H. Powell was the unanimous choice. Powell addressed the meeting and, in typical fashion, expressed his admiration of the sitting Tory members in personal terms. At the same time he did not think the Tories represented the views of the majority in the county of Carmarthenshire. He criticised the Tory government

Liberals meeting place: schoolroom at Water Street Methodist Chapel, Carmarthen.
(Courtesy Lon Owen).

of the day for wasting the surplus money handed to them on taking office and it was time for a return to power for Gladstone, Harding, Bright and others. And then he became his unassuming self, claiming that he did not agree with the meeting's choice of candidate (himself) because he did not consider he had 'the ability or the means for the position.' Powell said that he had hoped to see Pugh at the meeting, ready to accept the candidacy. 'Now in selecting me I fear you have done so out of gratitude for 1874 or perhaps you thought I was ambitious for the seat. I assure you I had no such ambitions then [1874] nor have I now.' He said that his candidacy in 1874 had been forced on him by Sartoris' last-minute threat to leave the Liberals without a candidate unless he (Powell) would stand as well, as 'two gentlemen present here this evening, Mr George Thomas [attorney and town clerk of Carmarthen] and Mr Prosser [leading member of Water Street Chapel and farmer of Tygwyn, Llangynnwr] can testify.' He had had to accept without even consulting his wife! Finally, Powell accepted the candidacy provided they all accepted him for what he was: 'a country man'. He worked up a bit of steam to end with: 'Once you unfurl the Liberal flag and place it in my hands it will not be taken down until we are conquered or victorious.' Among those 'noticed' at the meeting were the Reverend William Morgan, Reverend J. O. Davies, Reverend J. Jones, Reverend D. S. Davies (minister at Ramoth, Cwmfelin Mynach and Calfaria, Login, and a great friend to Powell) and several others.[10]

The *Carmarthen Journal* showed its Tory colours in a dreadfully biased report in its issue of 12 March 1880 when it attacked Powell in no uncertain terms: 'his sporting activities will not

Reverend J. Wyndham Lewis (1838-1895), minister
at Water Street Methodist Chapel, Carmarthen,
and a leading radical.
(*Hanes Methodistiaeth Sir Gaerfyrddin*. Dolgellau, 1911).

Reverend David Saunders Davies (1842-1917),
minister at Ramoth, Cwmfelin Mynach
and Calfaria, Login Baptist Chapels.
(Eddie Evans collection).

Ramoth Baptist Chapel, Cwmfelin Mynach. *Yr hen gapel*.
(Nansi Evans collection).

TO THE ELECTORS OF THE COUNTY OF CARMARTHEN.

GENTLEMEN,

A Dissolution of Parliament having been announced I now place my services at your disposal in compliance with the unanimous request made to me at the large and representative Meeting of Liberals held at Carmarthen in October last.

Believing that the internal welfare and the external independence of the Country has been seriously damaged by the acts of the present Government, I will, if elected, loyally support the general policy of the Liberal Party, to whose wise measures our country owes so much of its prosperity ond greatness, its Civil and Religious Liberty.

My Watchwords are Peace, Retrenchment, and Reform, as being singularly applicable to the present crisis, when the warlike and intermeddling policy of the Tory ministry has produced disquietude and distrust at home and abroad, whilst its extravagance and financial incompetence has greatly interfered with the material interests of the country.

Connected as I am with land, I have naturally marked with regret the depression of the Agricultural Interest, and any measure that might be introduced in order to give greater security to Tenants for the outlay of their capital, would meet with my hearty support. The simplification of the sale and transfer of Land would in my opinion greatly benefit both Landlord and Tenant.

Feeling that the inhabitants of the Counties are deprived of their just share in the election of their representatives, I am prepared to vote for the equalization of Town and County Franchise.

I think the ratepayers who contribute so largely to the County Stock should have control over its expenditure through elected County Boards.

In local matters it has ever been my aim to support all projects tending in any way to promote the prosperity of this and the adjoining Counties; and if returned as one of your representatives rest assured that my interest in these matters will be, if possible, increased.

I shall be unable to wait upon you all personally in the short time which now remains before the election, I beg, therefore, to solicit your vote and interest.

I have the honour to remain, Gentlemen,
Your most obedient Servant,
W. R. H. POWELL.

Maesgwynne, Whitland, R.S.O.,
10th March, 1880.   [8390

Etholiad Sir Gaerfyrddin.

AT ETHOLWYR SIR GAERFYRDDIN

FONEDDIGION,

Gan fod Dadgorfforiad y Senedd wedi ei wneyd yn hysbys, gosodaf yn awr fy hun ab eich gwasanaeth, yn gydunol â'r cais unfrydol a wnawd ataf mewn cyfarfod o gynrychiolwyr Rhyddfrydol a gynaliwyd yn Nghaerfyrddin yn mis Hydref diweddaf.

Yn credu fel yr wyf fod llesiant tufewnol, ac annibyniaeth allanol y wlad hon wedi eu niweidio yn fawr gan weithrediadau y Llywodraeth bresenol, bydd i mi, os caf fy ethol, gefnogi yn galonog wleidiadaeth y Blaid Ryddfrydol, i fesuran doeth pa rai y mae ein gwlad yn ddyledus i raddau helaeth am ei llwyddiant a'i mawredd presenol, yn gystal a'i Rhyddid Gwladol a Chrefyddol.

Fy arwyddeirian ydynt, Heddwch, Cynildeb, a Diwygiad, gan eu bod mor gymhwysiadol i'r adeg bresenol, pan y mae gweithrediadau rhyfelgar a therfysglyd y Weinyddiaeth Doriaidd wedi cynyrchu aflonyddwch ac anymddiried yn y wlad hon a gwledydd tramor, a phan y mae eu hafradlonedd a'u banallu i drefnu achosion arianol y Deyrnas wedi bod yn niweidiol iawn i lwyddiant ein gwlad.

Gan fy mod yn dal cysylltiad â thir, yr wyf wedi sylwi gyda gofid ar y Caledi Amaethyddol, a bydd i mi gefnogi yn galonog unrhyw fesur a ddygir i fewn i'r dyben o roddi rhagor o sicrwydd i denantiaid am osod allan eu cyfalaf (capital). Byddai symleiddio deddf pryniad a throsglwyddiad tir, yn ol fy marn i, lesau, i raddau helaeth, y Tirfeddianwr a'r Deiliad.

Yn teimlo fod trigolion y Siroedd yn cael eu hamddifadu o'u than gyfreithlawn i etholiad eu cynrychiolwyr, yr wyf yn barod i bleidleisio dros gydraddoli etholwyr y Trefia'r Siroedd.

Credwyf y dylai y trethdalwyr a gyfranant mor helaeth tuag at y County Stock feddianu llywodraeth dros ei dreuliad drwy Fyrddau Sirol etholedig.

Mewn achosion lleol, y mae wedi bod yn brif ymgais fy mywyd i gynorthwyo pob cynllun a dueddai yn unrhyw fodd i hyrwyddo llwyddiant y Sir hon a'r Siroedd cylchynol; ac os dychwelir fi fel un o'ch cynrychiolwyr, gallwch benderfynu y bydd i'm dyddordeb yn y materion hyn, os yn bosibl, gynyddu.

Ni fyddaf yn alluog i alw gyda chwi oll yn bersonol yn yr ychydig amser sydd o hyn i'r etholiad; gan hyny, nid oes genyf ond deisyf eich pleidlais a'ch cefnogaeth.

Meddaf yr anrhydedd i fod, Foneddigion,
Eich ufudd was,
W. R. H. POWELL.
(Yr unig Ymgeisydd Rhyddfrydol.)

Maesgwynne, Mawrth 10fed, 1880.

Powell's address for the General Election of 1880.
(Courtesy *Carmarthen Journal*).

recommend him to farmers, who are Nonconformists and his pronounced churchmanship will militate against his success. Tenants admire his dogs but not his principles . . . It is a pity that W. R. H. Powell should be forced from his retirement to contest Carmarthenshire. As a county gentleman he is worthy of esteem but as a politician he is nowhere. If questions in the Commons related to kennels and stables, fine . . . but in finance, foreign affairs and colonial matters he would be nowhere . . . like a round peg in a square hole!'

Canvassing was in full swing in March 1880 and at a Tory meeting addressed by one of their candidates, John Jones of Blaenos, Phillips of Clyngwyn, Llanboidy was present. Powell spent a day canvassing in Llandyfaelog, Meincie and Porthyrhyd and on the following day he was in Pontarddulais. In a speech, Powell said the Tories attacked him for keeping hounds but many voted for him because he kept hounds! In 1874, opponents attacked him for 'pulling down the church' but since then he and his Nonconformist friends had restored the church at Llanboidy and now they said he was too much of a churchman to represent Nonconformist Liberals! Supporting speeches were delivered by Mr Henry Jones, Mr Michael, Reverend Davies, Siloah, Reverend Rowlands, Moriah and Reverend J. Jones, Felinfoel.[11] Powell emphasised that he would advocate the extension of the franchise to every householder. He would, also, support the proposed Burials Bill. And he wanted to see County Boards established to control spending of local rates; an idea ridiculed by the Tory candidate, Lord Emlyn, who alleged that spending 'would not lessen one farthing'.[12] The Tory newspapers tried to make out that Powell was simply a 'sporting squire' and completely unsuitable to be an MP. When there was talk about Croydon (home to the prestigious Croydon Races) being made a parliamentary constituency, the *Western Mail* manufactured a joke at Powell's expense. Its columnist reckoned that it was almost a foregone conclusion that Powell would fail to win a seat in Carmarthenshire but he might stand a better chance in Croydon 'where he is well known. He used to take a great interest in the steeplechases there and he would be a fit and proper member for such a place. The Squire of Maesgwynne is fond of racing and betting and cannot well represent the land of butter, cheese and eggs. As the Hon. Member for Croydon he would be at home.'[13]

Powell's election address, printed in Welsh and in English in *The Welshman* of 2 April 1880, included the Liberal Party's watchwords of Peace, Retrenchment and Reform. He would support any measure giving greater security to Tenants for their outlay of capital. He wanted to see the process of the sale and transfer of land simplified as it would benefit both landlord and tenant. At the poll, a week later, there was great enthusiasm, with some outbreaks of fighting at some polling stations![14] The count took place at Llandeilo where the result was announced:

Powell (L)	4,101	elected
Lord Emlyn (C)	3,030	elected
John Jones (C)	2,712	unelected

Plumpers (those who cast one vote only):

For Powell	3,341
For Emlyn	146
For Jones	110

With over 3,030 electors voting for Powell only, he was the clear winner and Carmarthenshire was once again represented by a Liberal and a Tory. Carmarthen Boroughs (the towns of Carmarthen and Llanelli) was also represented by a Liberal, Benjamin Thomas Williams, who was returned unopposed. B. T. Williams was a barrister, born in Narberth, Pembrokeshire, and

MP for Carmarthenshire, W. R. H. Powell, at his desk.
(Thomas Lloyd collection).

was recorder of Carmarthen from 1872 to 1878 when he was elected unopposed at a by-election as MP for Carmarthen Boroughs. He resigned as MP in 1882 to become a County Court Judge.

The county result was a great disappointment to the Tories who, after extensive canvassing, were confident of winning both seats. But their reckoning did not take account of the fact that the ballot was secret. The Tory election agent was of the opinion that promises made to Tory canvassers had been 'broken by the thousands' and 'to my mind it will be useless to canvass again and an utter waste of money to do so.'

Wales' Liberal representation had been increased by 10 to 29 while the Tory numbers had reduced by the same number to 4. The Westminster Parliament consisted of 237 Tories, 352 Liberals and 63 Irish Home Rule members. The 1880 election results for Wales reflected the changing character of Welsh Liberalism with only a small minority of the twenty-nine members returned representing the Whig element, while eight members were Nonconformists.[15] Powell, although officially a churchman, had for decades championed Nonconformist causes. For example, he had long promoted non-denominational education for which purpose he had built a school at Llanboidy in 1863. He had declared his support for disestablishment of the Church of England in Wales in 1874 and as a member of parliament he renewed his call for action on the matter in speech after speech throughout Carmarthenshire. Powell's public pronouncements during the 1870s on the adverse effect of excessive drinking of alcohol on people's behaviour made him a natural supporter of the Sunday Closing Bill and the dissenters of Carmarthenshire backed him to the hilt. In his first term in Parliament he had the satisfaction of voting for the Burials Bill, opposed all the way by his co-member Lord Emlyn, and helped it become law before the end of the session. The Burials Act gave Nonconformists the right to a burial service in Anglican churchyards.

3.4 Spreading the radical message

1880: Llanboidy, Carmarthen, Llanelli

Powell was back in Llanboidy in time for the 1880 autumn agricultural shows and was able to report on his first parliamentary session during which he had voted in 146 divisions. Of the Welsh members, Lord Kensington, MP for Haverfordwest, topped the list having voted in 159 divisions. Powell's fellow MP for Carmarthenshire, Lord Emlyn, managed only 10 divisions and the *Carmarthen Journal* was quick to his defence pleading 'ill-health and other duties' in mitigation. We can only imagine the *Journal*'s reaction if the voting records had been reversed!

After her father's election to Parliament, Miss Caroline Powell took over the duties of Hon. Sec. of the Llanboidy Agricultural Society. At the 1880 show dinner, W. R. H. Powell referred to the 'abundant harvest' enjoyed that year. He emphasised that 'politics was properly excluded from these meetings and he should not infringe upon that rule.' He went on to claim that the increase in home produce was 'equivalent in value to a 'gift' of £15 per family'. He thought cheap produce benefited everyone, especially agricultural labourers whom he had always sought to assist in every possible way. He said that the farmer had been more talked about in the recent Parliament than for some time, and on both sides of the House. He hoped some of the measures (dealt with in parliament) were beneficial to the farmers.

For example, he had received a lot of correspondence requesting his support for the abolition of duty on malt and he agreed with the proposal because farmers would then, in addition to using damaged wheat or inferior barley as feeding, also be able to make it into malt or, with a 6s. licence, brew it into beer. If their house was over £10 (rateable value) they would need a 9s. licence. Many constituents had complained to him about the excise officer's valuation of their houses at more than £10, so he had insisted that an inspector visit the area and report on the Excise evaluations. The inspector had found in favour of the constituents and Powell got a tremendous round of applause from the appreciative diners! When told that a leading tenant farmer had claimed the Act would be of no benefit to farmers, Powell retorted that if this Act was not a boon, he despaired of ever satisfying the farmers!

The Ground Game Act allowed farmers to kill rabbits and hares on their land to protect crops from destruction and should 'cement the relationship between tenant and landlord.'

He reported on a visit he had made to the Aylesbury Dairy Company's butter factory in London. The eventual outcome of his visit was the exhibition of butter-making in the Market Hall, Llanboidy, described in Part II.

Powell voted for the Ground Game Act of 1880. It allowed farmers to protect their crops from destruction
by rabbits and hares. The rabbit trade grew into a substantial business in the twentieth century.
Left to right: Gwyn Sambrook, John Thomas, Brynderwen, Llanboidy and son William Thomas (Will Bach).
(Eddie Evans collection).

He also referred to a stroll he took in Tottenham Court Road where he witnessed 'thousands
and thousands of people buying some horrid looking compound' which they called 'jam'. It
occurred to him that they in Llanboidy 'ought to send hundreds of tons of blackberries every
year which would be eagerly bought by these people [in London] and some persons might make
a fortune out of the despised blackberry!'[16]

The *Carmarthen Journal* was not slow in attempting to make political capital out of Powell's
speech, claiming that he was using the shows to promote his political views: 'The Squire of
Maesgwynne has returned to his friends in Carmarthenshire after sticking most manfully to his
duties through a very long and trying session. At a dinner last week he said he did not wish to
introduce politics and immediately plunged into them forthwith. Among other things, he is
reported to have said that the extra produce of this season which he estimated at £1 million
would be equal to a present of £15 to every family in UK! There are 7 million families in UK
and it would puzzle even the magician of finance who lives at Hawarden [Gladstone] to give
£15 to every family out of £1 million. Perhaps Mr Powell was thinking of the county which he
represents which is only a small part of the UK.'[17]

A week later at the Carmarthenshire Agricultural Society Exhibition the president, Mr J. S.
Tregoning, reckoned that the show meetings were an ideal forum for 'hearing remarks on

questions of interest to the country' such as 'abolishing the malt duty, dealing with hares and rabbits (cries of no politics) and the Employers Liability Bill which was vital to employers of labour'. Powell took full advantage of the president's encouragement and said he felt it right to tell them of his endeavours on their behalf . . . he had never shirked his duties and had attended some 150 divisions. He thought of agriculture without (associating it) with politics. He thought the bills, referred to above, benefited landlords and tenants alike. In response to the concern about the depression suffered by agriculture in the country, a government commission consisting of a Mr Pell and a Mr Read had been sent to study the state of agriculture in America and Powell had a few copies of their report which he invited those present to take with them.[18]

When 16 cases of drunkenness and one case of assault on the Reverend R. T. Jenkins, vicar of Mydrim, had to be dealt with at Llanboidy Petty Sessions with John Beynon, E. Schaw Protheroe, J. Bagnall Evans and W. R. H. Powell on the bench, a *Carmarthen Journal* columnist could not resist taking a pot shot at Powell by claiming that '20 cases, some serious, and rumoured to have taken place over less than 3 weeks,' had been heard at Llanboidy. The columnist called for change in behaviour in the Llanboidy area and urged W. R. H. Powell MP to sort out his erring fellow parishioners when he returned from Parliament. He seemed to ignore the fact that Powell was already returned and had been on the bench which had in fact fined those guilty of breaking the law.[19]

The drunkenness manifesting itself at Llanboidy was probably no worse than that experienced in communities throughout Wales and Britain in those days. Data for 1880 showed that the annual consumption of beer in Britain at 32 gallons per head of population was second only to Belgium (33 gallons per head). The figure for third-place Germany was 22 gallons per head and France was way behind at 4.66 but the French probably made up their alcohol intake through wine drinking.

In November 1880 a meeting of the county Liberals at Llanelli was addressed by the two Liberal MPs returned from Carmarthenshire: the boroughs member, B. T. Williams and the county member, W. R. H. Powell. Powell referred to Acts passed during that year's session of Parliament which was his first experience of the place. According to Powell, the Employers Liability Act enforced proper care on the part of companies and individual employers of labour and was only common justice for working men and railway servants. The Burials Act which legalized non-Anglican burial services in Anglican churchyards meant, in Powell's view, that Nonconformists had the right which was the birth-right of citizenship and should not depend on religious belief but should be extended to Jews and free thinkers. He went on to claim that the principle of relative toleration should be upheld and therefore the Act required amendment.

Powell said that in the next session he hoped to see brought before Parliament the land laws, the bankruptcy laws, and the right of rate-payers to have some part in the management of county affairs and he hoped to see the county franchise enlarged in the same way as the borough franchise had been. 'Liberal principles, [Powell believed], were the only principles by which the great fountain of natural life could be safely guided to its unknown destination. The longer he lived the more he reflected and the stronger were his convictions and he could not better express them than in the words of Mr Gladstone . . . "The experiences of life convince me more and more that the political creed of the Liberal party is that which will most effectively increase the honour and strength of our nation and the stability of our constitution".'[20]

1881: St Clears, Llanboidy, Cross Inn (Ammanford), Carmarthen, Llandeilo

By the time the agricultural shows came round in the autumn of 1881, W. R. H. Powell was able to report on his first complete year as a Member of Parliament. For example, at St Clears Agricultural Show Dinner he reported that he had voted for the Irish Land Bill which granted fixity of tenure and arbitration on rents by a land court. Powell and others had been calling for similar measures for Welsh tenants and the passing of the Irish Act would have encouraged them to intensify their demands. He had supported the Wales Sunday Closing Bill which had passed into law with 28 of Wales' 30 members voting for it. The real significance of the Wales Sunday Closing Act was that it was the first time in history, that Wales had been treated as a national unit and Powell had played his part in the 'yes' vote. It was during the debate on the Sunday Closing Bill, that Osborne Morgan (Denbighshire) observed that 'people should understand that in dealing with Wales you are dealing with an entirely distinct nationality', more distinct than Scottish or Irish because of the additional barrier of language. In Wales, he said, crime was as little known as Conservatism! The early 1880s was the beginning of the growth of political nationalism in Wales.[21]

A week later at the 1881 Llanboidy Show, Powell reported that 'fault had been found with him . . . for bringing politics up' in his speeches at the shows, so he 'would merely allude to the work of the past session.' He then repeated his report given at the St Clears Show!

On 9 September 1881, a Liberal meeting was held at Cross Inn (nowadays known as Ammanford) to enable W. R. H. Powell to meet and address his constituents in that part of Carmarthenshire. He was received as the man who, at the election of the previous year, had come to Cross Inn, had seen and had conquered! He said that in the last session of Parliament they had sat for longer than at any time during the past 50 years but that relatively few bills had been passed because of the length of time allocated to the 'unhappy and disturbed state of Ireland'. He hoped that before long the people of Ireland would benefit from the Land Bill which had passed into law in the last session. He then referred to bills likely to come before Parliament in the coming session. One matter would probably relate to the procedure of business in the House of Commons. And he had no doubt that 'county government will soon be looked into and we shall have to consider the establishment of representative boards and probably the re-adjustment of local taxation.' Other matters which he considered important were the reform of the bankruptcy laws, the assimilation of county and borough franchises and 'no doubt important changes in our system of land tenure in general (applause).'

He reported how recent remarks on the subject of land tenure had attracted 'a howl of execration from the Tories here and elsewhere; but to me I assure you their praise is censure and their censure praise.' He re-emphasised his strongly held views by reading the report from *The Welshman* which had so incensed his opponents: 'I do hope to see some kind of fixity of tenure for Wales. I hope it will come to this: that farmers will feel that when they have to quit this world themselves, their wives and families will reap the advantage of the seeds which they have sown, and will not be turned out of what their forefathers have improved by their outlay (deafening and prolonged applause).' He went on: 'My meaning is this; that some sort of tenure should exist that would put the farmer in a different position from what he now holds, and would prevent a tenant being capriciously evicted by his landlord without receiving full compensation for all permanent and unexhausted improvements made by him on his holding . . .

And I do not approve of leases . . . because they terminate . . . without entitling the tenant to any compensation for the improved state in which he may leave his farm.'

Powell contended that as things stood, much farm land was in a very poor state because farmers were understandably reluctant to invest in improvements which at the end of the day would not belong to them: 'The land of the country, being a fixed quantity and incapable of extension, is by that very fact placed outside the category of ordinary property and in a wholly different position from that of personal estate. Hence the holding of land is a monopoly, and . . . the Legislature should step in to make such laws and fix such regulations for this monopoly as shall be of benefit to the nation at large (applause). . . . Why should a landlord, on evicting a tenant, have the power and privilege of sweeping up the whole of the property on a farm, much of it perhaps belonging to other people? The farm may be said to consist of the land, the stock, the crop, the horses, the implements, the seeds, the manures, the household furniture, and some other things. Why should the leter [sic] of one of these commodities, have a preferential claim over all the others? (applause). I am fully convinced that . . . the land laws in this country require radical change and reform; and first and foremost come security of tenure, and a perfect guarantee of repayment to the tenant for his improvements (great applause) . . . The real wealth of a nation consists in the fertility of the soil and the means taken to develop it . . . This is not a party question. For thirty years or more . . . its necessity [has been] understood [and] an equitable system of tenant right has been asked for, but in vain . . . The question is: should the population of a limited area like ours, rapidly increasing in its numbers and its wants, quietly allow such a state of things to continue and look passively on while the bone and sinew . . . and capital too . . . of the nation are driven from our shores to cultivate the land of foreign countries? (Applause). Should we render ourselves so dependent on foreign countries as we are now becoming for food which ought to be produced here at home, and continue to send millions of our country's wealth to other nations for the supply of our daily bread? (No! and renewed applause). No! . . . I hope the answer of all will be No! Then . . . let us be up and doing, before it is too late, and endeavour to avert this evil . . . let us discuss in a friendly and business-like spirit . . . and try to devise some means for helping our legislators . . . in promoting [our] country's welfare.'

He went on to say that he had 'been charged with holding communistic principles (laughter). Well, if a sincere desire to benefit all classes by just and equal laws means communism, then I must plead guilty to the charge (loud and continued applause) . . . The plain fact is, however difficult it may be for some people to realise it, we are leaving feudal times behind us with an accelerating impetus, and as education and enlightenment increase, so will all anomalies and imperfections in our laws be remedied. The principles of justice, equality and right are marching onwards like a great army, trampling under foot and burying in the sands of time . . . monopolies, injustices, incongruities, ignorance, prejudices and all the hosts of evil. It is the standard of this great army, led, as I believe, by Liberalism, that I would wish to unfurl with a desire to see constant fresh recruits enrolled. We have principalities and powers to contend with, but with right on our side we will go on conquering and to conquer (enthusiastic and long continued cheering)'.[22]

Powell was president of the Carmarthenshire Agricultural Show for 1881 and he took the opportunity of laying before those assembled for the dinner, some of his political views. He claimed that the previous night at Maesgwynne he had been thinking of what he should talk about. His thoughts had covered many topics such as the need to establish representative county boards so that people who provided the money (local taxation) would have some control over expenditure; a flood prevention bill was needed but would the upland inhabitants be prepared to pay extra tax for the benefit of lowlanders? There might be a need to re-distribute local taxation. He anticipated the amalgamation of highways boards and turnpike trusts and the government might introduce a tax for carriages so as to assist ratepayers in maintaining roads. Then there was tenants rights, fair rent and fixity of tenure.

He also thought of the 9,061 'extra souls' which the census had shown to live in Carmarthenshire (as compared to ten years previously). All had to be fed and this highlighted the need to spend more capital on the county's farms. With increased investment, '50% more corn, meat and dairy produce might be obtained.' The question was how to bring about the increase in investment. He had concluded that a 'Land Bill or something of the sort, some new system, would be of great advantage to Wales (loud applause). Something that would encourage the farmer to farm better and give him greater security for his outlay.' Lease was not the answer because a 21-year-lease granted to a young couple would probably result 'in them farming well for 7 years, keeping it steady for another 7 years and taking as much as they could out in the final 7 years.' Their children would not benefit for their labours at the end of the day. Powell wished to see some fixity of tenure for farmers in Wales. Farmers, when they quitted this world, should see their wives and families benefit and not be turned out of the house which their forefathers had made by labour and toil (applause). He asked the assembled diners to 'pull together to devise some system and to let their representatives know, and they would do their duty.'[23]

As might be expected his views were attacked the following week, in the columns of both the *Carmarthen Journal* and *The Welshman*. The *Journal*'s editorial argued against security of tenure . . . only the landlord's short-term interest mattered to the Tory newspaper. A letter in *The Welshman* complained about the political content of Powell's speech at the Carmarthenshire Show. The writer labelled it 'one-sided and inflammatory . . . tenants' rights, fixity of tenure, encouragement of Rebeccaism and land bills should only be discussed at party meetings . . .' The letter continued by claiming the Liberals were split on those matters because the Liberal MP for Pembrokeshire had dubbed talk about a Welsh Land Bill, tenants rights and other wild schemes as 'twaddle'. But another report in *The Welshman* confirmed that land reform was firmly on the political agenda in Britain: a meeting was to be held to discuss land reform in Scotland at which the English Farmers' Alliance would be represented.[24]

Then, as now, the reluctant and conservative Welsh had to be dragged kicking and screaming into the reforming arena; thank goodness there was a visionary like W. R. H. Powell to do some of the dragging.

At the 1881 Llandeilo Show, he said that he had been accused of talking about the fixity of tenure simply to get farmers on his side. He denied the accusation and said he wanted to get a discussion going between tenant and landlord who came together only at the shows which, like Christmas, came round just once a year! Far better to talk about farming matters than to just drink each others health! And if they could not talk about it then, how was he to know their views so that he could properly represent them? (cheers). His own views were stronger than those he had expressed in Carmarthen. Security of tenure would help in getting tenants to invest in their land and improve the holding's productivity. An improved holding would obviously benefit the landlord as well (cheers). Powell also made the important point that tenants in the Llanboidy area already paid fair rents but, even so, unless they had greater security of tenure they would not improve their land and would not, therefore, increase their profits.[25]

As the debate continued Powell acknowledged the need to safeguard landlords against unsuitable sitting tenants and he suggested that they should have power to evict on giving 12 months notice and paying compensation on improvements. That got the *Western Mail* on the warpath! The 'Radical member for Carmarthenshire' was accused, on the one hand, of trying to imbue the minds of his constituents with communistic theories in regards to tenant rights but, on the other hand, of being contradictory in his call to safeguard landlords![26]

In the mid 1870s tenant farmers had been subject to large rent increases just before a depression had hit the farming industry. The Tory government of the day set up a Royal Commission to investigate and report on the farmers' problems and it had taken three years before it announced its findings which were not particularly helpful to tenants. As a result tenant farmers in Scotland had formed the Farmers' Alliance to take their case forward and English tenants had followed suit. In December 1881 the Alliance had succeeded in getting a bill prepared and James Howard MP was to steer it through Parliament. When the *Western Mail* got wind of the matter it claimed in an editorial that James Howard's bill sought 'not only to transfer the rights of agrarian property from one class to another, but to rob the landlord of a portion of his estate in order to benefit the tenant.' And, interestingly, it was W. R. H. Powell that was identified by the *Western Mail* as the Welsh leader with similar views to Howard: 'Like W. R. H. Powell, Howard declares that the rights of property are to him the most sacred of all things sacred! The public however will not be deceived by such radical and hypocritical *rhodomontades*.' The editorial described Powell and Howard as revolutionists and accused them of propagating communistic doctrines.[27]

1882: Carmarthen, St Clears, Laugharne

It should have been no surprise that the Farmers' Alliance's first meeting in Wales was at Carmarthen. It took place in July 1882 and W. R. H. Powell took the opportunity to remind the audience of his views on land tenure which he acknowledged had been criticised by friends and in the press. That was fine by him, but he had not heard or read anything to change his views. He added that in his opinion the Law of Distress (which governed the collection of rent) was unjust and unfair. It was agreed to form a branch of the Farmers' Alliance in Carmarthen.[28]

An example of Powell and Emlyn working together as Members of Parliament occurred in June 1882 when they jointly presented a petition from the Portreeve and Burgesses of Laugharne against Lord Rosebery's Bill to abolish or alter unreformed corporations. Laugharne was saved as a corporation.

In September 1882, Powell presided at a meeting of the Blue Ribbonites which was a movement against alcohol whose members were identified by a piece of blue ribbon worn on their lapels. The meeting in the Assembly Rooms, Carmarthen was called to hear a lecture entitled 'Bread or Beer; Brewers or Bakers' by the Reverend J. W. Kirton, LL.D. Introducing the speaker, W. R. H. Powell explained that he was friendly with brewers and bakers and that his concern was the problem of excessive drinking. Nothing gave him greater pleasure than aiding the working man's cause and to work in any way to empty the gaols, the lunatic asylums and the Union Houses. With regard to work, he had, for the past 46 years, worked from 5.00 a.m. often until midnight for many years without taking any alcoholic stimulants. He was an example of one who could stand late hours in the House of Commons as well as many younger men. He had not joined any of the temperance societies, he was not a Blue Ribbon man, but he was a total abstainer and had been so for many years.[29]

High on the agenda of Wales' Liberal MPs in 1882 was the promotion of Intermediate and of Higher Education in Wales, as recommended in the report of a Departmental Committee chaired by Lord Aberdare and with Henry Richard MP for Merthyr Tydfil as one of its five members. However lack of time and finance hampered progress in Parliament and the frustrated Welsh representatives felt it necessary to send a deputation to lobby the Lord President of the Council, Mr A. J. Mundella, to try to speed-up matters. The deputation, led by Henry Richard with W. R. H. Powell among fourteen Commoners and nine Lords, met Mundella on 19 June 1882.

In the autumn of 1882 Powell was still smarting from the attacks made on him for including politics in his speeches at Carmarthenshire shows. However, he was unrepentant, as he demonstrated at the St Clears Show, where he said that he still thought that the show meetings were important forums for discussions and their views were vital for him to help make up his mind on the various matters.[30] A week later at Laugharne Show, Powell said that he would leave politics out of his speech and would 'only allude to one non-political matter . . . the bill regarding land tenure and compensation for tenant farmers, almost certain to come before Parliament.' He declared his support for the bill and was applauded to the rafters.

Ever the entrepreneur, Powell said that it occurred to him as he travelled from St Clears to Laugharne that day, that a railway, on the pattern of the Ffestiniog railway, could be laid from St Clears to make easily accessible the scenery, the sands, the castle and the cliffs at Laugharne and it could be extended to Pendine. In fact something told him that plans for such a venture had been drawn up . . . someone called out . . . no money. But Powell continued with another thought that if they went to Coigen rocks and continued the line to Llanboidy he would give them the land for nothing! He urged them to come to Llanboidy Show a week later and to cast their eyes around as they travelled up and think 'we'll get a line up and come up again'.[31]

1883: Finsbury, Llanboidy, St Clears, Carmarthen

In June 1883 Powell took time off from his parliamentary duties to chair a meeting at the Welsh Baptist Chapel, Eldon Street, Finsbury at which Miss M. A. Williams of Ferndale gave a lecture on 'The Influence of Kindness'. But he apologised for having to leave the meeting early in order to attend an important division in the House of Commons but not before expressing his delight to meet his fellow countrymen in the metropolis. And then he went somewhat over-the-top or perhaps it was nostalgia that made him say that he was reminded of the 'dear mother country of Wales . . . free of crime and where hands were raised against wrong doers'. Powell praised the zeal and efforts of Nonconformist ministers in making Wales 'a nation of Non-conformists' and in creating the 'happy state of Wales'. He claimed that Wales had set an example by its Sunday Closing Act which was then being followed in Durham and other parts of England. He explained that several matters of importance to Wales were expected soon in the House. One was an Education bill and another was a matter he would only allude to, so as to avoid bringing politics into his speech! On that subject (disestablishment) it was for the people to make their wishes known and then Mr Dillwyn (MP for Swansea) and Mr Henry Richard (MP for Merthyr Tydfil) would 'be found in the van!' and he himself would be one of their most hearty supporters'. The Welsh only had to continue their exertions to reap their rewards . . . perfect religious equality and liberty throughout the land. He received great applause.[32]

At the end of June 1883 Powell and Henry Richard were members of a deputation that lobbied the Privy Council to safeguard the future funding of the college at Aberystwyth in face of competition from the proposed college for north Wales.

Back in Llanboidy for the September 1883 Agricultural Show he was paid tribute by that year's show president, Lord Kensington the Liberal MP for Haverfordwest, who said that the life of a Member of Parliament had changed and had become very difficult to manage because of the introduction of all-night sittings. He assured the audience that W. R. H. Powell was invariably one of the last to leave the chamber (cheers). Kensington was pleased that Powell looked in better health than when he saw him in London and he hoped that 'his native air' would fully restore him. But there was no letting up on Powell's part and after advising the farmers on measures they should take to reduce the risk of 'importing' foot-and-mouth which was affecting England, he referred to the Agricultural Holdings Act and said that he had listened attentively to every amendment proposed and took part in every one of the 30 or so divisions. He was of the view that the Act would result in a great improvement in the farming of the country. He would meet the farmers after the harvest to go into the details (applause). The applause reflected the fact that legislation was little understood by the Welsh-speaking farmers; a situation taken advantage of by many landowners . . . but not by W. R. H. Powell. He went on! When tenants knew that whether they had to leave their farms or whether their rents were raised because of their own improvements, they had a legal security and would be compensated for the expenditure of capital, skill and labour which they had put upon the land . . . there had to be a very great change in the farming of the country. He hoped to see the day when two blades of grass grew where one grew now and that not only the farmer but the nation at large would benefit (applause). Lord Kensington as well as the former MP, David Pugh, agreed with Powell's assessment of the benefits to be expected from the Agricultural Holdings Act. Powell closed his address with a quip that he was glad that the labourers had beaten the farmers in the garden produce section!

In addition to drawing in the country air, Powell found himself chairing a meeting of the Licensing Session at Llanboidy in the company of Edward Schaw Protheroe of Dolwilym, J. Bagnall Evans of Nant-yr-Eglwys and W. Lewis Philipps of Clungwyn when they granted 35 certificates to taverns in the Llanboidy and Llangan parishes.

At the St Clears Show and also at the Carmarthenshire Agricultural Exhibition the two Members of Parliament for the county, W. R. H. Powell (Liberal) and Lord Emlyn (Tory), were present and exchanged compliments in their addresses. The president of the Carmarthenshire Show was the Swansea MP, Lewis Llewellyn Dillwyn (Liberal) and he labelled W. R. H. Powell a *radical* rather than a Liberal.[33]

Before 1883 was out, Llanboidy held its Christmas Show in December with a range of produce on display including pigs, sheep dogs, live poultry, dead trussed poultry and dairy produce. But the striking thing about the show was the presentation of a paper on 'Agricultural Education' read at the dinner by Henry John a 32-year-old farmer of Castellgarw, Llanglydwen. Henry was the eldest son of Jenkin and Margaret John of Llwyn-yr-ebol, Efailwen, Llandysilio Parish and had been to America for a few years before returning and marrying Martha Griffiths of the 204-acre-farm of Castellgarw. Henry had some knowledge of the science of agriculture and occasionally contributed to the press. He was also a staunch Liberal. W. R. H. Powell had for some time been agitating to have 'agricultural science' taught in schools as part of his vision to improve agricultural practice and it was he that invited his fellow Liberal to present his paper. According to Henry John, the scientific principles of agriculture were insufficiently understood by farmers. There was a need for education and this could be achieved in two ways. Books at reasonable prices had come on the market and secondly, school boards should be urged to introduce the subject into schools. Public elementary schools were within reach of all and there was a South Wales College for Higher Education and a bill was due to give Wales intermediate education. Henry John suggested that subjects like history and geography were not as useful as agricultural science. Furthermore, if agricultural science was taken as an extra subject in schools a grant of 4 shillings per head could be earned by all above the fourth standard. And he pointed out that Llanboidy was particularly lucky in having as headteacher of the local school a person, Mr Emsall, who had passed with honours in principles of agriculture. They should waste no time in forming a science class in Llanboidy. All would benefit from instruction although most would not have the knowledge of English necessary to sit examinations. In addition, Henry John was sure that W. R. H. Powell would assist in every way, including giving a scholarship to enable the best pupil to attend a two-year-course in an agricultural college. No doubt that Henry John had been well briefed by W. R. H. Powell. Henry's death in 1891 at the age of 40 was a great loss to the community.[34]

1884: Llanelli, Carmarthen, Brynaman

As already mentioned, in addition to his reports at the agricultural shows, Powell also gave an account of his stewardship as an MP to specially organised meetings. For example, in January 1884 he, together with Sir John Jones Jenkins, the borough member, reported to their constituents at Llanelli. Because of the overcrowding at the Athenaeum Hall, the meeting was moved to the Tabernacl Chapel which was 'well filled'. The chairman, Mr Joseph Maybery, referred to the need for a good public hall in Llanelli and he suggested the formation of a company with a capital of £3,000 in £1 shares, to erect a building which would accommodate some 15,000 people.

W. R. H. Powell opened his address in Welsh but explained that his lack of mastership of the language forced him to ask their permission to continue his report in English. Much of the Liberal government's legislative programme had been disrupted by the unprecedented delaying tactics of the opposition but despite this, the government had succeeded in carrying several very useful measures. Powell referred to one bill that Sir John Jones Jenkins had succeeded in getting passed in the previous session which ensured that employees of a public or limited company received preferential treatment for wage claims if the company went into liquidation. Previously, the employees had to compete with other creditors. He repeated his support for two measures expected in Parliament in the next session: the extension of the Franchise Bill and the County Government Bill.

Powell also referred to the question of extending education opportunities, of which he had been a life-long passionate supporter. The intention of the Government to introduce a measure on Intermediate Education in Wales had been thwarted by the disgraceful delaying tactics of the opposition but he expected the Bill to return in the next session because it was 'a measure which we are entitled to expect from the present Government.' But Wales had at least benefited from a grant of £8,000 a year for higher education and he was hopeful that the grant of £4,000 to Aberystwyth College (University College of Wales) would be continued. 'It is not too much to ask for; Aberystwyth deserves it and it will be a boon and benefit to central Wales.'

Powell declared his support for the 'Disestablishment and Disendowment of the Church of England in Wales'. He explained that his views on the Church had not changed since 1874 and went on: 'Myself a churchman, I am nevertheless thoroughly in favour of the Disestablishment and Disendowment of the State Church in Wales because I believe that . . . it would be an act of long-delayed justice to a large majority of our fellow countrymen who do not conform to its teaching or ceremonial. . . . [But] abolish Establishment, [and] you will then clear the way for a sincere and cordial sympathy between all classes of Protestants.'

Powell said he had voted in 259 divisions during the last parliamentary session and had done so as a matter of duty to support an administration which was determined to improve the condition of the people. According to Sir John Jones Jenkins, W. R. H. Powell was one of the most active members in the House of Commons and had been present at almost every division that took place in the last session. As a result of his close attention to the business of the House over some years, Powell was very knowledgeable about the tactics used to get a measure through the House and had provided valuable advice to Jenkins to get an amendment to the Companies Act 1862 on to the statute book.[35]

Powell's performance at Llanelli was praised in *Y Goleuad*, the radical newspaper of the Calvinistic Methodists. His speech was short (about twenty minutes), concise, very interesting and fearless. He had succeeded in convincing all that he had served his position faithfully day-and-night, to a large extent (. . . *dywedodd [Powell] ei brofiad yn fyr, cryno a hynod o flasus, ac hollol ddi-ofn, gan argyhoeddi pawb ei fod wedi gwasanaethu ei swydd yn ffyddlon, a hyny ddydd a nos, i raddau helaeth. Bu wrthi am ryw ugain munud yn trin y mesurau a basiwyd, ynghyd a'r gwrthwynebiadau a gafwyd gan y blaid wrthwynebol.*)[36]

The public meeting in the Shire Hall, Carmarthen, on Monday evening 28 January 1884 had been called by the mayor, Tory supporter J. Jenkyn Jones, in response to 'a requisition by a long and respected list of persons.' As he introduced the speakers, the mayor appealed for every assistance in preserving order at 'such a large meeting'. That was a reflection of the trouble usually experienced at political gatherings in those times. But he need not have worried because no mention of any disorder was reported in the newspapers. On the platform with the mayor were the two Liberal members Sir John Jones Jenkins (Boroughs) and W. R. H. Powell (County) together with 'a number of local leaders of the Liberal Party and a galaxy of Dissenting ministers.' Even though a Tory supporter, the mayor in his introduction was full of praise for the Liberal members whom he described as 'men who attended faithfully to their duties. As for Mr Powell he was such a stickler for the House of Commons that he [the mayor] was sure he injured his health by sitting up the late hours of the last session . . . sometimes up to Sunday mornings and his [Powell's] party should be very grateful to him for his faithfulness.'

In his address Powell recalled 'Gladstone's Midlothian speeches' in which he 'mercilessly exposed the hypocrisy and sham of the Beaconsfield (Disraeli) – Salisbury Tory administration, with its policy of feebleness, doing nothing at home and its reckless policy abroad.' Soon afterwards at the General Election of 1880, the Liberals had swept to power. And in the words of W. R. H. Powell, 'The policy of the Prime Minister [Gladstone] was the policy of the country at large. Scotland polled Liberal almost to a man and our own Wales . . . sent . . . members to swell and uphold the crushing majority won by the great Liberal party (loud cheers).' The Irish Land Act was passed which, according to Powell, was 'doing more to heal the wounds of Ireland than any other measure' on the statute book.

He condemned the Tory opposition for 'entering upon a malicious and unprincipled policy of obstructive blocking and delay' which meant that much of the 'business which the country was calling for, could not be done'. But income tax had been reduced to its 'normal level' and public debt had been diminished. And in the last session 'the way was cleared for a reduction in the price of inland telegrams (cheers)', and the passenger duty on railway fares paid by the working classes had been reduced (applause) and a change advantageous to the consumer had been made in tobacco duties (loud cheers).

Powell went on to say that in the next session he earnestly desired to see before Parliament the measure for the extension of the franchise to the counties and the promised County Government Bill. The extension of the franchise would probably result in a redistribution of seats and Powell was adamant that Wales should not lose any seats as a result. So far as disestablishment of the State Church in Wales, Powell reiterated his wholehearted support for disestablishment: 'What is asked for is religious liberty, freedom of action and the administration of equal and impartial laws (cheers) . . . it is unjust to tax the whole community at large for the support of religious opinions which the real majority of the people not only do not hold, but repudiate and disown.'

Powell closed his address by appealing to the Liberals in Carmarthenshire to unite. 'Separate, we must be beaten; united we cannot fail to win (loud cheers).' He reminded them that all those granted the vote had to register to claim the right to use it. He said the cry was 'Register, register!' And he urged them to form Liberal Associations 'in every polling district throughout the county and "Organise, organise!" (cheers).' Was Powell echoing the Reverend David Rees, Llanelli (1801-1869) who, during the time of the Rebecca uprising, urged the people to 'Agitate! Agitate!'

W. O. Brigstocke of Parcygors, Llandygwydd, said that no Member of Parliament was more assiduous or more constant in his duties in the House than Mr Powell. A Commons policeman once told him that Mr Powell was 'a regular sticker'. Brigstocke ended his contribution when he proposed that 'the meeting, having heard the political views of Mr Powell, desired to express its unabated confidence in him.' The proposal was carried unanimously.[37]

To a certain extent the strength of the Liberal party depended on its success in holding together its Whig wing, typified by the old country squires, and its radical wing of which the Nonconformist ministers were representative. The tension that could arise between the two groups manifested itself in Cardiganshire when the radical Nonconformists felt that the MP, L. P. Pugh, was not radical enough in his views and they were contemplating replacing him as candidate at the next election. But Pugh had his supporters too! Moderate Liberals were determined to keep him as candidate with one saying that: 'We are not going to be brow beaten by a lot of beggarly Radical preachers who have not a shilling at stake in the county'[38] Powell on the other hand was the embodiment of both wings of the party: a landed proprietor turned radical campaigner.

The Tories meanwhile kept up their attacks on Powell through their newspaper mouthpieces, warning that they were waking up in Carmarthenshire and claiming that if they had been as well-organised in 1880 'Powell's hunting and racing engagements would not have been interrupted and the old county would have saved the disgrace of being misrepresented by a good natured squire who [allowed] Dissenting preachers and Radical demagogues to lead him by the nose.'[39]

In early April 1884 Powell was among leading Liberals on the platform at a 'Great Meeting of Welshmen' in the Memorial Hall, Farringdon Street, London convened to support the motion of Mr Lewis Llewellyn Dillwyn MP calling for the disestablishment of the Church of England in Wales. The chairman, John Roberts MP, declared that the Welsh were now chapel-goers rather than church. In London there were about 20 chapels serving the needs of the Welsh in their own language. In Liverpool the number was 50. Sir John Jones Jenkins MP provided a record of attendance at churches, chapels and mission halls in Swansea on Sunday, 23 March 1884. The Church of England had 10 churches and 7 mission halls, while the Nonconformists had 62 chapels, 4 mission halls and 9 other buildings. In the morning a total of 20,102 attended a service of which 80% were Nonconformists. In the evening the total attendees was 29,464 of which 84% were Nonconformists. The figures for Swansea confirmed Powell's claim a year previously that Wales was 'a nation of Nonconformists'.[32]

In his address, Llewellyn Dillwyn claimed that the Welsh differed from the English in thought and feeling. He said that 'we in Wales were a people before the English came here.' They were distinct from the English and they intended to maintain their nationality. They were different in language; they were different in religion and they meant to maintain that religion. In fact it was not a question of religion. It was a question of Wales for the Welsh. In fact Lewis Llewellyn Dillwyn based his case for disestablishment firmly on Welsh nationality and disestablishment was one of the founding issues which later led to a nationalist programme for Wales.[40]

In the 1884 parliamentary session, the Tory opposition continued their delaying tactics to prevent the Liberal government getting bills through the Commons and when the Franchise Bill did get through, the House of Lords threw it out! It must have been particularly disappointing for Powell to see the Franchise Bill lost because it was one of those glaring injustices which he spent his life trying to eradicate. He continued his outstanding voting record in support of Government measures during the 1884 session which ended in August. There had been 216 divisions of which 105 were after midnight. Powell had voted 153 times which was the fourth highest of the thirty-three members from Wales and Monmouthshire, behind Lord Grosvenor (Flintshire) 201, Lord Kensington (Haverfordwest) 200 and George Osborne Morgan (Denbighshire) 161. Powell's fellow member for Carmarthenshire, Lord Emlyn, only managed to turn up 22 times while Carmarthen Boroughs' Sir John Jones Jenkins voted on 85 occasions. On average the Wales and Monmouthshire members voted in 69 divisions.[41]

3.5 Rural labourers get the vote

The Franchise Bill granted the vote to 'county labourers'. In other words labourers in rural areas were to enjoy the same rights as their urban brethren. The Lords' action in blocking the bill was the last straw. In early August 1884 the Liberals held a major conference in St James' Hall, London to consider their future actions on the matter. 'The cream of British Liberalism was there! The pillars of the cause in the shires and the boroughs!' Delegates from Liberal Associations in Wales, England, Scotland and Ireland numbering 2,500 attended and Wales 'was well represented by Osborne Morgan, W. R. H. Powell, Sir Robert Cuncliffe, Sir John Jones Jenkins, Mr Lewis Llewellyn Dilwyn and others.' It was a conference that 'no government should dare ignore its voice'. Under the chairmanship of John Morley, MP for Newcastle on Tyne, a decision was taken to organise country-wide protest demonstrations to highlight the grossly undemocratic action of the unelected House.[42]

On his return to Carmarthen, W. R. H. Powell got his friend and leading Carmarthenshire Liberal, Alderman W. de G. Warren, Druggist, Drysalter and Tea dealer of Carmarthen, to form and chair a 'Demonstration Committee' to plan for a 'Franchise Demonstration' in Carmarthen in the autumn.

Powell was, by that time, the leading radical orator in west Wales and was much in demand as a speaker throughout the area. For example, a district meeting of anthracite miners' delegates from Caerbryn, Rhos, Park, Cawdor, Raven, Garnant, Gwaun Cae Gurwen, Hendreforgan, Cwm-y-gwrach, Brynmorgan, Ystradfawr, Ynys Cedwyn and Seven Sisters, held at Tregib Arms, Brynaman, at the end of June 1884, and chaired by William Abraham (Mabon), Liberal MP for the Rhondda who was to become the first president of the South Wales Miners' Federation, decided to invite their Liberal MP, W. R. H. Powell, to address them at their annual demonstration at Tir Bach House, Cwmamman. He was to be supported by John O'Connor Power (Irish Nationalist MP for Mayo), W. F. Maitland (MP for Breconshire), L. P. Pugh (MP for Cardiganshire), Sir John Jones Jenkins (MP for Carmarthen Boroughs), William Abraham together with the Reverend Kilsby Jones of Llandrindod, Reverend J. Jones of Felinfoel, Reverend D. Onllwyn Brace, Watcyn Wyn, and others.[43]

The demonstration was held on Monday, 25 August 1884, when several thousand coal miners, tinplate workers and farmers marched in procession behind two bands to a field near Tir Bach House. Numerous banners were on display; one informed the crowd that: 'Cwmtwrch district demand a vote for two million.' Others bore the words *'Trech gwlad nac Arglwydd'* and *'Hir oes i Gladstone a Bright yw ein gweddi; Salisbury, ti a bwyswyd yn y glorian ac ath gawd yn brin.'*

The afternoon's business was got underway by Mabon conducting the assembled throng in singing *'Hen Wlad Fy Nhadau'*. The political grievance of the day was the rejection by the House of Lords of the People's Bill (extension of the franchise). A resolution was put to the mass meeting by J. Lewis, Gurry Manor, Llandeilo, which included a strong protest against the rejection of the Representation of the People's Bill, describing it as 'an arbitrary and dangerous exercise by the House of Lords'. At the same time, Powell was praised for his work as their MP: 'That this meeting desires to express unabated confidence in Mr W. R. H. Powell, the Liberal Member for Carmarthenshire, and thanks him for his unwearied attention to his parliamentary duties and pledges itself to do its utmost to return him triumphantly to Parliament at the next

General Election'. The resolution went further and expressed the opinion 'that a thorough reform of the House of Lords' had become necessary and that the 'present crisis' presented an opportunity 'which should not be lost' to consider 'the character and composition of that House'. On that point some in the crowd shouted 'mend them'; others went further with 'end them'! The resolution ended with the hope that during the proposed autumn session, the Government would use all constitutional means to get the Lords to pass the bill.

In his response, Powell said it was the greatest assembly he had ever seen since becoming an MP. He had received a great welcome in the area during the General Election of 1880 and he felt bound to accept their invitation to attend the rally even though his doctor had advised him to rest. As regards the recent Parliamentary session, he said he had attended 23 of the 25 divisions and had supported the Government's measures such as the scheme for county government and an Intermediate Education Bill for Wales. But the Tory opposition's delaying tactics prevented their passage through the Commons. The Government was continually attacked on its handling of affairs in Egypt and votes of censure followed one another 'thick as leaves in Vallombrosa! (The Tuscany Abbey of Vallombrosa and its autumnal leaves is mentioned in Milton's *Paradise Lost*).

The one bill that got through the Commons, the Franchise Bill, had been thrown out by the Lords because, so they claimed, it was not accompanied by a Redistribution of Seats Bill. The real reason for the Lords' rejection was to prevent rural workers getting the vote and putting safe Tory seats in jeopardy. Or as Powell put it 'in order to keep out a class of people, too long kept out of the administration of the affairs of the country.' He believed the people would never allow an oligarchy to dictate to the people, and when the shame and reproach of the matter had passed away it would be seen upon whom the responsibility rested and 'this great measure would soon have to become law (cheers).'

He mounted a scathing attack on the leading members of the Tory opposition such as Sir Stafford Northcote for their unprincipled and selfish delaying tactics. But the opposition member who provided Powell with ample ammunition for ridicule and scorn was the back-bencher Lord Randolph Churchill leader of a breakaway disaffected Tory group of six, who, during the debate on the Franchise Bill in the Commons, changed his stance from outright opposition to silent support as it dawned on him that expanding the franchise would help the Tories in his fancied constituency of Birmingham where the sitting member was the leading Liberal radical Joseph Chamberlain. Referring to Lord Randolph as the 'smart young man from Woodstock' and as the 'ducal cadet of the house of Churchill', Powell accused him of lacking the courage to speak up in support of the Franchise Bill, preferring to remain silent on the matter and attempting to curry favour with the Tory leaders by persistent attacks on the Government's policy in Egypt which he obstructed 'with an amount of fervour altogether disproportionate to his physical capacity to give expression to it'. He illustrated Churchill's attitude by paraphrasing some verses of Lord Macaulay's *Lays of Ancient Rome*. One verse will suffice here:

> Out spoke the brave young Churchill,
> The captain of the six,
> Whoever aids the Government,
> We'll into him like bricks.

Powell went on to say that Lord Salisbury would be no friend either of the Crown . . . or to the House of Lords, if he persisted in advising his followers to put themselves in battle array against the overwhelming majority of their fellow subjects (renewed cheering). The Liberal Party had not invited a conflict but having entered upon it, retreat or surrender were alike impossible (cheers). Time was on their side. The flag which might droop to-day would by tomorrow be caught up by eager hands, and held aloft by valiant arms – never to be surrendered until it proudly waved over the citadel of national right and national freedom.

The Home Ruler, John O'Connor Power, was pleased to have 'come from Ireland to join them in Wales in condemnation of the House of Lords' for depriving two million people of the vote. He claimed that the key to the Tory policy was Salisbury's hope that the prevailing voting system would return him to power. The Reverend J. Jones, Felinfoel, also weighed in to condemn Lord Salisbury claiming that he 'had been weighed in the balance and found wanting'.[44]

Powell's speech at Cwmamman upset the *Western Mail* which saw fit to devote an editorial to attacking Powell claiming it was 'extremely humiliating to find a gentleman like the senior member for Carmarthenshire indulging in such absurdities of statement and invective as he did at Cwmaman [*sic*] the other day.' He was described as a leading radical who was so imbued with his own infallibility that he 'could not extend to others the right of arriving at other conclusions' on certain matters. It was claimed that Powell Bach reckoned that there was nothing too mean or miserable in party matters for the sympathy of Lord Salisbury, Sir Stafford Northcote and Lord Randolph Churchill. 'One would imagine from Mr Powell's speech . . . that these three statesmen had only one desire in common . . . the destruction of the Empire and the annihilation of the working classes'. The *Western Mail* claimed that Mr Powell's description of how Lord Randolph Churchill had 'changed front on the Franchise Bill and his motives for doing so' was 'the most uncharitable thing that has come under our notice during the whole of this acrimonious discussion.'[45]

Powell answered the *Western Mail*'s charges in a speech at Carmarthen during a Liberal Rally in support of the Franchise Bill. The demonstration took place on a fine Tuesday, 7 October 1884, and several excursion trains brought people to Carmarthen where several large establishments and many shops had closed for the day. At least 2,000 'serious' demonstrators turned up as well as an equal number who came for a day out! Inevitably, excessive drinking by a few revellers led to some fighting in parts of the town but *The Welshman*'s reporter reckoned that 'such violence and intemperance that did appear was in the oratory of the leaders rather than in the conduct of the people'. Twenty marshalls eventually got the procession under way from the Parade at 2.00 p.m. and as is apt to happen with processions, it was 'led' by a 'group of about 150 small boys among whom were a few cattle drovers and other adult individuals well known in the town.' They were followed by 'forty or fifty larger boys' before the official leaders, Mr Marks' Brass Band, appeared in front of a group of formidable Liberal MPs: Lord Kensington (Haverfordwest), Henry Richard (Merthyr Tydfil), W. R. H. Powell (Carmarthenshire), Sir John Jones Jenkins (Carmarthen Boroughs), William Davies (Pembrokeshire) and Morgan Lloyd, Q.C. (Beaumaris). Accompanying them were Alderman Warren, Mr Lewis Morris, Superintendent of Police, Mr G. James, and former Independent MP, Mr David Pugh.

A blue banner carried aloft and bearing a picture of Prime Minister, W. E. Gladstone, 'looking as grandoldmanish and tribunitial as possible' separated the MPs from a group of 'a hundred or more, mainly ministers, occasional preachers and deacons, all dressed scrupously cap-a-pie in black. This, which was apparently meant to be the genteel and respectable part of the procession, looked extremely like a funeral which had got accidentally mixed with the multitude.' It was most apt that banners bearing the words 'In memory of the House of Lords' and 'Funeral march of the House of Lords' were nearby! To liven things up, brass bands from Glogue near Crymych, from Llanelly and Kidwelly set the pace for marchers representing the Llanelly Liberal Association, and the districts of Llanboidy, Llanelly, Llandeilo and Kidwelly.

The Welshman's reporter could not resist describing some of the marchers as a motley crowd among which were found 'a few men of a different character', such as 60-year-old Mr David Thomas, farmer of 275-acre Castelldraenog, Llanboidy, a tenant of W. R. H. Powell, and Mr Simeon Davies of Whitland (probably the proprietor of a private commercial hotel and posting establishment in the town). Another group included a few 'naturalised Welsh-Irishmen with possible aspirations after Home Rule'. They were followed by about 120 farmers and others on horseback.

Banners there were a-plenty. One, imitative of a tombstone, was inscribed 'To the memory of the House of Lords'. Others followed: 'St Clears Corporation: Respect law, not privilege', 'A vote for the country as well as the towns', 'The House of Lords ended or mended'. 'Peers or people's rights', seemed a curious question to the reporter and the couplet: 'The people's will, The Franchise Bill' on another banner, he attributed, tongue in cheek, to 'some famous poet'. The Llangadog Liberal Association's banner read 'Welcome to Gladstone. The Franchise Bill for the people'. And then 'a party of jolly fellows, more in love with their country and its music than with politics', sang *Hen Wlad fy Nhadau*. . . 'as loudly as they could scream.' Inscriptions on other banners proclaimed 'We will have the vote' and 'Down with the Lords' which the reporter felt 'sounded a little businesslike and it was not surprising that PC Rees trod close on the heels of the bold youths who carried this message of peace.' A banner inscribed 'The evictions of 1868 sealed the fate of Toryism in Wales' was labelled 'a legend' by the reporter. There were a number of banners bearing Welsh inscriptions and those were followed by one bearing the names of the most prominent local Liberals and another bore the fatal order 'Gladstone: apply the axe'.

The procession took 50 minutes to pass through Guild Hall Square. At Mr Norton's field a platform holding around 100 people was soon filled and Mr David Pugh opened proceedings by stating that they were there to support the enfranchisement of two million householders in the counties (i.e. the rural areas); to place them on a level with their brethren in the towns who were enfranchised in 1861.

W. R. H. Powell was the first speaker and he gave a detailed account of his attendance at the House of Commons in the previous session. The Franchise Bill had faced 25 divisions before being thrown out by the House of Lords. And the Conservatives now claimed 'the measure would have landed the country in untold horrors of unlicensed democracy and bloodthirsty communism'. Powell had voted for a resolution moved by a Mr Willis 'for relieving the prelates of the established Church from attendance in the House of Lords . . . I cannot for the life of me see what advantage can accrue to the state from the presence of what Sydney Smith used to call "a mob of bishops" in the House of Lords.' Strong words from the Member for Carmarthenshire.

Although a churchman, Powell was first and foremost a democrat as he had demonstrated regularly since siding with Rebecca's supporters 45 years earlier. The Lords' rejection of the Franchise Bill rankled with Powell. The *Western Mail* had charged Powell with 'want of charity towards my political opponents.' A charge 'wholly unsupported by the facts.' Powell maintained that he had simply stated a 'historical fact' and he was 'sanguine enough to hope that (Churchill would soon) be found devoting his undoubted talent to a nobler mission than the bolstering up of exploded Tory notions [and] that the champion of the new school of Conservatism may yet breathe the freer atmosphere of the Liberal benches.'

In another outburst he showed his contempt for the Tories claiming that the Liberals could afford to despise the maundering twaddle of a political party, one of whose shining lights wrote the imperishable lines:

> Let arts and learning, laws and commerce die,
> But give us still our old nobility!

Powell went on to blast members of his own class but not of his political persuasion: 'The great territorial families which are still allowed to exercise a malign influence in the return of members of parliament would have strained every nerve to preserve the rotten boroughs by means of which they have acquired many material advantages as well as social distinction. It is a scandal to our system of representation that such abuses should exist after two reform bills have been passed within our own time.' Powell promised that 'we, as your representatives . . . will continue to fight your battle, and you will, I know, do your part towards the accomplishment of the great work of human progress, which . . . is the inheritance of the Liberal party. Having set your hands to the plough you will not be diverted from your purpose until the field is tilled. Such is your mission here today . . . I know you will prove worthy of your traditions, and that Wales will continue to occupy a foremost place in the great struggle for the rights and the liberties of the people.' Powell then moved the first resolution to the effect that the meeting trusted that Mr Gladstone would not consent to a dissolution of Parliament until the Extension of the Franchise Bill had become law. The resolution was seconded by Sir J. J. Jenkins and was carried 'with only a few dissentient voices.'

Lord Kensington said that meetings throughout south Wales showed that the voice of the country was thoroughly in favour of the Government. Mr Henry Richard was loudly applauded and responded to calls of '*Cymraeg*' by speaking for some time in Welsh. He said he had no connection with Carmarthenshire (shout of 'You are the Member for Wales') but he came in obedience to his friends who so ably represented them in Parliament, W. R. H. Powell and Sir J. J. Jenkins. The gathering agreed unanimously that in Carmarthenshire they should pledge their undivided exertions to return to the next Parliament a colleague who will join Mr Powell in supporting Liberal principles and policy.[46] The resolution meant getting rid of Lord Emlyn in the two-seat Carmarthenshire constituency.

Henry Richard, MP for Merthyr Tydfil, unofficial leader
of Wales' Liberal MPs. He shared a platform with Powell
at the franchise rally in Carmarthen in 1884.
(By permission of Llyfrgell Genedlaethol Cymru/
The National Library of Wales).

In the subsequent session of Parliament a deal was struck between the Liberal Government and the Lords which linked the Franchise Bill with a Redistribution of Seats Bill and both became law. Rural householders would, for the first time, have the vote at the next General Election and the two-seat Carmarthenshire constituency was divided into two single-member seats of West and East Carmarthenshire. Powell, typically, refused the safe Liberal seat of East Carmarthenshire in order to contest the marginal West seat where he resided. The *Western Mail* could not resist being economical with the truth when it claimed that Powell would prefer the East but that party needs directed him to oppose Emlyn in the West.[47]

3.6 Powell defeats Emlyn in the 1885 Election

Fearing that the new voters in rural areas were likely to be Liberal sympathisers, the Tories organised public meetings in an attempt to woo the voters. A meeting at Whitland in June 1885 was chaired by J. Beynon of Trewern, who was supported by W. Lewis Philipps of Clungwyn, Llanboidy, W. H. Yelverton of Whitland Abbey, H. Davies-Evans of Highmead and H. S. Carver of Blaengors. The Reverend W. D. Phillips of Crunwere, Rural Dean, addressed the meeting. At the end of the Dean's speech the well-known Liberal heckler, Reverend Griffith Havard of Whitland got to his feet to a mixture of applause, hisses and cries of 'sit down'. He stood his ground and told the chairman that he did not have a question because there was nothing in the speech worth asking about! But he would like to pass some comments . . . request refused.

James Williams of Whitland said that when he came to Whitland he was a moderate Liberal but he found all the local Liberals to be extreme . . . and so he became a Tory . . . (shouts of support for Powell). The Reverend Havard again got to his feet but the chairman decided to close the meeting.[48]

The Nonconformists hit back at the Tories when the leadership of the county's Independent (Congregationalist) denomination, at their Quarterly Meeting on 13 and 14 August 1885, publicly declared their support for Powell and urged others to follow their lead: 'This conference urges every voter in West Carmarthenshire to undertake his right reasonably and sensibly in the forthcoming election, by voting for the Liberal candidate, a gentleman whose previous voting record in Parliament together with his manifesto provide enough proof of his complete adoption of our Liberal aspirations. May Powell Maesgwyn be our hero this time again.'[49]

Minute 7 recorded at the quarterly meeting of Carmarthenshire's Independent Denomination
held on 13 and 14 August 1885 at Bwlchnewydd.
(By permission of Llyfrgell Genedlaethol Cymru/The National Library of Wales).

Clearly, the older school of Independents were no longer as influential within the denomination as they had been in the 1860s when the Reverend Joshua Lewis of Henllan Amgoed
declared his opposition to horse-racing and, even more-so to eisteddfodau on the grounds that
'I consider the eisteddfod to be more injurious to the Church than is the "races" because it is a
greater attraction to young men of a religious persuasion.' By 1885 the Independent leadership
were delighted to have a horse-racing eisteddfodwr as their 'hero . . . again'![50]

In the 1885 General Election campaign, public meetings rather than canvassing was the
preferred way of appealing for support. The meetings were held in town halls at Llandeilo,
Carmarthen, St Clears and Whitland and also in village chapels. Lord Emlyn, probably fearing
the challenge from W. R. H. Powell, often held two meetings a day. And as Cragoe pointed out
'policies' had overtaken 'personalities' as a key to electoral success. On both counts Powell had
a distinct advantage. A Liberal meeting at Ammanford was told that W. R. H. Powell was one
of the best members in Wales. But he had already made up his mind not to accept their offer of
the safe seat and East Carmarthenshire would need to find a new candidate.

A Liberal meeting at St Clears in June 1885 was chaired by the Reverend Rees Morgan, the
local Congregational minister, who was supported by the Reverend L Jones, Brynbanc who
spoke in Welsh and Alderman W. de G. Warren, who addressed the meeting in English. J. Bagnall

Evans of Nant-yr-eglwys, Llanboidy, as well as W. R. H. Powell had sent their apologies for being absent. Warren said that in devotion to Liberal principles and in care for all the interests of his constituents, Mr Powell stood second to none (applause) and he would be returned at the General Election. The Reverend J. Williams, Salem, St Clears proposed that they should do everything possible to return Powell as their member. He was seconded by the Reverend R. H. Jones, 26-year-old Baptist minister of Zion, St Clears, and the motion was carried 'with acclamation'.

As might be expected the platform at Tory meetings displayed a gathering of the gentry. . . anglicised and Anglican, while the Liberal support was grounded in Welsh-speaking noncon-formism, led by the ministers and by leading farmers such as Henry John, Castellgarw, Llan-glydwen, Stephen Owen, Hafod, Llanboidy and John Williams, Penlan, Llangynin.

In August 1885 Earl Cawdor in his role as Lord Lieutenant of Carmarthenshire did his son, Lord Emlyn, no favours in failing to nominate any Nonconformists for appointment as Justices of the Peace for the county. 'This is the man who expects Carmarthenshire's Nonconformists to support his son to win a parliamentary seat and to do so against their sincere and faithful friend Mr Powell, Maesgwynne, the Liberal candidate.' thundered *Baner ac Amserau Cymru*'s columnist 'Gohebydd'. Petitions in favour of Nonconformist nominations had not even been acknowledged by the Earl. Claiming that only six out of 120 justices in Carmarthenshire were Liberals, 'Gohebydd' condemned Cawdor's treatment of Nonconformists and Liberals and urged the voters of Carmarthenshire to bear it in mind as a reason, additional to the fact that he was a Tory, for rejecting Lord Emlyn at the next election.[51]

At the end of August 1885 the *Carmarthen Journal* published the voting records for 'the 1885 session' of members representing west Wales constituencies plus Henry Richard, presum-ably because he was already being referred to as the 'member for Wales'. There had been a total of 266 divisions; '157 before midnight and 109 after.' Topping the list was H. G. Allen (Pem-broke) who had voted in 125 divisions. He was followed by Lord Kensington (Haverfordwest) 105, W. R. H. Powell (Carmarthenshire) 100, Llewellyn Dillwyn (Swansea) 100, David Davies (Cardigan) 72, Sir John Jones Jenkins (Carmarthen Boroughs) 68, Henry Richard (Merthyr Tydfil) 66, William Davies (Pembrokeshire) 40 and Lord Emlyn (Carmarthenshire) 39. Report-ing Powell's far superior voting record compared to Lord Emlyn's must have pained the editor of the Tory *Journal*.

Powell was busy during the autumn of 1885 doing the round of agricultural shows. The Carmarthen Show was his sixth of the season following Newcastle Emlyn, Llanboidy, Laugharne, Llandeilo and St Clears.[52] At Llanboidy he was once again emphasising the need to set up a butter factory in order to improve the consistency and hence the demand for Llanboidy butter. At St Clears Show, the Tory candidate, Lord Emlyn, was also present and the two exchanged pleasantries at the dinner. It was a time of depression in agriculture but Powell at Carmarthen tried to raise spirits by claiming that 'there are better times coming boys, only wait a little longer.' How that comment went down was not reported.

One day in October 1885 a committee of Nonconformist ministers and others representing the Liberal electors of west Carmarthenshire met in the afternoon in Water Street Chapel, Carmarthen. An evening meeting had been called by the mayor, Mr J. Lewis, in response to a requisition. In his introduction, the mayor said that in the coming election thousands in

Carmarthenshire would, for the first time, have the right to exercise the franchise and they would soon have the power by local government of saying how their taxes should be spent (applause). He had no doubt that both candidates (W. R. H. Powell in the West and D. Pugh in the East) would go back triumphantly to Parliament. No doubt then who the mayor was supporting! Powell said: 'I am for perfect freedom in religion as in politics – I shall continue to advocate disestablishment and disendowment of the Church and to support the setting up of county government . . . The Liberal party is determined that there shall be an end to this system of taxation without representation.' The 'land question' featured prominently in the campaign[53] and a letter in *Baner ac Amserau Cymru* called for Powell and Pugh to make their views known on land reform.[54] Powell had campaigned ceaselessly for the right of tenants to have security of tenure and full compensation for their investments. And to this end he had repeatedly called for a strengthening of the Agricultural Holdings Act of 1883. At the Carmarthen meeting he returned to the land question by comparing farms to banks: tenants should feel the farm was like a bank; what he puts in is safe and when he can no longer enjoy the interest of his outlay, what remains is his and not his landlord's. Tenant farmers should get full security of tenure.

J. Bagnall Evans of Nant-yr-eglwys, Llanboidy, in moving a motion of confidence in W. R. H. Powell reminded the audience that when Powell was offered the safe Liberal seat of East Carmarthenshire he had refused it inorder to fight the marginal West seat where he lived. Evans then moved that W. R. H. Powell be adopted Liberal candidate for West Carmarthenshire and was seconded by J. Lloyd Morgan and passed unanimously.[55]

A week later Powell was at Llandysul with David Davies, the famous industrialist from Llandinam and Liberal candidate in Cardiganshire. W. O. Brigstocke, barrister-at-law, of Parcygors, Llandygwydd, was in the chair. Powell told the meeting that both he and David Davies had voted to give women the vote but many Liberals were against it. The audience responded with shouts of '*Powell am byth!*' Powell said that he had always striven to elevate the labourer but he thought the 2-acre-allotment scheme would be a white elephant . . . 'too little to plough and too much to dig.' He was of the opinion that labourer's children should be educated free by a grant from the consolidated fund (that is, funded by the government) (applause). Powell admitted that he was conscious of his own boldness in opposing Lord Emlyn but it was a matter of duty to the Liberal Party and the noble Lord had not chosen to contest the division in which he resided (applause). David Davies retorted that Powell had acted manly and nobly in championing the Liberal cause against Emlyn and that it would be, to a Welshman, a national disgrace if he were not returned with an overwhelming majority (shouts of 'We will return him!'). Davies went on to disclose that Emlyn was the only member from Wales who opposed the Sunday Closing Act (shame!). The other Tory member, Sir Watkin Williams Wynn, was brought from his sick bed to the house to vote FOR closing but the young nobleman, Lord Emlyn, delighted and gloried in voting AGAINST (shame!). He hoped they would remember that Tories are no good for Wales and Scotland![56]

General Election meetings in those pre-radio and pre-television days were excitable affairs which sometimes spilt over into violence. In a meeting at the Ram School, Pencarreg near Lampeter, Powell, the arch disestablisher, encountered a body of over 50 Church of England students from Lampeter College. As soon as the students entered the cry went up 'out with the students' and a free-for-all ensued but the students stood their ground. The chair of the meeting,

Alderman Jones, advised the young fellows that they would soon have to feed on gruel because disestablishment would soon be upon them and their spirits would not be so elated. In the uproar that followed, student jibes of 'what about the duck pond Jones?' and 'how are the apples eating?', apparently referring to some escapade that the chairman had been involved with in Pembrokeshire, were directed at Alderman Jones. In response to an invitation to come along with them, Powell enquired where would they like to take him . . . 'Sudan, Khartoum or where?'. . . to which the reply was 'Croydon Races!'. . . a reference to Powell's success in the prestigious Croydon Open eighteen years previously . . . 'which created great laughter'. One of Mr Powell's respectable supporters advised the roughs (most of the audience) to evict the students but they were unable to dislodge them! A show of hands against Mr Powell enraged the roughs and they charged again into the students who then withdrew. A resolution supporting Mr Powell was then passed.[57]

During those few weeks, Powell visited Llanybri, Pontyates, Pontyberem, Whitemill, Llandyfaelog, Bancyfelin and Llanpumsaint. Another example of a rowdy meeting was that held by the Conservatives at Whitland during the final days of the election campaign. The meeting was chaired by the Reverend W. D. Phillips, vicar of Crunwere, who had a tough time controlling the audience once Lord Emlyn in his speech denied ever saying that 'no working man should have more than 1s.8d. a day'. He was immediately interrupted by a shout of 'Yes you did'. Emlyn challenged the man to say when and where he had made such a statement but the disturbance among the audience was so great that the chairman sent Emlyn to his seat. A stone 'of 5 ounces' flung through a window fell just over the edge of the platform. After some sort of order was restored, J. L. G. P. Lewes JP of Henllan near Newcastle Emlyn moved a vote of confidence in Lord Emlyn and was seconded. But immediately the Reverend Griffith Havard moved an amendment saying that only a Liberal was acceptable in West Carmarthenshire and pledged support to W. R. H. Powell. The Reverend William Thomas, Whitland seconded the amendment. After taking the vote, both sides claimed a two to one victory![58]

Two days later the Tories met at St Clears and Lord Emlyn was again interrupted by Liberal hecklers. When Mr Bowen, Cwmbrwynog, an excitable Tory, jumped on to the platform he triggered an outbreak of rowdyism in which a Nonconformist minister played a leading role. The Evans brothers of Treventy made their way to the platform and appealed to those present not to disgrace St Clears by following the disgraceful conduct of the people of Whitland, witnessed a few nights earlier.

A few nights later the Liberals gathered for a meeting at St Clears. When a carriage arrived, carrying Powell Bach together with the president of the St Clears Liberal Association, J. Bagnall Evans, W. Simons of Merthyr Tydvil, J. Lloyd Morgan of Carmarthen and the Reverends J. Jones of Felinfoel and D. S. Davies of Cwmfelin Mynach, the horses were removed from the carriage and high spirited supporters pulled it through the village accompanied by a torchlight procession 'on a small scale'.

Capel Mair was 'well filled' when J. Bagnall Evans called the meeting to order and proclaimed that he believed the 'labourers vote would change the misrepresentation of the county and make it impossible that a Tory should ever again sit for Carmarthenshire (cheers).' During his address, Powell claimed that Lord Emlyn was misrepresenting his views on tenants rights. He (Powell) was 'for land being as saleable as a ship with all the restrictions of the laws of princogenitive [*sic*] and entail swept away, and he wanted farmers to be able to regard their farms as a bank with perfect security for all their outlay and improvements (cheers).'

As regard the working man he did not think the three acre system would benefit him . . . but he wished to see the working man better housed with well stocked gardens, (joining) a club for sickness and old age and his children educated free by a grant from the consolidated fund. It was more important to invest in children's education than to provide extravagant pensions.

Powell went on to state that he did not seek a seat for his own interest for he was far happier and more comfortable at home, but (rather) because he did not wish to see a Tory returned for that division (cheers). He knew he had the strongest opponent in all Wales, 'but if they would rely on him, though he was only the *"dyn bach o Maesgwynne"* (loud and continuous cheers), he would carry the flag of Liberal principles to the front and never disgrace it by any act of his (renewed cheers).'

It soon became clear that Mr Simons from Merthyr Tydvil had been brought in to throw a few low blows at the Tories. He declared that the two prominent characteristics of the Tory Party were bloodshed and extravagance which had led to the huge National Debt and 'the taxing of everything which the people cared to look at, handle, touch or taste. The windows they looked through were taxed, the points of the women's bodkins, the laces of their boots, the buttons on the waistcoats, the women's scissors, and even the grave-clothes of the dead were taxed.' Simons claimed that: '"Tory" was an old word for "thief" (laughter and applause)' and that the party had 'well maintained its character'. He reckoned that the Tories were a select body living apart from the people.

In a meeting at Whitland the town's Reverend William Thomas read out an address prepared by the Whitland Liberal Association directed at their candidate, W. R. H. Powell: 'Sir, We have

not forgotten your faithful service in the House of Commons during the past five and a half years in voting for Liberal measures and against Conservative amendments and needless votes of censure. Your votes have convinced us that you are not a lover of Parliamentary honours without discharging Parliamentary duties, and that you believe you represent your constituents rather than advertise your idiocyncracies as a Member of Parliament.'[59]

During the campaign, Powell complained about the dirty tactics employed by the Tory landlords in attempting to coerce their tenants into voting for Emlyn. But on the other hand the Tories alleged that the Nonconformist ministers used their pulpits to influence their congregations into supporting Liberal candidates . . . the so called 'Nonconformist screw'.

On polling day the radicals were out in force on the streets of Whitland 'hooting and shouting' at any whom they suspected of belonging to the other party. One well-known local obstructionist and refreshment-house keeper went so far as to place a sign over his door, stating that

Reverend William Thomas (1832-1911), minister at Whitland's Soar and Tabernacl and Llanddewi's Bethel Independent Chapels. A leading radical, he backed Powell to the hilt. In 1889 he was elected as Whitland's first county councillor.
(*Cyfrol Goffa Gweinidogion Annibynnol Penfro.* Merthyr Tydfil, 1933).

dinners would be supplied at the following charges 'Liberals 1 shilling, Conservatives 1s.6d.' News of a Liberal victory in Pembroke was greeted by loud cheers and shouts from a group 'under the influence of John Barleycorn'. When W. R. H. Powell arrived at 4.30 p.m., supporters took the horses from his carriage and pulled it themselves to the railway station where Powell said a few words before leaving by train for the count at Carmarthen. About 500 had voted at Whitland.[60] No doubt most had put their cross for Powell and that was the pattern throughout the West Carmarthenshire constituency giving W. R. H. Powell a convincing victory over his Tory opponent Lord Emlyn.

However, *The Welshman*, a supposedly Liberal newspaper, carried a curious comment on the result: 'We repeat our apprehensions that the character of Welshmen for intelligence and due appreciation of noted talent will suffer in the eyes of the world when Lord Emlyn's defeat becomes known all over the kingdom' and that it was 'discrediting for Carmarthen if not all of Wales that a man like Emlyn should not have a pick of seats.' According to *The Welshman*'s report the emphatic victory was brought about by many Conservatives withholding their votes because of their personal admiration of W. R. H. Powell who was popular among people of every class and party. Although Emlyn was very able, Powell was the 'man of the people'.

But K. O. Morgan in *Wales in British Politics* saw it differently: 'In 1885 the crisis on the land was a major political question in Wales. In West Carmarthenshire, W. R. H. Powell, a Liberal landowner from Maesgwynne . . . defeated the Cawdor representative, the popular Lord Emlyn, in an election fought largely . . . on the Agricultural Holdings Act of 1883.' Powell had for a long time been calling for the Act, weakened at its passing by the acceptance of a Tory amendment, to be strengthened to give a fairer deal to the tenant.

There is no doubt that the newspapers did not give Powell the credit due to him for his stance on Liberal principles of justice in matters of religion, education, tenant rights and the well-being of the poor. The plain fact was that the so called Liberal *The Welshman* newspaper did not support many of the policies advocated by Nonconformist-backed Welsh Liberal candidates and had labelled some of them, such as disestablishment of the Church, destructive! Throughout his life, Powell's actions in the community were those of a radical and his acceptance of the radical Liberal programme should not have surprised anyone. In the 1885 General Election he had taken on the Tory and Liberal, or perhaps more correctly, the Whig establishment and, with the active support of the Nonconformist ministers, had trounced them, and *The Welshman*, to its shame, could not stomach it.

The result was announced from the balcony of the Town Hall at Carmarthen:

W. R. H. Powell (Liberal]		4568
Lord Emlyn (Tory]		2942
	Majority	1626

On the same balcony eighty-one years later another Welsh radical, Gwynfor Evans, made history by becoming Plaid Cymru's first MP.

Powell thanked all and spared a thought for his friend Pugh whom he expected to have a greater majority in the east. (Pugh did win the East Carmarthenshire seat standing as a Liberal.) And, perhaps stung by the many grossly unfair attacks made on him during the campaign, he expressed the hope that not a single Tory would be returned! No doubt mindful of his deteriorating health he assured the people that when 'y Dyn Bach Maesgwynne had no further health and strength to serve them in Parliament, he would resign into their hands the trust they had placed in him and assist them to elect another Liberal member for the County.'[61]

The 1885 General Election turned out to be the final nail in Lord Emlyn's parliamentary coffin. In 1889 he lowered his sights and became a member of the first Carmarthenshire County Council. But his complaint at the first meeting of the council that he did not understand a word of the council chairman's introductory comments in Welsh showed that he was not of the people he represented. That incident highlighted the difference between the Tory Lord and the radical Squire in their attitude to the language of their constituents. Powell understood Welsh and invariably apologised for his inability to deliver a speech in the language, but Lord Emlyn on the other hand not only did not understand Welsh, let alone speak it, but was clearly intolerant of those that did. Another difference between them was the way they spent their wealth. Emlyn spent his fortune on the Cawdor 'palace' of Stackpole Court in Pembrokeshire and also on building a luxury yacht for his own benefit. On the other hand, Powell spent his money on building a school, a market hall, labourers cottages and a hotel . . . all of which benefited the community of Llanboidy and district.

In the 1885 General Election, the swing to the Tories in England, where 16 seats were gained from the Liberals, was not repeated in Wales where the representation remained at 29 Liberals and 4 Tories reflecting the radical aspirations of the Welsh electorate. The Liberals were returned to power but with a reduced majority and the conversion of Gladstone to favour Home Rule for Ireland split the party. The Whig element formed the Liberal Unionist Party and joined with the Tories to defeat the Home Rule Bill on 7 June 1886 by 343 votes to 313. Radicals such as W. R. H. Powell (West Carmarthenshire), Tom Ellis (Meirioneth) and Henry Richard (Merthyr Tydfil) were among the 22 Welsh Liberal Radicals who supported Gladstone while seven Welsh Liberal Whigs including Sir John Jones Jenkins (Carmarthen Boroughs) voted with the Tories. Gladstone immediately dissolved Parliament and a General Election was called for July 1886 ensuring a short campaign. The Nonconformist ministers threw their weight behind Gladstone and Home Rule for Ireland rather than follow the breakaway Liberal Unionists.

3.7 Powell defeats Unionist in the 1886 Election

The West Carmarthenshire Unionists soon got into their stride with a meeting at St Clears attended by their candidate, Londoner Sir James Lawrence, a former Tory MP for Lambeth, who shared the platform with local Tory farmer, J. Bowen of Cwmbrwyn, who was well used to making a fool of himself at the local show. Another local farmer T. Evans of Treventy chaired the meeting. The few others on the platform were from outside the area. Among those in the crowded room were a number of Nonconformist ministers. The chairman spoke in Welsh and claimed he was a Blue (Liberal) radical but the crowd's surprise reaction 'Oh!' questioned his assertion. It was a noisy meeting and Sir James' attempt to address the crowd was hampered by what appeared to be an organised opposition by young men and others at the back who kept up an almost continuous interruption. The Reverend David Williams, Salem, St Clears, got up onto the platform and moved a motion of confidence in Mr Gladstone which drew three cheers from the crowd. The chairman declared the meeting closed and was manhandled as he left the hall. Outside, fighting broke out but it must have been a one-sided affair judging by the situation in the hall. The following morning the Unionists tried to organise an outdoor meeting but once again constant interruption forced them to give up.

Meanwhile the Gladstonian Liberal candidate, W. R. H. Powell, was at the Salutation Hotel, Newcastle Emlyn, together with Mr Bowen Rowlands the candidate for Cardiganshire; the sitting MP, David Davies of Llandinam was standing as a Unionist and was destined to lose his seat. A certain Dr Lloyd was in the chair and opened proceedings by declaring the need for a 'good Home Rule Bill for Wales' because 'if the present state [of decline] continued, Wales would soon be in as bad a state as Ireland (applause).' W. R. H. Powell said he was a strong advocate of Home Rule and if returned he would support Gladstone to do justice to Ireland and to Wales (great applause). The Methodist minister, Reverend Evan Phillips' proposal that the meeting approved the candidate's views was carried unanimously.[62] The following week, Powell addressed a meeting in Carmarthen chaired by Alderman Warren. Powell announced he was convinced by the argument for Home Rule although he did not say whether he was referring to Wales as well as Ireland. He reminded his audience that although the previous session of Parliament had been a short one, they still managed 143 divisions of which he had attended 127 (applause).

The Gladstonian Liberals organised well, thanks to an 'army' of Nonconformist ministers. Meetings were held throughout the constituency at places such as Pensarn, Bancyfelin, Laugharne, Brechfa and Llanybydder. Powell attended two meetings a day. At an evening meeting in Llangyndeyrn he was accompanied by the Reverend John Wyndham Lewis, minister of Water Street Methodist Chapel, Carmarthen and at Llansteffan he had the support of Alderman Warren, George Thomas and, again, Reverend J. Wyndham Lewis. At Kidwelly, David Stephens presided and Mr Cobb, MP for Rugby, joined Powell on the platform. Cobb had been talked of as a possible candidate for Cardiganshire but nothing came of it. Gladstone had sent a message to Cobb instructing him to ask the voters of Carmarthenshire if they retained confidence in himself and in Powell. Gladstone hoped the voters would answer by sending Powell back to Parliament with an overwhelming majority. Cobb laid into Sir James Lawrence alleging that: 'This puffed up London Alderman had come there to flaunt his money bags in the face of the people of Carmarthenshire . . . send Powell to Parliament and cause this . . . alderman-unionist to return home a wiser . . . man.' He produced voting figures for the two candidates during the 1884 Parliament when Lawrence was a Tory MP. Of 216 divisions, Powell had voted in 158 while Lawrence managed only 14.

During the course of the Kidwelly meeting, two major Welsh Liberal figures entered the hall. William Abraham,

William Abraham (Mabon), miners leader and MP for the Rhondda. Often shared a platform with the radical squire.

(By permission of Llyfrgell Genedlaethol Cymru / The National Library of Wales).

better known as Mabon the Liberal MP for the Rhondda, and David Randell a solicitor of Llanelli and prominent Liberal nationalist were returning from helping Thomas Edward Ellis, the rising star of Welsh Liberal nationalism win Meirioneth. They had called at Kidwelly to give Powell their support and they were heartily received.

Sir James Lawrence held meetings at Newcastle Emlyn, Llangeler, Kidwelly, Ferryside and Whitland where there was another 'rowdy meeting'. The fact that the chairman of the meeting at the Market House Whitland was from Carmarthen was evidence that support for Lawrence was rather thin on the ground. And he had been warned that he was in for a 'warm' reception. There were present a 'number of Reverend gentlemen' who 'acted in a manner not quite in accordance with those principles of fair play' which Liberals prided themselves on upholding. When the Unionist candidate arrived on stage, shouts went up for Powell and for Gladstone. Lawrence was continually interrupted and was at one stage advised to 'go back to London'. Much of the interruptions were made by dissenting ministers such as the Whitland pair, Reverend William Thomas and Reverend Griffith Havard, while the lone churchman, Reverend E. Rowland occasionally interrupted in support of Sir James.

Griffith Havard was a particularly colourful performer at political meetings. He had been a Baptist minister at Blaenavon, Monmouthshire and at Saundersfoot and at Beulah Chapel, Little Newcastle in Pembrokeshire. While at Beulah he encountered some difficulties which led him in the 1870s to give up the ministry and set up as a Chemist and Druggist at Whitland. He passed away in the 1890s.

The meeting at Whitland had already started when Havard arrived on the scene but his walk to the front of the hall halted proceedings when the whole audience got to its feet with 'cheers and waving of hats'. He raised his hat to Sir James who returned the compliment. Much of the remainder of the meeting was a slanging match between the pair. Havard's opening comment was to tell Sir James that he 'ought not to oppose one who is so popular everywhere as Mr Powell' which drew 'an uproar' of support. On the matter of Home Rule for Ireland, Havard told the Liberal Unionist that 'the Irish are trampled so low as to have to live upon potatoes and you are the sort to take even the potatoes away.' Sir James explained that he was opposed to Home Rule because he was against putting the Protestants in the hands of the Catholics. Havard's interjection implied that the Protestants had invited trouble by their past actions in going 'from farm to farm with guns and bayonets to collect tithes'. And he further alleged that the Union only came about because 'they bribed them'. The Reverend William Thomas of Whitland advised the candidate that 'we oppose you altogether. Mr Powell is too popular for anyone from London to oppose him.' And an attempt by a Mr Richards of Llanelli to speak in Welsh on behalf of Sir James had to be abandoned after Griffith Havard accused him of having 'come from Llanelli to betray a friend'. To add insult to injury the Reverend William Thomas proposed a resolution of confidence in Mr Powell, which the chairman blocked by declaring the meeting closed.

Outside the hall, a well-known Powell supporter, Mr Simeon Davies a private commercial hotel owner, mounted a heap of stones and sang '*Hen Wlad Fy Nhadau*' and as he sang Mr Powell arrived on his way to the railway station and was 'very heartily greeted by his partizans'.

The Reverend William Thomas was minister at the Independent Chapels of Soar and Tabernacl, Whitland and Bethel, Llanddewi Velfrey. At one time he was a tenant to W. H. Yelverton of

Whitland Abbey and at his home in Whitland he had enough land to keep six or seven cows. But when the Liberal William Thomas refused to vote for Yelverton during the 1874 election, he was evicted. The incident put steel in William Thomas' blood and he became an ardent Welsh nationalist and ultra radical Liberal politician who supported W. R. H. Powell to the hilt. When the county councils were set up in 1889, William Thomas was elected the first county councillor for Whitland.

After the Whitland meeting, three of Sir James Lawrence's entourage visited Llanboidy. Anticipating Sir James would put in an appearance the villagers displayed an effigy of the candidate with an epitaph in memory of 'Jimmy Lawrence' recording his 'death' at Whitland on 12 July 1886. But 'Jimmy' did not put in an appearance and as the three visitors left Llanboidy they had 'to run the gauntlet of a shower of eggs'.[63]

The result of the West Carmarthenshire election was declared at Carmarthen on 16 July 1886 at 1.30 p.m. and it was a convincing victory for W. R. H. Powell:

W. R. H. Powell	Gladstone Liberal	4181
Sir James Lawrence	Unionist Liberal	1916
	Majority	2265

After the declaration, Powell expressed his hope that throughout the Kingdom, in Wales, Scotland and England, the Liberal Party would soon be again united. He thanked his supporters for giving him an 'unprecedented majority' and left for Whitland where he arrived at 7.15 p.m. He was greeted by an enthusiastic crowd accompanied by the Llanfyrnach Brass Band. The MP walked to the Post Office and from the steps he addressed the crowd. There were also speeches from the Reverend gentlemen William Thomas (Whitland), D. S. Davies (Cwmfelin Mynach), David Rhys Davies (Rhydyceisied), Griffith Havard (Whitland) and William Thomas (Llanboidy).

Afterwards the brass band headed a procession in which Powell rode in his carriage pulled by the crowd, rather than the horses, for the whole of the six miles to Llanboidy! A large meeting ensued at the Market Hall with Mr J. Williams, Penlan, Llangynin in the chair. Mr Powell addressed the assembled multitude and among other speakers were Mr Palmer, Brynbanc; Mr Owen, Hafod; Reverend D. Jones, Whitland; Reverend David Rhys Davies, Rhydyceisied; Reverend D. Evans, Cwmbach and Reverend D. S. Davies, Cwmfelin Mynach.

In sharp contrast to England, where the Gladstonian Liberals lost 115 seats, Wales maintained its support for Gladstone and Home Rule losing only one seat (West Denbighshire) to the Liberal Unionists. Both David Davies (Llandinam), candidate in Cardiganshire, and Sir John Jones Jenkins, in Carmarthen Boroughs, stood as Unionists and lost their seats to Gladstonian Liberals. When the election expenses of the candidates were published it was found that Sir James Lawrence had spent £1,198 compared to W. R. H. Powell's £672. Powell spent much less than his opponent on agents because the Tories used expensive lawyers whereas Liberals could depend on a network of Nonconformist ministers and did not need to pay agents.

In August 1886 a demonstration by the Taf Vale Temperance Association was held at Llanboidy. A public meeting at 2.00 p.m. was chaired by W. R. H. Powell MP and he, together with Reverend Morris Morgan, Swansea and Reverend Williams, Bethania, Cardigan, addressed the crowd. A children's tea party was held in the Market Hall and Powell gave £3 to defray the cost. The day ended with an evening concert at the Market Hall.[64]

In January 1887 Powell presided at the Llanboidy Eisteddfod where his friend the Reverend D. S. Davies was the conductor. Before the end of the month he might well have been at Carmarthenshire Races where his 'Eveline' and 'Waxy' ran but without success. He was back in London in February 1887 attending a meeting of Welsh members called to discuss the legislative programme affecting Wales. The meeting was chaired by Henry Richard and members present included T. E. Ellis, J. Bryn Roberts, William Abraham, W. R. H. Powell and Stuart Rendel.[65]

But, then, on 18 February 1887 came the first indication that Powell's health was causing concern with the announcement in the *Carmarthen Journal* that the MP had 'paired' with the Hon. F. C. Morgan, Tory MP for Monmouthshire South. Powell and Morgan, despite their political differences, had been comrades of the turf over previous decades. Their friendship helped Powell to do his best for the Liberal cause by making sure that his missing vote was balanced by Morgan's missing Tory vote.

In fact the long hours spent in the House of Commons had been too much for Powell's, by then, rather fragile constitution and had induced severe heart palpitations which, for one thing, had ended his days on horse back. Another notice of pairing between Powell and Morgan appeared in the *Carmarthen Journal* on 8 April 1887, the pairing to be effective for ten days.

3.8 Powell presents anti-tithes petition but hayricks go up in flames

At that time, opposition to paying the church tithes was mounting throughout Wales and the rector of Llanglydwen, Reverend Samuel Davies, refused to pay the tithes then due, on the ground that the tithe payers had declined to pay the tithes without a reduction of 15%. An Anti-Tithe-League meeting was held at the Llanboidy Market Hall (by permission of W. R. H. Powell) in March 1887. Present at the meeting were tithe payers from nine parishes and they protested at the proposal by the Conservative and Unionist government to transfer payment of tithes from occupier to owner and they vowed to use every means to secure disestablishment and disendowment of the Church in Wales.[66]

Powell's health was sufficiently restored by early June 1887 to lead a delegation of Liberals from West Carmarthenshire to meet none other than the Grand Old Man, W. E. Gladstone, who had come to Swansea to meet his supporters in south Wales. In his speech at Singleton Abbey, Gladstone emphasised that Wales was a 'distinct nationality' for which he received applause.[67]

Powell's concern about the unfairness of the church tithe charges was reflected in his attendance in Parliament in early August 1887 to present a petition 'praying for the passing of the Tithe Rent-Charge Bill' in that session. He was recorded as representing the Rural Deanery of Emlyn. Similar petitions were presented by Bowen Rowlands MP for Cardiganshire on behalf of the clergy of the county of Cardiganshire and by a Mr Tomlinson on behalf of the Rural Deaneries of East Gower and Castlemartin in Pembrokeshire.[68] Two months later the *Carmarthen Journal* on 5 August 1887 reported that Powell's health had been 'affected by the recent heavy pressure of parliamentary work and that he had arranged to pair with F. C. Morgan to the end of the parliamentary session'. The publication in September 1887 of the voting records of Members of Parliament revealed how demanding the 1887 session had been. There had been 485 divisions, 73 more than in any previous session. But again, W. R. H. Powell had excelled by voting in 242 divisions and was third in the voting list for Wales and Monmouthshire members who had on average voted 122 times. Top of that list on 327 was the young radical from Meirioneth, Thomas Edward Ellis and he was followed by Admiral R. C. Mayne (Pembroke and Haverfordwest) on 254.[69]

Before the end of August 1887 Powell was well enough to chair a meeting of the Llanboidy Petty Sessions with three other magistrates E. S. Protheroe, J. Bagnall Evans and W. Lewis Philipps in attendance. The business 'was almost entirely with summonses against parents for not sending children to school'. Powell's health was sufficiently recovered for him to attend the Llanboidy Show in September 1887 but he admitted that he had been very unwell a few weeks previously, more unwell than he had been during the tedious parliamentary session. But he had paired and 'come down to his native air'. He had not attended the Newcastle Emlyn Show that year because in his state of health he could not face a journey of 28 miles each way. He had sent an apology and a subscription but, still, he had been found fault with and told that he should have been at Newcastle Emlyn to hear the farmers' grievances on the payment of tithes. He was clearly rather upset about the criticism. Perhaps the criticism from Newcastle Emlyn made him attend the St Clears Show when, as he admitted, he should have been at home because he felt so unwell. But he was concerned about rumours of the show's impending demise and came to declare his support for its continuation. He was looking forward to seeing them all at the following year's event.[70] Powell sent a letter of apology for his absence due to ill-health from Carmarthen Show and the show secretary, David Prosser, commented that he had seen Powell a few days earlier and was certain that Powell should not have been out on that day.[71] But Powell was committed to his public duties and on 11 November 1887 he was chairing a meeting of the Llanboidy Petty Sessions.

In January 1888 he was again fit enough to chair another petty sessions meeting at Llanboidy where thirteen men and three women were charged with assaulting Mr Roblin, the lay impropriator of certain tithes in the district, his son and Mr Collins, an auctioneer at tithe sales held at Llwyndewi Farm near Pont-y-Fenni and Pen-y-coed Farm near Whitland. A special body of police from Carmarthen was in attendance to keep order in the crowded court in the Maesgwynne Arms Hotel. Powell sought the advice of the advocates as to whether he should remain in the chair. There was no objection. The case for the the prosecution was that whilst trying to carry out the tithe sales Roblin, his son and Collins had been pelted with mud, dung and rotten eggs, huddled and assailed by a crowd of about 500 people. After the sales the harassment continued as they made their way to Whitland. It was revealed in court that on the day of the sales, Roblin had carried a revolver and his bailiff had a derringer. Powell delivered the court's verdict and it was clear that he, at least, had every sympathy with the injustice that gave rise to the protest. But he said that the court was responsible for upholding the law as it existed but would do so as leniently as possible. The defendants were fined £1 with costs; a verdict greeted with cries of 'Shame!' and 'Ah!'[72]

During May 1888 it was rumoured that Powell was about to resign his Parliamentary seat due to ill-health and that he had requested to meet with Liberal leaders in Carmarthenshire to discuss the matter. The meeting was arranged for the end of May but ill health prevented Powell from attending. A few days later, after considerable confusion, or so it was claimed by the blood-thirsty *Western Mail*, it was announced that talks with Powell had taken place and that he would be staying on as Member of Parliament.[73]

Powell was back at Westminster in June voting with colleagues Tom Ellis, D. A. Thomas and others, including a score of Conservatives, to defeat the Conservative Government on its proposal to undertake expensive reorganisation in public offices. And he was present at the Welsh Liberals' first meeting after the Whitsun recess in the company of Henry Richard (chairman), Lewis Dillwyn, Osborne Morgan, Alfred Thomas, T. F. Price, W. Bowen Rowlands, D. A. Thomas, S. Rathborne, William Abraham (Mabon), John Roberts, Samuel Smith, Stuart Rendel, T. E. Ellis and Arthur J. Williams. They unanimously agreed to oppose the clause in the Technical Institution Bill allowing voluntary schools to receive financial aid from the rates. Powell was a regular attender in the House of Commons until the end of the session in August 1888, but after that session ill-health prevented him from ever returning to Westminster.

The voting record of Welsh members for 1888, published at the end of December, showed that up until August, Powell had voted 147 times and was seventh highest attender out of the 35 Welsh members. However, he had not been well enough to return for the autumn sittings. While his health allowed, Powell was a thoroughly conscientious Member of Parliament.

The tithe war reared its head on the boundary of Llanboidy and Llanwinio parishes in September 1888. The trouble must have brought back memories to Powell Bach of his beginning as Squire of Maesgwynne and being 'welcomed' by the Rebecca uprising nearly half a century earlier. On Friday, 17 September 1888, tithe owner Lt. Colonel Howell of Penrheol, Mydrim, sought to cause the sale of hayricks at Yetygarn and at Blaenwaun Farm in the village of Blaenwaun in order to recover the tithes due him. To bring about the sales, twenty police-men drawn from Llanelli, Llandeilo, Carmarthen, St Clears, Laugharne and Whitland escorted the bailiff, Robert Lewis a tailor of Pendine, over the nine miles or so from St Clears to Blaen-waun.

At Yetygarn, the home of the Reverend Dan Evans, minister of Moriah Chapel, a wall was draped with a poster on which cartoons had been drawn depicting the bailiff and his relatives and carrying the legends 'Robert Lewis and Company' and *'Dim Degwm i neb byth mwy'*.[74] In addition a red bedcover was flying from the top of a tree; its erection a few hours earlier had been the signal for neighbours to attend the 'sale'.[75] A 'howling crowd' greeted the bailiff's party and insults and rotten eggs were thrown at them. The hooting made it impossible to carry out a sale of the hayrick and eventually a local farmer, W. Phillips of Castell Mawr, emerged from the crowd declaring that he had purchased the hay for £3.10s.7d. But the bailiff had accepted £3.10s.6d. in payment.

The bailiff, escorted by the police and followed by the bellowing crowd, walked the half mile to Blaenwaun Farm where the Reverend Dan Evans asked for silence to hear Mr E. H. James J.P. of Pontygavel, Glandŵr, read out a statement of protest signed by the outgoing tenant, Mr John Jones, intimating that the rightful owner of the two hayricks at Blaenwaun Farm was the incoming tenant, Mr William Lewis, and that the hay should therefore not be sold to recover tithes owed by the outgoing tenant. The bailiff took no notice and proceeded to sell the hayricks although a public auction was made impossible by the bellowing crowd. Eventually a man who had accompanied the bailiff from Pendine claimed that he had bought the ricks for £5. As the police attempted to steer the bailiff and his cronies out of the village a shower of clods and rotten eggs fell on them and retaliation by a couple of policemen was nipped in the bud by Inspector Williams who decreed an orderly withdrawal to avoid a riot.

After the party made their getaway, an open air meeting was chaired by E. H. James JP and several speeches were delivered and a collection realized £2.12s.2d. towards the expenses. But some protesters had a late night. And the following morning the villagers awoke to find the two hayricks at Blaenwaun Farm burnt to the ground and only smouldering heaps of ashes remained to mark the spot where the stacks had stood.

The end of the affair took place at Llanboidy Petty Session at the end of September 1888 when David Rogers, a labourer of Croesishmael, Llanwinio, was hauled before the magistrates charged with assault on PC T. V. Rees during the tithe distraint sale at Blaenwaun. Before commencing the case the chairman of the bench, W. R. H. Powell, withdrew from the court and took no further part in the proceedings. No doubt he was fully aware that his strong views on the utter injustice of the tithe system would have made it very difficult for him to remain impartial in dealing with the case. PC Rees explained that at the sale a number of people were hooting, yelling and throwing eggs and stones. A rotten egg hit him on the shoulder damaging his uniform and PC Philip Morgan was a witness to the fact that David Rogers was the egg thrower. Rogers was found guilty and was fined £1 with costs of 16s.8d.[76] It would be no surprise to find that Powell Bach helped Rogers deal with his punishment.

Powell was warmly welcomed to the St Clears Show in mid-September 1888 'after a very arduous [parliamentary] session'. And the show president drew rapturous applause when he reminded those present that it was Powell's jubilee year as MFH. Sir Charles E. G. Philipps of Picton Castle, Pembrokeshire, was president of the show and he may have been responsible for reintroducing the practice of 'endless' toasts. When his turn came to speak, Powell Bach could not resist taking a swipe at the time-wasting practice before turning his attention to the matter of tithes. And he showed himself to be a realist in having to accept that as things stood, tithes were lawful charges. His complaint was that the charges in Wales were manifestly unfair because they were calculated on the basis of the price of corn on the London markets rather than on the lower price obtained in Wales. He produced reams of figures to show that the arrangement was not 'right, proper or just'. For example, the average price of wheat in Middlesex was 16% higher than the average price obtained in Wales. And in Carmarthenshire the difference would have been even greater. Powell's remedy was that, as long as they existed, tithes should be regulated by the sales in the county in which the corn was grown. Furthermore, he thought that one of the duties of the new county councils should be to appoint 'a receiver of the corn sold with power to give a receipt and certificate to the purchaser and to the seller and to impose a fine on those who did not adhere to the regulations.'

The Liberals in Carmarthenshire were undoubtedly radical in their views and were active in making those views known. For example in September 1888 they met at Carmarthen to voice their support for Gladstone's policy of Home Rule for Ireland. The meeting was chaired by the Reverend J. Wyndham Lewis and the main speaker was local lawyer John Lloyd Morgan. The cases of Dillon and Mandeville had brought great discredit to the Tory-Unionist Government. John Dillon was the Irish Nationalist MP for East Mayo and was active in the Irish Land League movement for which he was often imprisoned. John Mandeville was a well-to-do farmer and Home Ruler from Mitchelstown. He was imprisoned for preventing some evictions of tenant farmers and spent five months in jail where he was brutally mistreated which resulted in his death six months after his release. He was dubbed 'another martyr to the Home Rule cause'. The Carmarthen Liberals were unanimous in their support for Home Rule and in their condemnation of the Government's policy and of its harsh treatment of Dillon and Mandeville.[77]

A month later in October 1888, the Liberals again met at Carmarthen, this time to discuss the forthcoming elections to the newly formed county councils. Lewis Morris MA, solicitor of Llangynnwr, Carmarthen, presided and about fifty persons attended. Dr Jones from Llanelli reported that East Carmarthenshire would fight the county council elections on political grounds provided West Carmarthenshire agreed to do likewise. He was informed that the Tories had, not only chosen their candidates, but had also decided who they would appoint as officers of the council! Barrister A. W. Jones said that the Liberals only had to stay united to get a majority of seats on the council and thus check-mate 'those little games'. Powell Bach urged them to treat the council elections as party political contests and if they avoided splits, they had nothing to fear from Primrose Leaguers and their toast and tea! And it was high time for the Liberals to get 'a share of the loaves and fishes' by appointing their men to key posts just as the Tories and the Liberals did in government. The Liberal Unionists came under heavy attack from the Reverend A. J. Parry who denounced them as the 'bane of the Liberal party' and should not be supported; a view shared by the Reverend J. Wyndham Lewis. But compromise was achieved, and the meeting agreed to select candidates 'of the broadest Liberal views'.[78]

3.9 End of the road

Powell continued to do his best to support the Liberals in Parliament and, while his poor health prevented him from attending at Westminster, he succeeded in November 1888 to pair with Colonel Hill to the end of the parliamentary sitting. His 'pair' may well have been Edward Hill, the Tory member for Bristol South whose son was to play cricket for Glamorgan. At the beginning of January 1889, Powell chaired the monthly meeting of Llanboidy Petty Sessions when William Jenkins of Penyback, Kiffig was fined 5 shillings and costs for being drunk at Whitland. But at the end of January he was not well enough to attend and act as president of the Llanboidy Eisteddfod. When his absence was announced, the crowd rose to their feet to show their respect. In Powell's absence, Edward H. James JP, of Pontygafel, Glandŵr, Llanfyrnach was voted to the chair. James was one of the first outside the enclave of the squires and the clergy to be appointed justice of the peace and was known as *Justys y Bont*. The adjudicators were Mr David Jenkins, Mus. Bac., lecturer in music at Aberystwyth College, for the music competitions and Reverend Benjamin Thomas (Myfyr Emlyn) of Narberth for the prose and poetry competitions.

In the same issue of the *Journal* the Welsh rugby team to meet Scotland was named and, as a keen sportsman, Powell would have enjoyed reading of the inclusion at forward of Rowland Lewis Thomas of Parciau, Henllan Amgoed, for the first of his seven caps. He had attended Llandovery College before becoming a medical student in London where he played for London

Back row, left to right: W. Watts, forward (Newport); J. Deacon, forward (Swansea); F. Mills, forward (Swansea); C, B, Nicoll, forward (Cambridge University and Llanelly); T. C. Graham, forward (Newport); J. hannen, forward (Newport). *Middle row, left to right:* T. W. Pearson, three-quarter back (Cardiff); R. Garrett, three-quarter back (Penarth); W. McCutcheon, three-quarter back (Oldham and Swansea); A. J. Gould, captain, three-quarter back (Newport); R. L. Thomas, forward (Llanelly); W. J. Bancroft, back (Swansea); A. W. Boucher, forward (Newport). *Front:* P. Phillips, half-back (Newport); G. Rowles, half-back (Penarth).

Rowland Lewis Thomas, Parciau, Henllan Amgoed, ready to do battle as a member
of the Wales XV that played England in 1892.
(Denley Owen collection).

Welsh. He was later to play for Llanelli and became a general practitioner at Parciau and coroner for west Carmarthenshire. He also became, with his great friend Captain David Garrick Protheroe of Glyntaf near Llanglydwen, a keen follower of the Carmarthenshire Hunt. When he passed away in 1949, his hunting clothes were placed in the coffin and the hunting horn was sounded at the end of the burial service.

In early February 1889, the Press Association reported that W. R. H. Powell was in a dangerous condition at Maesgwynne. And despite the family denying this and claiming that he had always been delicate, they admitted in the *South Wales Daily News* that he was very unwell and was confined to bed but was no worse than he had been for some weeks past. The report in the *Carmarthen Journal* on 15 February 1889 that Powell was 'weak and dangerously ill' was not disputed.

In May 1889, Lewis Llewellyn Dillwyn MP for Swansea, at long last, was able to bring his Bill for Disestablishment of the Church of England in Wales before Parliament. The Bill was lost by 284 votes to 233. Wales' MPs voted overwhelmingly in favour by 27 votes to 4 with 3 abstentions. Obviously, one of the absentees was Powell and he must have been disappointed with the result because he had campaigned for disestablishment for over a quarter of a century. On the other hand he would have welcomed the huge advance in support from the 45 that had supported the 1870 bill.[79]

At the Hunt Ball in 1948 but born in the age of Powell Bach. *Left:* Capt. David Garrick Protheroe, JP (1869-1951)
of Glyntaf, Llanglydwen, for 30 years Master of the Pembrokeshire and Carmarthenshire Otter Hounds.
Right: Dr Rowland Lewis Thomas (1862-1949) of Parciau, Henllan Amgoed, a famous
Welsh Rugby International, 1889-1892. They had followed the hunt in W. R. H. Powell's days.
In the centre is MFH, Lt. Col. W. H. Buckley.

'May they "keep the tambourine a'rolling" for many years to come'.

(Courtesy Carmarthenshire County Museum).

Powell's enthusiasm and commitment to his duties as an MP knew no bounds. J. L. Walters, chemist at Llanboidy, was with Powell at Maesgwynne a few days before his death. At one point it was thought that Powell had, in fact, passed away and Walters left the room. When he returned some time later he was amazed to find Powell busy writing letters and the excuse he gave for doing so was that 'he had no time to spare'!

W. R. H. Powell MP died at his home Maesgwynne, Llanboidy, on 25 June 1889 at 70 years of age. He had suffered from heart disease, and acutely so, for the previous two years. He had been a conscientious and radical Liberal Member of Parliament since 1880 and his complete loyalty to his duties led *The Welshman* on 28 June 1889 to claim that 'those that pressed him' after his health broke down in 1887 to go back to Parliament 'have been guilty of great cruelty . . . he might have been allowed to spend the rest of his days quietly in breathing the air of his native hills, which he loved so well.' The report went on to say that when his health was tolerable, hardly any member except the whips was present at so many divisions as W. R. H.

Powell to vote in the Liberal interest. But *The Welshman* still could not hide its Whig credentials as it repeated its line that he was not looked upon as a Liberal before 1874 but that 'of late years he adopted the whole of the extreme Liberal programme.' At the same time the report claimed that the 'Conservative squires who had hunted with him for 50 years esteemed him no less in his social capacity because of his political views.' *The Welshman* went on to describe Powell as a popular country squire who enjoyed his sport and was always planning some improvement for the benefit of his village of Llanboidy and the farmers living around. And it highlighted his efforts during 1874 and 1876 to establish a Benefit Society to help cottagers and labourers in west sWales. The *Western Mail* reckoned that 'Powell Bach Maesgwynne' had few if any personal enemies even though his fox hunting craze would not have have found favour with the 'prim Puritans' who, 'as Radicals were enrolled under his banner.' Although not a great orator, at least according to the *Western Mail*, he invariably drew large audiences whenever a political address by him was announced. 'His discourses, couched in simple, unaffected

Reverend William Thomas (Tomos Llanboidy) (1862-1931), minister at Trinity Independent Chapel, Llanboidy, from 1885. He was a radical who was elected county councillor for Llanboidy in 1913.

(Eddie Evans collection).

language, were delivered in an easy conversational style. They did not indicate previous preparation, but as a matter of fact he generally committed his speeches to writing.'

The funeral took place on Saturday, 30 June 1889. The family's public announcement that it was to be a private funeral failed to deter, not only the local community, but also leading Liberals and gentry of west Wales and further afield, from turning up to pay their last tribute to the popular Squire of Maesgwynne. Not unexpectedly, bearing in mind his life-long championing of the Nonconformist cause of disestablishment, the service at Maesgwynne Mansion was in the hands of his friend and local Baptist minister, Reverend D. S. Davies, Cwmfelin Mynach. The following Sunday afternoon Mrs Powell and family of Maesgwynne attended Trinity Independent Chapel, Llanboidy, to hear a memorial sermon delivered by the Reverend William Thomas (Tomos Llanboidy) to a large congregation.

3.10 The politician assessed

The *Carmarthen Journal* in its obituary of 28 June 1889 followed its usual line of admiring Powell as a country gentleman who played and worked hard in his locality but it could not resist showing its political hostility, even in its obituary report: 'As a politician, Mr Powell has not left any remarkable record behind . . . he had not given the required attention to politics that would have made him a man of judgement and insight.'

Others, however, thought differently. One of those was Independent minister and author, the Reverend Benjamin Davies, born in 1878 at Blaencwmfallen, Llanboidy. His parents were

Trinity Independent Chapel, Llanboidy, where Powell's widow and family attended a memorial service
conducted by the Reverend William Thomas.
(Courtesy National Library of Wales).

tenants of W. R. H. Powell and his father worked as a groom at Maesgwynne. In 1953, Ben Davies in his *Cofiant Tomos Llanboidy* wrote that 'Powell believed in Christianity's practical influence on life as a whole . . . the belief that politics was either too dirty to touch or it should be used under Christian principle to save the world.' Davies recalled that in W. R. H. Powell's time, the village (Llanboidy) was 'alive with support for Liberalism'.

One who knew Powell well was the Reverend William Thomas (Tomos Llanboidy) and he was full of admiration for Powell's thinking and actions in the field of education. As an MP, Powell had called for government money to fund free-schooling for labourers' children and for the school curriculum to be free of denominational influence. He also called for the inclusion of agricultural science as a subject in local schools because of its importance in improving farming practice. The Reverend Thomas maintained that Powell had been far ahead of his time in his thinking on education. He believed in educating the working class and 'had provided for the education of the neighbourhood [of Llanboidy] long before any government had dreamt of projecting [*sic*] a scheme.' Thomas summed up W. R. H. Powell as 'by birth, an aristocrat, by conviction a democrat, by faith a theocrat . . . [but] . . . by Christian necessity a reformer.'[80]

Land reform was high on the list of radicals' demands but the *Western Mail* was utterly opposed and the paper's identification of Powell as the leading advocate of reform in Wales together with its accusations that he was propagating communistic doctrines served only to underline Powell's considerable stature as a politician.[27] He was, undoubtedly, the magnet which attracted the reform-minded Farmers' Alliance to Carmarthen for their first meeting in Wales.[28]

112

Powell was relentless in calling for a Land Act for Wales and his warning that as things stood men and money were forced abroad to farm, making the home population dependent on foreign-grown food which should be home-produced, was more evidence of the insight which the *Carmarthen Journal* professed not to find in the MP.[22]

Further evidence that politics to Powell was a thinking-man's game was provided at a meeting of the West Carmarthenshire Liberal Association at the Assembly Rooms, Carmarthen on 1 July 1889. The assembled delegates heard the highly respected 50-year-old minister of Water Street Methodist Chapel, Carmarthen, the Reverend John Wyndham Lewis, say: 'Mr Powell was a very able man, far abler than many were disposed to admit. His ideas on all social and political questions were remarkably clear; and I have no hesitation in saying that he was as advanced in his views as any man in the House of Commons.' As an example he referred to a matter close to Powell's heart: '[He] was very advanced in his views on the land question; he went as far as to say that money deposited in the bank should receive no interest. Labour, in his opinion, was the only thing that should be rewarded.' Wyndham Lewis was of the opinion that Mr Powell was one of the best members that was ever sent from Wales to the House of Commons. 'He was a faithful and conscientious member. He knew when to vote without conferring with us and he knew when it was his duty not to vote without consulting the views and wishes of his constituents. I know of no man that could do this better than W. R. H. Powell.'[81]

Powell's attendance at divisions of the House was rarely bettered and his remarkable voting record together with his expert knowledge of the processes of getting bills through the House and on to the statute book made him a formidable parliamentary figure.[35]

Therefore, the *Carmarthen Journal*'s assertion that Powell 'had no judgement or insight' was not supported by the evidence from the above sources.

The same newspaper's claim that Powell had 'not left any remarkable record behind' was also contrary to the facts. In the first place, the *Journal* had often published Powell's voting record in the House of Commons admitting it was second to none. And, for the first time ever in the history of Carmarthenshire, those votes were invariably cast for the radical interests for which he was publicly praised by highly respected radicals in his constituency, such as the Reverend J. Wyndham Lewis of Carmarthen and the Reverend William Thomas of Whitland. Secondly, at home in the constituency Powell had regularly 'preached' the radical Liberal message at meetings throughout Carmarthenshire and had succeeded in transforming an expected Tory seat into a safe Liberal one. In fact Powell had laid the foundation for the seat to remain in radical hands as, in time, it passed from Liberal to Labour to Plaid Cymru. Thirdly, his work in assisting his constituents was certainly remarkable and was praised by numerous speakers at the Liberal gathering. For example, the meeting's chairman, W. O. Brigstocke, a barrister, said that: '"Trouble" was a word unknown to [Powell]. Not merely did he extend care and solitude towards his own personal supporters, but he also extended it to those who were his political opponents.' He added that as an MP, Powell 'frequently wrote from sixty to seventy letters a day. No man ever made an application to Mr Powell that did not get a cordial reply.'

Bagnall Evans of Nant-yr-Eglwys, Llanboidy, who knew Powell 'as a neighbour' reckoned that Powell spent his life working 'for the material help and for the social advancement of all classes of people about him . . . his own district and neighbourhood was, during his lifetime, turned from a comparative wilderness into a paradise entirely by his devices and plans . . . he

W. R. H. Powell, MP.
(Eddie Evans collection).

was always an early riser [and] until [well] into the night he was engaged in some way or other doing good to the district and to those about him. I know this country pretty well and I tell you that the equal of Mr Powell socially, politically and in many other ways is not to be found in the whole of the Principality.' Bagnall Evans recalled that Powell had, for years, called for local control of local taxes and the passing of the Local Government Act in 1888 setting up county councils had given him much pleasure. After the council elections of January 1889, the county councils became operative on 1 April 1889. To its credit, one of the first decisions made by Carmarthenshire County Council was to offer to nominate W. R. H. Powell to be an Alderman . . . and 'he felt deeply the compliment paid him.'

Therefore, contrary to the *Journal*'s charge, the evidence outlined above is that W. R. H. Powell, as a politician, had in fact left behind him a remarkable record. And even the *Journal* in its 5 July 1889 issue seemed to have had second thoughts, at least so far as his performance as a constituency MP was concerned, by its admission that: 'Perhaps Mr Powell's character as a politician showed best outside St Stephens . . . no matter how humble the constituent he could always obtain a hearing, a kind word and, if practicable the fulfilment of his desires. And his help and courtesy extended to friend and foe alike . . . political foe that is . . . personal foe he had none.'

The main purpose of the Liberals' meeting was to select a candidate for the by-election for the West Carmarthenshire seat. Bagnall Evans and others reminded those present of Powell's view that the great question before the people of Wales . . . the one great and absorbing question . . . was the disestablishment and disendowment of the Church. Furthermore, Powell had felt that the cause of disestablishment would be best secured in West Carmarthenshire by having a Nonconformist as his successor in Parliament. Mr Stephens of the Kidwelly Liberal Association and others expressed their support because it had been a matter of the greatest importance to Mr Powell and nothing would have pleased him more than to be succeeded in West Carmarthenshire by a Nonconformist Liberal member committed to disestablishment. Reverend Wyndham Lewis' final comment was: 'He [Powell] was all-together an exemplary character; and if we are anxious to respect his memory, we ought to select, this afternoon, an advanced Liberal and a Nonconformist to represent us in the British House of Commons (applause).' Their wish was granted with the selection of 28-year-old Cambridge educated John Lloyd Morgan, a barrister whose father, the Reverend William Morgan, born at the Forge, Whitland, had been a professor at the Carmarthen Presbyterian College and minister of Union Street Independent Chapel, Carmarthen. J. Lloyd Morgan duly won the seat and held it for 21 years before giving it up in 1910 to become a County Court Judge. He was succeeded by another Liberal, John Hinds.

3.11 END PIECE: A truly remarkable man of the people

The emergence of the Squire of Maesgwynne, W. R. H. Powell, as a radical Liberal politician in the 1870s and 1880s in Carmarthenshire was remarkable, bearing in mind that his ilk, the gentry, were in the first place usually in the Tory camp and, secondly were in serious decline as community and political leaders from the 1860s onwards. The second half of the nineteenth century saw the growth and development of a Welsh national consciousness based on Nonconformism, the Welsh language and the Liberal Party which left the aristocracy adrift in their anglicanism, English language and Tory politics.

But the Squire of Maesgwynne was an aristocrat apart!

He may have been an Anglican and gone to church on Sunday but for the rest of the week he was a Nonconformist. 'Wales is a nation of Nonconformists!' was Powell's proud boast in 1883 to the audience in Finsbury's Welsh Baptist Chapel in London. Some of his closest friends were Nonconformist ministers such as the Baptist D. S. Davies of Cwmfelin Mynach and the Independents William Thomas of Whitland and his namesake of Llanboidy.

In Llanboidy, Powell bridged the Nonconformist/Anglican divide in education by building and running a school at his own expense where the teaching of religious dogma was prohibited.

His action was in response to the Archdeacon's insistence that the Anglican catechism be taught in the village's existing church school, thus effectively barring Nonconformists' children from attending.

Powell's lifelong efforts to improve the lot of the poor and of the tenant farmers, and his constant advocacy of a fair and just deal for Nonconformists in the matters of church tithes and taxes, and his demand for local control over spending of local taxes made it natural for him to embrace all of the Liberal movement's radical policies. Indeed, his Friendly Society for west Wales labourers paid ill-health and pension benefits fully thirty years before a Liberal government matched it with a statutory scheme introduced by another Welsh radical, David Lloyd George.

The Welshman's professed surprise (see 3.2) at Powell's acceptance of radical policies it labelled 'destructive' showed the paper to be no more than a Whig relic.

His inability to make a speech in Welsh proved not to be the handicap it might have been to him becoming the Liberal member for the Welsh-speaking Nonconformist Carmarthenshire. The importance of the Welsh language in the developing national consciousness was simply that it was spoken in every home and in every chapel . . . warnings of its inevitable future demise in the face of English schoolmasters were still being largely ignored. Little wonder therefore that the immensely popular Powell's oft-made apology for his lack of fluency in Welsh was readily accepted by a mainly unconcerned public.

At the same time he played his full part in satisfying the community's linguistic and cultural expectations. For example, he gave his full support to the tailoring of church services in Llanboidy to meet the needs of a Welsh-listening congregation with the concession of the sermon being repeated in English. When the handful of monoglot English attenders complained at the length of the service and their inability to understand most of it, the vicar's curt reply of 'take it or leave' must have had W. R. H. Powell's full support. Welsh cultural events were backed to the hilt by the Maesgwynne family. They organised and performed in concerts at Llanboidy and attended concerts and eisteddfodau over a wide area of west Wales.

When all the above is taken into account, it can confidently be claimed that the Squire of Maesgwynne was not of his ilk. Rather, Powell stood with the common people and became the answer to their yearning for a spokesman implicit in the Rebeccaite's lament 'we have no voice'.

As early as 1866 ordinary people were clamouring for Powell to become the 'member for Wales' and they had their wish in 1880 with his election as MP for Carmarthenshire. His record as an MP was one of outstanding service and total commitment to the Liberal party in parliament, to his constituents irrespective of their political leanings or their social status and to spreading his strongly held beliefs in reform and justice throughout his constituency.

Through his lifelong actions as a leader determined to improve the lot of his local and wider community and by his persistent pronouncements in favour of the progressive programme of reforms of the Liberal movement, W. R. H. Powell can truly be said to have been Carmarthenshire's first radical Member of Parliament.

Part IV

THE RISE AND FALL OF LLANBOIDY RACES

4.1 Introduction

A T A DINNER in his honour in the Farmers' Arms, Llanboidy, in April 1848, the 29-year-old W. R. H. Powell was complimented for being a kind landlord, a good neighbour and as 'indefatigable in his exertions to afford sport'.[1] On the one hand, he was a typical squire in his uptake of sport to fill his spare time but on the other hand, his extraordinary efforts to provide 'good sport' for all to enjoy, again, made him a squire apart.

The growth in popularity of sport in the first decades of the nineteenth century had the beneficial social effect of enabling people of all classes, ages and background to meet and mix although, as Peter Radford in his *The Celebrated Captain Barclay* pointed out, the social gulf was too wide to be bridged easily. Cricket, for example, was a game in which the gentry produced teams made up of themselves and their employees. Frederick Prince of Wales played in such a team and in a match in 1751 when he was 44-years-old he was hit on the head by a cricket ball and died. So it was that George II was followed on the throne by his grandson rather than his son.

If cricket did not appeal to W. R. H. Powell, pigeon shooting, foxhunting and horse racing certainly did. In 1839 he was listed as a holder of a game certificate.[2] At Maesgwynne he had a lake, Llyn Maesgwynne, which attracted, for example, wild ducks to keep company with the home-bred water birds. He and his brother, Thomas Rees Oliver Powell, organised pigeon-shooting matches at Maesgwynne at which a dozen or more squires, from Carmarthenshire and adjoining counties, competed. However, for most of the gentry at that time, horse racing and fox hunting were the main activities which helped fill their ample free time. But Carmarthenshire was not well served in that respect. Horse racing was still to take off and although fox-hunting had become popular the packs of hounds in Carmarthenshire were usually small and some, such as Grismond Philipps' pack at Cwmgwili, were maintained for the pleasure of a few friends. W. R. H. Powell was to change all that. At Maesgwynne, he developed what has been described as a village-size complex to accommodate his sporting interests. It included 'a circular riding school, ranges of racehorse and hunter stables, carriage-houses, and kennels for hounds, terriers and spaniels.' There was a 'round Lodge' built in the 1840s with a thatched roof, similar to 'the one at nearby Glyntaf, now gone.'[3] (There was also a round house, still standing in the 1950s, near Dolwilym Mansion which was called Cottage, Llanglydwen, although it was more commonly known as *Y Tŷ Rownd*.)

In 1839, Powell took time off from seeking reconciliation with the Rebecca protesters and founded his own pack of foxhounds, the 'Maesgwynne'. Some years previously, probably

Cottage, Llanglydwen, a round house near Cromlech y Filiast on the Dolwilym estate of the Protheroes.
Known as *Y Tŷ Rownd*, it was still standing in the 1950s.
(Denley Owen collection).

Y Dyn Bach and his hounds.
(Thomas Lloyd collection).

during his time at Oxford, he had made contact with a legendary sportsman from Yorkshire, Squire George Osbaldeston, who had his own pack of hounds from the age of sixteen. W. R. H. Powell secured the services of Osbaldeston's famous dog 'Vanguard' and paired him with a bitch 'Mayfly' from a pack in Cynwyl, probably the pack founded by successful farmer and noted sportsman Evan Evans of Pant-y-Cendy near Abernant. The resulting litter was the basis of the Maesgwynne pack which was to dominate hunting in Carmarthenshire in the second half of the nineteenth century.[4] As Martin Johnes observed: 'Running a private pack and providing the dinners that were essential to a good day's hunting required wealth, and hunting was thus a way of actually signalling one's position in society. Working-class participation took the form of watching or following the grand spectacle of the huntsmen in order to brighten up what were otherwise often dull and hard lives.'[5]

In the early 1840s part of Carmarthenshire was hunted by the 'Carmarthen Hounds' (sometimes called the 'Carmarthenshire Hounds' in newspaper reports), a small private pack owned by Lieutenant Browne Edwardes and his father Captain David Edwardes Esq of Rhydygors, Johnstown, Carmarthen. The *Carmarthen Journal* of 18 February 1842 listed five packs due to meet at different locations during the following week: the Carmarthen Hounds at Green Court on Tuesday and at Bancyfelin on Friday; the Pant-y-Cendy scheduled for Castell Gorfod on Tuesday and the three others were the Tivy Side, the Begelly and the Pembrokeshire . . . no mention of W. R. H. Powell's hounds in that week's paper. On the death of the MFH of Pant-y-Cendy, the country previously hunted by his pack was taken over by W. R. H. Powell and he bought several drafts of the Pant-y-Cendy hounds. In 1843 *The Welshman* carried a report headed 'Powell's Hounds' and claimed that 'Fox-hunting seems to flourish here this season more than ever. Capital runs are as plenty as black berries were in September.' It went on to describe a meet where a fox was raised in Forge woods near Whitland Abbey. It went over Cwm-mynach to Cross Inn as if aiming for Kilsant but 'he turned left over Goitre to Esgerddwygoed, Vronysgawen, Rhydypark and on to Maengwynhir, over Clydey mountain to the village of Star and then, right over Nantycastell and Drysgolgoch, skirting plantations at Dyffryn and came to the end on the banks of the Cych a little above Cwm-morgan. A splendid run of 2 hours and 20 minutes without a single check.' Measured on a map that run covered about 20 miles![6]

Another prominent pack in west Wales was the one belonging to an interesting character, Captain James Mark Child the colliery-owning squire of Begelly, an 'occasional Nonconformist, former titular gamekeeper to Lord Milford, and cousin of Sir Richard Philipps . . . A Radical, he had protested against representation [of Pembrokeshire in Parliament] by a "stranger".'[7] (In 1838, Sir James Graham, a protégé of Sir Robert Peel's had been 'accommodated' as MP for Pembroke Boroughs after losing his seat in England.) The *Carmarthen Journal*'s hunting listings in the early months of 1843 included several joint meets of Mr Child's and Mr Powell's hounds. For example, at Milton Mill and at Tavernspite in January; at Trewern Gate and again at Tavernspite in February. The joint 'meets' were an indication that the two squires were on very friendly terms and were probably on the same wavelength politically. But it would be some time yet, before Powell Bach showed his radicalism in the political field. In January 1843 a 'Tremendous Run' resulted from a joint meet at the Commercial Inn, Llanddewi. The reporter's reference to 'Vron' quarry and the 'Tave' river gave the game away that he was completely ignorant of the Welsh language and was in all probability writing down the words 'Fron' and 'Taf' as they sounded in his monoglot English ears. The river claimed . . . 'about twenty gents dipped . . . and at Coedllys the cry on all sides was . . . bellows to mend.' Sixty riders had followed the hounds for two and a half hours over twenty-five miles. 'The scene homewards resembled the scattering of the twelve tribes of Israel. The horses from Tenby must have travelled at least seventy six miles.'[8]

4.2 Races at Meidrim

Running in parallel with the growth of fox hunting was the growth in horse racing: on the flat and over banks and hurdles. Steeplechasing got its name from the practice of racing across country from one church steeple to another and may have started in Ireland in the eighteenth century. The first 'Grand Liverpool Steeplechase' was organised by Aintree innkeeper, William Lynn, in 1836 but since it was run on only part of the Aintree course settled on in 1839, the dispute continues as to which was the first Grand National. Steeplechases were got up at Haverfordwest in 1834 and at Abergavenny in 1836.

In the early 1840s numerous additional annual steeplechases were promoted, and the sport became 'completely the rage'. The great events at Haverfordwest, Tivyside and Aberystwyth were joined by those at Carmarthen, Castlemartin, Narberth and 'lately Mydrim'. The *Carmarthen Journal* reporter rode about nine miles to Meidrim on a fine day, 26 April 1848, where he found vehicles of all descriptions including a 'four-in-hand' and a still more numerous host of pedestrians of all kinds, grades and qualities and a goodly company of ladies. The gentlemen he had 'noticed' as being present included, W. Chambers jnr of Llanelli, Timothy Powell, R. Lort Phillips of Lawrenny, Browne Edwardes, Xavier Peel, W. R. H. Powell, W. Protheroe of Dolwilym, Rice Pryce Beynon, St Clears, J. T. Beynon, Trewern, Lampeter Velfrey, Nathaniel Rowlands of Parke, Henllan Amgoed. Also there were the Reverends Evan Jones, minister of Ffynnonbedr and Rhys Jenkins, vicar of Meidrim. The start of the course was in a field on Carllegan Farm, home of Lawford Evans, about a mile above the village and the race was over three miles of country and consisted of two laps which took in between fifty and sixty leaps . . . 'not a few of which were regular raspers'. The race was a handicap steeplechase, of £1 each with no less than £15 added, for horses regularly hunted with the Carmarthenshire or the Maesgwynne Hunts.

Seven horses were entered but not necessarily by their owners. W. R. H. Powell's 'Cabin Boy', Mr Olive's 'Selim' and W. Prothero's 'Cadno' were all owned by W. R. H. Powell. Tom Davies of Hayes Farm near Pembroke, 'Hero of a Hundred Steeplechases', rode 'Cabin Boy', John Crymes James, solicitor of Haverfordwest, rode 'Cadno' and his brother James Rice James (Gipsy), farmer of Rogerstone, Nolton, Pembrokeshire, rode 'Selim'. The brothers were the sons of Haverfordwest attorney and solicitor Morgan R. James and his wife Mary Ann. 'Ponsonby', entered by Timothy Powell, was the property of E. Gwyn, Pilroath, Llangain. He was difficult to control so he had to put up with a special 'sharp bit' and his jockey George Griffiths, whip to Edwardes' pack, did not wear spurs. Tenant farmer, Mr D. H. Thomas of Derllys, near Travellers' Rest, two miles west of Carmarthen, was the owner and jockey of 'Dandelion' and with only 9st.12lb. to carry, 'Dandelion' attracted a lot of bets. After leading for most of the race six-year-old 'Cadno' carrying 10st.7lb. ran out of steam and eventually finished last. In failing to clear a fence, Browne Edwardes' highly favoured 'Nimrod' fell and interfered with 'Dandelion' thereby shattering many a punter's dream. The winner by half a length was aged but wild 'Ponsonby' carrying 11st.

Another race came off; it was a Farmers' Stake of 10 shillings plus £5 added. Farmers complained that the entry fee of 10 shillings was too high and only two horses entered. Their complaint was understandable because £1 in 1848 was the equivalent of about £100 today! The winner, 'Bob', was owned by tenant farmer Mr David Davies, Gelligeirad and the loser, 'Bess', was, according to *The Welshman*, the property of W. Protheroe, Dolwilym, although the *Journal* claimed that it was entered by a Mr Evans. During the evening dinner at the Fountain Inn arrangements were made to make the steeplechases a yearly event and nearly £50 in subscriptions was collected. It was also agreed, undoubtedly under the influence of Powell Bach, that the 1849 races would come off at Llanboidy and Browne Edwardes and W. R. H. Powell agreed to act as stewards. No record has been found of another steeplechase meeting at Meidrim but Llanboidy Races became established as an annual event, and so there is every reason to claim that the first 'Llanboidy Races' came off at Meidrim!

April 1848 was a busier month than usual for W. R. H. Powell because in addition to his twice-weekly fox hunts and attending steeplechase meetings, he was summoned to attend at the Farmers' Arms, Llanboidy at six o'clock on Tuesday, 25 April 1848. On the morning of that day a fine dog fox was turned out in front of Maesgwynne House at 10.00 a.m.; the unacceptable face of fox hunting laid bare. After the hunt, about forty gentlemen sat down to dinner at the Farmers' Arms with J. G. Lewis, barrister at law, of Henllan in the chair, assisted by W. Chambers, junior, of Llanelli. During the course of the evening, W. R. H. Powell was presented with a plate inscribed:

Presented to
W. R. H. Powell Esq
of Maesgwynne as a testimonial
of the high esteem and regard
entertained towards him by his neighbours
and friends and of their gratitude
for the pleasure afforded
them by his hounds.
April 25 1848[9]

About a week previously, members of the Carmarthen Hunt had paid tribute to their MFH, Browne Edwardes, at a dinner at the Golden Lion Hotel, Carmarthen.

Perhaps the most important decision made by W. R. H. Powell in 1848 was to employ John (Jack) Rees as a groom at Maesgwynne. John Rees, born in Abergwili parish in 1819, had been a jockey in the services of Bowen Davies, Maesycrugiau in Llanllwni parish since he was 15 years of age. Bowen Davies had the largest and most successful stable of racehorses in Wales and Jack Rees proved an outstanding jockey and enjoyed a string of successes on the flat at the old Carmarthen racecourse at Alltygog and at Aberystwyth, Haverfordwest, Cowbridge,

Brecon, Monmouth and Swansea. Further afield, Bowen Davies' horses with Jack Rees in the saddle were often victorious at Hereford, Ludlow and Wrexham. On the death of Bowen Davies, Jack Rees transferred his services to W. R. H. Powell, Maesgwynne and he became as successful a jockey over banks as he had been on the flat.

When he joined the staff at Maesgwynne in 1848, Jack Rees was put in charge of Powell's stud, and he was also appointed whip to the Maesgwynne pack of hounds under Powell as huntsman. And that remained the arrangement for the following nineteen years. There was a year's break during 1860/61 when Jack Rees took over the Lamb Inn and farm in Llanboidy.

4.3 Hunting and Racing at Llanboidy

Two races come off

The year, 1849, was historic in that on 10 April the first ever 'Llanboidy Races' took place. It is easy to imagine that it had excited a considerable degree of interest in the neighbourhood . . . and that it afforded some excellent sport. The stewards were the recently honoured MFHs, W. R. H. Powell and Browne Edwardes.

The first race was a sweepstake of two sovereigns each with twenty sovereigns added, for horses regularly hunted in Carmarthenshire. Gentlemen riders allowed 7lb. There were only four entries and the practice of running heats was used to extend the entertainment. The first horse to win two heats was the race winner.

RESULT OF THE FIRST EVER RACE IN THE FIRST EVER LLANBOIDY RACES HELD ON 10 APRIL 1849						
Owner	*Horse*	*Weight*	*Heat 1*	*Heat 2*	*Heat 3*	*Rider*
Mr Protheroe	Cabin Boy	11st. 7lb.	3	1	1	Owen
Mr Jones	Becca	10st. 12lb.	1	2	3	Griffiths
Mr Powell	Cadno	11st. 4lb.	4	4	2	Rees
Mr Howell	Dandelion	10st. 8lb.	2	3	dr	Woodman

Of the four horses entered, at least two, 'Cabin Boy' and 'Cadno', were owned by W. R. H. Powell.

The other race was a 'catchweight' between two horses; Mr Williams' 'Gilbert' ridden by Powell's star jockey Jack Rees, and Llanboidy GP, Doctor Charles Lewis Crosswell's 'Llanboidy Lass' with the country's top steeplechase rider, Tom Davies of Hayes Farm near Pembroke, in the saddle. 'Gilbert', being a far superior horse, won easily.[10] The races, probably, took place on land near Cefnbrafle, a few miles south-east from Maesgwynne. On the other hand it may have been the occasion when Llanboidy GP, Doctor Cresswell, rode his horse to victory and 30 sovereigns on Bronyscawen common a few miles north-west of Maesgwynne.

The day was likely to have been brought to a close with a dinner at the Farmers' Arms, Llanboidy.

The Maesgwynne 'crack pack' takes over

Before the end of 1849 the future of Browne Edwardes' Carmarthen Hounds was a cause for concern. After some initial contradictory reports in the newspapers as to the future of the pack, the fact that it was a meet of Mr Powell's Hounds, rather than Browne Edwardes', that kicked off the 1850 Carmarthenshire Hunt Week indicated that the Carmarthen pack was then defunct. In fact, by that time Powell had bought the Carmarthen pack and had taken over the country previously hunted by Browne Edwardes. The meet to start the Carmarthenshire Hunt Week was at the Plough and Harrow in Newchurch parish on the Conwil [Cynwyl Elfed] old road about two miles from town. 'The gallant pack, hunted by that most zealous sportsman and true Welsh Squire, W. R. H. Powell Esq of Maesgwynne, assembled at 10 o'clock'.[11]

It is likely that the dinner held in honour of W. R. H. Powell, MFH, during March 1850 at the Golden Lion, Carmarthen, was an acknowledgement of his commitment to securing the future of fox hunting in the county. Thirty-five gentlemen sat down to dinner at 6 o'clock having been denied a day's hunting by the atrocious weather.

Under W. R. H. Powell's leadership as Master of Fox Hounds, fox-hunting in Carmarthenshire became the sport, not only of the squires but also of the lesser gentry[10] and if Tom Rees in his *Racing Reminiscences* is to be believed, meets would also have given pleasure to 'every heart': 'Villagers come to their garden gates; labourers cease from their toils in the fields; children leave their tasks in the village academy, and everybody makes room for the hounds to pass. . . . Certainly there is no surer way of enraging a community than by doing an injury to a foxhound. Any man who does so is branded with the infamy of his foul deed.'[12]

But as already mentioned, maintaining a private pack was an expensive business and so it was for Powell Bach as implied by the following notice which appeared in the *Carmarthen Journal* on 23 August 1850, 'The Carmarthenshire Foxhounds: . . . W. R. H. Powell Esq. of Maesgwynne has handsomely consented to hunt the Carmarthen district with his celebrated pack provided the gentlemen of Carmarthenshire contribute their quota towards the increased expense . . . the neighbouring gentry should at once set the example by forwarding the amount of their subscription to the secretary.' His appeal is proof, if proof were needed, that W. R. H. Powell's reason for maintaining a pack of hounds had nothing to do with signalling his position in society but was entirely to do with his addiction to the sport. The appeal for funds was successful because a month later 'Mr Powell's Hounds' met at Llanddowror. By October 1850 the pack, sometimes referred to as 'The Carmarthenshire Foxhounds', was making successful visits to its expanded hunting country: 'The crack pack met yesterday morning at Ystrad Lodge. This being the first time the Hounds met in the neighbourhood of Carmarthen this season, a great number of the inhabitants of the town assembled to witness the meet. . . . We shall throughout the season give occasional reports of the runs.'[13]

Ystrad Lodge was about a mile west of Carmarthen and about fifteen miles from the pack's kennels at Maesgwynne and it is likely that on the day before the meet the whip, Jack Rees, would have brought the hounds to the kennels at Travellers' Rest, a mile or so from Johnstown, (named after John Jones yr Halen) to spend the night. One reason for referring to the pack as the 'The Carmarthenshire Foxhounds' was that Powell had by then started hunting the country previously hunted by the Browne Edwardes' 'Carmarthenshire Hounds'. In addition it may be that subscriptions had come in from far and wide and that 'Carmarthenshire' was a concession to such county-wide support.

During the first half of the 1850-51 season, meets were held twice a week at places such as Wenallt Lodge, Efailwen, Laugharne, Whitland Abbey, Llanddowror, Francis Well Turnpike Gate, Plas Panthowell, Trevaughan Bridge, near Whitland, Green Castle, near Llangain, Clogyfran Bridge, Llanfallteg Bridge, Maesycrigie Lodge, Cynwyl, Red Roses, Rhydyceisiaid Bridge, Lan Gate and, just over the border in Pembrokeshire, at Llangolman.

In February 1851 in a speech during that year's Carmarthenshire Hunt Week, of which he was the leading organiser, W. R. H. Powell emphasised the fact that he was not in the business of running a pack of hounds for the glory or the prestige associated with it. 'He [Powell] lived at a great distance and although he found it hard work in leaving home so early in the morning and returning late at night, he would still afford them all the sport in his power . . . [But] . . . He really thought they ought to have a subscription pack of foxhounds in the county and he wished some gentlemen would take the management of the hounds (cries of No, No). He considered that every county should possess a subscription pack and he, although his means were limited, would most cheerfully subscribe £50 to them, but so long as he continued as MFH he would most willingly show them all the sport in his power.' The chairman, David Jones of Pantglas, Llanfynydd, who became MP for Carmarthenshire in 1852, drew applause when he intimated that if Mr Powell wished he would be happy to support the hounds and hunt the county jointly with himself. David Jones also promised to subscribe £50 towards a stake in the following year's Carmarthenshire race meeting for horses bred in the county by farmers and ridden by tenant farmers. David Jones might well have thought it wise to boost W. R. H. Powell's spirits which had, probably, been dented by the dreadful weather during that year's Carmarthenshire Hunt Week, and the poorly-attended Dinner.[14] Some years later the pack was supported by a small subscription for three years but after 1860 Powell hunted the country at his own expense.[4]

Another race got up at Llanboidy

The final meet of the 1850-51 hunting season was at Llanboidy on Tuesday, 22 April 1851. But it was no ordinary meet because the day started with a horse race. '. . . a Scurry Steeple Chase Stakes was got up in honour of the occasion which was confined to members of the hunt and no trained horse was allowed to enter. The ground selected was near Llanboidy over two miles of fair hunting country. Eight gallant members were up in the pigskin (leather made from a pig's skin), and it was a well contested race throughout; Mr Powell, the MFH, winning with 'Cadno'. . . . Afterwards, all enjoyed a splendid cold collation at . . . Maesgwynne where they were received . . . by the Master of the Carmarthenshire Hunt and his accomplished, amiable and beautiful bride and where "all went merry as a marriage bell".'[15] Powell had recently married his second wife, Catherine Ann Prudence Philipps of Cwmgwili near Carmarthen. After the cold lunch they went hunting and killed three foxes near Dolwilym before ending the day with a dinner at 'the hotel at Llanboidy', which would have been the Farmers' Arms. During the season the pack had been out on 60 days; had run into 38 foxes in the open – 21 to ground, 13 lost and had only 6 blank days. The report ended with a lightly-veiled warning/appeal that 'It now

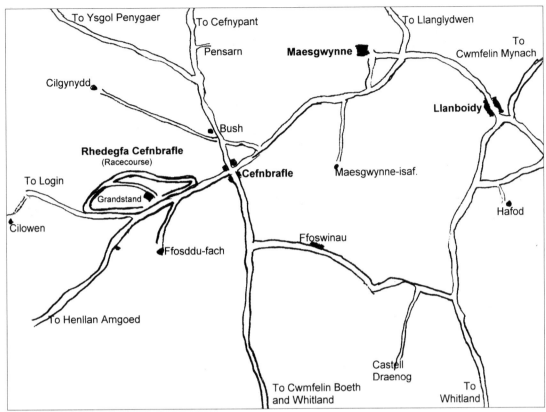

Rhedegfa Cefnbrafle (Racecourse plan).
(Denley Owen collection).

rests with the sportsmen of Carmarthenshire whether they [the hounds] be continued as Carmarthenshire Hounds or not'. The subscribers clearly needed some prodding to part with their money.[16]

The day's activities, of racing, luncheon at the mansion, hunting and dinner at the inn, undertaken in 1851 to celebrate the end of the hunting season, became the blueprint later developed into the week-long programme popularly known as Llanboidy Races.

On 16 October 1851 W. R. H. Powell attended what was advertised as a Public Hunt Dinner at the Ivy Bush, Carmarthen. Tickets (with bottle of wine) were 10s.6d. (52.5p). Presumably the dinner was an acknowledgement of W. R. H. Powell's service to hunting in Carmarthenshire. In the *Journal* report, W. R. H. Powell was referred to as the manager and he took the chair at the dinner and was supported by David Morris MP and the Hon. W. H. Yelverton of Whitland Abbey. In later years the amicable relationship between Powell and Yelverton was disrupted by the coming of the railway and the choice of a route for a rail link between Whitland and Cardigan.

The end-of-season races at Cefnbrafle, no doubt, encouraged W. R. H. Powell to act on his passion for horse racing by getting his own racecourse constructed. It was built in 1851 as was described in Part II and a few years later in 1857 the course was improved and a grandstand erected; evidence of W. R. H. Powell's determination to make the course second to none in Wales and, as we shall see, Llanboidy Races became an unique annual event in the racing calendar.

1852-1855 . . . A DAY at the races . . . great events at Llanboidy!

The first day-long programme of racing at Llanboidy took place on the new racecourse at Cefnbrafle on 30 March 1852. Newspaper reports made no reference to spectators being charged to enter the course. That was not surprising in the case of those on foot because it would be easy for them to gain entry over or through the hedges surrounding the course. Allowing them free entry would have also been consistent with Powell's continuous efforts to improve the lot of the ordinary people. On the other hand it would be easy to charge the visiting gentry in their coaches and that may well have been done. The meeting was well-organised with two army officers acting as stewards to supervise the action but there was no mention of bookmakers being present nor of beer tents and gaming booths on the ground to offer some alternative entertainment to the gathered throng.

'Probably the greatest amount of sport that has ever been witnessed in this part of the Principality in one day came off on Tuesday last at Llanboidy under the able stewardship of Major Hole and Captain Tighe of the 82nd Regiment of Foot. These races, . . . got up through the active exertions of . . . W. R. H. Powell Esq, took place . . . on the race course attached to the Maesgwynne estate about a mile-and-a-half above the pleasant village of Llanboidy . . . There had been snow on the previous Saturday and heavy rain on Monday. Tuesday morning was misty but the weather cleared about 2 o'clock. An immense concourse of spectators including several carriages of the neighbouring gentry and a goodly muster of officers of the 82nd Regiment together with most of the members of the Carmarthenshire Hunt assembled on the course to witness the great event of the day which was the much-talked-of match for £25 a side between Powell's mare "Esmerelda" ridden by the owner and, from Cresselly, Pembrokeshire, Mr Allen's horse "California" ridden by Mr W. Jones. The race was over two miles on the flat. Large sums of money were betted on this race which created much excitement.

Both riders had lost weight . . . and Mr Powell to a most extraordinary degree as when he came to the scales he was found to weigh only 8st.5lb. whilst Jones weighed 10st.5lb. This weight advantage it was thought would equalise the chances as "California" was known to be the swiftest horse. "Esmerelda" went off with the lead but after running a short distance, Mr Powell, who is near sighted, went the wrong side of one of the flags and was obliged to retrace his steps; this gave "California" a lead of some 50 to 100 yards [*Journal*] or some 200 yards [*The Welshman*] which he maintained throughout the race. Mr Powell was considerably amazed at the circumstances and offered to make a fresh match upon the same terms but this was declined by the opposing party.'

There were three other races which resulted in two wins for Powell. And then as *The Welshman* put it: 'A Donkey Race next ensued. . . . Mr Thomas' "Creeping Jane" won out of the eight Jerusalem ponies which started. A good deal of fun was created by the owner of each animal running behind it and continually thumping it with a large stick while the riders fully emulated their zeal in this respect.' (Jerusalem pony is a large species of donkey.)

After the races, an excellent repast was laid on at the Farmers' Arms, Llanboidy, by mine host Ben Griffiths at which W. R. H. Powell presided, assisted by D. F. Lewis Esq. of Carmarthen, and there was a packed attendance. Many of the attendees stayed over until the morning in order to go out with Mr Powell's hounds.[17]

The race meeting at Cefnbrafle in March 1852 would have brought great enjoyment to the local community who made up most of the 'great concourse of spectators'. The challenge race between the mare and the horse and the donkey derby must have provided topics for discussion in the locality for a long time afterwards. W. R. H. Powell was small of stature but *The Welshman*'s reporter was surprised when the Squire weighed in at only 8st.5lb. Therefore a strict diet must have been part of his preparation for the challenge race which is proof of his indomitable competitive spirit.

After the success of the day's racing in 1852 a period of consolidation took place over the following three years. The meeting continued as a one-day event of three races with two restricted to hunters of the Carmarthenshire Hunt and one open. The entertaining donkey race was discontinued after 1853. The prizes were standardized in terms of a sweepstake and added prize money. The races were limited to gentlemen riders so that, at that time, it was an amateur event compared to the Carmarthen and the Haverfordwest meetings where professional jockeys were allowed. [20,21]

The day's racing increased in popularity during those years and on Easter Monday, 9 April 1855 at 12 o'clock, it was to *Rhedegfa Cefnbrafle* that 'A vast concourse of spectators made their way. In fact at no former Steeplechase in the celebrated locality of Llanboidy has there been such an eagerness manifested to witness the fun as in this instance. Right well was all this anticipation repaid . . . the greatest possible credit is due on this as on all occasions to . . . W. R. H. Powell Esq, and to Oliver Powell Esq. [his brother] for the great pains and trouble they took in getting up these races, they having only had a fortnight's time for preparation and yet everything was in an orderly trim as if it had been put together a year previously.

The course . . . consisted of two miles of good hunting country interspersed here and there with turnip and ploughed fields, and with a great number of very stiff fences. This "line of march" had to be traversed twice in the case of the Hunt Steeplechase but only once in the Open Hurdle and the Hunt Hurdle.'

The three races were all of 3 sovereigns each with £20 added. In the Open Hurdle, W. R. H. Powell rode 'Esmerelda' to victory out of four starters but he could only steer 'Slave' to fourth place out of 4 runners in the Hunt Hurdle. Surprisingly, he had no horse among the eight that went in the Hunt Steeplechase.

Tickets for the dinner in the evening had been advertised at 5s.6d. (27.5p equivalent to about £27 at today's values); with places for 150. It was attended by 120 patrons who sat down at 5 o'clock at the Farmers' Arms, Llanboidy. Many toasts were proposed and all were exceedingly well received and singing and 'speechifying' continued for some time. On the following day, Tuesday, 10 April, the Maesgwynne hounds went hunting. [22]

MFH and Huntsman extraordinary

In recognition of his commitment, for over ten years, to the sport of fox-hunting a 'Public Dinner to W. R. H. Powell Esq., Maesgwynne, Master of the Carmarthenshire Fox Hounds' was held in his honour in April 1852 at the Ivy Bush Hotel where Mr Valentine Rees was the host. The president for the evening was David Browne Edwardes, Rhydygors and among those present were Grismond Philipps, Cwmgwili, William Lewis Philipps, Clyngwyn, Llanboidy and of course the guest W. R. H. Powell. The absence of the major gentry has been interpreted by Matthew Cragoe in his *An Anglican Aristocracy* as evidence that fox-hunting's appeal in Carmarthenshire was muted. However, the regular hunting by the pack over the previous dozen years and the record of the hunt presented at the dinner (see below) hardly support that claim. The president proposed the health of the guest and described him as a gentleman too well known to all present to require any lengthened 'eulogium' from him. Quite simply: 'Without W. R. H. Powell, fox hunting will never flourish'. As a sportsman he was unrivalled for his keen appreciation of the delights of the chase; as a gentleman, his customary courtesy and numerous social qualities were conspicuous, as a huntsman he knew how to do his work and performed it well. His hospitality was unequalled and there were few present who had not on some festive occasion or other partaken of it.

In reply W. R. H. Powell said that he had always done his best to promote amusement and to achieve what he conceived to be a public benefit to the county at large through keeping a pack of hounds within its confines. In the last season the hounds had been out 63 days with only 2 blank days. They had found 71 foxes although some may have been the same as previously hunted. Thirty-eight had been pulled down (26 dogs and 12 vixens), sixteen foxes earthed and 17 were unaccounted for. But he had a warning and an appeal to his co-diners regarding the future. Times were very bad and he would not be able to support the hounds single-handed but with their kind aid he would spare neither purse nor person to afford them good sport. He went on to say that last year he had spent £563 in keeping up the hunting establishment while this year it had cost £581.18s.7d. (Sums in excess of £50,000 at today's prices.) He had not charged for kennel, nor for use of his own property but merely for meal and for keep of horses and hounds. He wished it were possible for him to afford to defray all the costs but he had to remember that he had others at home to keep besides the pack![18] Further proof, therefore, that Powell was not in the fox-hunting business for prestige but for the 'good sport' it provided and for what he perceived to be a public benefit. The pack's main kennels were at Maesgwynne but for hunting the eastern parts of the county use was made of kennels at Travellers' Rest, a few miles west of Carmarthen.

Powell's indomitable spirit as a sportsman shone through a report describing a 'Clipper with the Carmarthenshire Fox Hounds'. A meet due at Llandysilio had been cancelled because frost and snow made it impossible for horses and humans. However, W. R. H. Powell had some friends staying at Maesgwynne and he was determined that they at least should have some sport. Nailed boots were put on and the hounds and followers soon found themselves at Alltybar down towards Cwmfelin Boeth village from Maesgwynne. A fox was raised and with the hounds on his brush went to Gellidogin and on to Glascoed by Henllan Chapel. Then back through Whitland Abbey covers and away along the banks of the Taf over Sarnlas, Lan, Dourder [*sic*] and Cwm-miles to Dolwilym covers. He then bore right for Maesgwynne and over Cilhengroes to Cwmfelin Boeth, across the Taf, under Trewern 'when that thorough good sportsman Mr Davies of Waundwrgi on his black mare joined them.' The chase ended at Plas-crwn, Llanddewi Velfrey and it had been a run of about three hours and at least of twenty-six miles. And all on 'impossible' frosty snow covered ground . . . at least in the morning in Llandysilio.[19]

'Conwil Mayfly' – foundation bitch of the Maesgwynne pack with pups from her first litter by Squire Osbaldeston's 'Vanguard', 1839.

Caroline Mary (8), W. R. H. Powell (junior) (5), W. R. H. Powell (30), Jack Rees (30).
Painted by James Loder, Bath, 1849.

Painting signed:
Yours obediently, Jack Rees.

Painting signed:
Yours faithfully, W. R. H. Powell.

Headstones of buried hounds at Maesgwynne.

The outstanding 'little horse' 'Hazard', with Jack Rees, won the Carmarthenshire Open in 1850, 1851 and 1853.

Silver Jugs donated by David Pugh MP for the United Hunt Club
Steeplechase at Llanboidy in 1859 and 1860. Both won by Powell's
B.G. 'Ready Penny' (Mr J. R. James).

The Llanboidy Challenge Cup value
50 sovereigns, donated by Mr Powell in
1860, became his property in 1864 after
three consecutive wins: B.G. 'Carew'
(T. Davies); B.H. 'St David' (T. Davies);
B.G. 'Bachelor' (J. Pope).

Powell paid 1,250 Guineas for 'Flyfisher'. He won
several valuable steeplechases including, in 1867,
the prestigious Croydon Cup (equivalent, it has been
claimed, to today's Cheltenham Gold Cup)
at 5/1 with Johnny Pope in the saddle.

CROYDON CUP
Nov. 27th 1867
won by
Mr Powell's C.G. 'FLYFISHER'.
RIDDEN BY J. POPE
[cup was the work of Richard Hennell]
(Courtesy Carmarthenshire County Museum).

Johnny Pope with the French-bred 'L'Africaine' . . . the supposed finest steeplechase horse in the world. According to his rider, George Holman, he would have won the 1886 Grand National but for interference from a loose horse. Hacked his way from Maesgwynne to Liverpool and back!

'Breach of Promise', another Powell winner in late 1860s, early 1870s.

Powell's outstanding hunter-steeplechaser 'Milton'.
[Painted by J. A. B. Jay, 1879].

1878 Ludlow Hunters Cup won by W. R. H. Powell's B.G. 'Milton'. Ridden by Mr R. Thomas.

Banner of the Three Counties Benefit Society, 1874-1953.
(Courtesy Carmarthenshire County Museum).

Left: Benefit Society Medal.
(Eddie Evans collection).

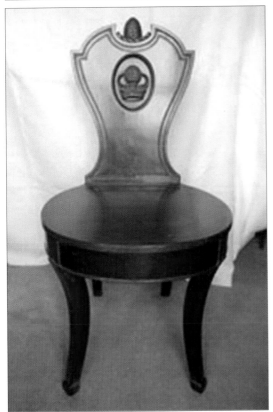

Maesgwynne Hall chair from a set of six.
Stamped M.B. (maker)

Water fountain memorial outside
the Market Hall, Llanboidy.

The Powell Maesgwynne
Coat of Arms.

Maesgwynne, 1983, with the late Major Francis Jones in the foreground.
(Thomas Lloyd collection).

4.4 1856-1865: The golden era of Llanboidy Races

1856: First Llanboidy Hunt Week: two days' racing at Cefnbrafle

As advertised in the *Carmarthen Journal* of 29 February the year 1856 marked a change from the one-day race meeting of the previous four years to a 'race week' at Llanboidy with two days of racing and two days of hunting. The races were for 'gentlemen riders' and therefore remained as competitions for the squirearchy. On Tuesday, 25 March, two races were scheduled: The Open Hurdle, over two miles, and a Hunt Steeplechase, both of 3 sovereigns each with £20 added. On Wednesday, Mr Powell's hounds were to meet and on Thursday, another three races were planned: an Open Hurdle, the Selling Stakes and the Consolation Stakes, all of 3 sovereigns each with £15 added. On Friday, the hounds were to be on the hunt again. It was pointed out in the advert that 'The six new two-stall stables are now ready at the Farmers' Arms, in addition to the excellent stabling there; and at the Lamb Inn for 30 horses.' In addition, Mr Ben Griffiths of the Farmers' Arms took advantage of the popularity of Llanboidy Races to put up for sale a prize stallion. He advertised it in *The Welshman*.

LLANBOIDY RACE WEEK.

To be Sold by Public Auction,

On THURSDAY, the 27th Inst., at the FARMERS' ARMS INN, LLANBOIDY,

At 11 o'Clock in the Forenoon,

The Property of Mr. BEN. GRIFFITHS,

THAT noted entire Horse "RAINBOW." He has travelled many seasons, and has proved himself a sure foal getter. His Stock have turned out first-rate Hunters and Coach Horses, and have fetched most excellent prices.

Also that celebrated Thorough-bred entire Horse "HAZARD," winner of the principal Open Steeple Chases in South Wales, having beaten the most powerful horses in the Principality. He has proved himself a sure foal getter, and his stock promises to turn out first-rate.

For further particulars and to view, apply to Mr. BEN. GRIFFITHS, Farmers' Arms, Llanboidy, at which place the Horses are now standing.

Llanboidy, March 20, 1856.

(Courtesy *Carmarthen Journal*).

There was no reference to the result of the sale in the newspapers but it was claimed that, apart from an easterly wind which caused many to 'lose the skin of his face', the meeting was 'probably the best in the southern Principality'.

On Tuesday in The Open Hurdle Race, only 3 horses started out of an entry of 9. In the Hunt Steeplechase, five ran and Mr Gwyn of Cwrt Hir, Llangain, on 'California' performed 'miracles' in remounting after two falls. He suffered the double handicap of an accident and a loss (of use) of part of a limb; it was the wonder of the day that he managed second place.

On Thursday, 'Stella' ran away with the Open Hurdle race in which five ran including Powell's outstanding 'St David' who finished second. Four ran in the Selling Stakes.

A total of 17 runners had taken part in the two days of racing in the first Llanboidy Race Week. The meeting had attracted the principal sporting gentry of the three counties in west Wales, officers of Militia Regiments and all the 'influential inhabitants of the locality'. Magnificent lunches had been laid on at Maesgwynne on each racing day and the *Journal's* reporter was clearly hoping for another invitation with his praise of Powell: 'he is true as steel in all matters . . . we trust he may never rust.' The week ended with a dinner at the Farmers' Arms in Llanboidy.[23]

There was no doubt that steeplechasing was on the up in west Wales at that time and the Carmarthenshire Steeplechases were then looked upon as a principal event in the sporting world in Wales and second only to the Abergaveny meeting. In fact, W. R. H. Powell had entered 'St David' for that year's Abergavenny and Monmouth Hunt Meeting. Hunting was also taking on an increasingly important role in Britain: 'Every season as it comes round, provision is made to hunt the various counties of England and Wales. Where is the district without fox-hounds or beagles? And then in connection with the hounds are the races – to test the mettle of the horses and to reciprocate those kindly feelings which bind together the gentlemen of distant counties.'[24]

Between the end of the previous hunting season in April 1856 and the start of the new one in October 1856, W. R. H. Powell's Maesgwynne pack had been re-named the 'Union Hunt Club Hounds'. One reason for founding the Union Hunt Club is likely to have been the need to look after compensation for farmers and tenants suffering losses to foxes venturing forth from their coverts in search of sustenance. The club would have covered the area hunted by the Maesgwynne pack which had been expanded to include the country hunted previously by the Pant-y-Cendy and by the Carmarthen packs. Setting up the club reflected Powell's concern for the welfare of ordinary people.

1857: A new hotel for Llanboidy

The coming of the railway to Carmarthen in 1852, and its extension to Haverfordwest in 1854, had made west Wales far more accessible to the wider world. Powell appreciated the new opportunities for further development of Llanboidy Races and of the area in general which resulted from the 'rail revolution'. He recognised that to make the most of the great attraction that 'Llanboidy Races' had become, the needs of the racing fraternity would have to be catered for. A high-class hotel was required to accommodate owners and their parties and to provide for holding of a dinner and possibly a ball. Accommodation was also needed for jockeys and grooms as well as for horses in order to attract entries from far and wide to race at Cefnbrafle. Only by offering the complete package could he hope to entice owners of the best horses to attend and compete at Llanboidy Races and only the best would satisfy the Squire of Maes-gwynne. At the same time it should be noted that Tom Rees, writing in 1916, stated that Mr Powell built the Maesgwynne Arms for the accommodation of hunt followers, 'The suites of rooms were well-arranged and furnished, and every modern convenience installed. There was a range of commodious horse boxes. Mr John Newell Moore, Lonlas, Neath; Mr William Henry Thomas, brother of the late Mr George Thomas, town clerk, Carmarthen, both keen riders to

Maesgwynne Arms Hotel, Llanboidy, built by Powell in 1856-57.
(Eddie Evans collection).

hounds; Mr Phillips and Mr Bidder, Neath; Mr George Noble, Captain Trefray, and several other gentlemen were in residence during the hunting season.'[12] It was in 1857 that the 'new hotel' first became available for use during Llanboidy Races and Hunt Week. Therefore, 1856 must have been a year of hectic building activity on the site of the new hotel. The Farmers' Arms was probably incorporated into the new building which was named Maesgwynne Arms. On the other hand the old Farmers' Arms may have been pulled down; certainly no more was heard of it on completion of the new hotel.

The *Carmarthen Journal*'s view was that 'when it is well known that such a refuge for the traveller or the sportsman who looks for good hunting with a crack pack exists the house will be well frequented and amply recompense the spirited proprietor for his outlay.' In the sale document of 1918,[26] the Maesgwynne Arms Hotel was described as having twelve bedrooms on the first floor and seven in the attics. There were five-stall stables with a large room above them where the Oddfellows Lodge held its meetings. There were other stables fitted with thirteen stalls. A coach house, saddle room and a cart house made up the remaining facilities for horses.

The historic 1857 Llanboidy Races at Cefnbrafle (or Cefnbraley as the papers misspelt it) came off with three races on Monday, 13 April, and another three on Thursday. The weather did its best to spoil the Monday event. There was rain, hail, snow and wind throughout the day, but even so, a goodly gathering of 'the right sort' braved the elements. Those allowed to ride the horses now included tradesmen and farmers as well as gentlemen but those who had ridden for hire were still excluded.

It was a highly successful meeting for W. R. H. Powell. As chief organiser he would have been delighted that a total of 48 runners were attracted to start in the six races. As owner he enjoyed four wins including a double by the star of the Maesgwynne Stable, 'St David', who won a 'splendid' Llanboidy Stakes with Mr R. Thomas up and after a day's rest repeated his success in the Cefnbrafle Hurdles Stakes with Powell himself in the saddle.

The Dinner was held at the new hotel when fifty gentlemen sat down to a 'splendid dinner' organised by landlord Ben Griffiths.[25] From newspaper reports prior to and during the following year's meeting it is clear that work on the hotel continued during 1857 and it was the visitors to the 1858 meeting that enjoyed the finished article. And the completed hotel would not be the only improvement in store for the 1858 visitors to Llanboidy Races.

1858: Biggest crowd so far at Cefnbrafle . . . 'better than anything seen in Wales'

Boosted by the success of the first two week-long meetings, W. R. H. Powell set about establishing Llanboidy Races as one of the top meetings in Wales. By the 1858 meeting: 'The course at Cefnbraley [sic] had been considerably improved, the ground levelled and all obstructions cleared away and . . . a grandstand of brick construction with weighing rooms beneath was erected which afforded a capital view of the racing' . . . and 'where refreshments of all kinds can be obtained.' For the first time, professional jockeys were allowed to take part with gentlemen riders allowed 5 lb. The prize money was increased with both the Handicap Sweepstake and the Open Steeplechase having £50 added. That amount of prize money was high enough to attract the best steeplechasers in Wales, England and Ireland to Cefnbrafle. There was a condition that at least three horses, the property of different owners, had to start each race or the added money would not be given. That condition meant that it would not have been possible for Powell's horses to be entered by persons other than Powell. The total added prize money for the seven races was £215 and much of the credit for raising it belonged to Oliver Powell the Squire's brother.

For the first time at Llanboidy Races, bookmakers were allowed to attend but the policy of no beer tents was to continue to distinguish Llanboidy races from, probably, every other race meeting in Wales, Ireland and England. Powell had strong views on the need to encourage people to live better lives. As a magistrate he would from time to time lament the fact that so many of the cases brought before him were of people, particularly the labouring class, having behaved badly while under the influence of drink. The provision of food and drink 'under the stand' would have been under the control of Benjamin Griffiths, mine host at the Maesgwynne Arms, a tenant of the Squire. Ben Griffiths could be trusted not to serve beer to those intent on making fools of themselves. For the races of 1870 and 1871 Powell felt it necessary to print on the advert for the meetings that 'Refreshments will be provided under the Stand, but no Booths will be allowed on the ground.'

During the week Powell's UHC hounds would meet on the Wednesday and on the Friday. The new hotel now had a name, Maesgwynne Arms, and a dinner was to be held there on the evenings of Tuesday, Wednesday and Thursday.

On the first day, Tuesday, fans made their way to Llanboidy on foot, on horseback and in four-horse carriages, flys, omnibuses and dog carts and about mid-day Maesgwynne Arms was thronged with guests. 'It is not many years since an attempt was first made to get up a Steeple

Chase in this district and few would have imagined that in so short a time the little village of Llanboidy would be able to put forth a programme for the week such as would puzzle many county towns to get up.'

According to the *Journal* there was much speculation about the outcome of the Handicap Sweepstake and of the Open Steeplechase: 'For the former some foreigners had been entered about which little was known . . . for the latter, 'Maid of the Glen', the winner of the Abergavenny and the Pembrokeshire was to meet with her old competitors in many a well fought field'. About 2 o'clock the bugle sounded for the saddling.

Nine ran in the Handicap Sweepstakes which was won by J. Davies' 'Minerva', ridden by the jockey (Thomas) that had recently ridden the winner of the prestigious Corinthian Cup at Kildare, Ireland. W. R. H. Powell's 'Wild Buck' (Capt. Baker) was second. Starting odds were '3 and 5/1 on the field'.

Six went in the Open and it proved a 'splendid race'. Powell's highly fancied 'St David' (Jack Rees) fell when looking good but his other entry, 'Deception' (J. James) at 5/1 ran the race of his life to beat the other highly-fancied entry, 'Maid of the Glen', also 5/1, to win the race.

An incident before the start of the Hunt Hurdle provided another example of the generosity of W. R. H. Powell. When someone pointed out that Powell's entry, 'Wild Buck', was far too good for the other six runners, 'Mr Powell, with that generosity which characterises all his proceedings, instantly withdrew him in order, as he kindly said, not to spoil the sport.' Another of the six withdrew himself because he bolted and made for home before the off. Betting was 3/1 on the field.

After another four races on Thursday a total of 37 runners had gone in the seven races.

The *Journal*'s verdict was that 'such a week of enjoyment seldom passed in the locality.' The last paragraph of the *Journal*'s report reflected the far-sightedness of W. R. H. Powell in promoting his new hotel, the Maesgwynne Arms for his own benefit and also for the benefit of the local community who could expect 'knock-on effects' from the Squire's outlay: 'Hint to sporting fraternity and tourists whether they are inclined for hunting with a first rate pack of foxhounds or, now that the season is over, they delight in fishing a stream second to none in the kingdom, all they have to do is to take a train to St Clears, drive to the Maesgwynne Arms Hotel, Llanboidy and there they are, with accommodation of a most superior class, for either man or horse, and sport at the door sufficient to satisfy any gourmand be he ever so avaricious. *Verbum sap* [Enough said].'[27,28]

1859: Most successful to date!

A notice in the *Journal* on 25 March 1859 signed by Jack Rees as clerk of the course of the Llanboidy Hunt Week and Steeplechases drew attention to the fact that entries for the races to be held on the 29 and 31 March 1859 could be submitted to the Hon. Sec. T. R. O. Powell at the Maesgwynne Arms at the start of the week. Post Office Orders to be made payable to the Hon. Sec. at the Llanboidy Post Office near St Clears. And, in case someone wondered where in the world the event was to take place: 'Llanboidy is within 5 miles of the St Clears, Whitland or Narberth Road Stations on the South Wales Railway.'

The following week, the *Journal* reckoned that: 'A more successful meeting has never taken place at Llanboidy. On Tuesday nearly all the vehicles in Carmarthen were requisitioned to convey the sporting fraternity to the scene of action . . . the [prize] money [£235] was greatly in excess of last year's and if this prosperous state of affairs goes on, the Llanboidy Hunt meeting will be second to none in the Principality.' In addition to money prizes, the county MP, David Pugh, gave a handsome silver claret jug.[29]

The added prize money was in fact 10% up on the preceding year and 33 horses went in the seven races. But it must have been disappointing to have attracted only four runners in the Open Steeplechase with two belonging to Powell taking the first and second places with 'St David' (Jack Rees) and 'Carew' (Mr J. James). The Maesgwynne stable steeplechasers were not easily beaten over a banking course; a fact which tempered the appeal of the prize money in the eyes of English and Irish owners.

When the hunting season started again with a meet on 7 October 1859 the Maesgwynne pack was listed as the Union Hunt Club Hounds (Mr Powell's).

1860: Llanboidy one of best in south Wales!

'Hunt Week' meetings of hunting and racing 'came off' in increasing numbers in the middle decades of the nineteenth century. For example, meetings took place at Abergavenny, Carmarthen, Tivy Side, Haverfordwest and Llanboidy. 'Races are receiving increasing support from all classes in the community – royalty and nobility, statesmen, men of science and literature and opulence. It is an error to associate these sports with blackguardianism, debauchery, black-legism, etc. – it is simply not the case.'[30]

The *Journal* was full of praise, 'if Abergavenny is still the top meeting in Wales, Llanboidy is catching up fast . . . now ranked as one of the most important Racing events in south Wales . . . [the 1860 meeting] was the most successful since the establishment of the races . . . added money being something extraordinary [275 sovereigns equivalent to about £27,000 at today's values] and as a consequence the class of horses brought together was first-rate.' The Open Steeplechase of 7 sovereigns with 70 sovereigns added attracted the 'Crack of Welsh Nags, pick of the Irish lot, Joe Maley, winner of the Warwick Open and one or two other English horses of no mean fame. . . . Tuesday morning was fine and by 12 noon the village of Llanboidy was alive with the constant arrival of carriages at the Maesgwynne Arms and we do not remember ever seeing so many sporting gentlemen congregated together as upon this occasion.'

However, a sudden change in the weather with a cold wind, overcast sky and drizzly rain followed by a 'fog which entirely shut out the view of all that was taking place and one of the best races on record was lost to the anxious spectators.'

Nine horses went in the Open, and as the *Journal* put it: 'From reports of riders, this was one of the best races that has ever taken place in this country but the spectators could only see the start and finish.' T. R. O. Powell's 'Carew' (J. Rees) 6/1, came second to the favourite J. McAdam's 'Joe Maley' 2/1, but W. R. H. Powell's 'St David' (J. James) 6/1 was unplaced.

Fifty sat down to dinner at the Maesgwynne Arms and 'several owners signified they would bring their horses next year and Mr R. Kerr, owner of 'Norma' who had won the Llanboidy Stakes, offered to give a stake of 25 sovereigns to be run over the flat next season – the offer was accepted.' Was this an attempt to counter the mastery of the Maesgwynne Stable's domination of banking races?

A special race was introduced in 1860 over four miles of good hunting country for horses bred in south Wales and the property of residents of Carmarthenshire, Cardiganshire and Pembrokeshire. It was a sweepstake of 7 sovereigns each to which Powell added a Challenge Cup, value 50 sovereigns. The Challenge Cup was to be produced at each successive Llanboidy meeting and not to become the property of any person until it was won three years in succession. Any number of horses, the property of the same owner, were allowed in this race. The Cup went to Mr Philipps' 'Frederick' (T. Davies), with W. R. H. Powell's 'St David' (J. James) second, T. R. O. Powell's 'Carew' (Capt. Crymes) third and Lort Phillips' 'Arthur' (Owner) last of the four runners.

A total of 37 runners went in the seven races and '[The Llanboidy week of] 1860 will be long remembered as one of the most successful that has yet occurred at Llanboidy.'[31]

Later in the year Powell, as one of 13 stewards, played a leading role in establishing the first ever Grand National Hunt Steeplechase at Market Harborough; an occasion which attracted 'an enormous attendance'. The Grand National Hunt Steeplechase was a race for *bona fide* hunters only (in contrast to the Grand National Steeplechase which was open to horses from public training stables) and it was hoped that farmers and hunting men would ride. The race was eventually incorporated into the Cheltenham programme. The other stewards at Market Harborough were the Dukes of Bedford and of Manchester, Earls of Stamford, of Warrington and of Scarborough, Lords Dacre and Tredegar, Sir Watkin Wynn, Messrs George Lane Fox, T. T. Drake, W. R. Stratton and W. W. Tailby. Thirty-one horses started.[32] No doubt, Powell took the opportunity to remind everyone of Llanboidy Races!

1861: 295 sovereigns added

For the first time at Cefnbrafle, an official handicapper was present for the Llanboidy week in April 1861 in the person of Mr R. Johnson from York.[33] The numbers entered and the added prize money made for startling reading. A total of 61 entries had been received for the 8 races which had yielded 220.5 sovereigns in entry fees. The prize money added amounted to a total of 295 sovereigns which equates to about £29,000 at today's values. A Sale of Hunters, etc. by Geo Goode was to be held on Thursday of the Hunt Week at Llanboidy.

The available prize money must have helped to attract the large numbers of entries and *The Welshman* reported that 'many of the horses were famous on the turf'. But the report also expressed the opinion that the success of the meeting was 'more attributable to Mr Powell of Maesgwynne than any other cause, for the sport owes its all to him. Standing as he does at the head of sportsmen in Carmarthenshire, it is almost a point of honour to wind up the season at the hospitable mansion of Maesgwynne where all are welcomed in the good old style.' The weather had been good and the 'gathering was immense. Never in the annals of Llanboidy has the programme so much sport. . . . "Llanboidy week", though in comparative infancy, has surpassed in a great measure similar events in places of greater magnitude and importance . . . mainly attributable to the energy and efforts [in collecting subscriptions] of T. R. O. Powell, Hon. Sec., brother of the worthy Squire . . .'[34]

Four of the races were open while the others were limited to horses from Carmarthenshire, Cardiganshire and Pembrokeshire. All five entered went in the Open Steeplechase of 8 sovereigns + 80 sovereigns added, over 4 miles. The race demonstrated once again the strength of the Maesgwynne horses over a banking course with Powell's 'Confederate' (J. R. James) winning from Captain Jordan's 'Little Monkey' with Powell's other entry, 'Ace of Hearts', ridden by Powell's stud groom, 22-year-old Lancashire-born John Wheale, in third place.

But that was Powell's only win at the meeting which saw a total of 48 runners go in eight races. Nine farmers coughed up 10 shillings (£50 today) to enter a horse in a race for farmers, tradesmen and yeomen within the UHC country for a prize of a saddle and bridle. It was run over 2 miles on the flat. Mr J. Thomas' 'Goblin' (Rees) won, and was sold for £60 at auction after the race.

1862: Fog, Rain and Champagne

In March 1862, two thoroughbred horses were available at Maesgwynne, Llanboidy to serve that season. The horses were 'The Confessor' and 'Anthracite'. '"The Confessor" will not be travelled. "Anthracite" will attend at Pembroke, Haverfordwest, Narberth, St Clears, New Castle Emlyn and Carmarthen if required by owners of mares who are requested to apply to William Purnell, Stud Groom. Good grass and boxes for mares and foals at one shilling per night. Barren mares five shillings per week.'[35] W. R. H. Powell was doing his best to improve the strain of steeplechasers in west Wales.

Fog and rain marred full enjoyment of the 1862 Llanboidy Races week although *The Welshman*'s report was full of praises and finished with the claim that . . . 'The races . . . excited, perhaps, more interest than usual from the fact that owing to the dense fog that prevailed nothing more of the racing could be seen than the entry into the field where the grandstand was placed.' That sentence reads as if it was composed, as it undoubtedly was, after the reporter had enjoyed the champagne lunch at Maesgwynne and had also sampled what Ben Griffiths had on offer in his bar under the grandstand![36]

The presence of Pryse Longden and his horses showed he had patched up his differences with Powell over an objection at Carmarthen earlier in the year. Of the four open races, W. R. H. Powell won two of them including the Open Steeplechase with his 'Confederate' (Tom Davies), evens, three ran. A total of 41 horses went in the eight races.

1863: Wales' Newmarket . . . almost

By the early 1860s Llanboidy Races commanded a place among the elite in the racing calendar for Wales, England and Ireland. The event was 'attended by several of the Metropolitan and Midland sporting fraternity and considered by the leading sporting journal, *Bell's Life in London*, worthy of a special representative to report it.' Its high standing was the 'result of the indomitable energy and perseverance of W. R. H. Powell as patron and T. R. O. Powell as Hon. Sec. . . . [and] under the present management it can progress to become the Newmarket of Wales.'[37] The *Bell's Life* reporter found that the newly-built hotel 'for size, edibles, comfort and civility might put to the blush many first class hotels, so called, in England or elsewhere' and the Cefnbrafle racecourse was 'one of the noblest in the Kingdom . . . [and] Mr W. R. H. Powell the pink of sportsmen in Wales . . . without whose ever ready and beneficent assistance the chase and field amusements generally throughout the district must long since have died out . . . Nor does generosity halt here, if we may judge from the rubicund faces of the clean and well clad poor, whose youngsters are about to be provided with free schools, now in course of erection at Mr Powell's own cost.' The reporter found 'the whole population in fact wearing an

STEEPLE CHASING.

STEEPLE CHASING FIXTURES FOR 1863.

FEBRUARY.

Scarborough 11	Newmarket 19	Lincoln 25
Reading 11	Birmingham..........23	Moreton-in-Marsh ..26
Aberystwith Hunt..16		

MARCH.

Brackley 3	North Wold 13	York 23
Royal Artillery (Woolwich) 5	Grand Military (Rugby) 16	Isle of Wight 24
Chipping Norton..... 5	Doncaster 17	Wharfedale & Otley.25
Liverpool Grand National 11	Bangor 17	Grand National Hunt (Market Harbro')..26
	Wetherby 20	

APRIL.

Colchester Garrison: 6	Liverpool Hunt Club.10	Cheltenham 14
Dorsetshire Hunt .. 8	Waterloo (Portsmouth) 14	Howden 16
Abergavenny 9		Llanboidy 21
Herts Hunt 9		

IRISH.

MARCH.

Elphin (mixed) 31

APRIL.

Galway Hunt 6	Kells 23	Springhill 23
Kildare Hunt 16		

MAY.

Nenagh (mixed) .... 6 | Tullamore .... 7 | Tipperary 27

JUNE.

Westmeath 2

AUGUST.

Roscommon (mixed) 26

SEPTEMBER.

Limerick (mixed) ......16 | Cashel (mixed) 30

OCTOBER.

Lismore .... 7 | Louth 23

NOVEMBER.

Tramore 24

Steeplechasing fixtures published in *Bell's Life in London and Sporting Chronicle* on 8 February 1863.
The Carmarthen meeting had taken place during the first week of February.
(Courtesy *Bell's Life*).

air of contentment, strong as the hills which encircle the quiet salubrious spot.' At 'the beautifully situated residence of Maesgwynne' he found a fine salmon stream, otter and fox hunting, lots of game and a wide range for shooting, abundantly vary if not prolong a country gentleman's life.' On a tour of the stables he found they were 'equal in appointments and convenience to that of any nobleman of the day.' They contained 'the ever-green 'St David' and 'Carew' (12 to 15 year olds), perfection itself 'Ace of Hearts' and a splendid four-year-old bought from Ireland.' The stud numbered 'nearly 30 horses, among them some of the best weight carrying animals extant', including the famous 'Esmerelda'.[38] In February 1863 *Bell's Life in London* reported that Powell had four steeplechasers, twelve hunters, and taking account of the 'colts, etc.', his total stud amounted to 34 horses 'under the care of Will Purnell.'[4]

At noon, Maesgwynne was 'thrown open without formality or distinction to every visitor to the races for a champagne lunch. Afterwards a vast number wended their way to the course in various kinds of conveyances besides hundreds of pedestrians, and on mounting the stand, the appearance of so numerous an assembly of the fair sex all attired in the height of fashion presented a scene brilliant in the extreme. Among those present were Mr Protheroe of Dolwilym [probably Edward Schaw Protheroe] and Capt. Morgan Lloyd and Miss Lloyd of Glansevin, Llangadog.'

At the course: 'a brick built stand and weighing rooms beneath [it cost 2s.6d. per race to weigh-in] afforded every facility for seeing and preparation. The banks too, some of them wide enough for a carriage to drive on the top were all that could be wished, sound as a bell, and with care, not precisely difficult to get over. By way of variety, made flying jumps here and there intersected the line, with two or three doubles, and a nicely turfed straight to finish.'

The fact that the meeting was subject to the 'new rules' of steeplechasing implied that W. R. H. Powell was closely in touch with those endeavouring to develop rules for the sport in those formative years.

The total added prize money of £305, the highest in the history of Llanboidy Races, helped attract 49 runners for the 8 races. Apart from the Challenge Cup race, every race in the 1863 meeting at Cefnbrafle had at least four starters, and two had nine, one of which was the Open Steeplechase of 10 sovereigns each with 80 sovereigns added, in which W. R. H. Powell's 'Ace of Hearts' (Tom Davies) evens, ran second behind the winner at 5/2. During that race the *Bell's Life* reporter noticed the partisan nature of the local crowd's support which he described in relation to the English horse 'Saladin' ridden by Mr Riddell actually completing the Open without mishap. 'The exceedingly patient handling by Mr Riddell of the Devonshire horse "Saladin" amounted to quite a marvel among the natives here who appear scarcely to comprehend the possibility of an English horse surmounting a Welsh country without some blunder or fall, neither of which befell the steeplechaser in question today, who, used to banks, won at South Molton on the 1st inst.'

Powell had three winners including 'St David' (Tom Davies) who beat T. R. O. Powell's 'Carew' (J. Pope) in the disappointing two-horse race for the Challenge Cup. The Squire 'declared to win' with 'St David' which confirmed that he was the true owner of 'Carew'.

At the end of the day the *Bell's Life* reporter reckoned it had been 'one of the best day's sport yet enjoyed in south Wales with glorious weather enhancing the splendour of the landscape of which the course forms, as it were, the centre.' Nor had the course completely cleared before:

Evening, too, with gown of pink,
Had stooped at Neptune's tap to drink,
Where Phoebus just before had been,
At this, his fam'd salt-water rim,
To give his horses corn and hay,
And rest from labours of the day,
To clear their feet of stones and gravel,
And fit them for the morrow's travel!

Back at the House 'hospitality ruled pre-eminent to the last with laden tables each day of substantial and choice viands with recherché wines to match, the esteemed host frequently hauling-in party after party from the lawn and otherwise attending to their creature comforts himself. And thanks to Mr Powell, the morrow brought the opportunity for a final run with the hounds. Although the hunting season had been over for some weeks, he decided to prolong the allotted time to show his guests 'good hunting and a good country to get over.'

The 1863 meeting at Cefnbrafle was the last time for the famous 'Carew' and 'Annie Laurie' to carry the orange and black colours of Maesgwynne, because Powell sold both to the well known horsemen from Devon, the Riddell brothers. At the Aberystwyth Steeplechases in February 1864, 'Carew' and 'Annie Laurie' and Powell's 'Miss Nightingale' filled ten of the twelve places in the four races that went at that meeting. Owners (not the above presumably) complained bitterly that the Aberystwyth course was too difficult with 'sixteen ploughed fields in the four miles'. Such conditions posed no problems for Maesgwynne-trained steeple-chasers!

1864: Like an Epsom spring meeting!
The April 1864 Llanboidy meeting, held a week after the Abergavenny races, was advertised in style in the *Carmarthen Journal*. The grandstand had been glazed for the comfort of the spectators and a saddling and dressing room added to the building. 'In fact every thing was as like a miniature Epsom Spring meeting as could be and when the representative of *Bell's Life* said that the Hunter Scurry, for which seventeen entered, reminded him of the Derby, there was no need to make further allusions to the class of races'.[39] The prestigious London-based *The Field: The Country Gentleman's Newspaper*, was represented, as it had been for many years, and the report carried in its 16 April 1864 issue described the occasion as: 'the last link in the long chain of Welsh meetings. We do not think any part of the United Kingdom [does] so much towards promoting the national sports of hunting and steeplechasing as the three western counties of south Wales. . . . There is a charm, however, about these western meetings which we have never met elsewhere. Llanboidy differs in some respect from its fellows . . . held as it is in a somewhat remote district, it is impossible to have the accessories of balls and concerts, but to make up for this deficiency Mr Powell throws his house open with true Welsh hospitality. His friends and neighbours, with strangers from a-far, rally round him, and on no course in Wales is so much rank and beauty seen as upon the picturesque, though somewhat barren, heath of Cefen Braly [*sic*]. The success of steeplechasing in the western part of south Wales is in no small degree attributable to the energy and perseverance of a single individual; jealousy creates

1864.

LLANBOIDY RACES & STEEPLE CHASES

WILL TAKE PLACE

On TUESDAY and THURSDAY, APRIL 12th and 14th.

(THE WEEK FOLLOWING THE ABERGAVENNY MEETING.)

TUESDAY.

THE LLANBOIDY STAKES.

A Handicap of 5 Sovs. each, if forfeit be not declared on or before Wednesday, March 30th, with FORTY SOVEREIGNS added. Entrance, 2 Sovs., to go to the fund. Second horse to save his stake. Five entries or no Race. The winner of any Race after the publication of the weights once, 7lbs., twice, or of any Race with 40 Sovs. added, 10lbs. extra, not to be accumulative. Those declaring forfeit in time pay only Entrance money. One mile and a half over the flat. To close March 16th.

THE OPEN STEEPLE CHASE.

A Handicap of 10 Sovs. each, half forfeit, if forfeit be not declared on or before Wednesday, March 30th, with EIGHTY SOVEREIGNS added. Entrance, 2 Sovs., to go to the fund. Second horse to save his stake. The winner of any Steeple Chase after the publication of the weights once 7lbs., twice 10lbs. extra. Five entries or no Race. Those declaring forfeit in time pay only Entrance money. Four miles over the Steeple Chase Course. To close March 16th.

THE U.H.C. STEEPLE CHASE.

A Sweepstakes of 3 Sovs. each, p.p., with a SILVER CLARET JUG added, value 9 guineas, the gift of DAVID PUGH, Esq., M.P. Entrance 1 Sov. to go to the fund. Second horse to save his stake. Five entries or no Race. For horses that have been regularly hunted in South Wales during this season, and have never been in a public training stable, or won a Race with more than £30 added (Garrison Races excepted), 4 years old, 10st. 7lbs., 5 years old, 11st. 5lbs., 6 and aged, 12st. A winner of any Steeple Chase or Hurdle Race once, 7lbs., twice, 10lbs. extra. Three miles over the Steeple Chase Course. To close March 30th.

THE HUNTER'S SCURRY.

A Sweepstakes of 1 Sov. each, p.p., with TEN SOVS. added by W. R. H. POWELL, Esq., for Maiden Horses, the property of Residents in Carmarthenshire, Pembrokeshire, or Cardiganshire, that have been regularly hunted, and have never been in a public training stable, or have ever started for any Flat or Hurdle Race or Steeple Chase value £20. Second horse to save his stake. 4 years old, 11st., 5 years old, 11st. 12lbs., 6 and aged, 12st. 7lbs. Gentlemen riders. Those who have never won a Race of the value of £50 allowed 7lbs. Two miles over the flat. To close March 30th.

THURSDAY.

THE CEFEN STAKES.

A Handicap of 3 Sovs. each, if forfeit be not declared on or before Wednesday, March 30th, with THIRTY SOVS. added. Entrance, 1 Sov., to go to the fund. Second horse to save his stake. Five entries or no Race. Those declaring forfeit in time pay only entrance money. A winner of any Race after the publication of the weights once, 7lbs., twice, or of any Race with 40 Sovs. added, 10lbs. extra, not to be accumulative. One mile over the flat. To close March 16th.

THE CAMBRIAN STEEPLE CHASE.

A Handicap of 5 Sovs. each, half forfeit, if forfeit be not declared on or before Wednesday, April 13th, by 10 a.m., with FORTY SOVEREIGNS added. Entrance, 1 Sov., to go to the fund. Second horse to save his stake. Five entries or no Race. Those declaring forfeit in time pay only entrance money. Four miles over the Steeple Chase Course. To close April 12th.

THE CHALLENGE CUP,

Value FIFTY SOVEREIGNS, added to a Sweepstakes of 7 Sovs. each, 3 forfeit, for Horses bred in South Wales, which have been the property of residents in Carmarthenshire, Pembrokeshire, or Cardiganshire since the 1st day of November last past, and have been regularly hunted during this season, and have never been in a public training stable. Any number of Horses, the property of the same owner, can start for this Cup. If four Horses start, the second to save his stake. 4 miles over a hunting country. 4 years old, 10st. 7lbs.; 5 years old, 11st. 5lbs.; 6 and aged, 12st. Entire horses to carry 3lbs. extra; Horses that have won £50, 7lbs. extra; £100, 10lbs. extra; £100 twice, or £200, 14lbs. extra, not to be accumulative. The Cup to be produced at each successive Llanboidy Meeting, and not to become the property of any person until he shall have won it three years in succession. A walk over not to count as a win. To close April 12th.

THE PRINCIPALITY HURDLE RACE.

A Sweepstakes of 3 Sovs. each, p.p., with TWENTY-FIVE SOVEREIGNS added, the gift of D. JONES, Esq., M.P. Entrance, 1 Sov., to go to the fund. Second horse to save his stake. Five entries or no race. For horses that have been hunted in Wales during this season, and have never been in a public training stable, or won a Flat or Hurdle Race or Steeple Chase with £30 added (Races run during this Meeting and Garrison Races excepted). 4 years old, 9st. 7lbs.; 5 years old, 10st. 5lbs.; 6 and aged, 11st. Winners extra as in the "U.H.C. Steeple Chase." Two miles over 7 flights of hurdles. To close April 12th.

CONDITIONS.

The Llanboidy Stakes, the Open Steeple Chase, and the Cefen Stakes to close and name to the Secretary, at the Maesgwynne Arms Hotel, Llanboidy, on or before Wednesday, March 16th. The Weights to appear in Bell's Life on the 26th of March. The U.H.C Steeple Chase, and the Hunter's Scurry to close and name on or before Wednesday, March 30th. The Cambrian Steeple Chase, the Challenge Cup, and the Principality Hurdle Race to close and name on Tuesday Evening, April 12th, by 8 o'clock. The Weights to appear the same evening by 10 o'clock. The Entrance Money and the Colours of the Riders must accompany each Entry, or the same will not be received. Weighing 2s. 6d. each Race. Three Horses, the property of different owners, to start for each Race, or the Public Money will not be added. The Flat Races will be run under the Newmarket Rules; and the Steeple Chases and Hurdle Race under the Grand National Steeple Chase Rules.

Mr. Powell's Hounds will meet on Wednesday and Friday.

An Ordinary on Tuesday, Wednesday, and Thursday, at the Maesgwynne Arms.

DAVID JONES, Esq., M.P.,
LIEUT.-COLONEL A. H. SAUNDERS DAVIES, } Stewards.
Mr. R. JOHNSON, York, Handicapper.
T. R. OLIVER POWELL, Esq., Hon. Secretary.

N.B.—Llanboidy is situated within five miles of the St. Clears, Whitland, or Narberth Road Stations on the Great Western Railway. All P.O. Orders must be made payable on the Llanboidy Post Office.

Advert for Llanboidy Races in the *Carmarthen Journal*.
(Courtesy *Carmarthen Journal*).

cavillers, and it is easy to sneer at the strength of the Maesgwynne stable, but were it not for Mr Powell we believe our duty as chroniclers would, as regards south Wales, speedily come to an end.' The report went on to challenge the unsuccessful owners to try again next year: 'There is an old saying "there are better fish in the sea than ever came out of it", so are there superior animals to turn the table next season and . . . deprive the "Ace" of the high honour he now holds, that of being the best horse in Wales.'

The Field's report then turned to the details of that year's Llanboidy meeting and in particular to a problem that had been encountered with the grandstand when its wooden shutters were open: 'it became a sort of palace of the winds; and colds and coughs were frequently traced to a visit to Llanboidy . . . so the wooden ones were removed and glazed ones substituted.' *The Field* reporter also referred to a dirty trick discovered prior to the first race when one of the jockeys questioned the accuracy of the scales in the weighing room. Upon examination by the stewards, a 3 lb. lump of lead was found nailed to the bottom of one side of the scales. It was noticed that an access to the weighing room was possible from the bar 'through a sort of buttery hatch' and it would appear that 'some rascal had got in that way. The incident was warning enough to the stewards that too much vigilance is not possible in all the details of a race meeting.'

The Welshman's report mentioned that a special area in the grandstand had been reserved for the press and the reporter wondered as to whether the increasing importance of the meeting had as much to do with the hospitality dished out by W. R. H. Powell as it did with 'the very excellent sport shown to lovers of the turf at Llanboidy.' A desk was fitted up in the weighing room for the press and *The Welshman*'s reporter expressed the hope that this facility 'will be followed in other places'. The total added prize money on offer was £300.

The great event of the first day was the Hunter's Scurry, a sweepstake of 1 sovereign with 10 sovereigns added by W. R. H. Powell. Named the 'Derby of Wales' it was for 'gentlemen riders' on maiden horses owned by residents in Carmarthenshire, Pembrokeshire and Cardiganshire, regularly hunted and never been in a public training stable. It was run over two miles on the flat and fifteen started! *The Welshman*'s report enthused that 'the varied gay and brilliant colours of the riders was a most pleasing sight'. The winner was Mr Hitchings' 'Newton' (owner) but an objection was lodged, claiming that Mr Hitchings had received payment as a jockey in previous races. The outcome of the objection had not been received at the time of *The Welshman* going to press. At the evening dinner M. A. Saurin of Orielton, Pembrokeshire and G. W. Baker from Berkshire agreed to be stewards for the following year.

The weather on Thursday was 'as charming as on the first day.' Before the start of the Cefen Stakes, an objection was made to Capt. Rhys' 'Newfoundland' on the score of forfeits of £5 each being unpaid for his horses, 'Rhoebus' and 'Butterfly' at the late Hungerford meeting. The stewards decided that the letter from Mr Dilke produced by J. Holman did not contain sufficient authority to stop 'Newfoundland' from racing and thus the objection fell. They certainly took their racing seriously. . . 'gentlemen' or not. Two extra races were put on and W. R. H. Powell's 'Nightingale' (J. Pope) ran out the winner in one. In the Challenge Cup for horses bred in south Wales and regularly hunted in Carmarthenshire, Cardiganshire or Pembrokeshire only two ran, both being Powell's horses. 'Bachelor' (Pope) beat 'Nightingale' (Riddell) and the Challenge Cup became the property of Mr Powell who had then won it three times in succession.

In view of developments in the following year it is worth noting that of the four open races in 1864, two were run over the banking course and two on the flat. A total of 58 runners went in the 10 races and *The Welshman*'s report finished: 'Thus closed one of the most brilliant and pleasant meetings it has been our fortune to attend. We augur that next year the fame of this year's doings will have gone forth and the Llanboidy Race week will more than ever be one of the "crack" weeks of the year.'[40]

The Hunt met at Maesgwynne on the Wednesday and it turned out to be a lengthy chase covering about twelve miles past Cefencelly covers to Goitre near Gilfach and on to Trelech church but a flock of sheep came to the fox's aid and the hunters returned empty handed!

1865: Changed times and a changed course . . . and the rain!

The success enjoyed by the Llanboidy Races from their inception up to 1864 owed everything to the huge promotional effort put in by W. R. H. Powell and his brother Oliver. Powell Bach for his part, supported race meetings all over the country by entering and running his horses and therefore, in return, could expect support for his Llanboidy meeting. He was also untiring in sending repeated reminders to owners of potential entries until the entries finally arrived! In addition he had, at Llanboidy, first class accommodation for visitors at the Maesgwynne Arms Hotel and on race days the champagne lunch at Maesgwynne was generally acknowledged to be an unmissable experience. Oliver Powell was a genius at collecting subscriptions so that the prize money at Llanboidy was incredibly high! It was important to fit Llanboidy Races in an appropriate slot with respect to the big meetings in south Wales such as Abergavenny, Carmarthen and Cardiff. For 1865 the Llanboidy Hunt, Races and Open Steeplechases were finally scheduled to come off on 2 and 4 May (the week following the Cardiff meeting).

But there were factors militating against Llanboidy and these were increasing in strength. There were more and more meetings coming off, particularly just over the border with England, tempting owners in those areas to attend meetings closer to their stables rather than undertake the long and expensive trip to Llanboidy. According to *Ruff's Guide to the Turf*, the number of 'jumps races' run in Britain more than doubled between 1861 and 1869.[41] Another disadvantage was the fact that racing over banks was exclusive to Wales (and to Ireland). In England, the races were over the flat, hurdles or flying courses. The Maesgwynne-trained horses were almost unbeatable over banks! The difficulties came to a head in 1865 when English owners announced they did not like the Cefnbrafle large banks and declined to compete!

The Squire would not give up that easily. He postponed the meeting for five weeks to allow the course to be altered 'to induce our English friends to bring their horses to run against our local ones.' An extra course was built on which all the heavy banks were replaced with flies consisting of low banks and gorse hurdles. *Bell's Life* reported that the new course had twenty-two fences, all doubles with intervening dykes, in the 4 mile route. They required 'doing' but 'the English and Welsh were now on even terms.'[42] The *Journal*'s view of the effect on the racing was: 'Although we do not like to see the good old style of steeplechasing done away with – the effect of the alteration was very improving – the UHC and the Open steeplechases were two of the best-contested races we ever witnessed – all the horses being together throughout, all jumping splendidly, the pace terrific and finishes exciting. The formation of the course –

being almost serpentine – meant horses passed near the stand – back and fore – a number of times and there was no need to use field glasses from the stand and elsewhere.' The advert in the *Carmarthen Journal* for the 1865 'Llanboidy Hunt, Races, and Open Steeplechases' made the point that both the Open Steeplechase and the open Cambrian Steeplechase were to 'be run over small flying fences and gorsed hurdles. No Banks.' Furthermore, the condition that 'Persons on Horseback will not be allowed on the ground to view the Races' suggested that mounted viewers had distracted competitors in previous years.

The pre-race champagne luncheon at Maesgwynne had been attended by over 200 guests. A sideboard was 'covered with presentation plate, racing and other trophies which Mr Powell had won during a long and honourable career.' According to *Bell's Life*, several of the visitors during the morning 'strolled through the worthy host's boxes, stables, kennels and contiguous farm. In one of the former, recently erected, stood four well-furnished three-year-old hunters by "Confessor" . . . 200 guineas had been refused for one of them.' Another, out of the famous 'Esmerelda' (destroyed some time back through infirmity) 'took the prize last year at Carmarthen for the best two-year-old hunter . . . Another two, 'The Duck' and 'The Dane', . . . 'will doubt-less be heard of as steeplechasers.' William Purnell, the head groom, was praised for his attention and tact throughout the visit. Further along on the tour, 'stood the high priced "Flyfisher", who since returning from Aintree has done walking exercise only, and next to him the notorious "Africaine" recently purchased for a good sum.'

The implied fragile physical condition of 'Flyfisher' was, no doubt, a reflection of the steeplechaser's exertions over the Grand National course at Aintree. The following year when 'L'Africaine' ran in the gruelling event he was hacked (ridden) the 320 mile return journey from Maesgwynne to Liverpool because of his aversion to being caged in a rail truck. We can only wonder at the length of time he took to recover from that ordeal.

According to the *Journal* it was a 'boisterous and drenching day . . . the fifteenth anniversary of this popular meeting.' They had splendid racing and there was a large assemblage, the majority of whom were wet to the skin before the day was over. Added prize money of £240 was spread over eight races.

The Open Hurdle (of 5 sovereigns +30 sovereigns) was won by Monsieur Vaillant's 'Heurlys' (Cox) and the owner was complimented by the *Journal* 'for his plucky spirit in bringing his horses [from Warwick] to run so far west.' The alterations to the course had done the trick!

The *Journal*'s correspondent complained about the delay caused by difficulties in the process of weighing for the sweepstake for ponies under 14 hands high (of 10 shillings each) which involved local owners, unused to orderly processes.

The Open Steeplechase of 7 sovereigns each with 70 sovereigns added, run over fences was 'a magnificent race'. It was won by the Hon. Godfrey Morgan's 'Persuader' (J. James), five ran.

There were 14 runners in the Hunters' Scurry (sometimes called the Cambrian Derby) (of 1 sovereign each +15 sovereigns) run on the flat and limited to hunters in Wales. There was, inevitably 'another long tedious delay in weighing, partly caused by the fact that the steward of the weighing room, Brigstocke, was himself a rider in the race.' The race resembled a miniature Derby! It was won by the Hon. Frederick Morgan's 'Adam' (owner) from Mr Bowen's 'Crusader' (W. Brigstocke).

The Morgans were the sons of Lord Tredegar and according to the report in *Bell's Life*: 'The victory of the Tredegar jacket brought down a burst of applause.'

Because the wet weather forced many to go home, soaked to the skin, only about thirty-six attended the dinner at the Maesgwynne Arms and 'the host, Benjamin Griffiths, must have been a loser' as a result. During the evening, Monsieur Villaume owner of 'Heurlys', speaking through W. R. H. Powell (who therefore could understand and translate French) asked for 'his health to be drunk in champagne and a liberal supply was brought out.' In reply, the Frenchman said that he felt greater pride in winning at Llanboidy than at other places in the country and he hoped he would win again there.

The next day provided further evidence of the uniqueness of the Llanboidy race meeting, when pigeon-shooting competitions were organised. The first event was an Open Sweepstake between two well-known sharpshooters, a Mr Ryder and a Mr Braithwaite and the Squire's brother, T. R. Oliver Powell who 'although very good, had never shot in public before and went in 'for a lark'.' Betting was on Ryder but in a turn-up for the books, Oliver Powell was the winner.

Thursday was a fine day for the final four races and Powell got his second winner when Johnny Pope rode 'Grantstown' to victory out of 5 starters in the Principality Hurdle. His 'Dandy' (J. Pope) had taken the UHC Steeplechase on the first day.

Fifteen ran in the Fox Hunters' Stakes (of 1 sovereign +15 sovereigns) for horses regularly hunted in Wales and never been in a public training stable. It was won by Mr Tom Rees of Llansteffan on his 'Trumpeter'.[43] Fifty-three horses had gone in the eight races for which the added prize money was £240.

As reported in *The Welshman*, a dinner at Maesgwynne Arms ended 'one of the best meetings of the season.' It is interesting that the altered course on which banks had been eliminated was only used for the two open steeplechases. The two steeplechases limited to hunters in Wales were still run over the old banking course. Banking courses were the favourite steeplechase tracks in Wales and in Ireland.[44]

4.5 The Powells go racing

W. R. H. Powell's intense involvement in hunting and steeplechasing did not mean that he neglected his family at Maesgwynne. We get a glimpse of the whole family at the Tivyside Steeplechases of 1866 in a journal kept by one Agnes Hermione Jennings of Gellideg in Llandyfaelog Parish. W. R. H. Powell, his wife Catherine and his elder daughter Caroline arrived on Tuesday evening 22 February at the mansion of Pentre, Boncath, Manordeifi (near Abercych) to join about twenty guests staying at the home of Saunders Davies.

On Wednesday morning the men left for the races but it was early afternoon before the ladies left, some, including Mrs and Miss Powell, in carriages and others on foot; the course was only about a mile from the mansion. 'There were five or six races amongst which was one for farmers riding their own horses, and a pony race. There were a good many carriages by the course, and in front of us was the Penlan carriage with four horses driven by Captain Jones and Miss Gulston, Mrs and Miss Boultbee and one of the little Jones inside. It was a very fine bright day, though cold and frosty. All our party in the break walked home with the gentlemen, we took a shorter way home through the fields. We saw the end of the pony race from the top of a bank, which they jumped over. We got home about 5.30 p.m. We had dinner at 7.30 p.m. We had singing and dancing in the evening.'

The following day breakfast was served at 9.30 a.m. after which everyone got ready to go to the meet of the foxhounds about five miles away. Some travelled by carriage and others by brake. W. R. H. Powell and his daughter were in hunting costume and rode in the brake to the meet where their horses were delivered by grooms. They arrived at the house near where the meet was held at about 11.00 a.m. and 'found a great spread prepared, which we did not feel inclined to partake of at that time in the morning.'

The riders and hounds soon left, leaving the rest to try to follow on foot or simply hang around for an hour or so. A certain Mrs Phillips amused herself as she 'chaffed Colonel Bunbury a good deal; a gentleman slightly inclined to corpulence.' The foot party were then carted back to the mansion and the gentlemen 'threw out halfpence to some children who were running behind the carriage, and which they scrambled for. We had luncheon about 2.30 p.m.'

'We stayed at home in the afternoon and had singing. One of the children frightened Mrs Powell by suddenly falling asleep in her arms. We had dinner at 7.00 p.m. Mrs Saunders Davies did not come into dinner because she was not dressed in time, so Mrs Powell took her place [as hostess I guess]. All the servants came into the music room to see us dressed [ready for the second Ball of the week at Cardigan, about seven miles away]. We went [by carriage in which they often carried hot water bottles] at 10.00 p.m.' At the Ball 'my dress was perpetually getting torn and I had to have it stiched up about eight times . . . we got home about 6.00 a.m.'

Next day, Friday, was departure day. Although there is no mention of the Powells travelling arrangements, it would have been by coach to Maesgwynne, about twelve miles away. Agnes Jennings 'got up about 11.00 a.m. and had breakfast and made preparations for our departure. I looked at the paper and some old 'Punches' till 2.00 p.m. The fly came round which we had ordered from Narberth and we left Pentre at 2.30 p.m. and drove to the Narberth Road Station [Clunderwen]. Got there about 5.30 p.m.. Train did not go till 6.15 p.m. so I walked with Lee to a shop and bought some biscuits. Mr Beckwith, who was going to London went with us as far as Kidwelly which we reached at 7.00 p.m., got home [to Gellideg, Llandyfaelog Parish] at 7.30 p.m.'[45]

4.6 1866: Powell tries to retire from the turf

It was a disappointment to the racing fraternity and the general public in the Llanboidy area to read and hear that there would be no races at Llanboidy in the spring of 1866. The course was to be improved with the intention of resuming racing in 1867.[46] And so, after sixteen years of continuous meetings at Cefnbrafle, horse racing at Llanboidy had come to an end. For nine years, from 1856 to 1865, the meetings had taken up most of a week, with two days of racing and two days of fox hunting . . . that was the golden age of Llanboidy Races.

As the year, 1866, progressed more bad news emerged from Maesgwynne. W. R. H. Powell suffered a serious illness as a result of which he was forced to miss the Llanboidy Agricultural

Society Show on Friday, 14 September, because he was recuperating in Ireland. In mid-November 1866, racegoers everywhere must have been saddened to read the following advert in the local papers:

STEEPLE-CHASE HORSES, &c.

MR. J. HOWELL THOMAS is instructed to offer FOR SALE at Whitland Station, on FRIDAY, NOVEMBER 30th, at Two o'clock precisely all the STEEPLE CHASE HORSES, the property of W. R. H. POWELL, Esq., together with some Prime Hunters, Brood Mares, and Colts.

Catalogues on application.

(Courtesy *Carmarthen Journal*).

It is more than likely that it was concern about his health that made him decide to sell his horses . . . a pretty momentous decision for a man so taken with sport.

As it turned out, Powell was not lost to racing because the November sale fell far short of the advertised aim. Only a few horses were sold such as 'The Friar', a four-year-old who fetched 195 guineas. But the reserve price was not reached for the best horses, such as 'Flyfisher', 'Daisy', 'Heurlys' – which he must have bought from Monsieur Villaume – and 'Ladybird'. It was rumoured that 'Fairyland' was sold privately for 1000 guineas. Therefore, Powell retained most of his remarkable stud.

Early in 1867, Powell was back in harness and was heavily involved with the revamped Carmarthenshire Steeplechases. But again, at that time, Powell was not enjoying the best of health and even though he claimed that 'a few of Taylor's Constitution Balls have set me right' his poor health and the excessive work load in getting up the Carmarthen meeting were, undoubtedly, factors in the failure to fulfil his stated intention to have races at Llanboidy in 1867. However, any thoughts of getting up a meeting at Cefnbrafle in April 1867 would have been dashed by the discovery of a fearful distemper affecting the hunters at Maesgwynne Stables. A seventh horse died from the infection in March. Powell had bought two hunters at Lort Phillips' sale and one of them named 'Crow' was thought to have carried the disease to Maesgwynne. 'Crow' had since died as had 'Newton', its partner from the Lort Phillips sale although it was 'Beeswing' that was the first to succumb. The other dead horses were the well-known hunter and Miss Powell's favourite ride, 'Confederate'; the promising and remarkably swift youngster 'Fawn'; the sprightly 'Lady Bird' and the latest to die was 'Moonbeam'.[47]

In April 1867 farmers and traders in the Llanboidy locality responded to the crisis by organising a testimonial for Powell, 'the leading sportsman in south Wales . . . chief promoter of the Carmarthenshire Hunt Week and of Welsh Steeplechases.' In addition Powell took a 'lively interest in magisterial business and in the politics of the County.' According to the *Journal*, 'many would be astonished to see the farmers and traders drawing out their 2, 5, 10 and even 15 pounds and giving with a zest that would be impossible to describe.' No subscription less than £1 was accepted and 'the money flowed in with one of the twelve districts soon reporting upwards of £160 collected.' At a meeting in Carmarthen Powell's hunting friends organised their own testimonial. By June the local testimonial had reached a sum in excess of £300.[48]

It would appear that the distemper may have been contained and limited to the hunters only, leaving the steeplechasers free of the disease because on 3 May 1867 Powell ran two of his best at the Cardiff Races and Steeplechases. In the Open Hurdle, Powell's 'Flyfisher' with Johnny Pope in the saddle was unplaced. But in the Open Steeplechase, his 'Flyfisher' with G. Holman up came first with 'Daisy' and Johnny Pope in second place in a field of six.

On 26 May 1867 there occurred one of the most remarkable Derby races ever witnessed at Epsom. The Lincolnshire landowner, Tory politician and racehorse owner Henry Chaplin had entered a dark chestnut colt, Hermit, although the horse had not fully recovered from a burst blood vessel. Written-off as a no-hoper, Hermit's starting price was 1000/15. On a miserable day of heavy showers, a field of thirty produced ten false starts which delayed the race for over an hour. Needless to say, Hermit, with John Daley up won by a neck after a late run. Decades later, local (Llanboidy) lore had it that Powell had reaped a small fortune from betting on Hermit and used some of the money to build Maesgwynne Arms and the Market Hall. But the actual dates of construction of those buildings (Maesgwynne Arms in 1856 and the Market Hall in 1881) do not support the tale and furthermore, Powell bet very little; his enjoyment was running his steeplechasers rather than gambling.

Later in 1867 W. R. H. Powell suffered another severe illness which limited his attendance at Llanboidy Agricultural Society Show in late September to a short visit to the field in his carriage 'to the unmistakeable joy of the people present' [meaning that the people were overjoyed to see him]. He was also forced to give up as huntsman of the Maesgwynne pack after doing the job for twenty-eight years! He handed over the horn and the job of huntsman to Jack Rees who remained as huntsman until the pack was sold in 1889 following the death of W. R. H. Powell. Jack Rees did have a break of a few months during the 1875/76 season when he broke a leg when going to covert on the first day of hunting. W. R. H. Powell took over as huntsman for a few months after which Jack Rees resumed his duties and Thomas (Tom) Davies, who lived at Plasybwci, Llanboidy, became whipper-in.

W. R. H. Powell and Jack Rees were on extremely friendly terms and Powell Bach would call at the Lamb Inn after attending church every Sunday morning for an hour-and-a-half's discussion. Powell often went to Ireland and, in the words of Tom Rees of Llansteffan . . . 'bought scores of well-bred horses, no doubt with the hopes of securing a Grand National winner in embryo. If the type of horse brought over did not turn out chasers, they became valuable as weight-carrying hunters. One horse, named "Fairyland" by "Greatheart", was sold simply as a hunter for a £1,000; he won several prizes in the show ring.' And when Tom Rees visited Cahirmee horse fair in Ireland he was asked by the principal Cork dealer, Tom Donovan, . . . 'what sort of man could Jack Rees be, as one qualification demanded by Mr Powell in all horses he bought, was their suitability as mounts for his famous huntsman.'[12]

Jack Rees' knowledge of bloodstock helped develop the large and successful breeding stud kept by Powell at Maesgwynne and, later, he went about introducing thoroughbred entires into the county and he kept some of the best-bred thoroughbred sires at the Lamb, Llanboidy, for the use of bloodstock breeders and farmers. The good work was continued by his younger son John Forsyth Rees, a veterinary surgeon at Carmarthen. His eldest son George Rees became a

147

veterinary surgeon at Staines near Windsor. He died at forty-one years of age in 1896. Jack Rees also trained several chasers at the Lamb, including 'Game Pullet', a bay mare which was one of thirteen starters in a memorable race at Cefnbrafle in 1870. Ridden by Tom Rees 'Game Pullet' had the better of the field and won by a head.[60] Jack Rees died at the Lamb in 1897.

In July 1868 an advert in the *Carmarthen Journal* indicated that big changes were afoot at Maesgwynne.[49]

SOUTH WALES.

MAESGWYNNE, SAINT CLEARS.

Important Sale of Renowned Steeplechase Horses and Hunters.

MR. J. HOWELL THOMAS has been favoured with instructions to offer for POSITIVE SALE, at MAESGWYNNE, on FRIDAY, the 17th July, 1868, the entire STUD of GRAND STEEPLECHASE HORSES and HUNTERS, comprising upwards of 30 Lots, the property of W. R. H. POWELL, Esq.

Full particulars will appear next week, when Catalogues, with every information, may be obtained from Mr J. Howell Thomas, Carmarthen; or W. R. H. Powell, Maesgwynne, where the Horses may be seen.

(Courtesy *Carmarthen Journal*).

Catalogues describing the animals were in circulation and patrons of the turf from all parts of the kingdom were expected to attend.[50] But despite a good attendance less than a third of the thirty or so horses were disposed of. 'Flyfisher' which had cost Powell 1250 guineas and had won the Croydon Cup and several other valuable steeplechases was knocked down for 153 guineas. The auctioneer soon realized that he was 'too far from "Tattersall's Corner" for these well- and carefully-bred horses to fetch anything like their real value.'[51]

Disappointing sale or not, it seemed clear that Powell was trying his best to retire from the turf. At the same time, in the field of fox-hunting he was still producing great sport with his Maesgwynne 'crack pack'. A meet at Llanddowror was reported as having been one of the best-ever runs by his pack. Whether or not his health allowed the MFH to have been out himself is not known.

There was no report of any activity on the matter of Llanboidy Races in 1868 or 1869 and according to the newspapers, W. R. H. Powell was at the time 'retired from racing'. But in fact he was far from finished with racing. For example, in April 1869 at the Aberystwyth Spring Steeplechases, Powell's 'Mayboy' ridden by Johnny Pope had great success, winning the Principality Stakes, where 4 ran, and coming second out of 6 runners in the Aberystwyth Stakes. At the Dinner W. R. H. Powell, in reply to a toast, said he had great pleasure coming to Aberystwyth and hoped 'to be able to come here for many years to come'.[52] It should be noted that no horses that had been in a public training-stable were allowed to run in the Aberystwyth meeting. But that did not prevent Powell from running his hunters which he continued to do, at least, at meetings within the three western counties. Clearly, the report of Powell having been 'retired from the turf' was premature! Powell had entered another horse at Aberystwyth. 'Fear', had been a favourite for success but she had hurt herself in the train on the way to the meeting. Although not badly injured it was deemed advisable not to take 'Fear' to Aberystwyth and Powell left her in the Abergwili stables of his brother-in-law, Grismond Philipps. So it may be deduced that at that time the brothers-in-law enjoyed cordial personal relations which were not always the case if Herbert M. Vaughan is to be believed. 'One of the many social scandals that in those far-off days shook the equilibrium of the countryside was occasioned by the late Captain Grismond Philipps of Cwmgwili calling out in a moment of unguarded wrath: "By G-d, he's being pulled!" in allusion to an incident towards the finish of an exciting race, the losing horse in question being the property of Powell, MP and MFH. There naturally ensued a considerable coolness (to put it mildly) between the two brothers-in-law . . . No doubt it was untrue; but there still persists a belief that the ethics of the racing world are not precisely those of the spiritual ditto.'[53] Grismond Philipps had considerable success with racehorses but, surprisingly, he had no runners at Llanboidy Races in 1854, 1855, 1856, 1870 and 1871.

The ineligibility of horses in public training stables applied to the 1869 Pembroke Races and Powell's success in winning the Hunter's Stakes with 'Mayboy' (Pope) has to be viewed in that light.

But yet again Mr Powell's 'retirement from racing' was cited in an editorial in *The Welshman* on 23 April 1869 as having contributed to the difficulties facing horse racing in west Wales: When the Maesgwynne Stable was up and running '. . . Mr Powell had in his stable the finest steeplechase horses in the country, and ran them at all the principal English meetings. As a consequence, the owners of English horses paid Mr Powell's country a return visit, entering their horses out of compliment to him. But Mr Powell having disposed of his horses . . . English owners lie no longer under a load of obligation, and therefore we did not see them at our late steeplechases.'

Another sale of Maesgwynne horses, this time of seven surplus hunters, took place on Saturday, 22 May 1869, at the cattle market at Carmarthen. There was a large crowd present from adjoining counties and more distant places.[54] All seven horses were sold for prices between 20 guineas and 200 guineas which must have pleased Powell in a way that his previous attempt in July 1868 to sell his 'entire stud' had not. However, newspapers' claims and statements to the effect that Powell had 'disposed of his horses' were rather wide of the mark; what was more likely was that, in addition to selling his surplus hunters, he probably reduced his stable of trained steeplechasers by private sales.

The numbers of horses at the Maesgwynne Stable and the depletion in numbers as a result of sales can be estimated from reports of visitors to Maesgwynne. For example, Agnes Jennings in 1870 reported upward of 40 horses at Maesgwynne. The date of her visit meant that 'upward of 40 horses' was the number left after the sales of the steeplechasers and the surplus hunters. Tom Rees on his visit in 1887 claimed that 'L'Africaine' had run in the Liverpool Grand National in 1886 but in fact it was in 1866 that the horse had been an also-ran in the famous race. Rees also reckoned that there were generally about 70 horses stabled at Maesgwynne with 20 being steeplechasers in training.[12] At first sight that comment by Tom Rees, made as late as 1887, is puzzling. By that time Maesgwynne had been past its peak as a steeplechaser training stable for about fifteen years. Tom Rees must have been referring to the number of horses stabled at Maesgwynne twenty years earlier, in 1867, when the Stable was in its prime and Powell was the leading owner and trainer of steeplechasers in Wales. On that basis it is reasonable to conclude that as a result of the public sale at Maesgwynne in July 1868 and subsequent private sales, Powell had disposed of many if not most of his 20 or so steeplechasers before 1870. Furthermore, he sold six hunters at Carmarthen in 1869 so that by the time of Jennings' visit to Maesgwynne in 1870, the 70 or so horses mentioned by Tom Rees would have been reduced by about 26 to 'upward of 40' as reported by Jennings.

In the 1870s, it is likely that most of the horses at Maesgwynne would have been hunters, but some would have been there as part of Powell's effort to improve the strain of hunters and of steeplechasers in west Wales in conjunction with Jack Rees of the Lamb Inn, Llanboidy. For example, a notice of sale in *The Welshman* of 2 January 1880 showed that steeplechasers were still being trained at Maesgwynne and four of them were offered for sale as 'maidens, never started; have been schooled and qualified and will soon be fit to run.' Another two were described as 'well known steeplechase horses – fresh and in work'. And a hunter named 'The Poacher' had the tag of 'winner of the Tivyside Hunt Steeplechase'. The 'retired from turf' tag applied to Mr Powell in 1868 probably reflected his decision to end his reign as a major racer of steeplechasers. The decision was forced on him by the changing scene in the world of steeplechasing which saw meetings concentrated mainly in England, and as a result it was no longer cost-effective for him to travel regularly over great distances to find races for his steeplechasers. But if the days were gone when Powell's colours of orange and black on a Maesgwynne trained steeplechaser remained a sight to be feared on racecourses everywhere he still enjoyed success in a few of the top-class races of the day as we shall see later.

4.7 1870: Llanboidy revived!

Horse racing enthusiasts would have been delighted to read, or hear about, reports in newspapers in late February and early March 1870 of the proposed revival after an absence of five years of Llanboidy Races, albeit confined to a single day, Wednesday, 30 March, of five races two of which were confined to hunters within Wales and Monmouthshire and the other three limited to hunters from the three counties of west Wales. No horse in a training stable would be allowed to run thus ruling out those steeplechasers in training at the Maesgwynne stables, if there were any.[55,56] Refreshments would be provided under the stand, but no booths would be allowed. The Dinner would be at the Maesgwynne Arms on the Wednesday evening.

In addition to the racing, a pigeon match was to be shot-off on the Thursday, by gentlemen of the three counties, and Mr Powell's hounds would meet on the Friday. The announcement was signed by W. R. H. Powell, Hon. Sec. Therefore, Llanboidy and the racing fraternity throughout Wales could look forward to three days of action at Cefnbrafle. But before that, in the middle of March, Powell ran his horse 'Count' in the Hunters' Stakes at the Pembrokeshire Steeplechases and took first place with his 19-year-old whipper-in Richard Griffiths in the saddle.

Having been starved for five years of the lavish pre-race hospitality dished out at Maesgwynne the local newspapers went to town in their reporting during the 1870 meeting. *The Welshman* claimed that past meetings at Cefnbrafle were 'amongst the most pleasing recollections in the life of the present generation of sportsmen' and that the meetings differed greatly from others in Wales. For example, the hospitality dispensed by the Squire and his family had not been surpassed 'anywhere in the kingdom'. Furthermore, the sport was always 'honest and interesting' and there was a 'complete absence of the hard business (betting and boozing?) seen at most other meetings'. The popularity of Mr Powell had been crucial in attracting owners to travel long distances to Llanboidy where the charm of T. R. O. Powell ensured a smooth solution to any problem that might arise.

At the 1870 champagne-luncheon, which lasted nearly two hours, a cake sent from London by Emily Catherine Powell (Powell's second daughter) was displayed and it carried the words 'Welcome to Llanboidy'. The weather was glorious and it was claimed that the meeting attracted the largest number of spectators ever assembled at Cefnbrafle.[57] One who was present was Agnes Hermione Jennings of Gellideg, Kidwelly, who recorded her observations in a journal. She had come by train from Cydweli to Narberth Road station on 29 March 1870 and was staying with a Mr and Mrs Gower at Clunderwen. On Wednesday, which was fine and bright but cold and windy, 'after breakfast we all went to Llanboidy Races, in carriages, 6 miles off. At Maesgwynne there was a large crowd who at 12 o'clock appeared as eager to devour turkey and to pitch into champagne as though they had not seen food for hours.' She was 'introduced to young Sartoris who was to ride Mr Powell's horses.' The crowd left the house at one o'clock for the race course and Hermione was driven there. She paid 2s.6d. (12.5p) 'to enter the grandstand which had windows all round.'[58]

Powell's principal jockey at the meeting was Greville Sartoris, son of the Liberal MP for Carmarthenshire. He went in three races and steered 'Count' to victory by half a length in the Principality Stakes out of nine starters. 'Count' was virtually unbeatable over Banks. Sartoris' connection with Maesgwynne was a short one on account of his untimely death after breaking his neck 'larking over a sheep hurdle'.[59]

The most populated race was The Hunter's Scurry with thirteen starters but none from Maesgwynne and 'A considerable time was necessarily occupied in weighing-out for this race, owing chiefly to the crowded state of the weighing room.' After another exciting race, 'Game Pullet', trained by Jack Rees, Lamb Inn, Llanboidy and ridden by Tom Rees of Llansteffan won by a length. 'Mr Rees was loudly cheered as he returned to the weighing room.' In his own account of the race in *Racing Reminiscences*, Tom Rees reckoned that twenty-five runners were at the off! In total, 35 runners had taken part in five races.

On the following day, a pigeon match was shot-off on the race course. And Agnes Jennings and the Gowers were back at Maesgwynne to see the match and more. After lunch at the mansion, Mrs Powell took them to see the stables which were very extensive and contained upwards of 40 horses. They were also shown the fox-hounds.[58]

A week or so later, W. R. H. Powell and his entourage were at the Tivyside races. He had two horses which were entered in three races. But in the Tivyside Steeplechase his horse was late arriving at the start and was refused permission to run. 'Everybody was sorry to find that Mr Powell's horse was left behind in consequence of his late arrival at the post. Though this arose from circumstances beyond the control of Mr Powell who is a tower of strength in all our local meetings, yet the managers cannot be blamed for showing that they are no respecters of person and that they are determined to enforce punctuality, the necessity for which on these occasions no one feels more than Mr Powell himself.' However, his horse 'The Count', with

Greville Sartoris up, won the Tivyside Stakes and Mr and Mrs Powell were present at the Hunt Ball held in the Guildhall, Cardigan.[60]

In April 1870, Powell was to prove that he still had top-class steeplechasers at Maesgwynne when his 'Daisy' ridden by England's leading cross-country jockey, Cheltenham-born George Stevens, won the prestigious Cheltenham Steeplechase. It was Stevens' third win in the race. A year later the 40-year-old Stevens was killed in a freak riding accident.[61]

Later in the year Powell's six-year-old 'The Hart' (6/1) ridden by Tony Pickernell (who rode the Grand National winner in 1860 and was to do so again in 1871) and carrying 12st.3lb. ran second to H. Chaplin's 'Schiedam' (4/1) with J. M. Richardson carrying 11st.8lb. in the 1870 Grand National Hunt Steeplechase at Cottenham, Cambridgeshire. Fifteen started. Considerable éclat was given to the meeting by the presence of the Prince and Princess of Wales, who were the guests of the Duke and Duchess of Manchester at Kimbolton.[32]

At the September 1870 Tenby Races, Powell horses started in two races and 'Septima' with Johnny Pope won the Attack Race. But it was at the dinner in the Coburg Hotel that Powell came into his own claiming he was there to help the meeting and that they would have had a dozen more horses if timely notice of the meeting had been given. Mr Scourfield revealed that Powell not only looked happy but he made others happy to look at him and that he imparted a lot of geniality and good humour to the proceedings of whatever meeting he was at. Powell informed them of his intention to have another meeting at Llanboidy in 1871 'to follow . . . the Carmarthen and the Abergavenny meetings so that they would have a little Welsh circuit.'[62]

4.8 Protect the foxes but compensate the farmers . . . insists Powell

The Union Hunt Club was disbanded in July 1870 at the Boar's Head, Carmarthen. It seems that the main purpose of the Hunt Clubs was to ensure that coverts (woods and/or undergrowth) were protected and maintained for foxes to breed and shelter in. Clearly the Union Hunt Club was not effective in this respect and it became clear during the meeting that it was W. R. H. Powell who was the main instigator of the call to disband it. But he also wished to set up a new club through which it could be arranged for the coverts to be protected and also for any losses of poultry suffered by neighbouring farmers to be compensated for. The meeting was chaired by Mr Grismond Philipps, Cwmgwili, and present were Mr Gwyn, Cwrt Hyr; Mr Carver, Wenallt; Mr Walters, Sarnau; Mr T. Morris, Coombe; Mr Llewellyn Ll. Price; Mr J. M. Jones, Llanllwch House; Mr J. B. Graves, Clare Hill; Mr D. R. Watkins and Mr J. Beynon jnr, Trewern. Mr Powell was not present at the meeting but he had written to Mr Gwyn stating that without coverts and foxes, no masters of hounds could show sport but if through preservation of coverts and foxes the cottagers suffered losses of poultry to the foxes, they should be compensated.

The discussions in the meeting provided another example of Powell Bach's powerful, indeed controlling influence in the field of fox-hunting in Carmarthenshire. Not only did the meeting agree to set up a new hunt club but it also adopted his idea that compensation for losses by farmers and cottagers should be paid directly by the squire responsible for a particular area and the squire could then claim back from the Club. That made life easier for the poor at the expense of the squires. Further discussion ensued as to the club's ability to pay compensation and it was decided that members should pay subscriptions of five guineas (presumably per year). And a name for the new club was not difficult to decide upon: 'it was only natural to call the new club the Maesgwynne Hunt Club.'[63]

There was no rest from hunting for Powell, even in the summer break from chasing foxes. In August 1870, W. R. H. Powell was advertising a 'meet of his Otter Hounds at Whitland on the Tuesday and at Blackpool Bridge on the Cleddau on the Friday of the same week.'[64] But the staple diet of 'good sport' for Powell Bach was, of course, fox-hunting and twice-a-week-meets were the order of the times. Occasionally a report in the local weeklies captured the intensity of the day's hunting in terms of the effort put in by the pack and the master, the huntsman and the whip together with some of the other mounted personnel as well as the undoubted pleasure it brought to hordes of foot followers. The whole activity needs to be viewed in terms of the accepted practices of the times: the nineteenth century.

4.9 The 1871 Llanboidy Races: the final fling at Cefnbrafle

Powell's announcement in Tenby in September 1870 of another race meeting in Llanboidy in 1871 may have been made under the influence of the after-glow of the highly successful day's racing of 1870. Six months later he explained that his decision to have a meeting 'once more' in Llanboidy was made in Carmarthen in February 1871 following requests from numerous friends, and those from Swansea had invited him to dinner and given him £50 towards the costs.[65]

The format of the 1871 meeting followed that of the 'golden-age': two days' hunting and two days' racing. Ten races were planned; a number equalled only once before, in 1864. Entries were restricted to hunters from south Wales and Monmouthshire, and racegoers flocked 'in great numbers' to Cefnbrafle.[66] Some arrived by train at Whitland and walked the four miles to the racecourse, others were driven from Whitland, Carmarthen, Saint Clears, Tenby, Haverfordwest and other places and the 'clean, neat little village was in a bustle at an early hour'.

In the afternoon 'the grandstand was crowded with ladies and gentlemen and . . . there was a long string of carriages occupied by many of the leading families' of west Wales. In addition there was a large attendance of the 'general public'. The 'gay and costly jackets of some of the riders' among whom were 'two or three professionals from England' provided a colourful scene.[67] Even though the meeting was restricted to the hunting fraternity of south Wales and Monmouthshire the added prize money of £255 ensured that races were as keenly contested as in an open meeting as confirmed by several 'incidents'. For example, an objection by the owner (C. B. Mansfield) of the second-placed horse in the Cefen Stakes on the grounds that the winner had not been 'regularly hunted' that season was admitted by its owner, Alfred Jones, who was subsequently disqualified and the race awarded to Mansfield. A more protracted protest resulted from the disqualification of Mr Henry Norton's entry in the 'race of the day', the Ladies Stakes. At the evening Dinner he demanded an explanation from the stewards but after 'some unpleasantness' it was agreed that the stewards' decision was final. At the same time the chairman for the evening, whose horse had won the race, announced that he was giving a plate 'of the same description to be run for on the Friday' by the same horses that had gone in the Ladies Stakes 'with the exception of his own horse'. The evening ended with 'a few songs'.

On the Thursday there was a meet of Powell's Hounds at Llanboidy with 'between 80 and 100 ladies and gents and a fair sprinkling of pinks.'

Although fewer attended the second day's racing because 'very few could leave their homes and businesses for two or three days in one week' those present saw C. B. Mansfield win 'a splendid' extra race with professional jockey J. Holman steering 'Jerry' to victory over 'Lancer' owned and ridden by Mr Gwyn.

Two of the races provided major incidents. In the Cambrian Stakes, 'Emperor' owned and ridden by W. R. H. Powell's son-in-law, W. F. Roch, bolted into the crowd close to the stand [they had no business to be there], knocked over a woman and then fell head-over-heels and rolled over his rider crushing him severely. Doctors present gave medical attention and it was a great relief that injuries were not as serious as originally thought. The final incident again involved C. B. Mansfield when his horse 'The Lamb' in the Consolation Stakes kicked and buck-jumped so much as to unseat his rider (Holman) and galloped wildly with the others into the winning field. When people tried to stop him he attempted to jump the entrance gate with all legs sideways and fell heavily on the road. He got up and galloped towards Llanboidy. Thus ended the incident-packed but highly enjoyable Llanboidy Races of 1871. A suggestion of having one day's racing in the spring and another in the autumn was left for Mr Powell to decide and 'we await the next merry meeting at Llanboidy.'[68]

The 'merry meetings' at Llanboidy in the 1850s and 1860s have been recalled by Reginald Herbert: 'There was scarce a meeting where W. H. Powell of Maesgwyn (close to Llanboidy) did not run something and he was known on every race-course in South Wales. He had some good horses too, amongst the best being Ace of Hearts, Flyfisher, Daisy, Fenton, and, in later years, Hussar, Milton and Minaret. Hussar was a wonder in hunters' flat races, and the weights he sometimes carried when he was beaten were, I believe, marvellous. . . . In those days the Abergavenny meeting was considered one of the best in Monmouthshire and South Wales. . . . Other meetings there were at Chepstow, Cardiff, Tenby and Llanboidy. The latter a typical Welsh gathering where they used to race and hunt on alternate days for a week, with very little bed for anyone. I have been told that on some occasions, though I never saw it, the competitors for the various 'chases were marshalled in front of the hotel in the village before the races and paraded through the streets of Llanboidy with their riders mounted and in racing colours . . . Llanboidy was the best fun of all the meetings, there being generally four or five matches to be disposed of before 'chasing began, mostly the result of a whole night sitting.' Herbert also referred to an incident which, he claimed, put paid to further meetings at Cefnbrafle: 'The meeting eventually was stopped in consequence of some blackguards, by way of a joke, forcing open the doors of the kennels in the middle of the night and letting all the hounds loose over the country.'[59]

However, it is most unlikely that the 'releasing of the hounds' incident was the reason for the ending of Llanboidy Races. Mounting difficulties in getting up the meeting had been experienced for some years. More and more race meetings had sprung up all over the country giving owners a choice of meetings close to home and the effort, in time and money, to induce owners to travel to distant places like Llanboidy had become prohibitive.

For W. R. H. Powell the evolving difficulties, outlined above, provided him with a double whammy because he was the lead-man in trying to maintain the highest standards of racing at both Llanboidy and at Carmarthen. In fact Powell was not in the best of health during those years and his extraordinary exertions in getting up the Carmarthenshire Steeplechases of February 1872 resulted in his serious illness at the start of that meeting. '. . . on the Wednesday only the faintest hopes, if any, were entertained of his recovery.'[69] Any lingering hope for another meeting at Llanboidy evaporated with Powell's collapse at Carmarthen. His recovery from illness took many months but eventually he was able to resume his leadership of the efforts to keep Carmarthenshire Steeplechases as one of the top race meetings in Wales.

However, time had been called on Llanboidy Races . . . horse racing at Cefnbrafle, spanning twenty-two years, was about to become a glorious memory.

LLANBOIDY RACES (Summary)								
Year	Duration	Added £	Races	Runners	Riders	Handi-capper	Grand Stand	Hotel
1848								
'49	morning		1	4	gents			
1850								
'51	morning		1	8	do			
'52	1 day		4+					
			donkey	14	do			
'53	do	£40.00	do	15	do			
'54	do	£60.00	4	20	do			
'55	do	£60.00	3	16	do			
'56	1 week	£85.00	5	17	do			
'57	do	£105.00	6	48	do			built
'58	do	£215.00	7	37	jockeys		built	
'59	do	£235.00	7	33	do			
1860	do	£275.00	7	37	do		improved	
'61	do	£295.00	8	48	do	yes		
'62	do	£295.00	8	41	do	yes		
'63	do	£305.00	8	49	do	yes		
'64	do	£300.00	10	58	do	yes	glazed	
'65	do	£240.00	8	53	do	yes		
'66								
'67								
'68								
'69								
1870	1 day	£180.00	5+					
			shoot	35	do	no		
'71	1 week	£255.00	10	64	do	no		

Part V

THE CARMARTHENSHIRE HUNT WEEK
AND STEEPLECHASES

5.1 1845-1849: The early years

THE *CARMARTHEN JOURNAL* of 4 October 1839 lamented that 'Until very late there were horse races at Carmarthen', but they had ceased because of a lack of money. It was to be another five years before a notice in the *Journal* announced that the Carmarthenshire Races were to take place on 25 and 26 April 1844. The stewards were Lloyd, Glansevin, Llangadog and Chambers, Llanelly House. However, the meeting had to be postponed because all of the promised subscriptions had not been paid into Morris' Bank.[1] The races were re-scheduled to commence on Tuesday 10 December 1844 and a meet of Gwyn Hughes' foxhounds would start the week's activities. On Wednesday, the Open Steeplechase (of 5 sovereigns each + 60 sovereigns) and a Pony Race (of 1 sovereign + Cup value 5 sovereigns) were to be run. And two more races, the Town Plate (of 3 sovereigns + 50 sovereigns) and a Sweepstake (of 1 sovereign. + Cup value 12 sovereigns), would complete the race programme on Thursday. The added prize money of 125 sovereigns would today be worth about £12,000. The week's activities were planned to end with a meet of Browne Edwardes' Carmarthen foxhounds on Friday. Hunt Balls were to be held on two evenings. In the event, only the balls went ahead because a severe frost put paid to the racing and hunting programme. No one from Maesgwynne was 'noticed' at the dances.[2]

The races at Carmarthen eventually came off on 22 and 23 January 1845. They were held on a field called Parc-y-Bryn on the farm of Pontgarreg, in today's Johnstown, within two miles of the town. Over 3,000 persons were present and the police and the 13th Light Dragoons kept the 'utmost order and regularity' where, because of the numbers present and the excitement 'there might have been a tendency to a slight departure from both.'

Four horses went in the Open, three in the Pony Race, eight in the Town Plate and three in the Sweepstake.[3] There was no mention in newspaper reports of W. R. H. Powell having entered any of the horses and neither was there for the Pembrokeshire and the Tenby Race meetings in August 1845.

Writing in 1916 Tom Rees of Llansteffan claimed that 'About 1845, steeplechasing came into vogue all over the country. There were meetings at Aberystwyth, Llandeilo, Pembroke, Narberth, The Tivyside and Carmarthen, the latter taking the foremost position.'[4] Tom Rees was probably a few years early for his claim for Carmarthen to be true.

In February 1846, the Carmarthenshire Hunt Week and Steeplechases at last got off to a successful week which included a 'splendid race' and a heated dispute![5] The meeting was held near Travellers' Rest a few miles west of the town and the course covered about four miles with between fifty and sixty leaps. The stewards were J. W. M. G. Hughes and D. B. Edwardes. A meet of Edwardes' Carmarthen Hounds kicked off the week's activities.

The Open Race (of 5 sovereigns each + 60 sovereigns) was won by W. R. H. Powell's 'Kangaroo' ridden by 25-year-old Tom Davies of Hayes Farm, Carew, Pembrokeshire and carrying 11st.11lb.; five ran. 'Kangaroo' was the only horse from Carmarthenshire, the other four were from Pembrokeshire and Tom's elder brother John rode the fourth-placed 'Giraffe' owned by Llewellin. And so, in the second year of the Carmarthenshire Steeplechases, Powell had succeeded in winning the Open. It turned out to be the start of a remarkable record of success for the Maesgwynne Stable which saw Powell win the Carmarthenshire Open 11 times in 25 years! He had a 'golden era' in the 1860s when only 'Fenton''s win in 1865 prevented Powell's horses from winning the Open seven times in succession! And less than a year prior to his win, 'Fenton' had been a successful member of the Maesgwynne Stable! It was also the first of six wins in the Open for jockey Tom Davies, his last being in 1865 at 44 years of age. Two of his winners were Powell horses.

On the second day of the 1846 meeting, the Town Plate (of 5 sovereigns each + 50 sovereigns) was again won by Powell's 'Kangaroo' with Tom Davies, this time carrying 12st.4lb. from Lewis' 'Tally-Ho' ridden by R. J. Dansey, a 31-year-old former 2nd Lt. 60th Rifles, then farming 90 acres at Glan-yr-Afon, Llanarth, Cardiganshire; nine ran. But Dansey disputed the result on the ground that 'Kangaroo', after passing the winning post first, turned back and walked outside the flags instead of between them. It seemed a very technical matter and the stewards found in favour of 'Kangaroo' and Tom Davies. A month later at the Pembrokeshire Steeplechases, 'Tally-Ho' and Dansey gained revenge by beating 'Kangaroo' and Tom Davies into second place.

The 1847 Carmarthenshire Hunt and Steeplechases, in the third year of their existence, were again troubled by inclement weather and had to be postponed for two weeks to 22 February. Although there was no mention in newspaper reports of Powell being present in any capacity it seems that his horse 'Chance' was taken there by his neighbour W. Protheroe of Dolwilym, Llanglydwen and won the Hunters' Stakes with Tom Davies; three ran. In the Open, Powell's 'Kangaroo' (Tom Davies) entered by Browne Edwardes was fourth; seven ran.[6]

A meet of the Carmarthen Hounds led by the MFH, Browne Edwardes, of Rhydygors near Carmarthen, a 29-year-old retired Army Lieutenant, opened proceedings for the 1848 Carmarthenshire Races Week held at Green Castle near Llangain. W. R. H. Powell had no horse entered in the Open but his 'Pioneer' ridden by Tom Davies won the Hunters' Stakes. For whatever reason it was W. G. B. S. Protheroe who entered 'Pioneer' in the Selling Stakes and Tom Davies again steered him to victory. The week's activities were concluded with a foot race between two men over the steeplechase course! The *Journal* was up-beat about the development of the Carmarthenshire Races over the 'few years' of their existence and although 'not yet at the level of Liverpool, Cheltenham and Worcester' the report was optimistic that in a few years the Carmarthen meeting would rank with the best.[7]

For the Pembrokeshire Steeplechases at Castlemartin in March 1848, Powell had entered 'Cabin Boy' and 'Pioneer', and Protheroe had 'Chance' on the card.[8] When a person other than the owner entered a horse, that person presumably paid the considerable fee to enter the horse in the race. Also it is possible that people like Protheroe allowed some of Powell's hunters to graze Protheroe's fields at Dolwilym during the summer break in the hunting calendar. (That was still a practice a century later in the 1940s when the then squire of Dolwilym, David Garrick Protheroe, had hunters (*ceffyle main*) belonging to others of the hunting fraternity farmed-out at Dolwilym over the summer months.)

W. R. H. Powell and Capt. Lloyd of Dolhaidd, Penboyr, had consented to be stewards for the 1849 Carmarthenshire Week. Clearly the 30-year-old Squire of Maesgwynne was developing as a leader in the sporting world of west Wales. A decision was taken to move the course from north of the river at Castell Moel (Green Castle) to south near Croesyceiliog village. Powell Bach had horses in two races and won the Scurry Race with 'Hazard' and John Rees out of four starters. It was Powell who chaired the dinner.[9]

5.2 1850-1853: Powell's hounds take over

It was becoming a tradition for the Carmarthenshire Hunt and Steeplechases Week to start with a meet. In 1850 after the demise of Browne Edwardes' pack it was W. R. H. Powell's Maesgwynne pack that took to the country. Monday and Friday were reserved for meets of Powell's hounds and Wednesday was allocated for Chambers' hounds (of Llanelli).[10] The racecourse that year was on land belonging to D. A. Saunders Davies MP at Wauncorgamfawr near Llanllwch. The weather for the races on Tuesday was wet and foggy and some owners did not want to go ahead with the races. But Lort Phillips who had come all the way from Lawrenny, Pembrokeshire threatened to walk his horse round the course and claim the prize; the other owners soon saddled their horses!

A list of entries for the Open Steeplechase published a few weeks earlier included W. R. H. Powell's 'Squire Ugly', which was destined to carry the heaviest weight of 12st. But the published results of the races showed that W. R. H. Powell had indulged in some 'horse lending' prior to the meeting. In the Open it was R. Lort Phillips' 'Squire Ugly' ridden by T. Davies that finished second to Jerry Olive, of the Boar's Head, Carmarthen's 'Hazard' (J. Rees) with Lort Phillips' 'Esmerelda' (J. Davies) in third. Among the six runners was W. Protheroe's 'Dandelion'. It is likely that the first three horses were the property of W. R. H. Powell. *The Welshman* summed up the racing in verse:

> Down down the precipice wild they break
> Where the foaming waters roar;
> And then up the brow of the mountain take
> Where horses never trod before.
>
> No checking hand to the rein he lends
> On slippery summits sheen,
> But ever and aye his head he bends
> At the plunge in some dark ravine.

In the ten-year-period 1850 to 1860, Jack Rees rode four winners in the Carmarthenshire Open and won the other big race, the Handicap, five times! He did the double on three occasions. Three of his victories in the Open were on 'Hazard', the first in 1850 for Jerry Olive of the Boar's Head. The horse was then bought by W. R. H. Powell and Jack Rees won the Open on it in 1851 and 1853. He won the Handicap on 'Hazard' three times, once in 1850 for Jerry Olive and in 1851 and 1853 for W. R. H. Powell. Jack Rees won the race twice more for W. R. H. Powell, on 'St David' in 1857 and on 'Carew' in 1860 when he was 41-years-old and by then he was landlord at the Lamb Inn, Llanboidy. 'Hazard' is reputed to have never lost a race! According to Tom Rees in his *Racing Reminiscences*, Jack Rees continued riding until 1866.

W. R. H. Powell was present at the Hunt Ball in the Boar's Head but, as a widower, he was unaccompanied. Capt. Grismond Philipps of Cwmgwili and his sisters were also there and no doubt the Squire of Maesgwynne got to know one of them, Catherine Anne Prudence, a little better.[11] By the time of the Pembrokeshire Steeplechases on 15 March 1850 it was W. R. H. Powell's 'Hazard' with John Rees up, that finished third in the Open race. A week later, Powell Bach must have doubted the wisdom of his 'horse lending' strategy because, in the Narberth Open Steeplechase at Sodstone Farm, his horse 'Hazard' with John Rees in the saddle was beaten into second place by R. Lort Phillips' 'Squire Ugly' with Tom Davies up.

The hope for a successful meet to open the week's proceedings in 1851 was ruined by 'snow, frost, storms and heavy rains.' Nevertheless, Powell, punctual as ever, was seen 'winding his way with huntsman and hounds to Raymond's Lodge . . . regardless of the pelting of the pitiless storm . . . [his] . . . delight to ride across the country in the wake of a well trained pack is proverbial.'

The Open on Tuesday had been expected to be a weight test for Mr Stokes' 'Baptist' described as 'the great gun' of the race. Would 12st.12lb. be enough of a handicap for 'Baptist' to be beaten? It was reported that: 'The splendid creature [Baptist] will to be piloted by Mr John Davies of Hayes whose brother Tom "the hero of a hundred races" will be on Lort Phillips' 'Esmerelda' (11st.5lb.) and Tom expects to be "there about the mark".' The previous year's winning partnership of 'Hazard' (11st.) and Jack Rees was going again and by 1851 the horse's owner was W. R. H. Powell who was 'universally beloved as a thorough sportsman and true type of the honest Welsh Squire.' In the end, 'Baptist' was scratched! There was heavy betting at the Golden Lion for Tuesday's races and although 'Cabin Boy' from Pembrokeshire was favourite, 'Esmerelda', 'Hazard' and 'Squire Ugly' attracted a lot of support. There were seven runners and on the day it was Powell's 'Hazard' with huntsman Jack Rees in the saddle that took the 1851 Open from Lort Phillips' 'Esmerelda' with the wily Tom Davies up. According to the *Journal* it was 'One of the most beautiful and well contested races ever witnessed at Carmarthen or anywhere else.'

But then a 'Most disgraceful fight took place between some soldiers of the 77th Regiment and some civilians who had been roughly handled.' But the reporter thought better than to elaborate because he felt certain the matter would finish up with the magistrates. Despite the unkind weather, Capt. Grismond Philipps of Cwmgwili and family which included his sisters were present on the racecourse and at the evening's Ball. Clearly the bad weather was not going to deter his sister, Catherine Anne Prudence, from showing her complete support for W. R. H. Powell whom she was to wed before the end of March. But the dinner was not well supported.

Only the mayor and one alderman represented the town, which was particularly disappointing bearing in mind that David Jones, MP, Pantglas, Llanfynydd, had come all the way from Paris to perform his duties as one of the stewards and to chair the dinner. The leading role played by W. R. H. Powell in the organisation of Carmarthenshire Races was again revealed when he announced at the dinner that by 'being an impudent beggar' (his words) he had persuaded 'his gallant friend' Capt. Grismond Philipps together with none less than Lord Emlyn, MP, to act as stewards for the 1852 meeting.

An interesting variation during the week of the 1851 meeting was a concert 'under the presence and patronage of the stewards,' held at the Town Hall, Carmarthen on the Wednesday evening at 8.00 o'clock, featuring 'The Celebrated Welsh Nightingale, Miss E. L. Williams.' Seats were priced at 2s.6d. (reserved), 1s.6d. (second seats), 1s.0d. (back seats). E. L. (Lizzie) Williams, born in Neath in 1836, was one of a number of outstanding Welsh singers of the day and often sang duets with the leading male singer from Dowlais, Robert Rees whose nom-de-plume was *Eos Morlais*. She was referred to in Welsh as a *pencerddes* (chief musician) and was known as *Llinos Cymru* and sometimes as *Llinos y De*. In 1858 she performed in New York. The concert was well attended and according to the advert, W. R. H. Powell would have been present. He had led the hunt meet at Travellers' Rest during the day but *Llinos Cymru* would have made sure he did not nod-off at the concert. As a man of initiative and action he may well have been instrumental in obtaining the services of the star singer.[12]

At the end of February 1851, at the Pembrokeshire Steeplechases, Powell's 'Hazard' was pipped by Lort Phillips' 'Esmerelda' in the Open, reversing their placings at Carmarthen. The buying and selling 'game' picked up pace during 1851 and 1852 – if that was the real explanation for the apparent change of ownership of the two star-horses 'Esmerelda' and 'Hazard'. At the beginning of 1851 Powell owned 'Hazard' and Lort Phillips owned 'Esmerelda'. However, in November 1851 a Mr Marshall entered 'Hazard' at Aberystwyth and the horse finished second in the Open with Jack Rees up. But by the time of the Carmarthenshire Races in February 1852, it was W. R. H. Powell who scratched 'Esmerelda' from the Open because he could not get the rider of his choice. The Maesgwynne stable jockey, Jack Rees, had been retained by Jerry Olive of the Boar's Head to ride his horse 'Hazard' in the Open and they finished in second place. In the Carmarthenshire Handicap, Powell's 'Esmerelda' with Archer in the saddle won, with Olive's 'Hazard' and Jack Rees unplaced. Five ran. But a month later, it was Powell's 'Esmerelda' and Powell's 'Hazard' that were entered in the Narberth Steeple-chases! It is reasonable to deduce that during 1851, 'Esmerelda' was sold by Lort Phillips to W. R. H. Powell. But the apparent switches of ownership of 'Hazard' during 1851 from Powell to Marshall to Jerry Olive and back to Powell is more difficult to fathom. Marshall and Olive would have paid the entry fees when the horses were entered in their names and it is possible that Powell got some form of sponsorship from them to help meet the costs of running his stable at Maesgwynne.

During the 1852 Carmarthenshire Races, a concert was held to raise funds for the Carmarthen Infirmary. The star performer was the musician, Brinley Richards, who was born in Quay Street, Carmarthen, in 1819. His father had a music shop and was the organist at St Peter's Church. As a young man Brinley Richards showed exceptional talent as a composer and succeeded in getting sponsorship from the Duke of Newcastle to study at the Royal Musical Academy. After further studies in Paris with Chopin, he returned to the Musical Academy where he eventually became a Director. He was considered the best pianist in Britain and gained fame as a teacher of piano playing. It was he that initiated the local examinations on behalf of the Academy and he acted as its examiner in Wales and in Scotland. He was a great supporter of the National Eisteddfod and often acted as an adjudicator. At the Carmarthenshire Hunt concert, Richards opened his presentation with a selection from *Les Huguenots* by the renowned Swiss-born composer Sigismond Thalberg and continued with a selection from his *Recollections of Wales*; the airs *Of noble race was Shenkin, Ar hyd y nos* and *Codiad yr Ehedydd*. 'Airs as familiar to us all as household words' and the audience was 'delighted with his exquisite performance.'[13]

More success followed in March 1852 for W. R. H. Powell's steeplechasers with Jack Rees riding 'Hazard' to second place out of 6 starters in the Open at Narberth but the same jockey could only manage third place on 'Esmerelda' out of 5 starters in the Llandeilo Open.

The proposed meet to start the 1853 Carmarthenshire Week was cancelled because of snow and frost and the disappointment of losing his day's hunting may have put Powell in the frame of mind to cause controversy in two races, in both of which he had entered two of his horses. In the Open, Mr Jones' 'California' was highly favoured but a fall put him out of the race. Two horses went on the wrong side of flags leaving Powell's 'Esmerelda' (Mr Crymes) and 'Hazard' (Jack Rees) to fight it out. At that time the mare 'Esmerelda' had the measure of the little horse 'Hazard' but, apparently, the Squire had 'declared "Hazard" to win' and 'Esmerelda' was pulled to allow the desired result! A similar incident occurred in the Handicap Chase except that it was Tom Davies who did the pulling on 'Esmerelda'. Bearing in mind that heavy betting was the norm at the Carmarthenshire Steeplechases it is difficult to understand how punters allowed Powell Bach to get away with such a ploy.[14]

In early March 1853, Powell was at the Pembrokeshire Steeplechases in Haverfordwest where his 'Esmerelda' was entered in the Open. The pre-race talk was of a walkover since no one fancied their chances against the redoubtable 'Esmerelda' but in the event three started and Jack Rees steered 'Esmerelda' to a comfortable victory. In the same month at the Narberth Steeplechases, 'Esmerelda' and Jack Rees repeated their success by winning the Open. Seven ran. A day's hunting with Powell's Hounds was part of the Narberth meeting in 1853. And to confirm his commitment to the steeplechasing cause he accepted the job of steward for the Narberth meeting for the following year of 1854; nothing was too much trouble for the sport-mad Squire of Maesgwynne.

5.3 1854-1857: Council Sponsorship Boost

By 1854 the railway and the electric telegraph were already benefiting Carmarthenshire Races as 'The South Wales Railway Co. ran special trains which conveyed immense numbers . . . [and] . . . the Electric Telegraph allowed . . . messages [to be] dispatched to the north in the morning as to which were the favourites and in the evening as to the results of the races.' That same year the meeting received a further boost from the Town Council's decision to sponsor the Open Race to the tune of £70 added-prize-money which in the following year was increased to £100; equivalent to about £10,000 today. That level of added-money placed the Carmarthenshire Open on a par with open races at Worcester, Warwick, Leamington, Birmingham and Cheltenham and bettered only by the Grand National at Liverpool. The council continued its sponsorship annually for thirteen years until the organisers, faced with difficulties in attracting top steeplechasers to Carmarthen, wavered yearly between open races and ones limited to local hunters. During the mid-70s council sponsorship ceased.

The 1854 Open attracted fifteen entries, including Powell's 'Hazard' and 'Esmerelda', of which nine ran, nearly double the numbers in previous years. For the next dozen years or so the council sponsorship helped attract to Carmarthen the best horses from Wales, Ireland and England and the resulting high standard of racing drew ever larger crowds to the town. In 1854 the crowd at the racecourse numbered not less than 2,000. A packed town was just what the keepers of shops, inns and hotels needed and such a boost to the town's economy justified the council's generosity. Another vital factor in attracting the best horses to Carmarthen was Powell's practice, as a leading owner, of taking his horses to the top race meetings in England, such as Cheltenham and Croydon, and 'he was known on every race-course in south Wales.'[15] As a result, owners from far and wide brought their horses to Carmarthen as a sign of their admiration and respect for Powell.

In the Open 'Esmerelda' (John Rees) at 18/5 came second to the 3/1 winner. In the Carmarthenshire Handicap, 'Hazard' refused at one jump but still managed third place. 'Esmerelda' went again but about two fences from home it fell in taking a fence and John Rees dislocated a wrist. But half an hour later John Rees was riding Powell's 'Slave' at 3/1 to victory in the The Trial Stakes![16]

The Hunt Ball was held at the Boar's Head and among those present were Mrs and Miss Protheroe of Dolwilym. They would have been 52-year-old Emma Hart Protheroe and her 20-year-old daughter Emma Arabella Ellen Schaw Protheroe. The absence of Emma Hart's husband, William Garrick Brydges Schaw Protheroe was, probably, explained by the fact that husband and wife were not on speaking terms for most of their married life. If the hope in attending the Hunt Ball was to find a husband for Emma Arabella, then it was not to be. According to Herbert M. Vaughan she never married and she shared her final years with a roomful of cats, two mangy dogs, a sick turkey and unbearable, at least to visitors, stench and noise. She died in 1920.[17]

The racing circus moved on to Haverfordwest in early March where 'Esmerelda' proved that her fall at Carmarthen was no fluke as she repeated the feat in the Handicap Steeplechase to finish fourth out of five. But she redeemed herself by winning the Hunters' Stakes with Mr Crymes in the saddle. Dense fog restricted viewing. Miss Protheroe of Dolwilym again made it to the Ball. In September 1854, W. R. H. Powell took his aged horse, 'Peacock' to Tenby Races but in the Corporation Plate 20 guineas race, it could do no better than finish fourth out of four runners.

Frost caused postponement of the February 1855 Carmarthenshire Races and they eventually took place at the end of March on a course east of the town, opposite Allt-y-gog on the other side of the river. It had Merlin's Hill as background.[18] Powell Bach ran three horses at the meeting, two of them in the Open. 'St David' carrying 10 stone with John Rees up finished second but was awarded the race after the first past the post, 'Master Frederick', was disqualified for fraudulent entry. He was proved to be a horse named 'Lottery', winner of several races in

Ireland. The dispute was finally settled before judge and jury at Carmarthen in July 1855.[19] 'Esmerelda' with John Davies won the Carmarthenshire Handicap.

Two weeks later Powell took two horses to the Narberth Steeplechases and in the Open, once again 'Esmerelda' with John Davies was pipped for first place and 'St David' with John Rees, finished fifth out of ten runners.

A committee was formed to organise the 1856 Carmarthenshire Races which were described as the best race meeting ever in the county of Carmarthenshire although it must have been disappointing that only one Irish horse, 'Maid of the West', showed. On Tuesday, the three-and-a-half-mile route to the course was thronged with people making their way to land just below Nantyci on part of Nantyrhebog and Maesprior farms between the road to St Clears and the South Wales Railway. Although the betting favoured Mr Powell's Stable, it was Lort Phillips' 'Deception' that took the honours winning both the Open (6 starters) and the Carmarthenshire Handicap (7 starters).[20]

Monday evening, 16 February 1857, at 'the Golden Lion (Tattersalls) was better than ever and eleven runners were announced for the Open. Among them were horses that had run well in England and in Ireland'.[21] Betting was steady at 5/1 on the field. 'St David', 'Old Screw' and 'Victim' were the favourites. In the Open, Powell's 'St David' (Archer) led, but fell two fences from home but redeemed himself by winning the Carmarthenshire Handicap with Jack Rees in the saddle.

5.4 1858 to 1860: first win for a 'stranger'

In 1858 a list of subscribers was published; it included W. R. H. Powell and his brother Oliver among the fifteen and was probably intended to attract further financial support to help pay the running costs of the meeting. The meeting was held on 8 February and, 'For the past fortnight, proprietors of hotels in the town were inundated with applications for beds, apartments, stables and loose boxes – every available space had been occupied and the difficulty was to find accommodation for guests arriving by every train – but no complaints ensued.' The meeting continued to grow in importance and 'ere long will rank with Warwick, Leamington and Abergavenny.' It was impossible to overstate the good it brought to trade in the town.[22]

On Monday night, organised betting took place at the Boar's Head but it was 'A slow affair'. On Tuesday, the town was alive! 'Flys, omnibuses and traps of every description were in great request as few relished the four-mile tramp through mud and the pitiless, pelting rain and wind to the course which was, as last year, under Derllys bank.' Mr Bullins' grandstand had been erected. Eleven ran in the Open but W. R. H. Powell's 'Carew' (Jack Rees) had to make do with second place while 'St David' (Archer) was unplaced. The race produced the first-ever English winner in Mr John's 'The Miner' (George Stevens). 'Prior to this it was firmly believed that no English steed or jockey had the smallest chance over a Cambrian banking country but "The Minor" and George Stevens broke the spell by vanquishing the largest field that ever stripped for steeplechasing in the southern Principality.'[34] George Stevens was the outstanding jockey of the era. He rode the winner of the Grand National on five occasions: in 1856 on 'Freetrader', 1863 on 'Emblem', 1864 on 'Emblematic', 1869 and 1870 on 'The Colonel'. The inclement weather and the rather low numbers running in some of the races makes the *Journal*'s claim that 'the meeting was one of the most successful that has taken place in Wales' to be somewhat over the top.

Train-loads flocked once again to Carmarthen for the February 1859 races. W. R. H. Powell and his UHC hounds started the week with a meet at Bronwydd Arms. But it was a lean race meeting for Powell. In the Open, both of his runners, 'St David' (J. James) and 'Carew' (J. Rees) fell but still finished second and third behind Lort Phillips' 'Arthur' ridden by Tom Davies, Hayes; seven ran. The two horses again fell in the Carmarthenshire Handicap in which five ran.[23] In May 1859, Powell had entered his six-year-old bay gelding 'The Martlett' at Bridgend Races.

At the end of January 1860, Powell and his horses were at the Aberystwyth Hunt Week and Steeplechases and his 'Fenton' (Chiffney) won both the Gogerddan Stakes and the Consolation Stakes and his winnings at the meeting amounted to more than £7,000 at today's values.[24]

The 1860 Carmarthenshire Steeplechases was an occasion when the *Carmarthen Journal* went-to-town in its praise of 'the Hunt', claiming it provided 'Healthful recreation' and that 'the humble peasant and the titled lord, the toil-worn mechanic and his affluent employer, the rich and the poor – all feel deeply interested in these national sports as everyone may participate in the enjoyment they afford. . . . Races are receiving increasing support from all classes in the community. . . . It is an error to associate these sports with blackguardianism, debauchery, blacklegism, etc. – it is simply not the case.' The meeting 'was as good as ever' and Powell had his 'St David' and 'Ace of Hearts' running two races each, but for the third year in succession he had no winners.[25]

Entries for the premier race meeting in Wales at Abergavenny, published in the *Carmarthen Journal* at the end of March 1860, included T. R. O. Powell's 'Carew' among the fifteen in the Club Stakes and W. R. H. Powell's 'Ace of Hearts' among the eleven in the Open. An item in the *Carmarthen Journal* of 2 November 1860 regarding the Carmarthenshire Hunt Race Week intimated that the stewards, D. Pugh MP, Lloyd Price and W. R. H. Powell intended 'sparing no exertions to get up an unusually brilliant affair in this town'.

5.5 1861-1865: 'Ace of Hearts' the perfect banker

The *Carmarthen Journal* reported that the 1861 Carmarthenshire Hunt Week started on a rainy Monday in early February and the evening gathering in the Long Room of the Boar's Head, 'better known in sporting phrase as the "Carmarthen Tattersalls"', was not well-attended and 'little business was done'. To make matters worse, the packet boat from Cork carrying two fancied runners 'New Broom' and 'Posthorn' broke down en route and had to return to port and failed to arrive in Carmarthen in time for the races. 'Powell's lot were favourites for many of the races.' Tuesday was again rainy and attendees were glad of the shelter of the stand hired from Swansea. The Open was won by W. R. H. Powell's 'Ace of Hearts' (Mr J. James) at 5/2 and he notched up another win in the Ladies Stakes with his 'St David' (J. James). Bearing in mind that the previous three years had been barren ones for Powell's horses the *Journal*'s comment at the conclusion of the first day was surprising: 'We congratulate Mr Powell on being again a winner although we should have preferred seeing the honours of the day divided.' On the second day's racing neither Powell nor his horses showed any inclination to please the *Journal* and he had another two winners with 'Ace of Hearts' and 'St David' both ridden by James Rice James.[26] Racegoers were not to know that 'Ace' would remain unbeaten for the next four Open races over the Carmarthen banks until settling for second place in 1865! After that 'Daisy' would come up trumps over the Carmarthen flying course to win a further two consecutive Open races for W. R. H. Powell! After the 1861 meeting Powell bought the highly-rated 'Confederate' from James Rice James and at the end of February ran him and 'Ace of Hearts' in the Tenby Open but with no success.

In the following year at the end of January 1862, W. R. H. Powell and T. R. O. Powell had horses entered for the Aberystwyth Hunt Week. The Carmarthenshire Open of 1862 provided a result which was 'hitherto unequalled in the annals of steeplechasing.'[27] Tom Rees recalled that 'The 1862 Open provided intense excitement by the dead-heat of [Powell's] "Ace of Hearts" and [Sir R. de Burgo's] "The Rug" [from Ireland].' The race was re-run and the judge's verdict was again a dead-heat. 'The Irishman wished to run-off again, but W. R. H. Powell had too great a regard for his gallant horse to allow him to undertake such a severe ordeal the third time. This is the only record in steeplechasing where a dead-heat has been twice run over a four-mile banking course.'[4] And the 1862 meeting was historic in another sense because it was: 'an Honest meeting . . . for the first time it was patronised by a lot of first class bookmakers . . . for example, Messrs John and W. Warrington from London and Messrs Turner and Andrews from the Midland Counties', which showed that the Carmarthenshire Hunt Week had increased in interest and importance and if it could, in future, attract some foreign horses, the meeting would 'eclipse any out of Liverpool'. Powell's 'Carew' (J. R. James), evens, was involved in a 'terrific' race in the Carmarthenshire Handicap but was beaten into second place; four ran. The next race, the Volunteer Plate, was delayed as a result of an objection by W. R. H. Powell regarding the weights for the race. He argued that since no acceptance had taken place the previous night, the race as it stood should be declared void and the highest accepting weight raised to 12st. Mr Pryse Longden of Gogerddan objected to anything of the sort being done and eventually Mr Powell allowed his horse to run. But before the start, the stewards declared all bets off, which created no little disappointment among the bookmakers. Four ran and Powell's 'Confederate' (J. R. James) led them home.

The racing 'bible' of the age, *Bell's Life in London* carried a colourful report as it looked forward to the 1863 Carmarthenshire Hunt Week and Steeplechases: 'it is solely in Wales that steeplechasing is preserved in its truest and most primitive form. There, blood, stoutness, and endurance abound, in striking contrast to the miserable non-staying weeds figuring lately in the lists elsewhere; and to the Principality must also be conceded the palm for steeplechasing in its entirety as a spectacle . . . [and] to the ancient capital of Wales [Carmarthen], the public are partly indebted for the reforms in this branch of sport at length about to be adopted at all respectably conducted meetings.' Referring to the previous (1862) year's never-to-be-forgotten double dead-heats the report claimed that 'the two game horses . . . [had made] Wales famous in sporting chronicles and in song.' On the Monday evening of the 1863 meeting visitors assembled in the room at the Ivy Bush but the 50 to 20 offered on the field by three well-known bookmakers in attendance did not find a single customer. The 'two game horses', 'The Rug' from Ireland and Maesgwynne's 'Ace of Hearts' featured again among six starters in the Open race but in 1863, 'Ace' was 6lb. worse off than in 1862 and 'The Rug' was favourite until it became known that Tom Davies, 'the star rider in Wales', would be on 'Ace of Hearts' – he went to 6/4 while 'The Rug' was on 2/1. However, when it came to the race, 'The Rug' (Capt. Macrath) fell and 'Ace' landed 'Mr Powell's colours victoriously.'[28] It was the fourth time for Tom Davies to win the Carmarthenshire Open following his successes in 1846 on 'Kangaroo', in 1857 on 'The Victim' and in 1859 on 'Arthur'.

At the dinner W. R. H. Powell, as the Open winner once again, struck a humble note in saying that since 1845 he had always started a horse at Carmarthen and had many times received a good licking! Replying to the toast to strangers, Sir Richard de Burgo hinted as to the improvement in steeplechasing in this country if the handicaps were not made too close; for instance he referred to the Llanboidy programme as an example of good practice.[29] In mid-April 1863, Powell's 'Annie Laurie' ridden by his 20-year-old stable lad, John Pope, came second out of seven in the Tivy Side Hunt Stakes.

'Ace of Hearts', reckoned to be 'the best horse in Wales' by *The Field* and labelled 'perfection itself' by *Bell's Life in London*. Three times winner (1861, '63, '64) of the Carmarthenshire Open and dead-heated in both race and re-run in 1862.
(Courtesy Robert King).

At the 1864 Carmarthenshire Races Powell's 'Ace of Hearts', well ridden by Johnny Pope, completed a remarkable four consecutive years of being unbeaten in the Open. 'Ace of Hearts' was probably the best banking steeplechaser to come out of the Maesgwynne Stable.

After a day's hunting with Powell's hounds on the Wednesday, racing resumed on Thursday with Powell having horses going in the three races. He had three among the six starters in the County Members Plate of 8 sovereigns each with 50 sovereigns added. The race was a triumph for 21-year-old jockey Johnny Pope: '"Annie Laurie" took up the running and Pope, making no shadow of a mistake, landed her a winner [just] as he liked by twenty lengths.' The pair gained their second victory in the Hunters' Stakes which developed into 'a race between "Annie Laurie" and "Jack", the former steered by Pope, who had been so successful and deservedly so by his splendid riding throughout the meeting, making the run-up and winning by about a dozen lengths.'[30]

For the February 1865 Carmarthenshire meeting a 'small number of gentlemen founded a joint stock company limited to meet the cost of over £400 to erect a Grand Stand.' It was 45 feet long and 95 feet wide with refreshment rooms, weighing rooms and a railed-off paddock. Two hundred persons could be accommodated and a portion of the stand provided with a fireplace and seats was reserved for ladies. The stand's second floor was its flat roof and it was intended for those with more than ordinary interest in racing. The boggy part of the course had been drained. In the Open, 'Fenton' (Tom Davies), at 2/1 and carrying 10st.1lb. recently sold by Powell to J. R. Riddell, beat Powell's 'Ace of Hearts' (Johnny Pope) at 3/1 and 12st.8lb. into second place; 10 ran. It had taken an extra two-and-a-half-stone to end 'Ace''s remarkable four-year unbeaten run in the Carmarthenshire Open. There was a 'disagreeable affair' when Lort Phillips was refused entry for his horse 'Newton' in the Golden Grove Stakes on the grounds that it had previously won a race to the value of £20. It was later pointed out that the win had been on 'the flat' and the rule referred to applied only to 'steeplechasing'. But then, Mr Olive, owner of the fancied 'Gentle Annie' objected to 'Newton' starting because he had been officially refused entry. However, at the weigh-in the rider of 'Newton' found that he could not get up sufficient weight to ride and the horse was withdrawn. Bearing in mind the large prize money on offer it was, perhaps, not surprising that a lot of 'in-fighting' went on between the 'gentlemen' owners. Powell had three winners at the meeting, with Johnny Pope on two of them.[31]

While the erection of a new grandstand might have suggested that Carmarthenshire Races was a successful undertaking, the reality was different. In the early 1860s the meeting was facing mounting problems in its efforts to stay the course as a major steeplechase event. The problem experienced with Llanboidy Races also manifested itself at Carmarthen with fewer and fewer 'strangers' (English and Irish owners) prepared to bring their horses to race. The reasons for the strangers' reluctance were similar in the case of both Llanboidy and Carmarthen. Carmarthen had a banking course, over which the Maesgwynne-trained horses were virtually unbeatable! According to Tom Rees in his *Racing Reminiscences*: 'banking steeplechasers which had any chance of success against the Maesgwynne stables were very scarce. The stable contained such perfect bankers as "Ace of Hearts", "Annie Laurie", "Fenton", etc.' Owners lost interest in travelling to Carmarthenshire Races only to witness almost certain defeat for their horses at the hands of Powell Bach's super chasers! For example, starting in 1861, Powell's 'Ace of Hearts' had won the Open four times in succession (although 1862 was a dead heat) and the 1865 winner, 'Fenton', had only been out of Powell's ownership for a short time. In addition, there were more and more meetings taking place just over the border in England and those were far more convenient for owners in those areas than was far-away Carmarthen.

During 1865 W. R. H. Powell came to the rescue of the troubled organisation and took over as the Hon. Sec. of the committee running the Carmarthenshire meeting. Naturally, he was most concerned to see the races flourish again. As he said in replying to a toast at the dinner at the Boar's Head Hotel during the 1867 Carmarthenshire Hunt Week: 'I was ready, willing and happy to take the office of Hon. Sec. . . . at a critical period (applause). I will not enter into particulars, for all our friends know the state of things – a state that was getting worse and worse. I saw that unless some alterations were made, the Carmarthenshire Steeplechases would soon become very poor . . . I will work night and day to serve the interests of the meeting; I will undertake all the dirty and the heavy work if you will appoint someone who will find the funds and collect the money, as it is not pleasant for me to have to write to make up the deficit (hear, hear). We have received liberal subscriptions from the county and borough members [MPs] and the latter gentleman has increased his stakes from £25 to £50 (applause), but still £260 is required before we can clear, and that is a large sum. I am willing to do all in my power to promote . . . these steeplechases and carry them on (loud cheers).'

The advice that he had tendered to the committee was that they should follow the same course of action as he had already implemented at Llanboidy. His advice showed what a genuine person he was; he sacrificed the expected continued success of his stable in favour of the well-being of Carmarthenshire Races. The committee accepted Powell's advice to alter the steeplechase course from a banking one to a flying course so as to attract English entries.

5.6 1866-1867: 'Daisy' and Pope and the quietest of smiles

The 1866 Carmarthenshire Hunt and Steeplechases was a historic event: 'Until this year Carmarthen races have been confined to the old Welsh banking country which in many ways precluded the English horses from contesting on equal terms . . . [and so to conform] with the exigencies of the times the committee determined, and very wisely too, to reconstruct the course and we are now able to offer supporters of the turf as fine a four mile of flying or banking country as any that can be obtained in Great Britain. The fences have all been reduced to low banks, surmounted by gorse hurdles and a water jump has also been constructed.'[32]

It was clear that Powell had pulled out all the stops to revive the meeting: 'Never before have we had so many strangers among us, never before have so many good horses contested the Open Steeplechase and never before have the Carmarthenshire Steeplechases raised so much speculation in London and other sporting circles . . . although the number of horses competing was not so large as was anticipated from the long list of entries, yet it is satisfactory to know that they all came from a distance, with one exception, that they are all clever, and although as is inevitable, success attended but one of them, their experiences will induce them to come again. . . . On Tuesday the streets began to fill as train-loads came from Swansea, Llanelly, Llandeilo, Llandovery, Haverfordwest, Pembroke and Cardiganshire.'

But reconstructed course or not, Powell's horses featured strongly in every race! And the 1866 Carmarthenshire Open (of 10 sovereigns each +100 sovereigns) over the new flying course was won by Powell's 'Daisy' with Johnny Pope at 6/1! There had been considerable confusion before the race. 'Ace of Hearts' which Powell had recently sold to R. C. Riddell from Devon had been scratched some days before the meeting; Powell's 'Flyfisher' was not at the ground and his 'Gay Lad', although at the ground, was not permitted to start. 'Bunbury' . . . 'for reasons best known to Mr Sumner' was withdrawn. The favourite, 'Goldfinger' at 2/1, finished fourth out of seven starters. The Hunters' Handicap Stakes over banks, for horses resident in Wales, was an excellent race with Powell's 'Dandy' narrowly losing out to Mr Gwyther's 'Chance'. Both were carefully ridden, the veteran 46-year-old, Tom Davies steering 'Chance' and Pope, a lad from the Maesgwynne stable but at the same time a splendid horseman, piloting 'Dandy'. 'Mr Powell's trainer complained that T. Davies and "Chance" had crossed Pope's path repeatedly in order to hinder him. Davies denied the charge.' At the dinner Powell said this was his twenty-sixth season and during that time he had done his best to provide the national sport of the country. He thanked Colonel Davies for granting the committee a long lease on the course and allowing them to erect a grandstand. On the final day of racing Powell enjoyed further success with 'Dandy' (Pope) winning the Borough Member's Plate for horses in south Wales; four started.[33] It is interesting to note that the three open races were run over the new flying course while the other races, limited to horses from Wales, went over the old banking course.

Powell, at that time, was at the height of his powers as a racehorse owner. Tom Rees on a visit to Maesgwynne sometime later described the stable in its heyday: 'No better managed and equipped racing establishment existed in the country.' He considered it a rare privilege to receive, as all visitors did, the warm hospitality and courtesy of Mr Powell. And he was delighted that Johnny Pope, the first jockey, was deputed to show him around the stables and breeding stud. Tom Rees went on: 'boxes were roomy, well drained, and ventilated, a covered ride, three laps to the mile, well laid with tan for exercising in wet and frosty weather, was a feature of the training grounds; so the horses in training had every facility for being perfectly fit, weather or no. The brood mares and young stock were a very promising lot, and well done.' Tom Rees revealed that there were generally about seventy horses stabled with twenty being steeplechasers in training. He added that: 'The cracks of the stable were "Flyfisher", a chestnut horse, for which Mr Powell paid 1,250 Guineas; he won the Croydon Cup and several other valuable steeplechases; "Laura", a real high class mare, was able to hold her own in the best of company; "Daisy", a most consistent performer, won the Open steeplechase at Carmarthen in two consecutive years, but the piece-de-resistance of the stable was "L'Africaine" . . . the supposed finest steeplechase horse in the world . . . He was a French bred horse . . . and Mr Powell advanced £1,200 to his owner, his security being the horse, its management and the right to run him . . . He ran in the Liverpool Grand National Steeplechase in 1866 won by "Salamander", carrying 10st.7lb. "L'Africaine", carrying 13st.2lb., George Holman in the saddle, who told me he would have won comfortably, if not for the interference of a loose horse.'

Tom Rees then described the disappointment of W. R. H. Powell when his friend, Mr Reginald Riddell from Devonshire who ran and rode several horses at Carmarthen and Llanboidy, 'arranged' with the owner of 'L'Africaine' to have him released from the Maesgwynne stable so that he could ride him in Holland and Belgium where small fortunes could be made in horse racing. For example, Riddell won 70,000 francs in one season with his horse 'Carew' and another 80,000 francs with 'Fenton', 'Miss Nightingale' and 'Annie Laurie', all of which he had bought from Powell! Little wonder that Riddell was anxious to get his hands on 'L'Africaine'.[4] Reginald Herbert summed up the situation: 'Powell at one time had a share in that well-known horse "L'Africaine", I fancy it was a sort of mortgage. Anyway, I remember there was a deuce of a row when Riddell, the original owner, wanted him back.'[15] But Riddell's luck was about to run out; 'L'Africaine' ran and won once in England before being taken abroad where he broke a leg at Deauville, France, and had to be destroyed.[4]

Bell's Life in London provided a short historical context to the 1867 Carmarthenshire Hunt Week and Steeplechases. 'Originally a purely local affair – perhaps more famous for indoor festivities than sport – the chases eventually caught the eye of Turfites in the Emerald Isle who in successive years crossed the channel with "The Screw", "The Old Rake", "Shanbally" and "New Broom" to do battle with the Welsh horses, but never beat them in the Open handicap, and so matters proceeded till "The Rug" in 1862 walked over and divided the principal prize, after two dead heats, with "Ace of Hearts". Prejudice, even then, was far from extinct and finding their interest at stake, the managers eventually cut down the much dreaded impediments [banks] to the fences now in use, which the most moderate of animals ought to get over. Other improvements followed – to wit the execution by shares of a new Stand, the suggestion we believe of Mr W. R. H. Powell of Maesgwynne, whose exertions for a lengthened period in promoting the Carmarthen meeting have won for him universal gratitude and esteem. This year, however, a further tax has been imposed on his generosity by his accepting the secretaryship of the chases . . . . That the right man thus stepped into his right place was happily borne out by the unprecedently [*sic*] numerous entries obtained for the past anniversary, the larger proportion of them being English horses, to say nothing of the influx to the old town of noble and influential patrons of the national pastime never before attending Wales. In accepting office, the indefatigable MFH was however compelled to throw up for the present his own [Llanboidy] meeting. Hotels filled fast, every bed was secured and private lodgings was at a premium. Evening in the Assembly Rooms – "Merrimac" was most fancied for the morrow, though at the close it became doubtful whether the good-looking "Aprillis", receiving his final preparations at Maesgwynne, was not as good a favourite.'[34] More 'strangers' than ever were attracted to try their luck against the local nags. One of the 'strangers', the Duke of Hamilton, was perhaps the leading racehorse owner in England and was apparently of a 'rudely ruddy complexion, had a powerful neck and seemed strong enough to fell an ox with his fist. He had a frankness of speech bordering on rudeness.' Clearly, he was the complete opposite of W. R. H. Powell. At the time of his visit to Carmarthen, the Duke of Hamilton was close to financial ruin, partly as a result of lost wagers. His horse 'Meerschaum's' running in the Carmarthenshire Open did not help his financial problems but a few months later at Aintree, his horse 'Cortolvin' ridden by John Page won the Grand National and in addition to substantial prize money he also took some £16,000 from the bookies, which restored his fortune.

The 1867 occasion at Carmarthen was described by Tom Rees writing in 1916:[4] 'several high-class chasers having entered, among the owners being His Grace The Duke of Hamilton, Mr Yates, Mr Fothergill Rowlands, Mr Ducrows [from Ireland], Mr Green Price, Mr Philip Merton, Mr Hobson, Capt. Shaw and other prominent owners and stables, so that the racing prospects were of the brightest. Naturally all the leading hostelries were full to overflowing; private houses were requisitioned by family parties at the handsome fee of fifty to seventy guineas for the whole week, while the majority of vendors took a holiday and hied themselves to London town to enjoy the sights and gaieties of the Metropolis. . . . Grocers, butchers, fishmongers, wine merchants, pastry cooks, etc. delivered their various commodities in large

170

quantities, sufficient for the week maybe . . . The gentry of Tivy Side, and other parts of Cardiganshire, Pembrokeshire, Glamorgan and Carmarthen all contributed their quota to the gay and festive crowd. . . . Directly concerned with the racing were the trainers, jockeys, stable-lads, bookies, touts, and tipsters, tic-tac men, and the usual hangers-on of the sports of kings . . . after the Liverpool Grand National, the most important steeplechases were Worcester, Warwick, Leamington, Birmingham and Cheltenham Grand Annuals, and the Carmarthenshire Open Steeplechases. They were mediums of ante-post betting. A horse could be backed as soon as the entries were out with the list men of London, Manchester, Liverpool and Bristol, to win a considerable amount.' Tom Rees went on: 'The streets [of Carmarthen] with their crowds of sportsmen from the surrounding districts, augmented by train-loads from further afield, presented a most animated appearance, all anxious to glean the latest news concerning the various competitors. The favourite [for the Open], "Merrimac", was greatly fancied, his past performances were very encouraging. It was whispered that "Aprilis" had won a wonderful trial at Maesgwynne, but several shrewd sportsmen could not believe that the veteran Tom Davies [46-years-old] would be able to do him justice over the flying course (over banks he had no equal); then there was "Flyfisher", one of the best-looking horses that ever looked through a bridle, winner of the Croydon Cup, and cost Mr W. R. H. Powell well into four figures; "Daisy" [from Maesgwynne], a most consistent performer, and with Pope [Maesgwynne's resident jockey] in the saddle, was a great local fancy . . . Crowds of pedestrians from early morn wended their way to the course. All sorts and conditions of men, some women, and many children succumbing . . . to the unfailing attraction of horse-racing, and its attendant chance of a gamble . . . many local schools had to chronicle numerous truants.'

Ten runners started in the Open. 'Arlescott' and 'Meerschaum' made the running, closely followed by 'Garus', 'Aprilis', 'Merrimac', 'Pensioner', and 'Mulberry' some lengths in the rear. After going about a mile, 'Garus' refused; 'Aprilis' came to grief; 'Arlescott' still led, the rest of the field close up. At three miles, 'Ballet Girl' shot her bolt. 'Flyfisher' held out signals of distress. 'Daisy' then went to the front, followed by 'Arlescott' and 'Mulberry'. They could make no impression on 'Daisy', who won by a length and a half, 'Arlescott' beating 'Mulberry' by three lengths. Pope came in for a great ovation, having ridden a well-judged race. But as reported in *The Welshman* the 'splendid ovation made no visible effect on him beyond drawing forth one of his very quietest smiles.'[35]

Johnny Pope had burst on the scene as W. R. H. Powell's number one jockey at the Carmarthenshire Steeplechases of 1864 when he did the double, winning the prestigious Open (nine runners) on 'Ace of Hearts' and the Carmarthenshire Handicap (six runners) on 'Annie Laurie'. He won the Carmarthenshire Open again in 1866 riding 'Daisy' (six starters). And it was on 'Daisy' that he produced his greatest performance when he took on and beat the best of the Irish and English steeplechasers over their favourite flying course in the Open of 1867 in, perhaps, the greatest race ever seen at Carmarthen. Not only had the course been changed to suit the 'strangers' but only 'Flyfisher', the other Maesgwynne entry, carried more weight than 'Daisy'; but Pope's good judgement carried the day. The star quality of Johnny Pope can also be gleaned from the writings of 'Augur' in the *Sporting Life* in 1891: 'Times may not be so merry in South Wales as they used to be in the days when the ever-to-be-respected Mr Powell, of Maesgwynne, was a kind of king in the land, when poor Jack Olive held the reins of government at the Boar's Head, at Carmarthen, . . . and the famous Welsh steeplechase rider, Pope, used to carry a big ball of string in his pocket, one end of which was fastened to the near side of his horse's bit, so that in coming to grief over the big fences that had to be negotiated he could pull his mount round within the same field as he lay on his back, take saddle again, and then go on and win. . . . One of Mr Powell's best horses was "Flyfisher", who would have distinguished himself over the old Croydon course under a big weight.'[36] Another source dates the ball-of-string trick to an earlier era and to another of Powell's jockeys. According to Reginald Herbert: 'Old Davies (Tom Davies of Hayes Farm, near Pembroke) used, in early days, to ride most of Powell's horses. He was a rare hand over the Welsh courses, always carrying a ball of twine in his breeches pocket, fastened to his horses bit, so that in case of a fall at one of the banks, and the horse getting loose, the line would pay out till Davies picked himself up, caught hold of it, began hauling in the slack, and so brought his mount to hand, a fall over the sort of country they had to negotiate by no means extinguishing a winning chance.'[15] It may well be that Johnny Pope who became Powell Bach's top jockey in the 1860s, learnt the twine trick from 'Old' Tom Davies.

CARMARTHENSHIRE OPEN STEEPLECHASE, 1867					
Weight st. lbs.	Owner	Finishers	Age	Rider	Position
12 5	Mr Powell	Daisy	aged	John Pope	1
11 11 (7lb extra)	Mr Williams	Arlescott	aged	Ellison	2
10 11	Mr Martin	Mulberry	aged	J. Holman	3
12 7	Mr Powell	Flyfisher	aged	G. Holman	0
11 12	Mr Yates	Merrimac	aged	Hobson	0
11 7	Duke of Hamilton	Meerschaum	aged	Page	0
11 1	Mr Rowlands	Garus	aged	Reeves	0
10 9	Mr Ducrows	Ballet Girl	6 years	Milward	0
10 7	Mr Owen	Pensioner	aged	Mr Thomas	0
10 7	Mr Lewis	Aprilis	aged	Tom Davies	0
Betting – 5 to 2 against Merrimac, 3 to 1 Aprilis, 6 to 1 Daisy, 6 to 1 Arlescott, 7 to 1 Meerschaum, 10 to 1 any other.					

The 'strangers' had come to Carmarthen in 1867 looking forward to meeting Powell's horses on a level playing field – no banks – so it was somewhat ironic that it was still W. R. H. Powell's horse that won the prestigious Open. As it turned out, 1867 was the end of a fabulous run of successes for W. R. H. Powell's Maesgwynne Stable in the Carmarthenshire Open. After 'Carew', with Jack Rees, had finished runner-up in 1858 and 'St David', with J. R. (Gipsy)

James, had done the same in 1859, the marvellous 'Ace of Hearts', with J. R. James, won the 1861 Open. 'Ace''s appetite was whetted and he went on to make it a record four wins in a row (one was a dead heat) which earned him the accolade of 'perfection itself' from the top racing magazine *Bell's Life in London*. 'Ace''s successful riders were James Rice (Gipsy) James, twice, the veteran Tom Davies, and Maesgwynne's own Johnny Pope. In 1865 'Ace of Hearts', with Johnny Pope, was pipped to the post by his old stable-mate 'Fenton', with Tom Davies. Subsequently, Maesgwynne's challenge in the Carmarthenshire Open was taken up by 'Daisy' with Johnny Pope and the pair rewarded W. R. H. Powell with two magnificent victories over all-comers in 1866 and 1867.

At the dinner William Morris MP was delighted that 'A large number of gentlemen from England and the adjoining counties have not only attended but have also brought their horses here . . . [it had been] a very successful meeting . . . thanks mainly to Mr Powell who had come forward in the most critical period in the history of the races and took on the heavy duties of Hon. Sec. . . . an office which I hope he will continue to fill.' The vice-chair, Herbert Evans of Highmead, said that: 'the whole success of the meeting . . . is entirely due to Mr Powell.' Powell informed the diners that he had not spared himself in getting up the meeting and 'unfortunately, I was a little knocked out of time . . . But I am happy to say that a few of Taylor's Constitution Balls have set me right (laughter and cheers).' He thanked the Duke of Hamilton, who had brought five horses, and all the other English and Irish visitors at the meeting for their support. Powell went on: 'Every man likes to win but I give you my word that I would rather not have won yesterday (laughter and cheers). I did not put a shilling on the horse; I did not speak to my man about him, and I never was more surprised than to see him coming home first.'

But then a Mr Verral from London sounded a note of caution about the future. After saying that he was convinced that the Carmarthenshire Steeplechases might be a great affair it was unfortunate that W. R. H. Powell was 'situated in an out-of-the-way place; if he were nearer London he could depend upon making any meeting with which he was connected the best in the country. Many could not afford to bring their horses a couple of hundred miles to Carmarthen.' The chairman then proposed a toast to the press present at the dinner: Mr Meyrick of *Bell's Life*, Mr Comyns Cole of *The Field* and Mr R. Ll. Jones of the *Carmarthen Journal*. (*Bell's Life in London and Sporting Chronicle* was, up to the 1860s, the leading sporting newspaper without which no gentleman's Sunday was complete. In the 1860s it faced competition from *The Field*, *The Sportsman*, the *Sporting Life* and the *Sporting Times*. In 1886 it was absorbed by the *Sporting Life*.) *The Welshman*'s post-meeting report claimed that 'W. R. H. Powell endeavoured to make it a great meeting and was eminently successful.'[35]

5.7 1868-1872: Powell 'retires' from the turf . . . Carmarthen in decline

Whilst the 1867 Carmarthenshire race meeting was undoubtedly 'eminently successful' the task of keeping Carmarthen at the forefront of steeplechasing was facing mounting difficulties. The proliferation of meetings at places much nearer than Carmarthen to the major stables of England put a greater onus on Powell's pulling-power on English owners to visit Carmarthen in return for his support of their meetings. Another factor was Powell's bouts of ill-health one of which, soon after the 1867 races, forced him to seek assistance from W. O. Brigstocke of

Gellydywyll, Newcastle Emlyn, who agreed to join Powell as joint Hon. Sec., saying that he was 'glad to repay some of the many kindnesses I have received at his hands.' A third factor manifested itself as a result of the negative reaction of a few English turfites to Powell's success at Croydon Races where he took two of his steeplechasers in December 1867.[37] In the prestigious Croydon Open, 'Flyfisher' at 5/1 with Johnny Pope in the saddle upset the odds in winning the much-sought-after Croydon Cup from the favourite Lord Poulett's 'Benazet' at 7/4 on. Towards the finish as Pope took up the whip 'Flyfisher' swerved across 'Benazet' and Lord Poulett lodged an appeal which was decided at Tattersall's on the following Monday after which the stewards issued a statement: 'We are of the opinion that the objection made by Lord Poulett to "Flyfisher" for the Croydon Cup has not been sufficiently proved by the evidence.' It was signed by Reginald Herbert (acting for Lord Coventry), H. Crawshay, and Chas Bevill (acting for Sir F. Johnstone). However, the alleged poor form shown by 'Flyfisher' in an earlier race at Croydon resulted in a controversial article in *Bell's Life* which charged Pope with having 'pulled' 'Flyfisher'. The article stung Powell to the core and left him contemplating disposing of his stud. To his credit the editor of the *Carmarthen Journal* wrote in support of Powell and expressed the hope of 'every person interested in sport in the county' that Powell would not 'part with his valuable stud of racehorses and will not retire from the turf.' W. R. H. Powell replied to *Bell's Life*'s charges in a letter to the paper:

Sir,

I need scarcely say I have been much annoyed by the comments that have appeared in the various sporting journals on the conduct of my jockey (Pope) at the late Croydon meeting and I trust you will allow me to say a few words in his defence and in vindication of my own character. I run my horses more for pleasure than anything else and bet very little; I only had £20 on 'Flyfisher' for the Cup and the same on 'Laura' for the Steeple Chase Handicap. My jockey assures me that the mare ran completely away with him, and for the greater part of the race he had not the slightest control over him, and he further alleges he was so much upset by the dispute which arose from the former race and the severe reprimand he received from my trainer, Purnell, for having ridden contrary to instructions that he lost his head and scarcely knew what he was about. All I can say in explanation of the inconsistent running of 'Flyfisher' is that he is naturally a gross horse, and on the occasion was short of work, having recently suffered from lameness. Under the circumstances I cannot think it surprising that he should have shown better form on the Thursday than on Wednesday, more particularly as the pace in the second race was not nearly so good as in the first. Personally I had not the slightest fancy for him for either event, and did not back him on the first day nor should I have even started him on the second day but for the urgent solicitation of a friend who informed me that 'Benazet' went short. As I only had a trifle £20 on him I am utterly at a loss what object I could have had – apart from the question of principle – in pulling him on the first day, seeing that, even if he had won he would not have been liable to any extra penalty for the Cup.

Yours
W. R. H. Powell.[38]

174

The unfavourable remarks on the Croydon incidents in papers such as *Bell's Life* hurt Powell deeply. At a meeting of the Carmarthenshire Hunt and Steeplechases committee in late December 1867, he referred to 'uncalled for remarks . . . in the sporting press' and went on: 'such untruthful remarks at my time of life are not easily borne and are keenly felt.' He was 48 years of age. He explained that he did not wish to subject himself further to such unjustified remarks and he would refrain from running horses any longer. 'My wish is (I do not say that I shall do so positively) to sell the whole of my horses if I can find purchasers.'[39] The *Carmarthen Journal*'s editorial on 27 December 1867 expressed the view that 'every person interested in sports in the county will hope that he [Powell] will not part with his valuable stud of race-horses, and will not retire from the turf.' The editorial went on to state that Powell was considerably annoyed 'and with good reason, at the attitude recently assumed by the Sporting Press towards him; but we trust that he will not, on those grounds alone, cease to occupy a position in South Wales which he has so long and so honourably filled.'

The advert which appeared in *The Welshman* on 3 January 1868, signed by the joint Hon. Secs., made clear that all the races for that year's Carmarthenshire Races were to be run 'over the new flying course (no banks) . . . Under Grand National Rules.' There were two open races but, for the first time since the meeting's inauguration some twenty-three years previously, there was not to be a race called the 'Carmarthenshire Open'. And there was no sponsorship from the Town Council. Dropping the famous title would appear to have been a glaring omission but it was ignored by the local papers.

The town was very lively on the Monday of the 1868 week with the arrival of county families, turf reporters, bookmakers, jockeys and general habitués of the racing world. For the large crowd of walkers to the course near Derllys there was a risk of being knocked down by the passing carriages. The harpist and soloist who usually entertained the crowd were absent that year but according to the report in the *Carmarthen Journal* 'there was a [black man] who sang one song over and over again while his wife collected the coppers; and there was a German band – four miserable looking fellows with lanky hair and attired in the blue coloured clothing peculiar to their kind.' There was a late start to the races because Donovan's 'Holly Boy' arrived half-an-hour late, his owner having been given the wrong information about the race time. Seven races did go and there were five starters in three of them. Two races had four runners and two had three. The Borough Member's Stakes was won by W. R. H. Powell's 'Tempest' (J. Pope) but only three ran. Four ran in the Ladies Stakes and Powell's 'Flyfisher' (J. Pope) came second out of four. At the dinner, W. O. Brigstocke claimed that their course was unsurpassed anywhere in England and Powell said that he hoped to carry on the work for some years to come. Powell's Hounds with himself as master and Jack Rees as huntsman met, as usual, on the Wednesday.[40]

The Welshman claimed that 'on the whole the meeting had been a success' with large numbers of London bookmakers in attendance but business was 'not large'. All respectable lodgings in the town had been taken and a few visitors had to travel to Ferryside to find accommodation. But if numbers of people was satisfactory, horses were 'pretty scarce' although those that did appear 'were clever and some fit for the very best company.'

Apparently, fields had also been small at many English meetings that season. But small fields were 'not to be wondered at considering how these meetings have multiplied in the country'.[41]

And to attempt to counter that problem with higher prize money was easier said than done. But worse was to follow, for the Carmarthenshire Steeplechases were designed to attract 'strangers' and the best horses in the country; a plan heavily dependent on Powell and his stable being involved in the turf. *The Welshman* on 26 June 1868 (see Part IV) advertised Powell's intention to sell all of his steeplechasers. As it turned out, the sale was disappointing and most of the horses remained in Powell's ownership. But disappointing sale or not, it was clear that Powell was reducing his involvement with the turf. And when a notice of another sale by J. Howell Thomas, appeared in *The Welshman* on 21 August 1868, this time at Gellydywyll, Newcastle Emlyn, the writing was on the wall for Carmarthenshire Races. Gellydywyll was the home of W. O. Brigstocke, joint Hon. Sec. with Powell of the Carmarthenshire Hunt and Steeplechases. The sale notice made it known that Mr Brigstocke was leaving Wales. Sometime during 1868, Powell and Brigstocke resigned as joint Hon. Secretaries and John S. Olive of the Boar's Head took over the job.

An advert in the *Journal* in January 1869 stated that the proposed 1869 Carmarthenshire Races would be run 'over the new flying course (no banks)'. So 'no banks' continued as the main selling point. The 'Carmarthenshire Open' was back on the card with £100 Town Council sponsorship restored. There was also a notice in the paper to the effect that Mr Powell did not intend running his horses, 'Primrose' and 'Tempest', at Carmarthen and they were being offered for sale. It was a curious notice; was W. R. H. Powell trying to reduce his influence at the meeting in order to persuade other owners to enter their horses? Whatever was Powell's intention, the 1869 meeting at Carmarthen was not a great success: 'The first blow was the retirement of W. R. H. Powell from the turf (which we hope is only temporary), followed by his retiring from the active management of this meeting.' The next blow was delivered by the newly elected Members of Parliament for the County and the Borough reducing their subscriptions from £50 to £25, thereby spoiling two of the best races of the meeting.[42] The races had been run that year on consecutive days which drew the comment from the *Journal*: 'it was a great convenience to strangers who send their horses so far west but we think the old system was better.' And then came the u-turn as the anti-strangers feeling was forcibly expressed in the *Journal*: 'There are plenty of good horses in our midst – why not return to the 'banks' and let the Carmarthenshire Hunt Week go off with the same éclat as in days of yore?' *The Welshman* reported that 'few bookmakers were present; one or two from Manchester and London.' In addition, on this occassion the Sudbury and the Edgware meetings were held 'on the same time'. It had to be remembered that for the English owners it was a 'long, expensive and tedious journey to Carmarthen.' On top of all there had appeared 'unkind statements in newspapers'. In the *Daily Telegraph* 'Hotspur' had written: 'The Carmarthen meeting was formerly quite a Cambrian carnival but the dissolution of Mr Powell's stud of steeplechasers and miserable management, appear to have dwindled it to utter insignificance.' In *The Welshman*'s view they had to choose between making the meeting strictly local with entries restricted to Carmarthenshire and neighbouring counties or, make it more public by increasing the value of stakes to attract distant horses. *The Welshman* professed to favour the latter approach as it was, 'more in keeping with the spirit of the times.' But it gave no indication where the extra prize money was to come from.[43]

Mr Powell was still hunting and between sixty and eighty mounted turned up for the meet at Penycoed near Trawsmawr on the Tuesday of the Carmarthenshire Hunt Week. Racing took place on consecutive days, Wednesday and Thursday to reduce the time that distant owners had to spend at the meeting. Only three horses went in the Open. The winner of the Cambrian Stakes was put up for sale but there were no offers. W. R. H. Powell's 'Tempest' and 'Primrose' were put up for sale and both 'were bought-in for 105 guineas and 140 guineas'. At the dinner Powell confined his remarks to hunting, saying that it was twenty-nine years since he began hunting in the county. There were three packs in the county at that time, but he had 'worn them all out!'. But the mystery about Powell's position remained. He had not been involved in organising the 1869 races nor did he run any horses there; yet when Sartoris, a newly elected MP, said that Powell had asked him to be steward for the following year's meeting it was pretty clear who was in charge at Carmarthen! An editorial in *The Welshman* pointed out that open races had also failed at Tenby whereas races confined to the three counties at Tenby and at Tivyside, at Pembroke and at Aberystwyth had been 'unusually successful. . . . Would not a race meeting – similar to that at Punchestown, – confined to the three counties, do still greater good?'[44] But so far as Carmarthen was concerned, opinion remained split in 1869 between retaining it as an open meeting or changing to one restricted to local horses.[45, 46] Meanwhile, in far-off Cheltenham to where he had removed from Newcastle Emlyn, W. O. Brigstocke, Powell's former joint Hon. Sec., could not forget Carmarthenshire Races. He must have had copies of *The Welshman* sent to him to enable him to follow the debate on the future of the meeting. In a letter to the editor, Brigstocke explained that he had come to the conclusion that 'the meeting should be remodelled' and he proposed that entries should be limited 'to Wales and Monmouthshire' but he strenuously advised the committee 'to stick to the flying one [course].' And then in his final sentence he underlined the commanding position enjoyed by W. R. H. Powell, retired or not, in regard to Carmarthenshire Races. 'I trust that by the time of the proposed [committee] meeting, Mr Powell and myself will have a programme sketched out, which will embody these principles, and will, when revised by a competent committee, prove acceptable to all who wish well to Steeplechasing in Wales.'[47]

The 1870 meeting was organised by a committee with advice from Powell and Brigstocke, and entries were confined to Wales and Monmouthshire. The banking course was re-introduced alternately with the flying one and no horses from a training stable were allowed. The restrictions pleased the *Journal*, 'for when gentlemen and farmers who breed horses find that there is a pecuniary chance of getting something back for their troubles and expense, then it will stimulate them to bring into the county the best sires that can be procured in order to improve the quality of their stock.'

Hard frost in the week before the meeting had raised the possibility of postponement but the *Journal* sounded an optimistic note that 'under the "new regime" a large majority of the horses entered belong to one or other of the three counties of Carmarthen, Cardigan and Pembroke and would run whether the races are postponed or not. This was not the case when we depended mainly on English and Irish horses. But there will be the usual large influx of visitors from all parts of the Principality, there being a strong conviction abroad that there will be more genuine sport at our meeting next week than has been seen here for some years past.' The racecourse had been moved from its site, east of town near Alltygog, to Pass By on the St Clears road. 'The Principality Stakes and Golden Grove Stakes . . . started in the field just below the stand above Glanygors, round the flag on part of Maesyprior, past the grandstand, skirting the chapel at

Pass By, across Nantyrhebog fields and round again, finishing opposite the stand . . . Stewards were very active . . . [but] must add to them Mr W. R. H. Powell with his sound practical advice and Mr Brenchley in the weighing room gave the most material assistance in furthering the success of the meeting. All races used Grand National Rules.'[48]

The Welshman reported that: 'The town on Monday was unusually quiet; few strangers had arrived. There was consequently no business done on Monday night in the shape of betting.' On Tuesday, 'There was a goodly field to meet the gallant Squire of Maesgwynne, who brought his hounds to Trawsmawr Gate punctually at half-past ten.' And the report was very complimentary to W. R. H. Powell: 'It should not be forgotten that [it is] to Mr Powell, of Maesgwynne, and Mr Brigstocke of Gellydywyll [that] the public are indebted for the programme which has this week been gone through; in fact, it is not too much to say that had it not been for their assistance, and the kindness of Mr Lewis, the mayor of Carmarthen, in offering to get in the subscriptions from the inhabitants of the town, the stewards would this year have had great difficulty in getting up a meeting.'

Thus, despite having had to abandon his 'open meeting' idea which had proved such a success a few years earlier, Powell was still utterly committed to making a success of the Carmarthenshire race meeting albeit as one confined to Welsh hunters. At the dinner Powell referred, briefly, to the ups and downs of the Carmarthenshire Races and urged young and old including himself to 'put our shoulders to the wheel, we shall yet succeed. . . . I hope we are going to revive the meeting, for the good of the town and the interest of sport in the neighbourhood (hear, hear). Anything I can do to help it on I shall always be most happy to do (cheers).'

Four of the races were over banks and three on the flying course. Powell had a horse running in four of the seven races but Johnny Pope who rode all of Powell's horses had to wait for a ride on Alf Jones' 'Milkman' in the last race, the Consolation Stakes on the flying course, before gaining his first win; six ran.[49]

Before the end of March 1870, Powell was at the Pembrokeshire Steeplechases. In the Hunter's Stakes, for horses regularly hunted in South Wales and Monmouthshire and had not been in a training stable, his 'Count' (R. Griffiths) won from five starters.[50] A month later it was reported that the Tivy Side Hunt Week and Steeplechases had attracted more interest than usual because both the Aberystwyth and the Tenby meetings had been discontinued.[51]

The condition of entry for the 1870 meeting would have signalled the end of the efforts to maintain Carmarthenshire Races as a leading open meeting attracting professionally trained steeplechasers from Wales and elsewhere. However, Powell, probably, could not give up trying to keep Carmarthen as a major fixture in the open steeplechase calendar. At the Dublin Horse Show in 1870 Powell persuaded a Captain Morgan to bring his horse to the following year's Carmarthenshire race meeting. Presumably, Powell had no trouble in getting the committee's agreement for two races in 1871 to be open to all-comers but there was no council sponsorship. The entries for the four races on each day were numerous and consisted of first class animals. The London and Birmingham 'divisions of professionals' was fully represented but it was 'necessary to eject one or two welshers from the enclosure.' (The origin of the term 'welsher' was provided by the well-known poet Ceiriog in a letter to the *Western Mail* on 16 July 1883: 'Sir, *In Bell's Life* about 25 years ago your readers will find an account of Jim Welsh, an Irishman who became notorious for cheating on the turf. His name, like that of his countryman

Captain Boycott (under a different set of circumstances) was used to distinguish an odious practice ever afterwards. I am etc., J. Ceiriog Hughes.').

Pope rode Powell's 'Frantic' to victory in the Carmarthenshire Open Handicap but in the Open Hunters' Stakes Pope was thrown by 'Septime' and was kicked in the face by 'Partisane' resulting in cuts above and below his right eye. He was stunned and was attended to by Dr Lawrence of the Grenadier Guards. The Selling Stakes for Hunters not in a training stable resulted in a dead heat between Oliver Powell's 'Ascension' (R. Griffiths) and W. R. H. Powell's 'Terror' (G. Holman) out of three starters. In the rerun (heat) 'Ascension' won easily.

At the dinner W. R. H. Powell said he was glad that the 'meeting was beginning to look up again' and they were indebted to owners who brought their horses from a distance; one, Captain Morgan, had come from Ireland. Morgan emphasised that it was entirely due to Powell that he had brought his horse over and he would be back next year together with some friends from Ireland. There was no better sport anywhere including Liverpool or Birmingham and he would tell his friends that they could expect kindness and fair play which was more than they would get at many places. Mr Ensor from Cardiff also praised the standard of sport at Carmarthen and 'in Cardiff their little sport could not vie with Carmarthen'. He went on to say that in 'Cardiff town and Glamorgan generally, there was no name more honourably or favourably received than that of Mr Powell of Maesgwynne.' The mayor of Carmarthen in his speech stated that 'Mr Powell did all the work.' According to *The Welshman* it was W. R. H. Powell who 'although he had no official office' was responsible for the 'excellent meeting.' The report claimed that the previous two or three years had been 'barren of sport' and it 'required a special effort to try a revival.' Money had been obtained but what about horses? W. R. H. Powell had agreed to contact owners in England and in Ireland and as a result a 'very creditable list of entries was published . . . meritous [*sic*] and good performers.'[52,53]

The start of the 1872 Carmarthenshire Week was promising in that every respectable lodging in the town was taken and there was every chance that the week 'would acquire a prestige beyond precedent.' The bright outlook was due to the hard work of W. R. H. Powell, 'the chief pillar of the Carmarthenshire meeting.' He worked hard, early and late, and his labours were crowned with success, although when he met the committee three weeks earlier he complained of pains in his head which prevented him doing active work and he was unable to follow his hounds. Through his energy 'peculiar to himself' he had secured a 'capital lot of entries'.[54] There were thirty-nine entered for both the Carmarthenshire Grand Annual Steeplechase and the Carmarthenshire Open Steeplechase. Both were handicap races. Mr Jones MP of Blaenos, Llandovery, and Captain Vaughan of Brynog, Llanfihangel Ystrad, Cardiganshire, were the stewards. But on Tuesday it became known that Mr Powell has been seized with a dangerous illness and 'on the Wednesday only the faintest hopes, if any, were entertained of his recovery.' Mr Powell had come to Carmarthen on Sunday evening and occupied apartments at Commerce House, Guildhall Square, intending to remain for the week. 'Although by no means in good health, it was impossible for one like Mr Powell – who never does anything by halves – to relax the strain upon his nerves, and on Monday night he broke down entirely with a severe attack of congestion of the brain. The best medical attendance the district could afford was at once summoned. Mr Crosswell of Llanboidy, his local medical adviser, was instantly called in and Dr Lawrence of the Grenadier Guards, an old friend of the family, had remained with the patient throughout Tuesday night and Wednesday morning. But when Mr Powell took a turn for the worse on Wednesday, it was deemed advisable to call in Mr Rowlands and Mr Hughes of Carmarthen.' By Thursday morning Mr Powell had regained consciousness and there was 'every reason to hope that the danger [would] be tidied over.' But the sports of the week had been 'deprived of their brightest and most genial promoter who for many years had been the life and soul of the gathering.' The hounds met at the Guildhall on Wednesday morning but the hunt was abandoned. And the dinner, proposed for Wednesday, was postponed. 'In short, the mechanism of the meeting was stopped, for everyone's mind was burdened with sorrow and unconditioned for festivity.'

Of the thirty-nine entries collected by Mr Powell five went in the Grand Annual with Powell's 'Garde Civique' (J. Pope) getting second place. W. R. H. Powell had more success in the Tally-Ho Steeplechase with 'Trampeter' (Mr E. P. Wilson) winning out of six runners. The attendance at Thursday's races was 'far short of Tuesday's and [could] only be accounted for by the melancholy tidings of Mr Powell's illness which spread far and wide as soon as it became known.' Five went in the Open out of the thirty-nine entries but Powell had no runner.

Overall it was a successful meeting with a total of forty-one runners going in the eight races. But there was 'only one draw-back to the complete success of the meeting. Scipio could be spared, we could do without the Marquis of Queensberry, but the absence of Mr Powell created a blank that could not be filled.'[55] The *Carmarthen Journal*'s editorial on 9 February 1872 began: 'Difference of opinions may exist respecting the utility of the Carmarthenshire Annual Hunt and Steeplechases; some may approve and others disapprove such sports, but everyone will regret the cause which has deprived the meeting during the present week of its usual life and mirth viz, the dangerous illness of Mr Powell of Maesgwynne. The event has created a gloom which will extend to every locality where Mr Powell is known, for where he is known, he is popular and deeply respected. This illness is partly, if not all-together, the result of his assiduous labours to further and ensure the success of the meeting.' Over the following three weeks, the *Journal* published reports on the state of Powell's health. On 15 February 1872 under 'St Clears news: The alarming illness of [Mr Powell] caused considerable anxiety throughout this locality where he is so popular and respected. Telegrams were sent to Carmarthen by anxious friends and sympathisers. We trust that the Master of the famous Maesgwynne Hounds – of the kindly face and warm heart – has yet many years to live, and that he may be spared to hear the welcome sound of "Tally-Ho" re-echo along the Tave for many a long day to come.'

On 23 February, under 'Local Intelligence: Mr W. R. H. Powell is gradually progressing towards convalescence and we hope soon to report his being able to return to Maesgwynne. He is naturally very weak but during the past few days he has been able to take carriage-airings which has resulted most favourably.' And on 1 March, under the heading 'Mr Powell's Hounds', the *Journal* reported on a meet at Whitland Abbey. It was an unusually small gathering, no doubt due to the absence of Mr Powell. Mr George Thomas, 52-year-old attorney and town clerk of Carmarthen, 'arrived after a ride of 15 miles with a cheering report of our Master's steady convalescence. Even Jack Rees' face brightened up with a smile.'

At the beginning of April 1872, at the Abergavenny Grand National Hunt Steeplechases, Powell's 'Hussar' (Mr Sartoris) carrying 12st.7lb. won the Open Hunters Flat Race over two miles out of six starters.[56] At the beginning of May 1872, Powell was at Cardiff Races and Steeplechases. In the Ely Hurdle, Powell's 'Partisane' with Mr Holford up, finished third out of six starters. In the Open Hurdle, Pope could only steer Powell's 'Garde Civique' to last place out of three. In November of 1872, Powell's 'Hope' (G. George) ran in the Tivy Side Stakes at the Tivy Side Hunt Week and Steeplechases but was unplaced.

5.8 Geography and changing times decide Carmarthen's fate

The new year of 1873 saw Powell back in charge of the Carmarthenshire Races and it was reported that he had 'laboured unceasingly to get the entries.' He had not been satisfied with sending one invitation to potential entrants but in some instances had backed up his initial invitation by half a dozen reminders 'so anxious [had] he been to secure the success of the meeting.' Although there had been more entries in the past it was gratifying to see so many (34 for the Open) at a time of such keen competition. Geography was against Carmarthen. There was a scarcity of horses at Birmingham, Cheltenham and Bristol and when they offered large stakes in such central locations 'we cannot expect any large measure of success here – 100 or 150 miles from anywhere.'[57] The races for the 1873 meeting had been advertised as being 'over an easy flying course – no banks.' Frost again interrupted the meeting and the stewards postponed the races to the following week. Telegrams were sent to owners to come with all speed but owners in England did not believe them – they were ice bound. By Tuesday everything had improved but Mr Powell could not leave his home – 'snow drifts impeded the roads'. Powell was 'sadly wanted' but all were 'glad that it was not last year's reason that kept him away.'

Eight races were got up – four on each day and a total of thirty-four runners got off. At the dinner speakers expressed their pleasure at seeing Powell restored to health and they wished him 'many years of life, not only for the purpose of supporting these meetings but also to continue the many other good things he did in the county (applause).'[58] W. R. H. Powell thought that a flying course was best for this country because it did bring in more people at a time when it was difficult to get people to come from afar because of a great increase in steeplechase meetings. But Mr Gwyn of Cwrthir, Llangain, disagreed and did not mince his words in claiming that, while he was sorry that the meeting had been a failure after W. R. H. Powell's hard work, they had to face the fact that the county gentlemen were tired of seeing horses that never were hunters coming down to Carmarthen and running against the hunters of Carmarthenshire and taking away all the money. The gentlemen would subscribe to see a good race between hunters on an equal footing but not otherwise. He had told Mr Powell that he must have two races over banks for real hunters. If they gave stakes of £80 and put the entrance at 1 sovereign they would get plenty of horses. The Castlemartin men would come to run over banks. Mr Gwyn had no doubt that people in the county were tired of seeing screws coming down to take all their money. Mr Gwyn had made a clear call to return to the closed meeting tried in 1870. W. R. H. Powell's reply was that he agreed with all that was said! Was that reply a sign of the politician showing through? In the General Election held in February 1874, he was an unsuccessful Liberal candidate for Carmarthenshire. He said he should like to see £100 added for a race over banks and another £100 for a flying course and he advised the committee to do that the following year. He was confident that Lord Cawdor, of Stackpole Court, Pembrokeshire, would give something handsome if there were races over banks on both days. Clearly, Powell kept his politics separate from his sport. He was about to stand against the Lord's son, Viscount Emlyn, in the 1874 General Election.

The Welshman's verdict on the 1873 meeting was that 'it might have been worse.' And it emphasised the disadvantage placed on Carmarthen by its location far from the principal stables. It was absolutely necessary to change, however reluctant the promoters to dispense with the services of 'famous' horses'. Changing the course 'as suggested by Mr Powell of Maesgwynne [seemed] the only escape from a difficulty.' The course should be 'three fold'. They might still get the occasional horse from a distance to go over the flying course. There was always a goodly number of hunters in the district ready for a banking course as in former days. And a flat course would satisfy all.

The start of 1874 must have been pretty taxing on Mr Powell with his involvement in the General Election and at the same time striving to get up another good hunt week at Carmarthen. To *The Welshman* it was a 'duty and pleasure to record the fact that Mr Powell of Maesgwynne has been again at the front, as he has been for many years. As a worker on these occasions he is unmatched and how much the Carmarthenshire meeting depends on his exertions.'[59] In 1874, seven races were over the flying course and two over banks. Powell had only one horse at the meeting and he ran him in two of the races but without success. A total of forty-five horses ran in the nine races. The stewards were Viscount Emlyn, W. R. H. Powell and six others and the joint Hon. Secs. were J. Olive and Tom Rees. Lord Cawdor and the gentlemen of the Penllergaer Hunt had been very liberal in their donations. The meeting was hailed as the best for many a day.

The following year's event was even better and once again Mr Powell and the Hon. Sec. had been busy. The 1875 meeting was described as excellent, even though the two open races fell through. On Monday it was discovered that the Licensing Act allowed the extension to opening hours to inn-keepers during race week and the inns of Carmarthen remained open until midnight during the week. A few horses arrived on Sunday and Monday but the trains on Tuesday brought a large number and businessmen were in greater force than for some years. Hotels rapidly filled by Tuesday night. The failure of the open races to fill led to talk of making the following year's meeting a purely local affair which, in *The Welshman*'s view, would be a great mistake.[60]

Powell's hounds with himself as MFH met on Monday to start the week. Of the eleven races, five were on the flat with the others equally divided between banks, hurdles and flying. Powell ran horses, all ridden by Mr Thomas, in five races. The total added prize money for the 1875 Carmarthenshire Races was in excess of 370 sovereigns (about £37,000 at today's values) and all the prize money paid out went to owners within south Wales.

There were no races at Cefnbrafle to celebrate the end of the hunting season in the Spring of 1875. But there was a special meeting at the Lamb Inn, Llanboidy, to mark the occasion when a testimonial was made to the universally-respected huntsman Mr Jack Rees.[61] The Maesgwynne Hunt Club met at the Lamb Inn at 9.00 a.m. on Monday for the last meet of the season. Proceedings started with breakfast in the Lamb. William E. B. Gwyn, JP, of Plas Cwrt Hir,

Llangain and Mr Henry Thomas of Swansea had acted as principals in the matter but support had come from past and present members of the hunt and also from farmers and breeders of the country. Jack Rees had been a faithful servant to Mr Powell for twenty-seven years, thirteen of them as huntsman. Rees commented that he had been with his master for seven-and-twenty years and would like to be another twenty-seven. He first worked for Bowen Davies of Maesycrugiau before moving in 1848 to Maesgwynne, and looked after the hounds, first as whip and then as huntsman. He was well known as a successful steeplechase rider and his struggles with Tom Davies were famous. He was first known as Jack Maesycrugiau. He had his first mount at Carmarthenshire Races in 1848 although there was no record of it. In 1849 he rode 'Maid of Lawrenny' to second place behind 'Baptist'. At that time, Tom Davies was an experienced rider and had been successful on 'Kangaroo' and others. Jack Rees' most successful mounts were 'Hazard' and 'St David' from Mr Powell's stable which had turned out some of the best steeplechasers ever seen in Wales. He had now given way to younger riders. Rees always spoke freely and called a spade a spade but he never used offensive language. He was doing much to improve the breed of horses in his district and farmers and breeders owed a debt of gratitude to him for the excellent stud horses he brought out every year. His reward was a service in plate costing 100 guineas. Rees' monogram was engraved upon each article and the centre of the salver was engraved with: 'Presented to Jack Rees by the members of the Maesgwynne Hunt Club and other friends in token of their esteem and in recognition of his long and zealous services as huntsman to Mr Powell's hounds. April 1875'.

W. E. B. Gwyn made the presentation and W. H. Thomas called out 'Long life to you Rees and may you die in harness'. Rees replied by thanking them and claiming that he owed more thanks to farmers than to others because he often tore down their gaps and broke their fences and they got no sport! Jack Rees referred to the birth, the previous evening at Maesgwynne, of W. F. Roch's son and heir to the Butterhill and Llawhaden estates. (W. F. Roch was married to W. R. H. Powell's younger daughter Emily Catherine). W. R. H. Powell reported on a successful season in which 38 foxes had been killed in the open and 100 run to ground. And he was as energetic as ever in looking forward to the following season.

Before the end of April, at the Tivy Side Hunt week, Powell's 'Lucy' (J. Pope) won the Cardigan Stakes of 4 sovereigns each with 30 sovereigns added; 5 started.

W. R. H. Powell had worked as hard as ever to get up the 1876 Carmarthenshire Races and succeeded in getting the best entry ever seen there! Seventy-two horses in total went in twelve races for which the total prize money added was £490.[62] But at the same time it was evident that the open handicap races could not be filled and it was time to confine races to hunters (local horses). It was an unlucky meeting for the Maesgwynne Stable because the horses had influenza and stayed at home, thus robbing the meeting of one runner from nearly every one of the dozen races. And Powell's horses had been expected to win two or three of the races. His top jockey, Johnny Pope, was there and rode for other owners. But around that time tragedy struck for Johnny when his wife of two years died in childbirth. The attendance at the dinner was poor and Mr Powell said it was 'paying a very bad compliment both to the meeting and also to the hunt (applause).'

On Easter Monday 1876, Powell was a steward at Llandeilo Races but he did not have any horses running. He was again at the Tivy Side Steeplechases where Johnny Pope rode in three races but with no success. Mr Powell's hounds continued to hunt regularly during the 1870s.

For the 1877 Carmarthenshire Steeplechases (under Grand National rules), W. R. H. Powell as Hon. Sec. had enticed a new name to act as one of the stewards. Crawshay Bailey of Maindiff Court, Abergavenny, was the son of the ironmaster and MP for Monmouth Boroughs (1852-1868) of the same name.[63] The 1877 races came off on the old course near Derllys about three-and-a-half miles from Carmarthen and according to the *Carmarthen Journal* 'were it not for W. R. H. Powell, these races would have been ere now on the way to "the dogs".'[64] A total of thirty runners started in six races.

The dinner, chaired by Crawshay Bailey, was well attended which had not been the case for many years. Lort Phillips, one of the stewards, in his speech said he had done virtually nothing because Powell had done everything! Powell deserved their thanks, first in the hunting field as well as the racing field and as the chief promoter of every good county sport. Lort Phillips went on to claim that Carmarthenshire Races were 'quite equal to the Puncheston meetings in Ireland and the Liverpool meetings in England. Some of the best horses come to Carmarthen and we had plenty of horses we are not ashamed to send out to run elsewhere . . . Most of the credit was due to Mr Powell (loud cheers).' Others endorsed the praises of Mr Powell and Crawshay Bailey summed up his qualities and said that no man had a better heart or a more active mind, an example to all younger sportsmen. 'If you were at Monmouthshire Hunt tonight you would find that no name received a warmer welcome than the renowned name of Mr Powell,' and so it would be at hundreds of other places. They were proud of him and rejoiced in the number of Carmarthenshire horses he had brought to Abergavenny. Powell, in reply, mentioned the difficulties of getting up a meeting at Carmarthen. There were not so many men running horses locally as there were in the 'old times'. In the old times there was 'hardly a tithe [tenth] of the racing men in England that there are now, and of late owners of horses have more money added to races within a short distance of their stables, so it is very hard to persuade them to come to out-of-the-way Carmarthen.' Mr Berry, representative of *Bell's Life*, was again present and he backed up the others in praise of Powell. In all the places he had been to, there was no man of the turf whom he esteemed more than Mr Powell.

On the second day W. R. H. Powell had runners in four of the six races and he had two winners. The Harkforward Flat Race, was won by 'Milton' (Mr E. P. Wilson) out of four starters, and the Who-Whoop Hurdle was won by 'Tenby' (Johnny Pope) out of five runners.

In April 1877, Powell had 'Tenby' with Johnny Pope up, running in two races at the Llandeilo Races but had to be satisfied with third place in both races.

Sometime in the September quarter of 1877, W. R. H. Powell's brother and close co-worker in the golden days of Llanboidy Races, Thomas Rees Oliver Powell, passed away at only 45-years-of-age.

The number of entries for the 1878 Carmarthen Races was good but the depressed state of the country was thought to account for the poor attendance at the meeting of members of the middle and lower classes.[65]

In the 29 March 1878 issue of the *Carmarthen Journal*, John Rees of the Lamb Inn, Llanboidy, advertized that he had two stallions available for cover that season.

But around that time, John Rees' wife Ann passed away leaving a husband and seven children aged from twenty-three to eight years of age. The loss of his wife was probably the reason why,

1878.

To cover this Season, that superior Blue Roan
Cart Horse,

EARL OF SEFTON,
LATE YOUNG SAMPSON,

Excellent foal getter, at £2 2s. each mare, and 5s.
the groom, the property of John Rees,
Llanboidy.

1878.

To cover this Season, that superior Brown Pony
winner of the third prize at Liverpool Royal
Show, 1877,

CYMRO BACH O'R ARCH,

At £1 1s. each mare. Groom's fee, 2s. 6d., the
property of John Rees, Lamb, Llanboidy.

(Courtesy *Carmarthen Journal*).

a month later on 26 April 1878, John Rees held a Sale of 'young Hunters, Colts, Entire Pony, Dairy Cows, Sheep, Pigs, Dry Timber, etc.' including 'Cymro Bach' at the Lamb Inn, Llanboidy. But he continued to farm and to be the innkeeper at the Lamb.

W. R. H. Powell's support for steeplechasing was illustrated by his entry of six for the Cardiff Races on 1 May 1878. He actually took one horse to Cardiff and, 'Milton', with Mr Trewent in the saddle won the Grand Stand Hunters' flat race of 50 sovereigns out of three starters. In the 1878 Abergavenny Races, Powell had two horses and Johnny Pope rode 'Milton' to victory in the Clytha Selling Hurdle of £25. 'Milton' completed a hat-trick of major victories in 1878 when he won the Ludlow Hunters Cup ridden by Mr R. Thomas. The pair repeated their success at Ludlow in 1880.

In the 1878/79 Hunting season, Powell's hounds did not appear in the *Journal*'s list of hunting appointments until 29 November 1878. It is possible that John Rees, the huntsman found it difficult to cope with all his duties at the Lamb Inn and farm after the misfortune of losing his wife in the early part of 1878.

At a meeting of the committee of the Carmarthenshire Hunt Week in December 1878, W. R. H. Powell agreed that it would be best to hold the 1879 races during the first week of

February since that would be 'just before the Croydon, Birmingham and Sandown Park meetings.' It was further agreed to run six races on the first day but since the Borough Member of Parliament, Mr B. T. Williams, had declined to subscribe, the loss of the Borough Member's race meant that only five races would be run on the second day.[66] Powell's leadership resulted in a reasonably successful race meeting in February 1879 although frost again caused a week's postponement. Personally, he had a very successful week, with four winners! His first jockey, Johnny Pope, rode 'Nightingale' to victory in the The Cambrian Hunters' Steeplechase where five ran, and rode 'Milton' to victory in both the Who-Whoop Stakes out of three runners, and the Gone Away Stakes where three ran. In the Derllys Stakes, Powell's 'Milton' went again but ridden by Mr Trewent and came home first out of four starters.[67]

An advert in early January for the 1880 Carmarthenshire Hunt Week listed entries for ten races. It was signed by W. R. H. Powell as Hon. Sec. On 9 January 1880, the auctioneers J. Howell Thomas and Thompson offered for sale at Whitland Junction ten of Powell's steeplechasers and hunters. Three were sold and the other seven entered for the 1880 Carmarthenshire Races. Powell's horses won three of the races and Pope rode two of the winners: 'Nightingale' in the Tally Ho Stakes of 60 sovereigns over the flying course (5 ran), and 'Priestcraft' in the County Members Hurdles of 50 sovereigns (3 ran). Mr Thomas rode 'Milton' to victory in the Derllys Stakes on the flat (4 ran).

However, the meeting was not a success: 'There are times and season for all things. February is the wrong time to run the races. The grand object of horse racing is to keep up the breed of horses and not to open a field for betting and it cannot improve breed to run them in February. When races do not fill and fields are small – "something is rotten in the state of Denmark".'[68] It had taken over forty years to question the suitability of holding the races in the month of February!

Another sporting event took place at St Clears in July of 1880 which consisted of two track races, one over 440 yards and one over 880 yards between a Mr W. Harry and a Mr John Lloyd for £10 a side. They were allowed an hour's break between the races which were run at the Mansel Athletic Grounds, St Clears.[69]

Powell's hounds were not listed in the local papers' hunting appointments for 1880. They probably did hunt but W. R. H. Powell was otherwise engaged with the matter of the General Election which took place between 31 March and 27 April 1880. He was successful in winning one of the two Carmarthenshire County seats for the Liberal Party; the other successful candidate was Conservative Lord Emlyn. In the autumn Powell would have been involved at Westminster and therefore unable to follow the hunt as he had done for 40 or so years. From January 1881, Powell's hounds' hunting appointments were again listed regularly in the local papers.

The Carmarthenshire Hunt Week and Steeplechases had to be postponed in 1881 because of the 'Great Storm'. The meeting got under-way at the end of February but Powell's involvement was understandably reduced compared to previous years because of his parliamentary duties. But he had five horses running and two of them went in two races. He had three winners.[70] Powell brought his hounds to the Guildhall on the Wednesday and a good hunt followed. And he still managed to attract the label of 'Chief Promoter of the meeting' from *The Welshman*'s correspondent.

But times were changing and other sporting activities such as athletics and bicycle racing were growing in popularity. On Easter Monday 1881, the Carmarthen Athletic Sports Club organised a meeting at 'people's park' which provided a mix of foot and cycle races. The winner of the 440 yards foot race for boys collected 10 shillings (50p) and the runner-up got 5 shillings. First place in a three-mile bike race was worth £2 and second place £1. The winner of the high pole jump cleared 8ft 10ins and won 7s.6d. (37.5p). The one mile handicap foot race's first prize of £1 was a bit mean.

In April, Powell found time to attend Pembrokeshire Steeplechases although he had no horses running. Two months later, on Wednesday, 22 June 1881, there was a sale of 'noted steeplechasers and hunters' at Maesgwynne attended by a crowd from far and wide.[71] The first in the ring was 'Nightingale' who fetched a 'fair' price of 110 guineas. 'Hazard' followed and went for 80 guineas 'to the emphatic declaration of "Jack Rees"' which reminded everyone that it was the huntsman's mount. The 'made' horses, 'Skipper' and 'Sailor', sold for 150 guineas each as did the Master's favourite, 'Mallet', sold to Mr Weatherby, of the world-renowned racing firm, for his own use. Jack Rees' 'The Priest' and 'Roly Poly' and others averaged 100 guineas. Offers for the young unbroken stock of 3 and 2 year-olds were too low and Powell would not sell. The gathered throng enjoyed the flowing champagne and nut-brown ale!

By the time the 1882 Carmarthenshire Races came off, Powell had effectively retired from 'activity in the field' because 'Politics permeates the whole structure of our system, our money market is ruled by politics and our every day trade and some even carry it into their places of worship and make it a part of their devotions. Horse racing does not escape the touch of politics either. Mr W. R. H. Powell, MP, knows this very well and, induced by a combination of several circumstances – such as his parliamentary duties and others – he has retired from activity in the field. Not long ago W. R. H. Powell sold several of his horses by auction and thus hinted that he did not intend for the future to be such a prominent leader in this part of the country.'[72] W. F. Saunders of Glanrhydw took over as Hon. Sec. from Powell.

But Powell was far from finished with sport. His hounds met with their usual flourish during the 1882 Carmarthenshire Week and although he had only two horses running on the first day, both carried the orange and black colours of Maesgwynne to victory; 'Chorister' over Powell's beloved banks and 'Milton' on the flat, both ridden by Pope.

The *Journal* reflected the huge esteem felt for Powell in reporting that all were glad to see him win that day and they hoped that increasing age, parliamentary duties nor anything else would ever take Mr Powell away from the Carmarthenshire Races. At the dinner it was Powell who spoke on behalf of the Members of Parliament and he reminisced on the years gone by . . . on the battle between 'Kangaroo' and 'Tally Ho', on the time a jockey claimed his saddle was made of india rubber which was why he sprang off and fell! – and there was the memorable event in which 'Ace of Hearts' figured . . . In those days the jumping was far better . . . there were no horses now that jumped banks as those did in the old days . . . he had tried his best to return to those days . . . but every dog had his day and he had had his . . . now it was Mr Saunders' turn. Mr Berry of *Bell's Life* magazine spoke and Dr Hughes gave a rendering of 'Pale Young Curate' which song was 'well received'.

On the second day's racing, Powell had two horses going but without success. In the County Members' Hunters Hurdle of £30 (£25 from W. R. H. Powell, MP), his 'Kalmin' (Pope) failed to recover his owner's outlay by finishing third out of four.

In August 1883 Powell's photograph adorned the front cover of the London-based *Baily's Monthly Magazine of Sports and Pastimes* in which appeared a biographical sketch and a signed photograph of the sporting great; a sure tribute to Powell's past prominence in the world of racing and hunting.[73]

Powell's hounds were listed regularly in the local papers' hunting appointments during the 1882/83 and the 1883/84 seasons, but he was not mentioned in the reports of the 1883 Carmarthenshire Hunt Week. It may well have been that his parliamentary work did not permit him to be present. But he was present at the 1884 Carmarthenshire Week and presented his hounds at the Guildhall and 'good sport was expected for our worthy member and his excellent huntsman Mr John Rees.'[74] There were fewer attendees in 1884 but the racing was pretty good although Powell's sole entry was an also-ran.

John Rees acted as starter at Carmarthenshire Races during the 1880s.

Powell had two horses running in the Carmarthenshire meeting of 1885 but no winners.[75] However, two races did not fill. Between 40 and 50 attended the dinner in 1885 and in his speech Powell said he was getting too old to be in the saddle much with the hounds but he was glad to think that he had helped to maintain hunting in the county for the past 46 years.

No Powell horses were entered for the 1886 Carmarthenshire meeting and frost caused the meeting to be postponed. He had two runners but no winners in 1887.[76] Powell's Maesgwynne pack's meets continued to be listed regularly during 1885/86 and 1886/87 but it is unlikely that Powell himself was a regular attender by that time.

In an attempt to secure some sort of future for the struggling Carmarthenshire Hunt Week and Steeplechases J. Howell Thomas, the auctioneer, called a meeting in December 1887 at the Boar's Head with the declared aim that they must not let the old Carmarthenshire go down.[77] A new programme in which only a single day's racing was included was drawn up. The meeting was to start on a Tuesday with a meet of the Penllergaer Hunt to be followed on Wednesday by a day's racing and a dinner. Thursday was to see a meet of Powell's hounds with a Ball in the evening. The Penllergaer hounds would meet on the Friday to finish off the week. In the event, frost disrupted the 1888 Week and the races were spread over two days as in the past. A new race on the programme was the Maesgwynne Hunters Steeplechase Plate of 45 sovereigns (£25 from W. R. H. Powell, MP) over the flying course.[78] No horses were entered from Maesgwynne for any of the races. Powell's hounds met at Nant-y-ci on Monday, 6 February 1888, and he was still following the hounds in December 1888, albeit on wheels.

By that time Powell's health was a cause for concern and it may well be that his last meet was the one arranged at Maesgwynne on 8 January 1889.[79] The day began with a 9.00 a.m. breakfast at the mansion followed by a meet at Vron, Llanboidy, at 11.00 a.m. Powell would have enjoyed the breakfast but then he would have waved goodbye to his beloved pack. The following month brought no joy to the ailing Squire. For one thing, the Carmarthenshire Hunt Week and Steeplechases in early February 1889 was a low key affair judging by the scant coverage given it in the local papers.[80] Jack Rees was still the starter but John Francis had taken over as Hon. Sec. Perhaps the high point of the races was the Maesgwynne Hunters Steeplechase of 50 sovereigns (£25 from W. R. H. Powell, MP) over the flying course in which seven ran. No horses from the Maesgwynne Stable started in any of the races and no reports of a dinner or of a Ball appeared in the papers. The Week was clearly a pale shadow of those enjoyed when W. R. H. Powell was in charge.

Another matter that must have hurt the feelings of the Squire was the outcome of the attempt to prepare a testimonial for him by his hunting friends. At a gathering in Carmarthen in

Outside Maesgwynne in the late 1880s. Ready for an otter hunt. W. R. H. Powell is seated in the middle with (possibly) his grandson George Powell Roch (b.1875) on his right. On the other seat, left to right, are Caroline Mary Powell (elder daughter), William Francis Roch (son-in-law) and Emily Catherine Roch (younger daughter).
(Denley Owen collection).

Final instructions for the hounds. The man on the left is the huntsman,
Thomas Davies (b.1843), who lived at Plasybwci.
(Denley Owen collection).

November 1888 chaired by T. Morris, Coombe, and supported by W. J. Buckley MFH, Penyfai and Baldwin Protheroe of Dolwilym, Llanglydwen, the idea of a testimonial to Powell Bach for his service to sport in the district received support from T. Jones, Llanfair Grange, Llandovery, who thought a testimonial was due in recognition of Powell's amazing record of having hunted the country for fifty years.[81] J. Beynon, Trewern, had been to see Mr Powell and had suggested that a portrait of Powell on horseback surrounded by his hounds might be appropriate. Powell's response was that such a portrait was not quite representative of himself in 1888! Powell had informed Beynon that the village of Llanboidy was rather short of water and that he wanted to bring water to the village. Perhaps they could erect a fountain with a suitable inscription as his testimonial. Beynon added that Powell did not press any particular idea and left it to them to decide. Beynon thought the expense of the water scheme too much to entertain; a surveyor would cost between £20 to £30. It was decided to wait and see how much money the subscriptions would bring in. In early February 1889 it was resolved at a meeting in the Ivy Bush Hotel, Carmarthen, to consult again with Powell about the form the testimonial should take. A couple of weeks later his friends gathered again on a Saturday afternoon at the Ivy Bush. Mr Tom Morris, Coombe, took the chair, and others present were J. Beynon, Trewern, Capt. Lloyd, Glangwili, H. J. Lawrence, Waungron, W. Lewis Hughes, Carmarthen and John Francis, Myrtle Hill.[82] It was reported that the subscriptions collected at the time amounted to £220. J. Beynon reported on a meeting he had had with W. R. H. Powell at Maesgwynne when Powell had been well enough to converse freely for a long time and they had talked about the proposed testimonial. Powell had said that since it was only some of his old friends that were contributing and that it had not been taken up by the county generally, he would be glad if they let the matter drop. J. Beynon told the gathering at the Ivy Bush that he was surprised that so few farmers had subscribed. Only eight names had appeared on the Llanboidy list. There were hardly any names on the Tenby list. It was resolved to return the subscriptions that had been collected. The lack of response to the proposed testimonial was, almost certainly, a reflection of how badly it had been organised rather than evidence of a collapse in respect for W. R. H. Powell. After all, the 'organisers' were the people who failed in the 1850s to keep up their subscriptions towards maintaining a county pack of hounds and left Powell to run the pack at his own expense. They were the people who allowed the hunt compensation fund to dry up in the 1870s leaving farmers and smallholders to pay for damage by foxes and horses until Powell stepped in to correct the situation. And they were the people whose lack of organising ability almost finished Carmarthen Races in the 1860s. Again, Powell came to the rescue.

But the *Western Mail* saw the fiasco through politically-tinted glasses which focussed on the radicals! 'We are sorry for the ridiculous collapse of the proposed testimonial to Mr W. R. H. Powell MP of Maesgwynne, the Member for West Carmarthenshire. Mr Powell has represented the constituency in Parliament for eight years, and was probably the only man whom the Radicals could have brought forward in 1880 who could have hoped to oppose with any prospect of success the powerful territorial interest of the Emlyns. The representative of an old county family, a most popular landlord, the holder of shrievalty when he was thirty – now something like 40 years ago – and one whose intense love of the chase constantly brought him into contact with all sorts and conditions of people, we should have thought the Squire of Maesgwynne the very man of all others whom the "democrac" would have delighted to honour after the particular fashion which some of its leaders had contemplated. But the business never really "took on". A paltry £150 or so was all that could be collected, and we were not surprised in the least to find the proposed recipient suggesting – we can imagine with ill-concealed disgust – that the whole business had better be let drop. It is only another instance of Radical ingratitude. They get the strongest man to fight their toughest battles for them, and when the victory has been secured the victor can just go hang. He has served the momentary purpose for which they wanted him, and when, as has been especially the case with Mr Powell, they see him old and ailing and not likely to be of much further use, they toss him aside with as little compunction or ceremony as they would any other sucked orange. Eight names on the Llanboidy list and practically none at Tenby were sufficiently discouraging for even the most sanguine stomach. How many of these were Conservatives, history sayeth not, but we dare be bound that a goodly proportion of them were. They are all to get their money back – "less the amount of expenses incurred". A miserable fiasco, truly.'[83]

Bearing in mind that the idea of a testimonial originated with the mainly Tory hunting gentry, it was a bit strong of the *Western Mail* to castigate the radicals for its collapse! And particularly after it had reported a few weeks previously that 'the gentry and farmers, without distinction of party, [were] subscribing as liberally as [could] be expected in those times.' However, it is likely that politics did play a part in the fiasco. The Tories were still smarting from the drubbing they had received from the Liberals when Powell had taken more than 60% of the vote in defeating Lord Emlyn in 1885, and had increased his share to 68% in trouncing Sir James Lawrence in 1886. And in early 1889 the Tories and the Liberals were having a go at each other in the campaign for county council seats. Therefore, the churchgoing Tory landlords at the Ivy Bush meeting, although friends with Powell on a personal basis, would probably have been reluctant to publicly canvas for subscriptions towards his testimonial bearing in mind Powell's strong support for the disestablishment of the Church in Wales and his repeated calls for a Land Act giving security of tenure and compensation for tenants.

But the reality was that there was no one with Powell's organising ability, initiative and energy to make a success of the proposed testimonial to himself in the way he had worked to recognise the achievements of his friend and employee, Jack Rees of the Lamb Inn, in 1875 and again in 1886. And so it was that W. R. H. Powell was allowed to fade away from the sporting scene in Carmarthen without a final official recognition of his towering achievements during the previous half-century. Without him, Carmarthenshire Hunt Week and Steeplechases also faded away and the event was destined never to regain the glory it had enjoyed under the dynamic leadership of Powell Bach, Maesgwynne.

But in the minds of steeplechase enthusiasts the triumphant days of the Carmarthenshire 'Open' in the 1860s would always remain as a real memorial to the genius of W. R. H. Powell.

		CARMARTHENSHIRE STEEPLECHASES: WINNERS OF THE OPEN HANDICAP, 1845-1873			
Year	Added Sovs.	Horse	Runners	Rider	Owner
1845		Kitty	4	Cadwallader	Lort Phillips
'46		Kangaroo	4	Tom Davies	W. R. H. Powell
'47		The Baptist		R. Powell	Mr Stokes
'48		The Baptist		Tom Davies	Mr Stokes
'49					
1850		Hazard	6	Jack Rees	J. Olive
'51		Hazard	7	Jack Rees	W. R. H. Powell
'52		California	6	Martin	Mr Rees
'53		Hazard	5	Jack Rees	W. R. H. Powell
'54	70	Petworth	9	W. Archer	Capt. Pryse
'55	100	St David	7	Jack Rees	W. R. H. Powell
'56	do	Deception	6	Mathias	Lort Phillips
'57	do	The Victim	10	Tom Davies	Dansey
'58	do	The Miner	11	Geo. Stevens	Mr John
'59	do	Arthur	7	Tom Davies	Lort Phillips
1860	do	Confederate	10	J. R. James	Mr M. Jones
'61	do	Ace of Hearts	5	J. R. James	W. R. H. Powell
'62	do	Ace of Hearts	6	J. R. James	W. R. H. Powell
		The Rug			Sir R. de Burgo
'63	do	Ace of Hearts	7	Tom Davies	W. R. H. Powell
'64	do	Ace of Hearts	9	Johnny Pope	W. R. H. Powell
'65	do	Fenton	8	Tom Davies	R. C. Riddell
'66	do	Daisy	6	Johnny Pope	W. R. H. Powell
'67	do	Daisy	10	Johnny Pope	W. R. H. Powell
'68		No Open			
'69	do	Whitehall		Stevens	R. G. Price
1870		No Open			
'71	80	The Robber		P. Merton	Mr Doncaster
'72		No Open			
'73	70	Scrub		J. Ruddy	Mr Doncaster

Most successful riders:

Tom Davies 6 winners (2 for Powell); Jack Rees 4 (3 for Powell);
Johnny Pope 3 (3 for Powell); J James 3 (2 for Powell).

THE FUNERAL OF W. R. H. POWELL

EXTRACTS FROM THE account in the *Welshman,* of 5 July 1889, of the funeral of W. R. H. Powell which had taken place at Maesgwynne and St Brynach's Church, Llanboidy, on Saturday, 29 June 1889.

(Courtesy *Carmarthen Journal*).

FUNERAL OF MR W. R. H. POWELL, M.P.

The funeral of Mr W. R. H. Powell, M.P. of Maesgwynne, Llanboidy, took place on Saturday afternoon. It had been published by the press that the sad duty would be privately conducted. This, however, was not to be. Not only did the old and young of the poorer classes of the community from the neighbouring districts assemble near and in the burial ground on this occasion, but the leading gentry of the united counties of South Wales, and many from a greater distance, attended to pay their last tribute of respect to one who in his day and generation had lightened the burdens of the labourer, and created cheerfulness and happiness in his humble sphere, and had met the wishes of the well-to-do by affording great facilities for the enjoyment of one of the most exhilarating of sports ever promulgated.

At one o'clock the funeral rites were commenced at the mansion by the Rev. D. S. Davies, Baptist minister, in accordance with the express wish of the deceased, who read a portion of Scripture (Psalm 16), and offered up prayer. The mournful procession then left the residence in the following order:

1. The Rev. William Rees, vicar of Llanboidy, and the Rev. D. S. Davies [Baptist minister at Ramoth, Cwmfelin Mynach and Calfaria, Login.]

2. Friends – Mr Alderman George Thomas, Carmarthen; Mr W. O. Brigstocke, chairman of the Carmarthenshire County Council; Mr Alderman Thomas Thomas, official receiver, Carmarthen; Mr John Hughes, F.R.C.S., Carmarthen; and Dr Phillips, Whitland.

3. The tenants.

4. The workmen.

5. The undertakers (Mr Jabez Thomas, the Shop, Llanboidy, and Mr Evans, joiner, Llanboidy.

6. The hearse, on either side of which were Stephens, the butler; Williams, the bailiff; Thomas Davies [stableman of Plasybwci]; Higgins, the gardener; John Rees [Lamb Inn, Llanboidy], Pope [Johnny Pope, stud groom and star jockey]; T. Davies, the kennel keeper [of Plasybwci]; and Henry James, the stableman [of Maesgwynne upper lodge].

7. Private carriage containing Mrs Powell, Miss Powell, Mrs Roch, and Master Roch.

8. The relatives: the Rev. E. H. Powell [brother], Hewish, near Bristol; Mr Randolph; Capt. Grismond Philipps, Cwmgwili; Mr W. Philipps, chief constable of Carmarthenshire; and Mr T. Roch.

9. The domestic servants.

On its way to the old parish church, the *cortege* was augmented by a numerous gathering, amongst which were noticed: Mr William Davies, M.P. for Pembrokeshire; Mr Thomas Morris, Coomb; Mr W. H. M. Yelverton, Whitland Abbey; Dr H. J. Lawrence, Waungron; Mr J. Beynon, Trewern; Mr Schaw-Protheroe [Dolwilym]; Mr Bagnall Evans [Nant-yr-Eglwys]; Mr H. W. T. Howell, Glaspant; Colonel J. R. Howell, Noyadd; Capt. Mansfield, Llysonen; Mr Philipps, Clyngwyn; Mr Gwynne-Hughes, Tregib; the mayor of Carmarthen (Mr Howell Howells); the Rev. J. Wyndham Lewis, Carmarthen; Mr Walter Jones, barrister, Llandovery; Mr J. Lloyd Morgan, barrister; Dr Howell Rees, Tyrbach; the Rev. W. Thomas, Llanboidy; Mr R. Carver, late of Wenallt, now of Cheltenham; and Mr H. S. Carver, Blaencorse.

On arrival at the churchyard the procession opened out, and the coffin was borne into the church amidst much genuine sorrow and sympathy; and whilst the vicar proceeded with the usual prayers, Mrs Powell and Miss Powell stood at the head of the bier, nor did they leave their rightful place until the body was consigned to the family vault hard by. As the mortal remains of the dear old 'squire were being interred, that beautiful hymn, "Now the labourer's task is o'er," was most pathetically sung by the choir, there being a notable predominance of female voices. This portion of the ceremony was truly sorrowful. There was a tremulousness in the singing of every one who took part that was most touching, and no spectator that had known the "Dyn Bach o' Maesgwynne" could help being overcome with the deepest emotion.'

A very large number of costly crosses and wreaths were placed around the vault. One cross in particular was magnificent. It was, we heard, made by Miss Powell herself.

It must have been somewhat consoling to the deceased's family to witness such a manifestation of profound sympathy by Mr Powell's staunch friends, who, to use their own words, could not, in spite of any wish to the contrary, stay away from the funeral of 'the very best fellow' they had ever known.

The following is a complete list of the floral wreaths, &c., laid on Mr Powell's coffin and placed in the vault: 'Mrs and Miss Powell, cross; Mrs Roch, wreath; Mrs Roch's children, cross; indoor servants, wreath; the gardeners, wreath; the Revd E. H. and Mrs Powell, cross; Miss Randolph, cross; Miss Kate Philipps, wreath; Mrs and Miss Gwynne Philipps, cross; the Revd W. and Mrs Rees, wreath; Mr John Rees, huntsman, cross; the villagers of Llanboidy, wreath; "In memory of our beloved Founder" from the Friendly Society, wreath; Mr John Evans, carpenter, wreath; Mrs Robert Thomas, wreath; Mr and Mrs Thos. Thomas, wreath; Mr J. Lewis, Commerce House, wreath; Liberal Association of the Western Division, wreath; Liberal Association of the Borough of Carmarthen, wreath; Mr J. Howell Thomas, wreath; Mrs Olive, wreath; Mr and Mrs Thomas Jenkins, wreath; Mr D. R. Morgan, wreath; Mrs Powell, Penycoed, cross; Mr Nicholas, Penycoed, wreath; Mrs O. Powell, cross; Mr and Mrs Protheroe, Dolwilym, wreath; from his young friends at Dolwilym, cross; Miss Schaw Protheroe, wreath; Mrs Leach, wreath; Mrs Norton, wreath; Mr and Mrs Gwynne-Hughes, Tregib, wreath; Miss Roch, Cheltenham, wreath; Mr and Mrs Logan, wreath; Mrs Maltby, wreath; Mr W. O. Brigstocke, wreath; Mrs Sparrow, wreath; Mrs Schomberz, roses; Professor and Mrs Braudt, cross; Revd C. Hesketh Knowles, wreath; Captain Mansfield, wreath.'

UNVEILING A MONUMENT TO HIS MEMORY.

On Saturday a monument, erected to the memory of the late Mr. W. R. H. Powell, of Maesgwynne, was placed without ceremony at the head of the family vault in the Parish Church of Llanboidy. The commission had been entrusted to Mr. William Goscombe John, of Cardiff and London, and this, his latest work, will favourably compare with any of his previous efforts. In front of a perpendicular slab of white marble, upon the surface of which has been faintly traced a cross, stands a draped female figure, with bowed head. The face, with the exception of the upper portion of the forehead, is hid by the right arm, which is deftly drawn across the eyes, while the left arm is gracefully thrown over the head, with the fingers listlessly drooping. The drapery is most skilfully treated, and every detail of this beautiful specimen of the sculptor's art displays the handiwork of a master.

Western Mail report on 29 September 1891 of the unveiling of *Grief* at St Brynach's church, Llanboidy.
(Courtesy *Western Mail*).

MEMORIAL TO W. R. H. POWELL

Grief by William Goscombe John

AFTER THE DEATH of W. R. H. Powell, the Maesgwynne family commissioned a memorial sculpture from William Goscombe John, the young Cardiff artist, whose father was a woodcarver employed at Cardiff Castle by the third Marquis of Bute. Goscombe John attended Cardiff Art School for ten years before moving to London in 1881 where he worked with Thomas Nicholls until 1886. He won a gold medal in 1889 which provided funds for an extended tour to Europe and north Africa. He remained in Paris in 1891 where he studied in the studio of Auguste Rodin. The Paris Salon honoured him with gold medals in 1892 and 1901.

After his return to London Goscombe John became a sculptor of national and international fame, executing numerous important commissions including the altarpiece of St John's, Cardiff, completed in 1891 and many public monuments and statues of public figures such as the shipping magnate and philanthropist John Cory, erected in front of the City Hall, Cardiff. He also designed the *Corn Hirlas* for the National Eisteddfod as well as the monument to the composers of *Hen Wlad Fy Nhadau* in Pontypridd. Two of his most celebrated works are his sculpture of Owain Glyndŵr in the City Hall in Cardiff and his memorial in Llandaf to the dead of the First World War. He was made a Royal Academician in 1909, was knighted in 1911 and became corresponding member of the French Institute.

Goscombe John considered the memorial to W. R. H. Powell to have been his 'first commission of any importance'.[1] The marble figure was conceived and modelled in Paris between 1890 and 1891.[1] The memorial was unveiled, without ceremony, on the Powell family vault in the churchyard of St Brynach's at Llanboidy on Saturday, 26 September 1891. In a short report in the *Western Mail* on 29 September 1891 the statue *Grief* was described as consisting of a perpendicular slab of white marble, upon the surface of which is a faintly traced cross, in front of which stands a draped female figure with bowed head. The face, with the exception of the upper portion of the forehead, is hid by the right arm which is deftly drawn across the eyes while the left arm is gracefully thrown over the head with the fingers listlessly drooping. The drapery is most skilfully treated and every detail of this beautiful specimen of the sculptor's art displays the handiwork of a master.

A similar grieving figure appears on Goscombe John's memorial to the musician Sir Arthur Sullivan placed, in 1903, on the Embankment in London. 'The grieving female figure [in the Sullivan memorial] is very French in style and a more fluid adaptation of the Powell monument figure. It calls to mind the work of Mercié.'[2]

During 2011, the memorial to Powell was relocated and *Grief* can now be found inside St Brynach's Church at Llanboidy.

---

1. Letter from W. Goscombe John to George Eyre Evans, Secretary of the Carmarthenshire Antiquarian Society, dated April 1, 1927 (Mr Michael Vaughan, private collection) (see below).
2. Fiona Pearson, *Goscombe John at the National Museum of Wales*, Cardiff, 1979.

Letter dated April 1, 1927, from sculptor William Goscombe John to George Eyre Evans,
Secretary of the Carmarthenshire Antiquarian Society.

(Courtesy Michael Vaughan).

'Grief' by W. Goscombe John (now relocated inside St. Brynach's Church, Llanboidy).
(Eddie Evans collection).

TIME LINE

1789   Walter Powell of Bristol was left Maesgwynne in the will of his cousin Walter Rice Howell.

1795   Walter Rice Howell Powell (senior) born at Maesgwynne.

1797   Elizabeth Jane Oliver Hungerford Powell born at Maesgwynne.

1799   Margaret Maria Georgiana Powell born at Maesgwynne.

1800   Death of Walter Powell at Maesgwynne. Buried St Clears.

1813   W. R. H. Powell (senior) at Christ Church, Oxford.

1817   W. R. H. Powell (senior) married Mary Powell at Brislington Parish Church, Bristol.

1819   W. R. H. Powell (Powell Bach) born at Foley House, Haverfordwest.
       Eliz. J. O. Powell married cousin Timothy Powell.

1821   Maria Jane Powell born at Foley House, Goat Street, Haverfordwest.
       W. R. H. Powell (senior) High Sheriff.

1822   Georgiana Mary Powell born (probably at Maesgwynne).

1825   Edward Henry Powell born at Maesgwynne.

1832   T. R. Oliver Powell born at Maesgwynne.

1833   W. R. H. Powell (Powell Bach) fell from bedroom window at school in Swansea.

1834   W. R. H. Powell (Senior) died at Maesgwynne, buried in Llanboidy churchyard.

1837   W. R. H. Powell (Powell Bach) at Christ Church, Oxford.

1839   W. R. H. Powell at Maesgwynne. Talked to 'Rebecca'.
       Founded the Maesgwynne pack of Hounds.

1840   W. R. H. Powell marr. Emily Anne Skrine in Marylebone, London.

1841   Caroline Mary born at Stubbings. W. R. H. Powell, wife and daughter settle at Maesgwynne.

1842   Branch of Ivorite Friendly Soc. at Llanboidy.

1844   W. R. H. Powell (the 3rd) born at Maesgwynne.

1846   Emily Anne (29) died at Maesgwynne.
       W. R. H. Powell's 'Kangaroo' (Tom Davies) won Carmarthenshire Open.

1848   Jack Rees made whip of Maesgwynne pack.
       Steeplechases at Meidrim.

1849   W. R. H. Powell made High Sheriff of Carmarthenshire.
       First Llanboidy Steeplechases.

1851   W. R. H. Powell married Catherine Ann Prudence Phillips.
       Cefnbrafle Racecourse built.

1852   Railway reached Carmarthen.

1854   Railway reached Haverfordwest.

1855   Son and heir W. R. H. Powell (11) died at Maesgwynne.
       Emily Catherine Powell born at Maesgwynne.

1856   Start of week-long Llanboidy Races.

1857   Maesgwynne Arms Hotel built at Llanboidy.

1858   Grand Stand built on Cefnbrafle Racecourse.

1859   Powell formed the Llanboidy Agricultural Society.

1861   'Ace of Hearts' (James James) won Carmarthenshire Open for first time.

1862   'Ace of Hearts' (James James) dead-heated twice in Carmarthenshire Open.

1863	'Ace of Hearts' (Tom Davies) won Carmarthenshire Open.
	Llanboidy School built and opened by W. R. H. Powell.
1864	'Ace of Hearts' (Johnny Pope) won Carmarthenshire Open.
1865	End of 'golden era' of Llanboidy Races.
1866	'Daisy (Johnny Pope) won Carmarthenshire Open.
	Clunderwen Eisteddfod.
	'L'Africaine' foiled at Aintree.
1867	'Daisy' (Pope) won the greatest Carmarthenshire Open.
	'Flyfisher' (Pope) won Croydon Cup.
	'Hermit' won the Derby.
1868	Mary Powell (mother of Powell Bach) died at Maesgwynne.
	Powell expresses opposition to hiring-fairs.
1869	Nos. 5, 6 Plasybwci built.
1870	'Daisy' (George Stevens) won the Cheltenham Steeplechase.
	Race Meeting and Pigeon Shoot at Llanboidy.
1871	Llanboidy Races held for the last time.
1872	W. R. H. Powell seriously ill at Carmarthenshire Races.
1874	Powell formed the United Counties Friendly Benefit Society.
	Emily Catherine married W. F. Roch.
1875	Llanboidy and Llangan United School Board formed.
1877	T. R. Oliver Powell died at Waungron.
	Grand Eisteddfod at Whitland.
	Memorial stone unveiled at Cefnypant.
1878	Powell refurbished St Brynach's Church, Llanboidy.
1879	Mary Catherine Roch born at Llangwm, Pembrokeshire.
	Eisteddfod Gadeiriol at Crymych.
1880	W. R. H. Powell elected MP for Carmarthenshire.
	Piccadilly Square, Llanboidy built.
1881	Powell addressed Ammanford Liberals.
	Llanboidy Market Hall built.
1882	Butter-making demonstration at Market Hall.
1883	Penygaer School opened.
1884	Powell at Cwmamman workers' rally.
	Powell, Henry Richard and others at Carmarthen franchise rally.
1885	W. R. H. Powell elected MP for West Carmarthenshire.
1886	W. R. H. Powell re-elected MP for West Carmarthenshire.
1887	Powell presented anti-tithe petition to Parliament.
1888	Tithe sale at Yetygarn. Hayricks in flame at Blaenwaun Farm.
1889	W. R. H. Powell died at Maesgwynne. Buried at St Brynach's Church, Llanboidy.
1890	Water-fountain memorial unveiled by granddaughter Mary Catherine Roch.
1891	'Grief' by Goscombe John, unveiled at St Brynach's Church, Llanboidy in memory of W. R. H. Powell.

REFERENCES

Part I:.
MAINLY FAMILY MATTERS

1. Eddie Evans, private collection.
2. J. Graham Jones, *The Carmarthenshire Antiquary*, vol. XXXV, 1999, p. 82.
3. Francis Jones, *Historic Carmarthenshire Homes*, 1987, p. 125.
4. Matthew Cragoe, *An Anglican Aristocracy*, Oxford 1996, p. 15.
5. *The Carmarthenshire Antiquary*, vol. III, p. 105.
6. *The Gentleman's Magazine*, July 1799.
7. *Maesgwynne Estate Records*, GB 0210 MAENNE, National Library of Wales [NLW].
8. *Carmarthen Journal*, 6 July 1821.
9. Thomas Lloyd, private communication.
10. *The Buildings of Wales, Carmarthenshire and Ceredigion*, Thomas Lloyd et al, Yale University Press, 2006.
11. David Howell, *Pembrokeshire County History*, vol. III, p. 256.
12. 'Alumni Oxoniensis 1715-1886', Cymdeithas Hanes Teuluoedd/Dyfed Family History Society.
13. Brislington Parish church records, Bristol Record Office, Bristol.
14. 'Diaries of a Doctor's Wife', *The Carmarthenshire Historian*, vol. XVIII.
15. *Carmarthen Journal*, 2 July 1819.
16. *ibid.*, 9 July 1819.
17. Records of St Thomas' Church, Haverfordwest. County Archives, Haverfordwest.
18. *The Welshman*, 28 June 1898.
19. Rev. John Jones, *Newport Castle and other Short Poems*, Carmarthen 1886 (Thomas Lloyd, private collection).
20. *Carmarthenshire Notes*. Edited by Arthur Mee, vol. I, 1889, p. 163, Cyngor Sir Caerfyrddin, 1997.

Part II:
WORKING IN THE COMMUNITY:
GLIMPSES OF THE SQUIRE'S INVOLVEMENT

1. D. J. V. Jones, *Rebecca's Children*, Clarendon Press, Oxford, 1989, p. 96.
2. *ibid.*, p. 98.
3. Russell Davies, *Hope and Heartbreak*, University of Wales Press, Cardiff, 2005.
4. D. J. V. Jones, *op. cit.*, p. 104.
5. David Williams, *The Rebecca Riots*, University of Wales Press, Cardiff, 1986, p. 139.
6. *Report of the Commission of Enquiry for South Wales*, 1844, p. 205.
7. D. J. V. Jones, op. cit., p. 206.
8. *Carmarthen Journal*, 13 September 1839.
9. *ibid.*, 18 February 1842.
10. Elfyn Scourfield, *The Carmarthenshire Antiquary*, vol. vii, 1971, p. 102.
11. Eddie Evans, *Llanboidy*, Carmarthenshire County Council, 2001, p. 37.
12. Thomas Lloyd et al, *The Buildings of Wales: Carmarthenshire and Ceredigion*, Yale UP, 2006.
13. *Carmarthen Journal*, 11 April 1856.
14. *ibid.*, 23 October 1863.
15. *ibid.*, 6 February 1863.
16. *ibid.*, 21 February 1868.
17. *Carmarthen Journal, The Welshman*, 9 October 1863.
18. *Carmarthen Journal*, 23 October 1863.
19. *ibid.*, 11 September 1863.
20. *The Welshman*, 18 September 1863.
21. *ibid.*, 22 September 1865.
22. *ibid.*, 18 September 1868.
23. *Carmarthen Journal*, 7 June 1867.
24. *The Welshman*, 15 March 1867.
25. J. F. Jones, 'The Schools of Llanboidy', *The Carmarthenshire Antiquary*, XXVIII.
26. *The Welshman*, 12 October 1866.
27. *Y Goleuad*, 2 Ebrill 1881.
28. *The Welshman*, 11 May 1866.
29. *ibid.*, 19 April 1867.
30. *ibid.*, 31 May 1867.
31. *ibid.*, 26 April 1867.
32. *Carmarthen Journal*, 18 September 1868.
33. *ibid.*, 23 October 1868.
34. *Western Mail*, 13 September 1869.
35. *The Welshman*, 28 May 1869.
36. *ibid.*, 19 September 1873.
37. *ibid.*, 1 September 1876.
38. *Carmarthen Journal*, 5 September 1873.
39. *The Welshman*, 27 February 1874.
40. *The Welshman, Carmarthen Journal*, 26 March 1875.

41. *The Welshman*, 9 April 1875.
42. *Western Mail*, 2 June 1875.
43. *The Welshman*, 22 December 1876.
44. *ibid.*, 11 May 1877.
45. United Counties Friendly Benefit Society, Carmarthenshire Archive Service, Ref. DSO/100.
46. *The Welshman*, 22 June 1877.
47. *Carmarthen Journal*, 13 December 1878.
48. *Western Mail*, 26 June 1879.
49. *Carmarthen Journal*, 21 December 1877.
50. *ibid.*, 13 September 1878.
51. *ibid.*, 2 January 1880.
52. *ibid.*, 6 February 1880.
53. *ibid.*, 17 September 1880.
54. *ibid.*, 31 December 1880.
55. *ibid.*, 6 December 1878.
56. *ibid.*, 14 November 1879.
57. *ibid.*, 16 September 1881.
58. *ibid.*, 5 December 1879.
59. *The Welshman*, 11 May 1877.
60. *Carmarthen Journal*, 26 December 1879.
61. *ibid.*, 18 March 1881.
62. *Carmarthen Journal, The Welshman*, 8 September 1882.
63. *The Welshman*, 15 September 1882.
64. *ibid.*, 22 December 1882.
65. *ibid.*, 9 September 1881.
66. *Carmarthen Journal*, 27 October 1882.
67. *ibid.*, 10 September 1886.
68. *ibid.*, 17 September 1886.
69. *The Welshman*, 2 October 1885.
70. *South Wales Daily News*, 6 January 1886.
71. *The Welshman*, 15 January 1886.
72. *Carmarthen Journal*, 24 July 1970.
73. Tom Rees, 'Racing Reminiscences', *Carmarthen Journal*, 1916, Cwmnedd Press 1977.

PART III:
CARMARTHENSHIRE'S FIRST RADICAL MP

1. D. J. V. Jones, *Rebecca's Children*, Clarendon Press, Oxford, 1989, p. 330.
2. *Carmarthen Journal*, 25 August 1837.
3. *The Religious Census of 1851*, vol. I, Cardiff, University of Wales Press, 1976.
4. *Carmarthen Journal*, January 1850.
5. *ibid.*, 11 October 1850.
6. *Western Mail*, 6 May 1859.
7. Kenneth O. Morgan, *Wales in British Politics*, University of Wales Press, Cardiff, 1991, page v.
8. *The Welshman*, 30 January 1874.
9. *The Welshman*, 13 February 1874.
10. *ibid.*, 24 October 1879.
11. *ibid.*, 29 March 1880.
12. *Western Mail*, 29 March 1880.
13. *ibid.*, 3 April 1880.
14. *The Welshman*, 9 April 1880.
15. Kenneth O. Morgan, *op. cit.*, page 40.
16. *The Welshman*, 2 September 1881.
17. *Carmarthen Journal*, 17 September 1880.
18. *ibid.*, 24 September 1880.
19. *ibid.*, 8 October 1880.
20. *ibid.*, 5 November 1880.
21. Kenneth O. Morgan, *op. cit.*, p. 42.
22. *Carmarthen Journal*, 16 December 1881.
23. *ibid.*, 23 September 1881.
24. *ibid.*, 30 September 1881.
25. *ibid.*, 23 September 1881.
26. *Western Mail*, 13 December 1881.
27. *ibid.*, 16 December 1881.
28. *ibid.*, 31 July 1882.
29. *ibid.*, 22 September 1882.
30. *Carmarthen Journal*, 8 September 1882.
31. *The Welshman*, 15 September 1882.
32. *Carmarthen Journal*, 8 June 1883.
33. *ibid.*, 14 September 1983.
34. *ibid.*, 21 December 1983.
35. *The Welshman*, 18 January 1884.
36. *Y Goleuad*, 26 Ionawr 1884.
37. *Carmarthen Journal*, 1 February 1884.
38. *Western Mail*, 28 July 1884.
39. *ibid.*, 22 February 1884.
40. Kenneth O. Morgan, *op. cit.*, p. 69.
41. *Western Mail*, 23 August 1884.
42. *Baner ac Amserau Cymru*, 6 Awst 1884.
43. *Western Mail*, 1 July 1884, 18 August 1884.
44. *Carmarthen Journal*, 29 August 1884.
45. *Western Mail*, 28 August 1884.
46. *The Welshman*, 10 October 1884.
47. *Western Mail*, 12 May 1885.
48. *Carmarthen Journal*, 12 June 1885.
49. LL.G.C. *Mân Adnau 1130B, Cwrdd Chwarter Annibynwyr Gorllewin Sir Gâr, tud. 207.*
50. E. T. Lewis, *Efailwen to Whitland*, vol. 2, Carmarthen, 1976.
51. *Baner ac Amserau Cymru*, 22 Awst 1885.
52. *The Welshman*, 2 October 1885.
53. Kenneth O. Morgan, *op. cit.*, p. 57.
54. *Baner ac Amserau Cymru*, 12 Awst 1885.
55. *The Welshman*, 23 October 1885.
56. *ibid.*, 30 October 1885.
57. *Carmarthen Journal*, 30 October 1885.
58. *The Welshman*, 6 November 1885.
59. *Carmarthen Journal*, 13 November 1885.
60. *Western Mail*, 3 December 1885.
61. *The Welshman*, 4 December 1885.
62. *Carmarthen Journal*, 9 July 1886.

63. *ibid.*, 16 July 1886.
64. *ibid.*, 20 August 1886.
65. *Western Mail*, 25 February 1887.
66. *Carmarthen Journal*, 25 March 1887.
67. *ibid.*, 10 June 1887.
68. *Western Mail*, 5 August 1887.
69. *ibid.*, 17 September 1887.
70. *Carmarthen Journal*, 16 September 1887.
71. *ibid.*, 23 September 1887.
72. *Western Mail*, 12 January 1888.
73. *ibid.*, 1 June 1888.
74. *Carmarthen Journal*, 14 September 1888.
75. Wil Ifan, *Bro Fy Mebyd a Cherddi Eraill*, Gwasg Gee, 1996.
76. *The Welshman*, 21 September 1888.
77. *Carmarthen Journal*, 21 September 1888.
78. *ibid.*, 26 October 1888.
79. *Western Mail*, 16 May 1889.
80. *Carmarthen Journal*, 4 July 1890.
81. *The Welshman*, 5 July 1889.

Part IV
THE RISE AND FALL OF LLANBOIDY RACES

1. *Carmarthen Journal*, 21 April 1848.
2. *ibid.*, 27 September 1839.
3. Thomas Lloyd et al, *The Buildings of Wales, Carmarthenshire and Ceredigion*, Yale UP, 2006.
4. *Bell's Life in London* 8 February 1863.
   Daphne Moore, *Carmarthenshire Foxhounds and the Pembroke and Carmarthen Otterhounds*, Reid-Hamilton, London.
5. Martin Johnes, *A History of Sport in Wales*, University of Wales Press, Cardiff, 2005.
6. *The Welshman*, 6 January 1843.
7. *Pembrokeshire County History*, IV.
8. *Carmarthen Journal*, 27 January 1843.
9. *ibid.*, *The Welshman*, 28 April 1848.
10. *ibid.*, 13 April 1849.
11. *ibid.*, 5 October 1849; *The Welshman*, 22 February 1850.
12. Tom Rees, 'Racing Reminiscences', *Carmarthen Journal*, 1916, Cwmnedd Press 1977.
13. *Carmarthen Journal*, 11 October 1850.
14. *ibid.*, 7 February 1851.
15. *ibid.*, *The Welshman*, 25 April 1851.
16. *ibid.*, 11 October 1851.
17. *ibid.*, *The Welshman*, 2 April 1852.
18. *The Welshman*, 23 April 1852.
19. *ibid.*, 18 February 1853.
20. *ibid.*, 15 April 1853.
21. *ibid.*, 21 April 1854.
22. *Carmarthen Journal*, 13 April 1855.
23. *ibid.*, 28 March 1856.
24. *ibid.*, 20 February 1857.
25. *ibid.*, 17 April 1857.
26. Maesgwynne Estate Sale Document, 1918.
27. *Carmarthen Journal*, 23 April 1858.
28. *The Welshman*, 23 April 1858.
29. *Carmarthen Journal*, 1 April 1859.
30. *ibid.*, 10 February 1860.
31. *ibid.*, 30 March 1860.
32. W. C. A. Blew, *A History of Steeplechasing*, London.
   MDCCCCL Internet Archive web site, 18 November 2011.
33. *Carmarthen Journal*, 15 March 1861.
34. *ibid.*, 19 April 1861.
35. *The Welshman*, 28 March 1862.
36. *ibid.*, 4 April 1862.
37. *Carmarthen Journal*, 24 April 1863.
38. *Bell's Life in London* 26 April 1863.
39. *Carmarthen Journal*, 15 April 1864.
40. *The Welshman*, 15 April 1864.
41. Paul Davies, *The Course of Chasing in Gt Britain*, in *Thoroughbred Heritage*, web site as at December 2011.
42. *Bell's Life in London*, 6 May 1865.
43. *Carmarthen Journal*, 5 May 1865.
44. *The Welshman*, 5 May 1865.
45. *Carmarthenshire Historian*, XI, 1974, p. 27.
46. *Carmarthen Journal*, 30 March 1866.
47. *The Welshman*, 29 March 1867.
48. *ibid.*, 14 June 1867.
49. *Carmarthen Journal*, 26 June 1868.
50. *ibid.*, 3 July 1868.
51. *The Welshman*, 24 July 1868.
52. *ibid.*, 16 April 1869.
53. Herbert M. Vaughan, *The South Wales Squires*. Methuen, 1926.
54. *The Welshman*, 28 May 1869.
55. *ibid.*, 25 February 1870.
56. *ibid.*, 4 March 1870.
57. *ibid.*, 1 April 1870.
58. *Carmarthenshire Historian*, XII, 1975, p. 43.
59. Reginald Herbert, *When Diamonds Were Trumps*. Walter Southwood and Co. Ltd., London, 1908.
60. *The Welshman*, 8 April 1870.
61. Richard Lawrence, *The Rise and Fall of Tenby Races*, CPW, 2003.
62. *The Welshman*, 30 September 1870.
63. *ibid.*, 15 July 1870.
64. *ibid.*, 12 August 1870.
65. *Carmarthen Journal*, 10 February 1871.
66. *ibid.*, 17 March 1871.
67. *The Welshman*, 31 March 1871.
68. *ibid.*, 7 April 1871.
69. *Carmarthen Journal*, 9 February 1872.

Part V
THE CARMARTHENSHIRE HUNT WEEK
AND STEEPLECHASES

1. *Carmarthen Journal*, 12 April 1844.
2. *ibid.*, 13 December 1844.
3. *ibid.*, 24 January 1845.
4. Tom Rees, 'Racing Reminiscences', *Carmarthen Journal*, 1916, Cwmnedd Press 1977.
5. *Carmarthen Journal*, 18 February 1846.
6. *ibid.*, 26 February 1847.
7. *ibid.*, 18 February 1848.
8. *ibid.*, 17 March 1848.
9. *The Welshman*, 16 February 1849.
10. *Carmarthen Journal*, 11 January 1850.
11. *ibid.*, 1 February 1850.
12. *Carmarthen Journal*, 7 February 1851.
    The Welshman, 24 January 1851.
13. *Carmarthen Journal*, 13 February 1852.
14. *ibid.*, 4 March 1853.
15. Reginald Herbert, *When Diamonds Were Trumps*. Walter Southwood and Co. Ltd., London, 1908.
16. *The Welshman*, 24 February 1854.
17. Herbert M. Vaughan, *The South Wales Squires*, Methuen, 1926.
18. *Carmarthen Journal*, 23 March 1855.
19. *ibid.*, 27 July 1855.
20. *ibid.*, 29 February 1856.
21. *ibid.*, 20 February 1857.
22. *ibid.*, 12 February 1858.
23. *ibid.*, 18 February 1859.
24. *ibid.*, 27 February 1860.
25. *ibid.*, 10 February 1860.
26. *ibid.*, 8 February 1861.
27. *ibid.*, 7 February 1862.
28. *Bell's Life in London*, 8 February 1863.
29. *Carmarthen Journal*, 6 February 1863.
30. *ibid.*, 5 February 1864.
31. *ibid.*, 10 February 1865.
32. *ibid.*, 2 February 1866.
33. *The Welshman*, 2 February 1866.
34. *Bell's Life in London*, 9 February 1867.
35. *The Welshman*, 8 February 1867.
36. *Carmarthenshire Notes*, Edited by Arthur Mee, vol. III, 1891, p. 20, Cyngor Sir Caerfyrddin 1997.
37. *Carmarthen Journal*, 6 December 1867.
38. *ibid.*, 13 December 1867.
39. *ibid.*, 27 December 1867.
40. *ibid.*, 7 February 1868.
41. *The Welshman*, 7 February 1868.
42. *Carmarthen Journal*, 5 February 1869.
43. *The Welshman*, 5 February 1869.
44. *ibid.*, 23 April 1869.
45. *ibid.*, 14 May 1869.
46. *ibid.*, 21 May 1869.
47. *ibid.*, 28 May 1869.
48. *Carmarthen Journal*, 25 February 1870.
49. *The Welshman*, 25 February 1870.
50. *ibid.*, 25 March 1870.
51. *ibid.*, 8 April 1870.
52. *Carmarthen Journal*, 10 February 1871.
53. *The Welshman*, 10 February 1871.
54. *Carmarthen Journal*, 9 February 1872.
55. *The Welshman*, 9 February 1872.
56. *Carmarthen Journal*, 5 April 1872.
57. *The Welshman*, 17 January 1873.
58. *Carmarthen Journal*, *The Welshman*, 7 February 1873.
59. *The Welshman*, 6 February 1874.
60. *Carmarthen Journal*, 5 February 1875.
61. *The Welshman*, 23 April 1875.
62. *ibid.*, 4 February 1876.
63. *Carmarthen Journal*, 16 February 1877.
64. *ibid.*, *The Welshman*, 23 February 1877.
65. *ibid.*, 8 February 1878.
66. *ibid.*, 6 December 1878.
67. *ibid.*, 21 February 1879.
68. *ibid.*, 13 February 1880.
69. *ibid.*, 2 July 1880.
70. *ibid.*, 25 February 1881.
71. *The Welshman*, 24 June 1881.
72. *Carmarthen Journal*, 3 February 1882.
73. *Baily's Monthly Magazine of Sports and Pastimes*, No. 282, Vol. XLI, London, August 1883.
74. *ibid.*, 1 February 1884.
75. *ibid.*, 6 February 1885.
76. *ibid.*, 28 January 1887.
77. *ibid.*, 9 December 1887.
78. *ibid.*, 3 February 1888.
79. *Carmarthen Journal*, 11 January 1889.
80. *ibid.*, 8 February 1889.
81. *The Welshman*, 23 November 1888.
82. *Carmarthen Journal*, 15 February 1889.
83. *Western Mail*, 26 February 1889.

INDEX